WOMEN AND LANGUAGE IN LITERATURE AND SOCIETY

WOMEN AND LANGUAGE IN LITERATURE AND SOCIETY

edited by

Sally McConnell-Ginet
Ruth Borker
Nelly Furman

PRAEGER

PRAEGER SPECIAL STUDIES • PRAEGER SCIENTIFIC

Library of Congress Cataloging in Publication Data
Main entry under title:

Women and language in literature and society.

   Includes indexes.
   1. Women--Language. ~~Addresses, essays, lectures.~~
2. Language and languages--Sex differences. ~~Addresses, essays, lectures~~. 3. Sexism--Language. ~~Addresses, essays, lectures~~. 4. Feminism--Language. ~~Addresses, essays, lectures~~. I. McConnell-Ginet, Sally.
II. Borker, Ruth. III. Furman, Nelly.
HQ1206.W872   305.4'2   80-20816
ISBN 0-03-057892-2
ISBN 0-03-057893-0 (pbk.)

Published in 1980 by Praeger Publishers
CBS Educational and Professional Publishing
A Division of CBS, Inc.
521 Fifth Avenue, New York, New York 10017 U.S.A.

0123456789   145   987654321

Printed in the United States of America

ACKNOWLEDGMENTS

This book grew out of the editors' association as colleagues in the Cornell Women's Studies Program and their shared intellectual and feminist interests in the general area of language. Many people have helped at different stages in the preparation of this book. Michele Dominy, Carl Ginet, Daniel Maltz, Kathryn S. March, and Barrie Thorne commented on substantial portions of the editorial materials. For reading the entire manuscript with care and acumen, the editors especially thank Susan Milmoe and a number of anonymous reviewers.

Nelly Furman's editorial work on the volume was done in part while she held a fellowship at the Society for the Humanities, Cornell University, 1977-78. She wishes to thank the director of the Society, Michael Kammen, and the staff for their support. Sally McConnell-Ginet has been helped with correspondence and other clerical details of manuscript preparation by the staff of the Department of Modern Languages and Linguistics, Cornell University; special thanks are due to Kristen Bieber and Jane Bryner.

Without the superb work of Ruta Noreika, the original typescript might never have turned into these printed pages. She not only gave considerable editorial help in preparing the final manuscript for production by Praeger, but she also took on the staggering job of preparing the index.

There would, of course, be no book without our contributors. We thank them for their patient cooperation throughout the long and often tedious editorial process. Most of all, we are grateful for the essays they have written.

Finally, we have learned much from one another during our work on this book. We have argued at length and often—not always—achieved consensus. Each of the editors wishes to thank the other two. We are unable to decide who should be blamed for any shortcomings that may remain.

—the editors

CONTENTS

LIST OF TABLES AND FIGURES

Table

INTRODUCTION

Marianne was silent; it was impossible for her to say what she did not feel, however trivial the occasion; and upon Elinor therefore the whole task of telling lies when politeness required always fell.

—Jane Austen

Language is the substance of social life and personal relationships: the fabric that connects individual lives is woven of words and silences.

I come forth to speak about Women's Rights, and want to throw in my little mite, to keep the scales a-moving. I know that it feels a kind of hissing and tickling to see a colored woman get up and tell you about things, and Women's Rights.

. . .

I wanted to tell you a mite about Women's Rights and so I came out and said so. I am sitting among you to watch; and every once in awhile I will come out and tell you what time of night it is.

—Sojourner Truth

Cultural values and prejudices shape the contexts of public discourse, yet language is a potent weapon in any struggle to change the conditions of people's lives and the ideologies that frame them.

This is the oppressor's language

Yet I need it to talk to you

—Adrienne Rich

Both in literature and in daily life, language articulates consciousness, orders experience, and makes possible shared consciousness and transformed experience.

Women are the subjects of this book. The connecting tissue, however, is language and the linguistic processes that help give women's lives form and meaning. Language works both for and against women, and the essays in this book explore only a few of the many ways in which the position and experience of women affects and is affected by language and its use in diverse settings.

The rebirth of feminism in the middle sixties has had an extraordinary impact on many women's lives and is making itself felt not only in personal relationships and in larger political arenas but also in scholarship and the arts. Feminist discourse has suggested both negative and positive implications of language in women's lives. Language, many claim, plays a crucial role in defining and maintaining a "man's world" while delineating and enclosing "women's place." In trying to move beyond that confining place, many women are attending to and changing the verbal realities of their daily lives. Women across America are adopting the new title *Ms.*, affirming independent identities through name choices and changes, protesting a perpetual "girlhood" verbally conferred, and supporting one another in "speaking up." Consciousness-raising, the distinctive political strategy of the new feminism, is predicated on the power of talk in small groups to translate the particularities of each individual's personal problems into collective awareness and potential action.

The intellectual and artistic activities of contemporary feminists also show a preoccupation with language and a dissatisfaction with our familiar linguistic resources. Not surprisingly, many women writers find the forms and "the oppressor's language" they've inherited inadequate to their expressive needs. To try to create alternative modes of expression, women are experimenting with new forms of writing and speaking. Language is seen as both problematic and potentially powerful in the development of alternatives to political, aesthetic, and intellectual traditions shaped by and for men.

Why has language played such a major role in so many different aspects of recent feminist activity? How can we explain the concern with words and their use in the context of protests against cultural stereotypes and social constraints that limit women's lives? What is meant by charges that men "control" or have "appropriated" language? If language is not independent of society and culture, what are the connections? The new feminism has raised such issues, and a number of the essays in this book begin to address them.

Scholarship on women's relation to language has by no means been confined to consideration of the views and linguistic practices of women who identify themselves as feminists. Careful analysis of what women say (and write) and how they say it is proving a very powerful tool for gaining insight into women's lives. Coupled with attention to what others say to and of women and how it is said, such investigations show that women's experience is not always expressed in the ways that male-centered analyses might lead us to expect. In literature, women's position as writers and as readers is being critically reexamined through consideration of language and linguistic processes. A variety of sophisticated theories of language and methods for studying it are used to understand women's sociocultural position and the import of language for changing women's lives.

The fundamental question is simply: *what can a focus on language tell us about women in literature and society?* How are women's situations and their concerns, their aims and strategies for achieving them, illumined by attention to language and its use?

Most of the essays in the book also suggest, however, a second question: *what can a focus on women tell us about language in literature and society?* Does incorporating women's perspectives and experiences challenge conventional models of language and language use, give us an appreciably different picture of the life of language? Women frequently do not use or interpret their language according to accepted norms.

This question points to the other current that feeds into this book: a revitalization of inquiry into language and its use. Language seems to have captured the imagination and engaged the intellect of many of our century's best minds. This reflects in part the growing sophistication of modern linguistics and the exciting possibilities it offers in a variety of academic disciplines and areas of intellectual life. Linguistics, of course, is defined as the science of language. Ferdinand de Saussure articulated its basic foundations at the turn of the century, and the Saussurean conception of language as a structured sign system has been developed and extended in a variety of ways in different intellectual traditions. The Chomskian revolution in theoretical linguistics, for example, was generated in the middle fifties within the major American tradition of structuralist linguistics, a tradition that ultimately derives from the work of Saussure. Both American and European structuralist and post-structuralist frameworks continue to provoke challenges and undergo revisions. The study of language has been transformed in the twentieth century, making it possible to relate linguistic investigations to more general theories of the human mind and social interaction. Psychologists, sociologists, anthropologists, philosophers, and modern literary critics have all looked to linguistics for models of language and for analytic techniques. When available linguistic theories have proved inadequate for explaining the role of language in thought and in social and cultural systems, scholars in other disciplines have proposed new approaches, some of which are feeding back into linguistics.

In trying to understand women's experience, scholars have drawn on methods and theories that connect the study of language to more general investigations of social life and symbolic systems. At the same time, they have also drawn from the new scholarship and thinking about women to help refine familiar concepts and develop innovative frameworks for language study. Scholarship on women is seldom satisfactorily confined to conventional disciplinary boundaries; the study of women's relation to language provides an unusual opportunity to begin understanding interrelations among the diverse approaches to language that have recently developed.

This book represents a convergence of the new scholarship on women and a variety of different streams of language-centered research and theorizing. It joins empirical investigations and conceptual analyses of language in social life with critical discourse on language in literature because they seem to shed light on one another and give a richer and more intricate picture of language in women's lives than any single approach could provide. Although methodologies and theories differ radically, there is a common focus on women's experience as producers and interpreters of language and on women's views of linguistic norms and practices and there are recurring themes and insights. We hope that this book may initiate more fruitful dialogue across some of the boundaries that have divided, for example, experimental scientists from literary artists. Different approaches, however, retain their integrity: this book does not propose a "comprehensive" theory or claim a "complete" description of language in women's lives. Instead it offers theoretical discussions of the particulars of a handful of women's linguistic situations, suggesting connections among those different situations and the frameworks within which they are considered.

One of the most complex and controversial issues raised by our book is just how literary and other uses of language are related. Among the advantages of juxtaposing discussions of language in literature with discussions of language in ordinary life is that it forces us to face the fact, which American linguistics has often ignored, that there are important differences among the diverse uses to which language is put. Recognizing that literary uses of language are crucially different from other uses can lead us to see that nonliterary uses of language are also heterogeneous. Perhaps most surprising to many is the suggestion that "communication" in the narrow sense of transfer of information is probably not the predominant use of language even *outside* literary contexts. We flirt, scold, exhort, implore, protest—and talk just to connect ourselves to other selves, to reduce our isolation. Within literature as well, uses of language are diverse: genre and period, for example, will be important not only for the patterns of language used but also for the kind and amount of attention paid by authors and readers to language itself. To see diversity in kinds of use leads us to expect that sex will interact with language in a variety of different ways that link to particular kinds of use.

In literature, however, there are not the feedback possibilities between producer and interpreter that sometimes help clarify the contextual specificities of speech interactions. Literary texts are encountered in many different settings by many different readers with no access to authors. Language can indeed help create its own contexts, and literary texts tend to be elaborated and self-conscious about potential interpretations in ways in which nonliterary uses of language generally are not. Nonetheless, literature only gives an illusion of having escaped its grounding in the inter-subjective social and cultural contexts in which it is produced and which it is read. Readers bring their own literary (and other) experience to a text along with their assumptions about its author and her (or his) aims, capabilities, interests. The author initially constructs the text, of course, against a backdrop of literary, linguistic, and other sociocultural traditions. That is, writing itself can be seen as involving creative reading.

Language itself is not usually an overt concern outside literary contexts. In most other uses of language, we pay relatively little conscious attention to the formal structure of what we have uttered or heard. This does not mean that the formal structure is therefore unimportant in such situations but simply that, in contrast to what is usually the case with literature, it is not a primary interest. Indeed, it may be because the importance of verbal form is seldom explicitly recognized and also because many linguistic choices (especially in ongoing speech) are not consciously attended to, that the social uses of language can play such a critical role in structuring women's lives. To separate manifest content from its particular formal expression is always to run the risk of over-looking or distorting the function of a particular linguistic act. A number of the essays suggest ways in which verbal minutiae and discourse structures of ordinary uses of language help to create and maintain social systems and cultural values. Although form plays different roles in literary and nonliterary contexts, it can safely be ignored in neither.

Thus, while literature and social life raise quite different issues about language, both domains suggest the importance of taking language itself seriously, making it clear that "what" is said is inseparable from "how." Both also suggest that linguistic forms in themselves do not necessarily determine what is conveyed, that language is not an inert "container" for transmitting messages but that both producers and interpreters, situated in particular socio-cultural contexts, create its significance. We have placed language *in* literature and society because this book offers alternatives to the view that language is a lifeless structure that simply provides labels for independently existing cognitive, social, and cultural realities.

Many other questions, some of them familiar and some new, are also raised in this book. Do women and men in our own sociocultural setting cultivate different types of discourse with different goals and criteria of evaluation? If so, why? If not, why do we persist in thinking that they do? Can the social and cultural realities of women's situations generate "feminine" styles of language use? How can such styles be exploited for literary purposes? What is the relation of social power and cultural conceptions of "powerful" speech to actual and assumed language use by women and men? How do women talk to one another? To men? In public? In private? What is the role of language used toward and about women in transmitting and maintaining cultural values? Are women more likely than men, because of their marginal social positions, to recognize diversity and change in language, to see the multiplicity of possible interpretations? Do women-centered approaches shift our views of literary discourse? Of scientific discourse? Of the articulation to ourselves and others of our own experience and perceptions?

Because we are all interested in bridging the gaps that separate us from one another, none of the authors has assumed an audience initiated into the mysteries of a particular discipline or specialized tradition. The book is organized into four parts, each of which begins with a brief introduction and presentation of the essays it includes. Any organization, of course, structures reading, selectively emphasizing connections among the articles, and developing certain themes at the expense of others; our book suggests ways to begin reading it.

To study language, we have to use it: paradoxically, language is both object and instrument of the investigations in this book. Thus these very investigations are undoubtedly themselves shaped by beliefs and cultural biases embedded in our system of linguistic practices. And this can happen in ways we did not intend and do not recognize. There can be no "last word" here, no tidy conclusion to hand to our readers. To offer a definitive study of women and language in literature and society is to offer an illusion.

Language enters into women's lives in complex, varied, and subtle ways. Women, in turn, breathe life into language. Women are both the subject and the subjects of this book: their voices echo in its pages.

PART I

VIEWS FROM AND TO
THE DISCIPLINES

INTRODUCTION TO PART ONE

Different disciplines bring distinctive perspectives and methods to the investigation of women and language. The editors' articles in this section review the contributions of linguistics, anthropology, and literature and show how taking women's experience and interests as central has begun to transform existing theories of language use and methods of analysis within each of these disciplines.

In "Linguistics and the Feminist Challenge," Sally McConnell-Ginet sketches the study of language and women by scholars in linguistics and "sister" disciplines—for example, psychology, sociology, and philosophy. She begins by reviewing discussions of language as both mirror and instrument of sexist society. She also considers proposals for changing our "father tongue," emphasizing the importance of the fact that in verbal communication speaker and hearer both rely not only on their knowledge of a linguistic code but also on a wealth of extralinguistic beliefs and attitudes. Language development and language change in relation to women can only be understood, according to McConnell-Ginet, by looking at women's and men's use of language. Although it is commonplace to claim that the sexes use distinct "languages," she argues that it is more helpful to view women and men as applying (potentially) different strategies to use of a common code.

Ruth Borker discusses the special contributions made by anthropological research on women and language in "Anthropology: Social and Cultural Perspectives." She starts by reviewing studies of the impact of women's social roles and relationships on their speech; next she looks at how women use language to (re)construct their social worlds and then discusses how social contexts can

1

lead the sexes to develop distinct ways of speaking. Finally, she considers the cultural dimensions of gender and language, comparing ideas and evaluations of language and the sexes in several different cultural settings.

Although language is the very stuff of literature, many critical approaches ignore the question of linguistic processes, as Nelly Furman observes in "Textual Feminism." Textual criticism, however, makes the verbal medium its center of interest. This change of focus, Furman argues, leads to major changes in our critical perspectives. It makes construction of a text the work of readers as well as author, for example. Investigations from readers' viewpoints of women's participation in the literary tradition not only point out the sex-biases embedded in our literary canons but reveal as well the underlying assumptions that shape our reading practices.

Linguistics calls itself a science, literature is a humanistic discipline, and anthropology draws on both humanistic and scientific methods of inquiry. Social and behavioral sciences are committed to the development of empirically testable theories of the why and how of human experiences. In contrast, the humanistic tradition is concerned with offering imaginative (re)visions of complex human problems rather than finding evidence to verify hypotheses. The essays in Part I and in the rest of the book, however, show that some general insights into the nature of language and language use emerge as common across the disciplines in spite of such fundamental differences in aims and methods. For example, both scientific and humanistic studies of women and language draw attention to the importance of language users (their thought, their particular histories) and to their interactions with one another. There is an increased concern with interpretation and with evaluation as significant and potentially problematic processes, and more attention is paid to the contexts in which language use is situated. Part I provides background and conceptual frameworks for thinking about the problems discussed in the rest of the book.

1
LINGUISTICS AND THE FEMINIST CHALLENGE

Sally McConnell-Ginet

Social and political movements frequently provoke debate about language and its place in human life, and changes in social and cultural structures are often connected to linguistic changes. Because it raises questions about so many of our most basic assumptions, the contemporary women's movement has given rise to especially impassioned and wide-ranging discussion of the connection of language to social life and to individual psychology. Letters to the editor bemoan *chairperson* or protest the use of *girl* to refer to a mature female person. Transsexuals seek training in "women's language." Writers talk of a "new language" to replace "our father tongue." To the many people educated in a view of language as apolitical and sexually neutral, such discussions and activities are difficult to understand.

Linguistics, which takes language as its defining subject matter, might seem the discipline that could provide some clarification of such matters. Yet the predominant theories and methods for studying language in modern linguistics do not seem particularly relevant—at least not at first glance. Recent linguistics has emphasized the study of general principles governing the sorts of units and kinds of structural relations among them that go to make up human language systems. By looking at features of language that do not depend on the specificities of the social and psychological contexts of its use, linguists have been able to develop precise and detailed formal theories that characterize pan-human language capacity. Given a focus on the abstract character of language as a rule-governed system that is represented in people's minds (an internalized "grammar"), we would not expect to gain much insight into the interaction of gender (or social inequality) with language. We do not find sex differences in the kinds of rules that can, for example, relate actives and passives or specify the structure of syllables.

But the discipline of linguistics does contribute to the study of women and language in important ways even if its scope is quite narrowly conceived and "technical." By specifying the general form of language systems, it directs attention to the possible parameters of variety among language systems, to the kinds of features that might distinguish the language of women and men in diverse situations. Most crucially, perhaps, it provides a framework within which we can explicitly describe the linguistic forms women and men use in particular contexts: it gives us a rich vocabulary for representing linguistic elements and rules. Investigations of the social and cultural significance of language must look at people's uses of language, how we speak and write, read and hear. But without some understanging of what it is being used, we can't even describe those uses, let alone try to explain them.

Thus technical linguistics provides a vital tool for the investigation of language in literature and society. Linguistics and scholarship in a variety of other social science and humanistic disciplines have entered into partnerships that are proving productive in the study of a wide variety of uses of language and of "linguistic politics," the implications of inequality among speakers and investigation of the adequacy of available linguistic resources to the needs of different speakers.[1] There is now substantial work in the new interdisciplinary specialization of sociolinguistics and the related, sometimes overlapping, interdisciplinary areas of the ethnography of communication, the sociology of language, anthropological linguistics, psycholinguistics, and stylistics.

The recent explosion of research on the complex interactions of language and sex has drawn methods and theories from these newly created fields.[2] Much of this work stems from feminist-inspired concern to understand the roots and mechanisms of male dominance, and more generally, the place of language and its use in women's experience.

It has frequently been thought that the main issues raised by feminist discussions of language are whether and how language *affects* social and cognitive structures. Many have taken it as obvious that language *indicates* (past or present) attitudes, beliefs, and values: arguments have centered on which psychological, social, or cultural phenomena a particular linguistic fact indicates and on whether those phenomena are buried in the past or continue to exist. In other words, it is commonly assumed without argument that social and cognitive structures have import for language development and change.

But in fact, we do not really understand how language is affected by extralinguistic factors any better than we understand the supposedly more problematic opposite direction of influence. The major challenge that feminist scholarship on language poses is to explain how there could be any interaction at all between language and an individual's thought, on the one hand, and the social and cultural contexts in which language is used, on the other. Research on language and sex has already drawn a rich and complex picture of such interactions, providing considerable evidence that such connections do indeed exist. And, in trying to provide explanations for what is actually observed, many of these studies are contributing to the development of theories of language with greater claim to social and psychological "reality" than the ones that are usually presented in introductory linguistic texts. It is not that these older theories are to be discarded but, rather, that they must be refined and adapted if we are to understand how language works in human life. Rather than an exclusive focus on language as a static *product* of the human mind (and of its socially situated experience), this research suggests the importance of linguistic *processes* in connecting individual human minds in a larger socio-cultural order. It also points to the important issue of how product and process, language structure and language use, interact with one another. We begin to get some insights into the nature of this interaction through looking at connections between the two major questions that have dominated research on language and the sexes. First, how are women spoken of and to? Second, how do women (and men) speak?

"SEXIST LANGUAGE?": SOCIAL AND CULTURAL MEANINGS

Since languages live in their users, it seems more appropriate to speak of language users as sexist, not the languages themselves. It is, nonetheless, revealing to look at the relation between the linguistic resources available in a community and the social differentiation of the sexes in that community. Most charges of sexism in language structure are aimed at the vocabulary, a component of langauge that has only recently begun to be systematically studied by linguists.

Although there is not a well-established tradition of serious investigation of such lexical phenomena as the coining of new words or the extension of existing vocabulary to new uses and meanings, linguists have long recognized the vocabulary as an important repository of social, cultural, and historical information about the people who have used it. Linguists who were also anthropologists and thus directly concerned with cultural and social phenomena have frequently based inferences about a community's life on the evidence of the linguistic resources available in that community—mostly looking at vocabulary, which can be thought of as indicating the system of "pre-packaged", "well-used" concepts. Following in this tradition, language and the general patterns of its use can be taken as an *index* of culturally shared or predominant attitudes and values connected with women and men, with sexuality, and with the sexual distribution of social roles and statuses. The range of forms of expression available for speaking of a particular topic (terms that refer to prostitutes, for example) and their interconnections can be viewed either as a cultural *artifact*, bearing testimony to the past, or as a *mirror* of sociocultural patterns widely operative in the contemporary situation (or both).[3]

Where we have clear-cut evidence about a semantic shift, we can make plausible conjectures about the lives of our foremothers and, in some cases, about past cultural conceptions of femaleness and maleness. For example, we know that *lady* descends to us from a form *hlaefdige* in Old English, which in turn was compounded from roots that meant 'bread' and 'kneader' (modern *loaf* and *dough* continue these earlier roots); we know that *hussy* and *housewife* derive from a common source (*huswif*), that the modern forms *wife* and *weave* are historically related, and so on. A formal connection existing within a contemporary language may point to an earlier semantic link: for example, *spinster* and the verb *spin*, an analysis suggested for the modern speaker by the use of -*ster* as an agentive suffix in forms like *prankster* and *songster*. In this case, the inference from internal evidence available to modern speakers leads in fact to a conclusion that we know (on independent grounds) to be sound.[4]

Feminists looking to semantic change for evidence of cultural conceptions have generally been careful not to confine themselves to isolated lexical items but have instead considered general patterns of semantic shift recurring in semantically related lexical items. A number of investigators have pointed to such phenomena as the sexualization of terms referring to women and the prevalence of acquisition of negative connotations (*hussy*, cited above, is not an isolated example) as evidence for (man's) preoccupation with woman's sexuality to the exclusion of her other attributes and as evidence of widespread misogyny.[5] What can we conclude? Although some scholars have considered the methodological and theoretical problems involved in using linguistic evidence to enrich our knowledge of the past, there is little in the way of systematic principles to explain semantic changes and to support cultural/conceptual inferences from them. And because language historians have seldom questioned popular assumptions about women's place in the social order, many of the explanations that have been proposed for attested linguistic changes are no stronger than the sex-biased beliefs and attitudes on which they depend.[6]

Why do some changes recur again and again? It seems plausible, for example, that the acquisition of negative (and often specifically sexual) meanings by once neutral terms for denoting women that we have just noted is somehow connected to widespread misogyny and views that women are mainly sexual beings. What is not clear are the mechanisms through which such sentiments lead to linguistic changes of this kind. *How* can linguistic meaning be changed because of people's background assumptions, knowledge, experience, and the like?

Analysis of the relation between contemporary language and cultural conceptions might seem more straightforward than linguistic reconstruction of the past, but even as a mirror of current attitudes and beliefs, language is somewhat problematic. Some extremely suggestive facts have been unearthed by recent investigators who have drawn our attention to significant lexical gaps (*henpecked* but no *cockpecked*), lexical asymmetries (*mothering* is a long-term affair but *fathering* the act of an instant), and nonparallel distribution of items that pattern similarly in some environments (linguist Robin Lakoff gave the inspired *cleaning lady/garbage gentleman*).[7] Do such phenomena reflect present-day attitudes, or are they simply the residue of our sexist past? (Spinsters no longer do much spinning.) To what extent, for example, is the "euphemizing" value of *lady* still operative in current usage (for at least some contexts and some speakers)? Such a question is unlikely to be resolved by appeal to speakers' intuitions as to whether "*lady* connotes triviality and frivolity," which is what Lakoff has claimed.

Although speakers' insights into connotations are useful in guiding the analyst, only a detailed study of actual language use (examination of the contexts in which *lady* occurs, its opposition to *woman, girl, broad,* and so on) can shed light on features of meaning that are at best implicit for speakers and, quite possibly, denied at a conscious level. In addition, of course, speakers vary in the systems underlying their language use. There may well be even greater variation in semantic nuances than in other aspects of the language system because these depend heavily on the availability of closely related lexical alternatives. This means that we cannot speak of "the" cultural conception that underlies a particular pattern of uses without taking account of the competing conceptions underlying alternative patterns of usage that may also exist. Careful investigation of who says what to whom in which contexts is a more reliable method than asking directly about meaning for sorting out the factors that differentiate expressions that are referentially equivalent (such as *lady* and *woman*).

The scholarly establishment and much of the general public have not taken seriously the suggestion that language (use) might perpetuate and maintain sex-typing, the subordination of women, and adherence to androcentric values. The idea that language affects social reality is mistakenly thought to depend on the belief that words—spoken or written forms—can in themselves, independently of their use by human beings to say something, influence the course of events. Critics also wrongly suppose that views of language as contributing to sexism imply that people whose linguistic resources were not overtly "sexist" would find it difficult to express the view that "those bra-burners oughta stay home with the kids" or be unable to hold an opinion.[8]

No one, of course, maintains that language is the *only* influence on people's ways of thinking or that a person can achieve all her or his desired social ends armed only with linguistic resources. But it is in part because the connections of language to thought and to social life are seldom explicitly recognized that language use can enter into the transmission and preservation of attitudes and values that are seldom explicitly articulated. Many—probably most—of our linguistic choices in ordinary conversation are not consciously reflected upon. This means that many of the messages we convey and receive are "loaded" with import beyond their overt content and perhaps beyond what the speaker intended. Overt messages are, of course, important but they do not raise any interesting theoretical questions. Any husband can say to his wife: "I'm the boss around here."* Any child may hear "you're just a dumb broad" often

---

*Note that "I wear the pants around here" originates as an expression that indirectly asserts authority through directly asserting masculinity (or, rather, male-typed clothing and thus, metonymically, maleness). This could only "work" linguistically against an assumption of male authority.

enough to come to believe that it must be an apt characterization. Such open grabs for power and blatant expressions of misogyny are always possible and can, of course, have tremendous impact. Yet it is the covert messages that are most difficult to resist, that we may unwittingly send ourselves, and that are easiest for the dominant group (sometimes sincerely) to deny.

Language may be effective in socializing newcomers to traditional ways of viewing the world in part because they assume it is an index of values and attitudes. Just as we can suppose the young child is an incredibly talented linguist, comparing rival hypothesized grammars against the evidence she encounters in the speech around her, so we can suppose that the child has some talent as a linguistic anthropologist, figuring out the cultural clues dropped in language use. So long as the child's inferences aren't obviously contradicted by (nonlinguistic) experience or by the bulk of the overt content of people's utterances, she or he can assume that "this is how people think around here." It doesn't even matter if most of the adults consciously accept the values attributed to them by children: the child may incorporate as basic assumptions a variety of principles that powerfully influence later behavior and beliefs and which can only be rooted out with great difficulty, thus insuring the continued influence of cultural belief systems that have long since been rejected at a conscious level by large cultural subgroups.

We still know virtually nothing about this process, but it is important to realize that we need not suppose that our language-learning experience determines what we think in order to say that patterns of language use encountered by children contribute substantially to forming their way of viewing themselves and their world. Philosopher Elizabeth Beardsley has suggested that "genderization"—marking sex in a referring or characterizing expression whose primary function in the utterance is independent of sex—plays an important part in the centrality of sex to self-identity and in our views of others and their behavior.[9] Genderization is said to occur when sex-marking is obligatory, by which Beardsley means that reference to sex can only be eliminated through use of expressions that are (for various other reasons) unsuitable or somewhat odd in the context. For example, English pronominal reference to a definite individual is (necessarily) sex-marked. It would therefore be extraordinarily difficult to do something like write a letter of recommendation with no mention, if only implicit through use of *she* or *he*, of the candidate's sex.* We have mainly

---

*An academic department in a major university attempted to do this by appending a note to the recommendations it sent out on behalf of graduate students that indicated a policy of initials for first names and a so-called "generic" *he* for later references. Many forgot, and the obtruding *s* was clearly visible under the correcting fluid. Reference to specific inidividuals with *he* is marked for masculinity at this stage in the history of English: see Sally McConnell-Ginet, "Pronouns, Prototypes, and Persons," in *Ethnolinguistics: Boas, Sapir, and Whorf Revisited* ed. M. Mathiot (The Hague: Mouton, 1979), pp. 63-83.

anecdotal accounts of the effects of these phenomena on the developing child, but it is not implausible to suppose that many children make the obvious inference: if people's sex is so critical in speaking of or about them, it must more generally be a centrally important personal characteristic.

Most widely discussed is the question of the so-called masculine generic: the use of *he* with sex-indefinite antecedents ("the conscientious citizen") and *man* in contexts where people in general are clearly involved ("only men have capability of speech").[10] These practices are connected with a more general phenomenon: the tendency to universalize forms with male reference (a modern example is *guys*, now widely used in direct address to a group which may be all female). Terms with female reference, instead of losing their sex-specificity, tend to lose their special distinguishing characteristics that discriminate among women and, thus, they become homogenized as in the extension of *lady* and of *girl* to refer to females of any status or age, respectively. In particular cases, there are detailed explanations that may be offered for such shifts but these two general patterns suggest a tendency, on the one hand, to equate humanity with the male sex and, on the other hand, to assume that femaleness defines women, whose individuality becomes submerged in categorizing principles that treat all women as identical. Universalization and homogenization are both aspects of a male-centered perspective on language.

Although it is primarily the vocabulary that has been held to transmit traditional assumptions about the sexes, psychologist Finn Tshudi's research suggests that this phenomenon may be linked to other levels of linguistic structure.[11] Tschudi has investigated judgments of the linguistic acceptability of "similarity statements" that compare the sexes. He finds, for example, that "Men can care for children just as well as women" sounds linguistically unremarkable to his experimental subjects whereas "Women can care for children just as well as men" is judged distinctly bizarre. Such asymmetries attest to the conventionalized reliance of language users on traditional views of women's and men's traits and activities. Even language users who overtly deny both the adequacy of these familiar stereotypes as descriptive models *of* real women and men and their desirability as normative models *for* real women and men often make unwitting reference to stereotypical Woman and Man. Such reference seems likely to reinforce such stereotypes (subliminally, as it were). It may also, as in the cases discussed earlier, help acculturate the young child to an awareness of them and (at least initially) a belief in their accuracy and/or desirability. Such hypotheses must, of course, be tested, but the data are certainly suggestive.

Tschudi's results draw our attention once again to the interaction of the language system with what speakers and hearers take to be shared experience and assumptions, commonly held "background" models of the world they each live in. Language achieves its communicative efficiency through our not having to spell everything out, our being able to rely on stereotypes and presuppositions to help us convey complex messages in a compact form. The problem is that we may convey more than we intend. It takes both conscious effort and considerable ingenuity to disavow particular stereotypes and presuppositions that are well established and that are invoked in conventionalized linguistic formulae like those above. Language is inherently conservative, at least with respect to changes that require conscious attention to what has been taken for granted. Change cannot be instituted simply by virtue of a speaker's using a new form or using an old form in a new way: others must recognize what it is the speaker is trying to say. Only if hidden assumptions are brought into plain view and made explicit is it possible for alternative world-models to become commonplace enough that they can function presuppositionally and help us form alternative stereotypes.

Although particular linquistic forms and structures are not sexist in themselves, the range of linguistic choices readily available in a community both reflects and contributes to maintaining traditional views of the sexes. The explanation is the same in both cases: namely, that language relies on (usually implicit) conventionalized models of the world. Changing those conventionalized models is an integral part of changing the system of linguistic choices: the two kinds of change are inextricably linked, each one leading to and depending on the other.

LINGUISTIC REFORM:
FEMINIST PROPOSALS AND RESISTANCE

In discussing feminist suggestions for various linguistic changes, even linguists have sometimes forgotten the rule they avowedly adopt for themselves: Do not prescribe how people *should* speak but describe how they *do* speak. And the important observation that the present state of a language must be considered on its own terms, without reference to past states of which present traces may or may not exist, is also sometimes forgotten.

Why, for example, do such coinages as *herstory* and *himmicane* arise? Spelling and, to a limited extent, pronunciation provide the formal link in the case of *history*. The conceptual connection lies in the traditional approach to history as the story (selective and romanticized in the tradition of fictions) of great men and their great deeds, an approach that fails to illumine the lives of foremothers (and, indeed, tells us little of the experience of the vast majority of our forefathers). In the case of *hurricane*, there is both a phonological connection to *her* and the additional formal link provided by the practice of dubbing these wild and destructive forces with female first names which serve as antecedents for feminine pronominal forms (this practice was recently changed, and names of both sexes are now used). To speak of *himmicanes* is to protest the conception of femaleness implicit in the naming practice and to draw attention to an index of antiwomen sentiment persisting in the culture. These are lexical innovations with point and purpose that capitalize on form in order to reinforce function. They need not be seen, as some linguists have seemed to think, as based on analyses of previously existing linguistic structures or beliefs about actual language history.

To counter the suggestion that *man* is not adequately generic, etymology is often brought forth inappropriately. It is true that *man* derives from a genuinely generic form that designated human beings with no opposition to a form designating only female human beings. In Old English, for example, compound forms distinguished female-men from male-men when the need arose: *wifmann* and *wermann*, respectively. The simple forms *wife* and *were* could also be used, the latter historically linked with Latin *vir-*, appearing in *virile* and *virtue*.* *Man* may have acquired its present strongly masculine sense at around the time that *person* became available to serve generic purposes when they arose.[12] Both the last citations of *were* and the first citations of *person* (in the sense 'human' and not specifically 'actor') in the Oxford English Dictionary are from the thirteenth century. These historical facts are of interest insofar as they provide some guide as to the kinds of change that can occur, but they do not establish the current "genericness" of *man*. In many contexts, sex-indefinite interpretations of *man* are now unavailable: the child who says, "Mommy is a man" will be corrected (unless Mommy has undergone a sex-change operation or in some other way been admitted to the male sex). If I say to you, "A man is at the front door asking for you," and you find a woman, you will conclude that I was mistaken or deceptive but not that I was simply uninformative. Thus the history of earlier uses is simply beside the point.

There is considerable evidence that both *man* and generic *he* do, in many contexts, fail to be genuinely non-sexed. Thus many people have begun to use substitutes (*person*, singular *they*, *s/he*, and coinages like *E*) and to advocate that others do likewise. In response many self-appointed keepers of the "father tongue" interpret such proposals for future usage (and instances of present usage) as demands that we deny past usage—that we "rewrite Shakespeare and the Bible." As both Shakespearean and Biblical scholars are well aware, the processes of linguistic and social change (along with, in the case of the Bible, repeated translations between radically different languages) have already created problems of interpretation for modern readers. We might someday need to remind English users that *he* in mid-twentieth-century texts was sometimes used in sex-indefinite contexts so that they would not misinterpret what they read. We now spend a significant teaching effort trying to convince elementary and secondary school students that masculine forms are always potentially generic and that *they* should not be used in singular contexts. Linguistically sounder pedagogy would not have to falsify present facts in order to try to preserve by authority an archaic system. Teachers must now explain away singular *they* in such sources as Shakespeare and Austen. Generic *she* goes unnoticed: the same person who tells a class that "*he* must always be used when males are potential

---

*The following anecdote suggests how the historical connection can be (mis)used. A young woman casually mentioned taking karate lessons in conversation with a learned but less than enlightened man. He: "But, my dear, that's not ladylike." She: "I wasn't aware that being ladylike was a virtue." He: "It's the *vir*-tue open to a woman."

referents" can send a notice home informing parents of "a teacher's expectations of her pupils" in a school where teachers of both sexes are employed.[13]

Changes in language (use) need not involve extending the lexicon or even using forms in radically new contexts. Many of the presently available guidelines for "nonsexist language" use offer suggestions for avoiding objectionable locutions that will not offend the sensibilities of those who find novel words shocking and singular *they* unthinkable.[14] Guidelines are just strategic suggestions, ideally based on careful analysis of present language use. Whether proposed changes are adopted depends on many factors: others' identification with the originating group, the usefulness of the proposed change in furthering some communicative purpose that a significant number of language users pursue, and the extent and kind of resistance offered by the various institutional and individual conservators of language.[15] When the move to get women the vote began to look as if it might succeed, the neutral term *suffragist* was replaced in the press by the diminutive (and belittling) term *suffragette*. The columnists and letter writers who protest the "barbaric" *chairperson* seem not to be bothered by *libber* (again, a diminutive offered in lieu of something like *liberationist*).

Why is new vocabulary proposed? An obvious though often neglected point is that language is our main way to make personal knowledge social and, more generally, to transcend the limits of individual experience. New terms like *sexism* and *male chauvinism* suggest parallels between racial and sexual inequality, between the super-patriot's complete exclusion of possible claims of non-compatriots in a blind allegiance to country and the unthinking male-centered identification of humanity with men. Such coinages yield intellectual interest,[16] establishing a direction for investigating and talking about the social and cultural world in which we live. New literary genres, new ways of dealing with familiar linguistic materials, metaphors that draw from women's experiences and perspective—language provides resources for sharing new insights and building on them.[17]

To understand how language can be both a source of information about women's lives and a force that helps to shape experiences in positive as well as negative ways, it is essential to look beyond the elements of the structured system that comprises a language to the people who use it. Linguistic structures do not exist in grammars and dictionaries but in the minds of the women and men who give them significance through their socially and culturally situated acts of language production and interpretation. We must consider the sexes as language users.

"GENDERLECTS": DISTINCTIVE LINGUISTIC IDENTITIES

Do women and men use language differently? If so, what sort of explanation might be found for these differences? One possible account is that the sexes operate with different structural systems or codes, that they have different "languages." To emphasize the close relation between so-called women's and men's languages, they have been dubbed "genderlects."* At relatively superficial levels, individuals have their own unique systems or idiolects, but the genderlect model posits a structural unity that systematically differentiates women's idiolects from men's.

The most familiar examples of different codes involve communities that have little or no communicative contact with one another. There are also cases where what we recognize as two distinct systems are preserved even though communicative contact exists and most members of the community are competent in both. My speaking the variety of English I do marks me as an American rather than a New Zealander or a Japanese. If I also spoke Yiddish, that would mark ethnic identity as a Jew. To view sex-linked differences in language use in terms of the genderlect model is to suppose that they arise from 1) membership in single-sex communicative networks during critical developmental stages, 2) reference groups and norms based on the language use of same-sex models, and/or 3) sex-based innate differences in linguistic competence. The hypothesis is that sex-class membership determines a basic linguistic identity whether the ultimate explanation is social, cultural, biological, or some combination thereof.

Twentieth-century linguists have argued (successfully, in my view) against any biological determinants of the features that differentiate such languages as Xhosa and Navajo, Greek and Hungarian. A child of any racial stock can learn any language. Since there certainly are biological differences between the sexes, the biological is a mode of explanation that some choose to account for virtually all differences in women's and men's behaviors. Language is rooted in the biology of the human organism, so it is not inconceivable that biology plays a role in differentially shaping the sexes' language. The place to look for empirical evidence would be in studies of language development and in neurolinguistics,[18] which deals with the neural correlates of language and language disorders. So far, however, there is absolutely no evidence that would suggest the sexes are pre-programmed to develop structurally different linguistic systems.

The earliest accounts of "women's languages" came from seventeenth- and eighteenth-century missionaries and travelers, who found sex-differentiated forms of language use in the native languages of the Americas, Africa, and Asia unfamiliar to Europeans. Early twentieth-century anthropologists and linguists produced more sophisticated descriptions.[19] Often, investigators found a fairly large number of commonly used vocabulary items restricted to women's speech with synonymous but phonetically quite different items used by men. Occasionally, there were systematic differences of the kind that might distinguish closely

---

*I'm not sure by whom: it has probably arisen independently more than once to designate a system of co-occurring, sex-linked speech features.

related regional dialects of a language. It was common to describe communities showing such sex-differentiated speech as having women's and men's languages, although the differences were usually quite superficial from the viewpoint of linguistic structure. Men's speech was often held to manifest the "proper" language with "women's language" considered a deviation.

Otto Jespersen, a noted Danish linguist whose investigations of English grammar still stand as a major contribution to linguistic scholarship, has a chapter called "The Woman" in his general and popular volume *Language: Its Nature, Development and Origin*. "The Woman" keeps company with "the child" (to whom several chapters are devoted) and "the foreigner": "the man" is strikingly absent. Jespersen's discussion ranges from a report of tabus among the Zulus on a woman's uttering words sounding like the name of her father-in-law to a claim that "women exercise a great and universal influence on linguistic development through their instinctive shrinking from coarse and gross expressions and their preference for refined and (in certain spheres) veiled and indirect expressions."[20] A near universal dislike by women of "coarse and gross expressions" may well be linked to the widespread use of sexual insults by men as a potent weapon to wield against women; explanations of the frequency of indirectness in women's speech appeal to social and cultural conceptions of power.[21]

In spite of his sometimes simplistic explanations and his frequent overt sexism, Jespersen succeeded in drawing attention to many important kinds of phenomena now being investigated more systematically in language and sex studies. He noted the significance for language use of educational opportunity, culturally prescribed roles, social mobility, and the like. He discussed bilingualism, languages reserved for religious or ritual uses, and linguistic change. Finally, Jespersen was well aware that women and men in on-going, established communities share at least one common code, even where readily apparent differences in their vocabulary and/or pronunciation can be found. Genderlects don't really help us understand most of these phenomena, but the dual-language framework persists as a model for thinking about differences (either observed or imagined) in the way women and men use language. This is true even when sociocultural modes of explanations have replaced the biological.

The model is particularly appealing where there are frequently occurring linguistic forms whose use is reserved exclusively for women or men (or, for example, for conversations with women present or for speech directed to women). In such speech communities, few verbal exchanges fail to convey information about the sex of conversational participants (in addition to whatever else they convey). There are or have been speech communities for which certain grammatical processes mark the sex of conversational participants. The most detailed analysis of such a phenomenon is still Edward Sapir's "Male and Female Forms of Speech in Yana," written some 50 years ago.[22] Like a number of other American Indian languages, Yana showed systematic categorical differences in pronunciation of "the same" form, depending only on the sex of the conversational participants (actual or assumed). One class of forms was used in female-present situations; the other class of parallel forms was reserved for all-male interchanges.

Sapir noted that several distinct processes of shortening and suffixation all had the surface effect of producing shorter forms for use with women present and tentatively suggested that "the reduced female forms constitute a conventionalized symbolism of the less considered or ceremonious status of women in the community."[23]   Both sexes apparently shared the linguistic competence—knowledge of Yana—which the rules of shortening and suffixation represented.   Men actually used both sets of forms in their own speech, and women, in contexts like story telling where a male character appeared in speech with males, could also use the male-only forms.   This particular kind of sex-linked meaning which expresses sexual composition of the conversational group, and is articulated through regular grammatical processes to create lexical alternates, is apparently rare.   It is, as Sapir pointed out in the opening section of his "Abnormal Types of Speech in Nootka," similar to the better-known phenomenon of morphological markers of deference and, more generally, of social relations among interlocutors shown in such languages as Indonesian and Japanese.[24]   The familiar Indo-European languages that distinguish second-person pronouns (the *tu* and *vous* of French, for example) as expressive of social relationships show an analagous though less pervasive grammaticalization of language users' "place."   That is, the grammar provides a way to superimpose communication of social messages on utterances whose main purpose is something else.   Devices of this sort insure attention to social roles and relationships, and children may well acquire their understanding of social space in large measure from learning to manage the relevant linguistic forms properly.

Genderlects could be recognized in Yana, although an adequate analysis would have to say something further about the social meaning involved in the "code-switching."   It is in part because the differences in Yana are apparently categorical—certain forms are only used in the female-present situations whereas others belong exclusively to the male-only system—that the dual-grammar approach seems appropriate to many investigators.   Where the inventories of forms are the same for both women and men, but certain forms are used more often by one sex than the other, it may still be possible to represent the differences in terms of two distinct systems.   Although she does not spell out in any detail what women's and men's grammars might look like, linguist Robin Lakoff seems to have a "frequency" model of genderlects in mind when she speaks of "women's language" in English and talks of women's being forced to become "bilinguals" if they are to make it in the man's world.   Where alternatives exist, certain forms may be picked more frequently by one sex than the other or certain constructions used more often.   To say that such differences in frequency constitute a "woman's language" suggests that to speak habitually using rather different frequencies of the sex-sensitive expressions than expected for a member of one's sex would make one sound sex-inappropriate or "odd" in some way, rather like speaking with a foreign accent.

How we speak or write, given different options existing in the community, depends on a number of factors. Contact is a necessary condition for use of a particular variety, and access to certain linguistic varieties will depend on social networks, education, and the like. Perhaps most important, we tend to talk like those with whom we identify and those whom we admire. Other social meanings attached to particular varieties of language can also prove important. In American English, for example, there is some evidence that intonational patterns enter directly into the expression of gender identity.[25]

We can thus hypothesize that, where sex differences exist in varieties of language used, such differences are either directly expressive of gender identity or reflect some other feature of the sexes' different social positions. The term *genderlect* can be appropriate in both instances because gender—the cultural meaning attached to sexual identity—frequently interacts with other socio-cultural identities. Working in a highland Guatemala village, Anne Farber found that Indian women proficient in Spanish were often perceived as rejecting their traditional roles as women, roles for which Cakchiquel (the native language) was quite adequate.[26] In other words, a gender meaning can be superimposed on other meanings attached to use of a particular variety of language.

"Women's language" is sometimes said to consist in part of sex-differentiated vocabulary. Although some lexical items may be perceived as more appropriate for use by one sex than the other, in many cases sex-differentiated lexicons are clearly the consequence of sex-segregated social and occupational groupings, of sex-typed activities and interests. A woman in contemporary America is much more likely than a man to have detailed knowledge of sewing, a social fact indicated linguistically by her mastery of a lexicon that includes such words as *gusset, interfacing, placket, shirred*, and the like. Some have suggested that fear of seeming/being gay—"homophobia"—keeps men from learning female-typed vocabulary (for example, specialized color words—*magenta*—or *lovely* as a general evaluative).[27] There is some literature on language of sexuality used by women and men and ways of talking about such topics as menstruation.[28] But we know very little about the extent to which sex-differentiated vocabularies exist and what their implications are for cross-sex communication.

Why are linguistic repertoires—the varieties and alternatives easily accessible for speech or comprehension and the social meanings attached to their use—sometimes sex-differentiated? What significance is attached by the community to such differences? As noted above, only rarely are systematic sex differences in language use primarily expressive of gender-identity or relationships. More often, sex is correlated with language use (either in reality or in cultural norms and stereotypes) because sex is connected with specialized domains and specific activities, which in turn link in various ways to kinds of language use and extent of linguistic repertoires. In large and diverse societies, gender interacts with other social identities so that women do not form a coherent social grouping of the sort "women's language" tends to suggest. To label differences by positing two separate sex-specific languages or to include sex among the conditions of grammar is sometimes useful, but genderlects do not explain how language functions in the lives of women and men and why the sexes' systems show the features they do.[29]

STYLES AND STRATEGIES: LANGUAGE AT WORK

Often when the sexes are said to speak different "languages," it can be more illuminating to speak of different styles or strategies or preferred patterns of language use. The shift in terminology is meant to reflect a shift in emphasis: rather than an assumption that linguistic alternatives are somehow fixed by the sex of the speaker, the focus is on the communicative significance speakers (and hearers) attach to the linguistic choices made in particular discourse settings. The members of the speech community are being viewed not only as the occupants of certain social positions (which may, of course, delimit the repertoire from which they can draw) but also as actors on the verbal stage, performing with linguistic resources available and developing new resources for use in future performances. The shift is from a focus on the individual speaker/ hearer, who possesses a particular (socio)linguistic identity, to her social relationships and interactions with others as those are realized in language use. From an investigation of static linguistic structures, a first step, we turn to investigation of dynamic processes of discourse.*

As psychologist Virginia Valian has pointed out, most of the differences between the speech of women and men hypothesized by Lakoff lie in the domain of language *use* rather than in the domain of language in the narrower structural sense that would imply different grammatical systems.[30] That is, in many cases women and men are doing different things with shared resources for producing and interpreting, exploiting in somewhat different ways a basically common code. The study of language use is, however, an important way to gain insight into the semantic structure of language. Differences in use of language by women and men can lead us to ask what it is about the function or meaning of a particular expression that might explain why women and men use that expression in different frequencies or in somewhat different contexts.

---

*Note that the genderlect model does not work well for differences in language use other than those correlating with speaker's sex. For example, the "women's language" Sapir observed in Yana is badly misnamed since the forms involved are expressions of an audience including women and are used by both women and men. It is speaker's or writer's gender identity that has been the preoccupation of much recent work on so-called "women's language" (for example, Robin Lakoff's and many subsequent studies). Some studies have found, however, addressee's sex a better predictor than speaker's of the distribution of certain forms supposedly characteristic of "women's language." See, for example, Dede Brouwer, Marinel Gerritsen, and Dorian De Haan's "Speech Differences between Women and Men: On the Wrong Track?", *Language in Society* 8 (1979), 33-50.

Experience with actual frequency counts suggests that many of the sex-linked differences that investigators have expected to find do not actually exist. Tag questions ("it's a nice day, *isn't it?*"), for example, have been fairly extensively investigated on the basis of Lakoff's suggestion that women use them much more frequently than men or in a wider range of contexts.[31] On the whole, these studies have not supported Lakoff's hypothesis. But to find no sex difference where one was predicted is significant. Such results force us to ask what features of cultural stereotypes about women and men and of our explicit beliefs about how languuage works (in this case, the function of tag forms) led to hypothesizing a connection between this aspect of language use and sex. The tag form, for example, is now seen to have multiple uses: it may convey hesitancy or it may constitute an invitation for the hearer to engage actively in the conversation, or both. Concern to understand whether the sexes use tags differently, and if so why, has forced investigators to attend more closely to the communicative function these forms serve. In other words, through looking at women, we have refined our view of a particular aspect of a particular language.

Japanese is one of the most frequently cited cases where there are striking differences between women's and men's usages. Although it is widely believed among the Japanese that there are many categorical differences in women's and men's language use, linguist Eleanor Jorden has found that this is seldom true and that the bulk of sex-differentiated frequencies in the use of particular forms can be explained in terms of women's speaking more politely than men. Such an account does not, of course, rule out the possibility that differences in politeness level may themselves play a role in expressing gender-identity. Jorden has noted that high frequencies of certain particles connected to politeness and formality (so-called "women's language") are much more likely to occur in certain contexts than in others. For example, a young woman talking to a male class-mate at a social event will speak far more "politely" than when talking to that same young man in a classroom setting. Older women (past child-bearing years) use these forms far less often than they did in the courtship and early marriage stages of their lives. That is, part of presenting oneself as "feminine" in Japanese is apparently sounding "polite," yet simply to label the phenomenon "women's language" would be to obscure the important connection with politeness.[32]

In many cultural settings, women's speech is said to be more "polite" than men's. This phenomenon is partly to be understood in terms of men's socially superior position, although there are other factors involved as well.[33] Sociologists Pamela Fishmay and Candace West, among others, have applied the ethnomethodological "turn-taking" view of conversational structure to explain findings that men are more successful interrupters and women more easily interrupted, that men talk more in mixed-sex groups (both private and public), that men are more successful at initiating topics than women, and the like.[34] Empirical studies of nonverbal communication and of address forms show similar phenomena: not surprisingly, men tend to communicate with women as the socially powerful communicate with those whom they dominate.[35] Yet many of these sex differences in communicative style are not completely explained by male dominance. Evidence from all-female contexts is especially important for establishing a complementary view of conversation as potentially a collaborative rather than simply a competitive activity. Studies suggest that women often do more than men in comparable settings to establish and maintain conversational links. Devices used include certain kinds of tags, murmured *mmhmms*, and use of question forms.[36] The predominant theory of conversation in social life tends to stress competition for turns. In this framework, conversation is seen as a game of conflict, with women as perennial losers.* An alternative might be to view it as a game of coordination, of which women are highly skilled players. Real communicative interaction, of course, is a mixture— as are real people in their collaborative vs. competitive orientations toward linguistic exchanges.

Many studies of language use as socially situated action are drawing on the newly developing area of linguistic pragmatics, the analysis of speech acts (what we do by speaking—for example, ask, persuade) and of the interaction of context and the linguistic system to produce such actions. For example, it is well known that directives can be issued in a variety of forms that range from the bald, "unmitigated" imperative to the allusive and indirect "hint" ("I'm cold" as a directive to close the window—or not to open it); what forms are used depends on the relationship of the interlocutors, the nature of the action being asked of the addressee, and so on. Susan Ervin-Tripp, a psycholinguist, has studied the structure of American English directives in some detail and does not find sex differences as such in how directives are issued but, instead, finds women and men similarly differentiating their directives according to familiarity with addressee, relative ranks, whether compliance is expected, and so on.[37] Rich information on particular relations and roles can be gleaned from analysis of directives, but a simple correlation of forms with speaker and/or hearer sex is unlikely to be particularly revealing because it cannot take account of the multiple contributions of contextual factors.

Even very young children use language to order their social lives. Ervin-Tripp reports on a study of directives issued by a two-year-old, who not only differentiated between her own age group and the three- and four-year-olds

---

*Rather than seeing women as perennial "losers," a terminology suggesting a fair competition, politically more sophisticated analyses see this disadvantage as some kind of victimization or oppression of women by men in the conversational arena. Fishman, for example, proposes an interesting Marxist-type model of women as the exploited workers who produce the surplus value enjoyed by men in the conversational economy. Her analysis is more subtle than this summary indicates, and some such model is certainly useful for explaining certain features of the structuring of cross-sex conversations. My point is that the economic or exchange model of conversation does not account for the full gamut of verbal interactions. The view that women and men tend to develop different cultural models of conversation in the American context, models both arising from and helping to create their different social worlds, is presented in Daniel Maltz and Ruth Borker, "A Cultural Approach to Male/Female Miscommunication," Paper delivered at Pitzer College, 1979.

at her nursery school, but showed a striking tendency to use many more politeness forms to her father than to her mother, showing her "not yet having been properly trained in the equality of the sexes."[38] Fathers themselves, in contrast to mothers, tend to speak to their children much as "strangers" do.[39] This suggests that conceptions of the relatively elevated status of males may arise in part from the relative inaccessibility of the male parent in a child's world (and, more generally, of adult males): even if familiarity does not breed contempt, distance probably promotes deference in speech and other behavior.

Communication proceeds by a series of inferences as to what the other participants intended to do in saying whatever was said. As William Labov and David Fanshel put it, "Conversation is not a chain of utterances, but rather a matrix of utterances and actions bound together by a web of understandings and reactions."[40] Misunderstandings, deriving from many sources, sometimes tangle the web. Even where a basic interpretive system is shared, communication can breakdown because of differing background assumptions or somewhat different strategies for achieving a common communicative goal. Consider the following case:

A: John's having a party. Wanna go?

B: OK.

A: (Later) Are you sure you wanna go?

B: OK. Let's not go. I'm tired anyway.

This exchange resulted in the couple's not going to the party, with each feeling the decision had been made as a favor to the other. As John Gumperz and Deborah Tannen point out in discussing this example, the *OK* and *anyway* in B's second remark could have told A that B was giving in to what B thought was A's preference. A, however, focused on *I'm tired* as indicative of B's desire not to go. B, on the other hand, mistakenly interpreted A's repetition of the initial query as dissatisfaction with the initial response, whereas A intended the repetition to serve the purpose of insuring that B was not simply trying to be agreeable but had had adequate encouragement to express B's real feelings about the matter (or some such).[41] Examples of this sort can easily be multiplied. Miscommunication between women and men of this kind is likely if indeed, as suggested earlier, the sexes have somewhat different approaches to "doing things with words," different conceptions of the significance of particular conversational gambits.[42]

Microanalysis of verbal form can also help elucidate certain aspects of a literary work. What, for example, has a particular woman built into her text? How does she exploit the linguistic resources available to her and shape her own formal patterns to serve particular aesthetic and literary purposes?[43] From such stylistic investigations of literary texts may emerge certain quite general tendencies that correlate with the author's sex.* Yet such results are uninformative

_____

*Such correlations are highly unlikely unless one restricts attention to a sharply delimited genre and period.

unless the correlations can be explicated, and this demands attention to literary meaning, which can only be studied by close examination of literary works and not by extracting isolated formal linguistic features from their literary contexts. Quantitative studies of both literary and social texts, which necessarily "decontextualize," derive their import from the detailed "contextualized" analyses that are required to determine significance (function or range of functions) of those particular formal linguistic features that a researcher has chosen to count.[44]

In neither social nor literary uses of language is there a determinate meaning associated with particular linguistic forms. What is said is formed against a backdrop of linguistic experience and knowledge and of the speaker/writer's view of the hearer/reader. What is understood is actively created by the hearer or reader, drawing not only from a somewhat personal perspective on language but also incorporating various assumptions and cultural biases about the person taken to be the source of the utterance.[45] Linguistic structures themselves are impotent: individual thought and socioculturally situated linguistic processes of production and interpretation endow them with significance and turn them into weapons—or tools.

A popular view of language makes it rather like the Morse Code: a system of labels that a particular community has decided to attach arbitrarily to independently existing messages, which the Code then allows community members to convey to one another neutrally and efficiently. This picture is misleading: language is used not just to tag experience but to organize thought and social life in various ways. Linguistic "codes" are constantly changing, not through legislation but through women's and men's strategic uses of them, uses embedded in society, history, and culture. Indeterminacy and multiple meanings are not the exception but important features of linguistic systems that underlie the role of language in changing society, culture, and personal consciousness. Once the simple labeling view is seen to be inadequate, it is possible to recognize *why* and to begin to investigate *how* language is of central importance in women's lives.

NOTES

1. See Dell Hymes, "Speech and Language: On the Origins and Foundations of Inequality Among Speakers," in *Language as a Human Problem*, ed. Einar Haugen and Morton Bloomfield (New York: W. W. Norton, 1974), pp. 45-72. See also Sally McConnell-Ginet, "Linguistics in the Feminist Context," presented as part of *Women and Language* Forum, 1978 MLA meetings.

2. Complete bibliographic treatment would require another book, but the following sources cover a representative range of linguistically influenced research on language and the sexes. Much of the research draws from linguistics but is based in other disciplines. Robin Lakoff, *Language and Woman's Place* (New York: Harper and Row Torchbooks, 1975) is a linguistic analysis that has spurred considerable research; Mary Ritchie Key, *Male/Female Language* (Metuchen, N.J.: Scarecrow Press, 1975) grew from the first linguistics course in this area and contains an interesting bibliography. Barrie Thorne and Nancy Henley, eds., *Language and Sex: Difference and Dominance* (Rowley, Mass.:

Newbury House, 1975) is an interdisciplinary collection with a thorough review article and annotated bibliography. A second volume, Nancy Henley, Barrie Thorne, and Cheris Kramarae, eds. is scheduled for publication in 1981. Other books include Douglas Butturff and Edmund L. Epstein, eds. *Women's Language and Style* (Akron, O.: University of Akron Press, 1978); Betty Lou Dubois and Isabel Crouch, eds. *The Sociology of the Languages of American Women* (San Antonio, Tex.: Trinity University, 1976); Barbara Eakins and Gene Eakins, *Sex Difference in Human Communication* (New York: Houghton-Mifflin, 1978); Barbara Eakins, Gene Eakins, and B. Lief-Brilhart, eds., *Women's (and Men's) Communication* (Washington, D.C.: Speech Communication Association, 1976); Casey Miller and Kate Swift, *Words and Women* (New York: Anchor Press/Doubleday, 1976); Alleen Pace Nilsen, Haig Bosmajian, H. Lee Gershuny, and Julie Stanley, eds., *Sexism and Language* (Urbana, Ill.: National Council of Teachers of English, 1977); Judith Orasance, Manay K. Slater, and Leonore Loeb Addler, eds. *Language, Sex and Gender: Does "La Difference" Make a Difference?* Annals of the New York Academy of Sciences, 327 (New York: New York Academy of Sciences, 1979). Volumes announced for publication in 1980 include Mary Vetterling-Braggin, ed. *Sexist Language: A Modern Philosophical Analysis* (Totawa, N.J.: Littlefield, Adams, and Co.) and Cheris Kramarae, *Women and Men Speaking: Frameworks for Analysis* (Rowley, Mass.: Newbury House). In conventional professional journals as well as in such new women's studies publications as *SIGNS: Journal of Women in Culture and Society*, papers on language and sex are appearing in increasing numbers. For example, *Women's Studies International Quarterly* 3.2 (1980), is completely devoted to this topic. *Women and Language News*, Department of Linguistics, Stanford University, lists both published and unpublished work, and reports on conferences, workshops, panels, and symposia as well as courses.

3. See Julia Penelope Stanley, "Paradigmatic Woman: The Prostitute," in David L. Shores and Carol P. Hines, eds., *Papers in Linguistic Variation* (University of Alabama: The University of Alabama Press, 1977) for many examples. Muriel Schulz, "The Semantic Derogation of Women," in Thorne and Henley, *Language and Sex*, pp. 64-75, discusses the general phenomenon of sexualization and degradation in terms referring to women.

4. I have used *The Compact Edition of the Oxford English Dictionary* (Oxford: Oxford University Press, 1971) and *The American Heritage Dictionary of the English Language,* ed. William Morris (Boston: Houghton Mifflin Co. and American Heritage Publishing Co., 1969).

5. It is not only modern feminists who note this trend. See, for example, Karl Jaberg, "Perjorative Bedeutungsentwicklung im Franzosischen," *Zeits. Rom. Phil.* 25 (1901), 27 (1903), 29 (1905). Cited in Stephen Ullman, *The Principles of Semantics* (Oxford: Basil Blackwell, 1951), p. 183, n.1.

6. Susan Wolfe (Robbins), "Patriarchal Paradigm for Language Change," presented at 1978 MLA meetings, suggests alternatives to the usual view that common Indo-European vocabulary provides evidence that our forebears some 5000 years ago had a strongly patriarchal culture and society. Such a view is presented, for example, in Emile Benveniste, *Le Vocabulaire des Institutions Indo-Europeennes* (Paris, 1969) and more accessibly, in Calvert Watkins, "Indo-European and the Indo-Europeans," *The American Heritage Dictionary,* pp. 1496-1502.

7. This and subsequent mentions of Lakoff refer to *Language and Women's Place.*

8. See Cheris Kramarae, this volume, for discussion of such misinterpretations.

9. In Elizabeth Beardsley, "Referential Genderization," *The Philosophical Forum* 5 (1973): 285-93. See also Beardsley, "Traits and Genderization," in *Feminism and Philosophy,* ed. Mary Vetterling-Braggin, Frederick A. Elliston, and Jane English (Totawa, N.J.: Littlefield, 1977), pp. 117-23.

10. See the research reported in Wendy Martyna, "The Psychology of the Generic Masculine," this volume.

11. In Finn Tschudi, "Gender Stereotypes Reflected in Asymmetric Similarities

in Language" (paper presented at American Association of Psychology meetings, Sept. 1979). Tschudi draws on the work in Amos Tversky, "Features of Similarity," *Psychology Review* 84 (1977): 327-52.

12. Suggested to me by Don Foreman.

13. See Wendy Martyna, this volume; McConnell-Ginet, "Pronouns," discusses generic *she;* see Otto Jespersen, *A Modern English Grammar on Historical Principles* (Kobenhave: Ejnar Muksgaard, 1909-49; rpt. London: George Allen and Unwin, 1961 and 1965), Part II, Syntax, First Volume, 5.56, for many examples of singular *they* from distinguished sources. Ann Bodine, "Androcentrism in Prescriptive Grammar: Singular 'they', Sex-indefinite 'he', and 'he or she'," *Language in Society* 4 (1975): 129-46, discusses the general issue of resistance to *they* in singular contexts. Donald MacKay, "Birth of a Word," unpublished manuscript, UCLA Department of Psychology, proposes *E*.

14. For example, APA Taskforce on Issues of Sexual Bias in Graduate Education, "Guidelines for Nonsexist Use of Language," *American Psychologist* 30 (1975): 682-84; *Guidelines for Creating Positive Sexual and Racial Images in Educational Material* (New York: Macmillan, 1975); *Guidelines for Equal Treatment of the Sexes in McGraw-Hill Book Company Publications* (New York: McGraw-Hill, 1974); "Nondiscriminatory Language," Appendix B, Guide to Manuscript Preparation (New York: Praeger Publishers, 1978).

15. See Cheris Kramarae, this volume, for discussion of the relation of the speech situation to success in attempted linguistic innovations and related issues connected with change and resistance to it. William R. Littlewood, "Linguistic Change During Interpersonal Interaction," *Lingua* 41 (1977): 1-11, points to ways that personal relations and the situation of communication may have an impact on language change, a general point of some importance in understanding how the views of the dominant social group are hard to challenge through lexical innovation unless members of the subordinate group interact and spread the innovation widely among themselves.

16. See Marilyn Frye, "Male Chauvinism: A Conceptual Analysis," in *Philosophy and Sex*, Robert Baker and Frederick Elliston, eds., (Buffalo, N.Y.: Prometheus, 1975), pp. 65-79, for an insightful discussion of conceptual distinctions to be made between sexism and male chauvinism.

17. See Naomi Scheman, "Anger and the Politics of Naming," this volume, for a philosophical analysis of language as a central component in personal and political perspectives on experience; Annette Kolodny, "Honing a Habitable Languagescape," this volume, suggests that women on the American frontier created domestic metaphors to help themselves view their strange surroundings as more familiar and less hostile.

18. In many cultures girls are said to speak earlier and have fewer speech disorders than boys, but the explanations are not very clear, and the data are murkier than I used to think. See, for example, J. H. Block, "Issues, Problems, and Pitfalls in Assessing Sex Differences," *Merrill-Palmer Quarterly* 22 (1976); H. Fairweather, "Sex Differences in Cognition," *Cognition* 4 (1976): 231-80; Ronald K. S. Macauley, "The Myth of Female Superiority in Language," *Journal of Child Language* 5 (June 1978): 353-63. (I owe these references to Patricia Brotherton.)

19. See A. Bodine, "Sex Differentiation in Language," in Thorne and Henley, *Language and Sex*, for a good review of the research. Actually, claims about sex-based differences in speaking far predate the European explorations of the New World, appearing in ancient sources.

20. Otto Jespersen, *Language: Its Nature, Development, and Origin* (London: George Allen & Unwin, 1922), p. 245.

21. Kathryn S. March suggested the relevance of sexual insults to me. Ruth Borker and Penelope Brown, this volume, deal with indirectness as a features of women's speech, suggesting why it might tend to recur in many different linguistic communities.

22. Reprinted in *Selected Writings of Edward Sapir*, ed. David G. Mandelbaum

(Berkeley: University of California Press, 1951), pp. 206-12.

23. Ibid., p. 212.

24. Ibid., pp. 179-96.

25. Carole P. Edelsky, "Question Intonation and Sex Roles," *Language in Society* 8 (1979): 15-32; and Sally McConnell-Ginet, "Intonation in a Man's World," *Signs* 3.3 (1978): 540-59.

26. Anne Farber, "Language Choice and Sex Roles in Highland Guatemala" (paper presented at 1974 meetings of American Anthropological Association). See also Ruth Borker and Patricia Nichols, this volume, for further discussion of bilingual situations.

27. Barrie Thorne tells me that a male member of the gay caucus of the American Sociological Association suggested this possible line of research to her.

28. For example, Virginia Ernster, "American Menstrual Expressions," *Sex Roles* 1 (1975): 3-13; Nancy G. Kutner and Donna Brogan, "An Investigation of Sex-Related Slang Vocabulary and Sex-Role Orientation among Male and Female University Students," *Journal of Marriage and the Family* 36 (1974): 475-84; Janice Moulton, "Sex and Reference," in *Philosophy and Sex*, ed. Baker and Elliston, pp. 34-43; R. H. Walsh and W. M. Leonard, "Usage of Terms for Sexual Intercourse by Men and Women," *Archives of Sexual Behavior* 3 (1974): 373-76.

29. Note Sapir's suggestion as to possible symbolism underlying Yana sex-differentiated forms. See Howard Giles et al., this volume, for impressions people form of women on the basis of how they speak.

30. Virginia Valian, "Linguistics and Feminism," in *Feminism and Philosophy*, ed. M. Vetterling-Braggin, Elliston, and English, pp. 154-66.

31. See, for example, Betty Lou Dubois and Isabel Crouch, "The Question of Tag Questions in Women's Speech: They Don't Really Use More of Them, Do They?" *Language in Society* 4 (1975): 398-94; and Marie Baumann, "Two Features of 'Women's Speech'," in *The Sociology . . .*, ed. Dubois and Crouch, pp. 33-20. A number of empirical studies look at other Lakoffian claims; see William M. O'Barr and Bowman K. Atkins, this volume, for a study set in the courtroom. Francine Frank, "Women's Language in America: Myth and Reality," in *Women's Language and Style*, ed. Butturff and Epstein, pp. 27-61, discusses the status of a variety of claims about sex differences in American English speech.

32. Eleanor H. Jorden, class lecture and "Language—Female and Feminine," in *Proceedings of a U.S.-Japan Sociolinguistics Meeting*, ed. Bates Hoffer (San Antonio, Texas: Trinity University, 1974), pp. 57-71. In the same volume see also Mary Sanches, "The Genesis of Sex-Role Style Markers in Children's Speech: The Children's Utterances," 101-11. Other recent discussions of Japanese include Sachiko Ide, "Language of Inferior Status: A Universal Feature of Women's Language," Japan Women's University and Motoko Y. Lee, "The Married Woman's Status and Role as Reflected in Japanese: An Exploratory Sociolinguistic Study," *Signs* 1 (1976):991-99.

33. See Penelope Brown, this volume, for an explanatory account of the connection between social structures and politeness.

34. For example, Pamela Fishman, "Interactional Shitwork," *Heresies: A Feminist Publication on Art and Politics* 1 (May 1977): 99-101; and "What Do Couples Talk About When They're Alone," in *Women's Language and Style*, ed. Butturff and Epstein, pp. 11-22; Don H. Zimmerman and Candace West, "Sex Roles, Interruptions, and Silences in Conversation," in *Language and Sex*, ed. Thorne and Henley, pp. 105-29 and West and Zimmerman, "Woman's Place in Everyday Talk: Reflections of Parent-Child Interaction," *Social Problems* 24 (1977): 521-29. Linguists have drawn on this tradition to advantage: see, for example, Marjorie Swacker, "Women's Verbal Behavior at Learned and Professional Conferences," in *The Sociology . . .*, ed. Dubois and Crouch, pp. 155-60. A useful "self-help" book that is aimed at arming women for public speaking contexts is Janet Stone and Jane Bachner, *Speaking Up* (New York: McGraw-Hill, 1977).

35. See Nancy Henley, *Body Politics* (Englewood Cliffs, N.J.: Prentice-Hall, 1977) for a discussion of sex and power differences in nonverbal communication; Sally McConnell-Ginet "Address Forms in Sexual Politics," in *Women and Language*, ed. Butturff, pp. 23-35, and Cheris Kramarae "Sex-Related Differences in Address Systems," *Anthropological Linguistics* 17.5 (1975): 198-210; both find parallels between status and gender differences in address usage as do Nessa Wolfson and Joan Manes, this volume; William M. O'Barr and Bowman K. Atkins, this volume, explore the link between what Robin Lakoff dubbed "women's language," which includes certain markers of deference, and power in the courtroom setting.

36. Lynette Hirschman, "Female-Male Differences in Conversational Interaction" (paper read at 1973 LSA Winter Meetings) and "Analysis of Supportive and Assertive Behavior in Conversations" (paper read at 1974 LSA Summer Meetings) finds such results. Women are seen building a joint conversational product by Susan Kalcik, ". . . like Ann's gynecologist or the time I was almost raped," *Journal of American Folklore* 88 (1975): 3-11; and a similar collaborative approach is taken by the young girls in Marjorie Goodwin's study, this volume. Goodwin makes it clear that the girls can also compete successfully.

37. Susan Ervin-Tripp, "Wait for Me, Roller-Skate!" in *Child Discourse*, ed. S. Ervin-Tripp and Claudia Mitchell-Kernan (New York: Academic Press, 1977), pp. 165-88. See also Susan Ervin-Tripp, "'Is Sybil There?': The Structure of Some American English Directives," *Language in Society* 5 (1976): 25-66; and Marjorie Goodwin, this volume.

38. "Wait for Me, Roller-Skate!" p. 183.

39. See Jean Berko-Gleason, "Fathers and Other Strangers," in *Developmental Psycholinguistics*, ed. D. Dato (Georgetown Univ. School of Language and Linguistics, 1975).

40. William Labov and David Fanshel, *Therapeutic Discourse: Psychotherapy as Conversation* (New York: Academic Press, 1977): p.30.

41. John Gumperz and Deborah Tannen, "Individual and Social Differences in Language Use," to appear in *Individual Differences in Language Ability and Language Behavior*, ed. William Wang and Charles Fillmore (New York: Academic Press).

42. See discussion in Deborah Tannen, "An Indirect-Direct Look at Misunderstandings: a Matrimonial and Cross-Cultural View" M.A. thesis, Univ. of California, Berkeley, 1976. See also Ruth Borker, this volume, for discussion of indirection.

43. See, for example, Paula Treichler and Bonnie Costello, this volume.

44. For somewhat more detailed discussion of these issues, see Sally McConnell-Ginet, review of Mary Hiatt, *The Way Women Write*, in *Language in Society*, 8 (1979): 466-69.

45. Nancy Miller, Caren Greenberg, and Peggy Kamuf, this volume, all discuss these issues in the literary context. Nelly Furman, this volume, deals with the question of language in literature from the perspective of literary criticism.

2
ANTHROPOLOGY:
SOCIAL AND CULTURAL PERSPECTIVES

Ruth Borker

While linguistics focuses on the rules which govern the internal structure of language and a literary analysis begins with written texts and explores the self-conscious processes by which they are constructed, the anthropological study of language explores the role of words in human social-cultural experience. The unique contribution anthropology can make to the study of language and gender is its exploration of how language use informs and is informed by the larger social and cultural patterns of which it is an element. It provides us both with range—making comprehensible the different realities to be found cross-culturally and expanding our conceptions of social and cultural possibilities—and depth—creating models of the web of interlocking factors that shape language use in particular human communities.

Anthropologists have been concerned with language because of its centrality in people's lives and because it provides a means for systematically linking macro- and micro-levels of social process. They have viewed women's and men's speech patterns as expressions of larger social and cultural patterns and as mechanisms for perpetuating those patterns at the individual and interpersonal level.

Anthropologists looking at women's language use have focused on two central concerns that parallel those in the anthropology of women. First, they have asked how a woman's social position in any particular community or institution affects her speech. Second, they have asked how the cultural ideas

I would like to thank Daniel Maltz, Mario Dávila, Kelsey Clark, Sally McConnell-Ginet, Fred Myers, and Bette Clark for comments on earlier versions of this chapter. Some of the ideas discussed here were first presented in my paper "Power in Speech: A Review of Women's and Men's Speech."

and models of language, of gender and of power and status give meaning to language use and shape linguistic behavior.

I begin my review with those studies exploring the social dimensions of women's speech, looking first at studies showing the degree to which women's social position determines their language use, then moving to studies showing how women use language to cope with their social situation, and finally considering how women do distinctive things with words as a result of their social experience. From these questions, I turn to studies that explore the ways cultural ideas shape speech by creating a system in which speech is produced and interpreted, focusing particularly on cultural models of men and women, power and language.

SOCIAL DIMENSIONS OF WOMEN'S LANGUAGE USE

In saying that anthroplogists look at social position I mean they look at the roles and relationships that link people together; at the norms that define appropriate social behavior; at the rights, resources, and obligations roles provide; and at the kinds of situations in which interaction takes place. In terms of the problem of language use and gender, they are concerned both with the ways this social complex shapes speech and the comparative placement of women and men in the social system.

Anthropologists have asked three types of questions about the impact of the social world on women's speech: 1) how is women's speech determined by their social position, 2) how is speech a means of coping with their position, and 3) to what extent do the differing social experiences of men and women lead them to use language in differing ways and to do different things?

Within any social system, some roles are sex-specific, some are simply associated with a particular sex, and still others are sex-neutral. In no society are individuals defined only by gender, but also in no society is gender irrelevant to social identity and position. That patterns of language use vary with differences in social position is a well-documented fact of sociolinguistics, and it is therefore not at all surprising that differences between the speech of men and women have been frequently reported. But two different social processes are at work in assigning different patterns of speech to the two sexes, and they should be distinguished. Whereas some features of speech are acquired as part of learning to speak and act "like a man" or "like a woman," other features, although they also correlate with the sex of the speaker, are primarily the result of social position and social experience. Thus a study of differences between the speech of male doctors and female nurses might choose to emphasize either the gender differences or the occupational differences between the two sets of speakers.

Robin Lakoff, for example, maintains that features which distinguish the speech of women from that of men in the United States are a direct function of American gender roles.[1] Women's speech, she argues, is related to their social position by a two-part process. First, women learn to use specific linguistic features as part of the process of learning to act "ladylike," to behave like acceptable women. Second, the specific linguistic features that they learn prevent them from asserting themselves in conversational interaction and limit them to being powerless and ineffectual members of society.

At least two anthropological studies of specific institutions within the United States have provided potential challenges for Lakoff's equation between "women's language" and the language of powerlessness. William M. O'Barr and Bowman K. Atkins (in this volume) look at the speech of court witnesses to see whether they used the features Lakoff had identified as typifying women and as expressing women's insecurity and lack of power.[2] They did in fact find such features were used by many women, but by no means all, yet they also found that a number of men used them as well. The key social fact correlating with use of these features was not gender, but social status. Speakers of low status used them, and because of the position of women in American society this was true of more women than men. They also found through experimentation that this speech was in fact "powerless" in a second sense; not only is it the way people without social power speak, the speech itself is powerless—less convincing and less believable than speech without such features.

Brenda Mann examined the speech in a very different setting—an urban bar.[3] She found that waitresses spoke in different ways from bartenders and that each spoke differently from customers. Speech is a central part of the job, it is a function of social position because it is a major component of the social role. And these roles were available to people on the basis of sex: only men could be bartenders and only women could be waitresses. Further, the roles provide unequal access to resources and authority. Bartenders controlled resources that were essential for waitresses to fulfill their jobs. Only by being willing to verbally defer to bartenders, by enacting in speech their social subordination regardless of their possible greater verbal skill, could women do their jobs. Although these speech patterns are a function of the social structure of the bar, the victories of bartenders over waitresses are often interpreted by the participants as being a result of gender, not social differences, and are seen as proof of male superiority.

If particular uses of language are a function of position, then these can only be changed by changing the social roles or the placement of women or men within the social system. Clearly the social system in such situations sets strong constraints on the actions of individuals. Such constraints are particularly important because the language use itself, while determined by the social system, also has social consequences—it affects interaction in particular ways and has particular meanings for community members. If women as a function of their position speak in ways that are systematically different from those of men, speech can serve as a marker of sexual identity and an indicator of basic differences in the nature of men and women. In such cases language use may not in fact be perceived as determined by social position but as determined by gender defined biologically, with important implications for male-female relations. The case of the United States is instructive. As O'Barr and Atkins show, key features that have been seen as distinctively women's speech depend not on gender but on social position, and the differences in women's and men's frequency in using them is the result of the unequal distribution of social status and positions of power between the sexes. But as Mann shows, socially determined differences can be interpreted as gender—based, as grounded in biology and immutable, thereby justifying social inequality between the sexes.

While studies of language as a function of social position demonstrate the existence of major constraints on women's speech, it is also true that there is some flexibility in the ways women can respond linguistically to the constraints posed by their social position. A number of researchers have shown that some language use characteristic of women can be seen as a means of coping with their social situations. These studies shift our focus from the social system to the individuals within it and the situations they confront.

This orientation has been taken in a number of studies of language choice in multilingual or multidialectal communities. In the past it was taken for granted that women were more likely to be monolingual than men in contact situations. Many ethnographers have noted that in the particular multilanguage situation they studied, men had greater contact with outsiders, giving them a greater need for, access to, and knowledge of the national or colonial language. Women's monolingualism in such situations was seen as a function of their restricted contact with non-local language speakers as a result of their involvement in domestic and locally based activities, in contrast to men's involvement in public politics and such economic activities as migrant labor. Recent studies by Anne Farber[4] and Susan Gal[5], however, make it clear that code choice is shaped by women's responses to their specific, locally defined social position.

Farber shows that Indian women in Guatemala have little to gain from speaking Spanish (unlike men) and are positively motivated to deny their knowledge and present themselves as more monolingual than they are. In fact, Farber and others suggest that ethnographers have probably misjudged the extent of women's bilingualism in many communities.[6]

Studying a rural community in Austria that is bilingual in German and Hungarian, Gal examined the less common situation of women leading the process of code change.* Gal makes clear that young women's greater use of German reflects their active rejection of peasant status, which is associated with Hungarian, in favor of worker status, associated with German. She argues that women accurately perceive the male-dominated structures of peasant life and the disadvantages at which it places them, and seek the greater ease afforded by the status of worker or worker's wife. While men in this community may find

---

*The Gal study is discussed from a slightly different vantage point in Patricia Nichols, this volume, as is Keenan's research, which I discuss in a later section. Nichols focuses on the question of the contribution of women to language change.

economic independence in the generally devalued peasant life, it has no such promise for women. These studies make clear that women's choice of language code must be understood in terms of the responses to the life situations women face in particular communities and that the facile generalizations of the past are no longer tenable.

Researchers have also looked at women's speech in specific social contexts as communicative strategies. From this perspective speech is seen as a means by which women seek particular interactional ends, given the linguistic resources they have available and the constraints operating on them as a result of their social position.

Karen Larsen in her study of speech in rural Norway explores the ways women speak in the home.[7] Women are recognized as having authority in the home, especially over children, but in asserting that authority they cannot be overtly verbally aggressive as such speech is regarded as inappropriate for women. Women do have a variety of linguistic resources available to them, however, and speech is seen by Norwegians as a feminine area of concern. Larsen found that women used an indirect strategy of switching to the standard dialect within their utterances to give added force to their statements and demands. Larsen argues that this use of indirection is not "hedging or modifying the force of one's speech," but a way of "redefining temporarily the frame in which a message is to be read."[8] The local dialect is associated with intimacy and personal involvement. The standard dialect, in contrast, is associated with social distance and implies that a speaker is conveying general information as a public representative rather than speaking as an individual. Thus when women switch to the standard they strengthen the force of their statement by "removing the utterance from the realm of personal communication and giving it both the import and impact of generally accepted knowledge."[9] This strategy allows them to invoke the irrefutable power of society and their own authority within it without using the direct and aggressive speech forms deemed only appropriate for men.

Brown's analysis (in this volume) of politeness in Tenejapa, Mexico, represents the most systematic attempt to show how use of specific linguistic features reflects women's strategies for dealing with their social position.[10] Using a strategy model of politeness, she predicts that given their social vulnerability and the strong norms of male authority, women should employ more politeness. She not only found that women were more polite but also that there was a distinctively feminine style of politeness that included greater use of irony, rhetorical questions, and negative assertions to convey positive meanings. She also found a high level of politeness for both parties in cross-sex conversations, which she speculates results from factors that attenuate male authority. What is most exciting in her study is her demonstration of how use of very specific linguistic features are systematically linked to aspects of women's social position.

The focus upon speech in terms of the conscious strategies women use to deal with particular situations emphasizes basic similarities in the ways women and men use language, even when the actual speech produced is different. It assumes that women and men share the same language tools, or communicative repertoire, and that both exploit the resources available to them to achieve desired ends in particular contexts.

But the different social experiences of women and men may have a more lasting effect on their speech patterns as well. From their different experiences, members of each sex learn to be proficient in different language skills and to do different things with words. Marjorie Goodwin's study (in this volume) of speech patterns in children's play groups demonstrates that girls and boys organize friendly interaction in different ways and that these differences are expressed in the use of different linguistic forms.[11] Boys, for example, express hierarchy through direct commands, while girls deny hierarchy through suggestions phrased "as proposals for future activity." Expanding on Goodwin's argument, Daniel Maltz and Ruth A. Borker have argued that many of these sex-differentiated rules for friendly conversation learned in childhood may be carried over into adulthood as gender-specific verbal cultures which provide a basis for miscommunication in cross-sex interaction.[12]

The most detailed examination of the relation between women's speech patterns and the social context in which they are developed can be found in Susan Harding's brilliant paper on women and words in a Spanish village.[13] The men and women of the village live in largely separate social worlds: men's lives revolve around land, women's around people. These differences shape their words and thoughts. Women's "intuition," Harding argues, is, in fact, a set of verbal skills women develop as they interact daily with husbands and children, learning to anticipate their needs. Women's subordinate position to men leads them to develop skills of finesse (the fine art of teasing out information) and subterfuge (fragmenting their demands and talking around issues). Women in the village do different things from men, in different places, with different people, and as a result they do different things with words.

Even when the content of women's and men's talk is the same, differences in the contexts of speech can lead to sexually distinct patterns of language use. James Faris, for example, describes a Newfoundland community in which all-male gatherings in the community store are the only occasions when people gather in groups to exchange information.[14] Because women talk privately in pairs in their homes and gardens while men talk publicly before a larger audience, they develop different styles of speaking. Men's talk is called "telling cuffers" or transmitting "news" while women's is labeled "gossip."

Insofar as women and men live in different social worlds—interacting with different types of people, in different places and times for different purposes-they are likely to develop different ways of using words. Marta Weigle, in reviewing material on women's "verbal art," points out that many researchers have failed to recognize the more conversational and "mundane" verbal genres that are distinctively women's.[15] She shows that attention to speech in everyday life leads to the discovery of a wide range of such genres. Researchers working in a number of communities have noted that women engage in distinctive forms of bawdy humor and storytelling[16], or use distinctive styles of humor such as irony.[17] In some communities, women fill social roles of mediators or match-makers based on their unique verbal skills[18]; in others, women exhibit distinctive styles of story- and myth-telling.[19]

One of the fullest explorations of distinctively female speech is Susan Kalčik's study of women's rap groups.[20] She shows that women in such groups follow a particular set of conversational rules based on a cooperative and collaborative model of talk. Questions and interjections from the "audience," the elaboration by each speaker of themes introduced earlier, and other mechanisms give a unity and form to the group's discourse. Within this framework, she argues that a distinctively female form of personal narrative, which she calls a "kernal story," can be identified. Such stories have emergent structures, taking specific form and focus in each telling from the particular situation and the interaction between teller and audience.

Gossip, talk about other people, is the most frequently cited women's genre of speech,[21] especially in the rural communities of Southern Europe. Because gossip is so often mentioned and covers a whole range of speech behaviors that are associated with women in many communities, it is a topic worth examining in some detail. Such an examination can show how women's social experience creates a context for their speech that is very different from the one in which men speak. By focusing on this use of words in a set of related communities in a single cultural area, the shaping of women's speech by the organization of their daily life can be seen clearly.

Researchers working in Portugal, Spain, Malta, France, Sicily, Italy, and Greece have all commented on "gossip" as a way of talking associated with women in the villages they studied.[22] Throughout southern Europe, researchers have noted the separation of women's and men's social domains as a prominent feature of social life. Women and men engage in different types of activities—both at work and leisure. They move within different areas of physical space within the village or occupy them at different times. Women's social life is centered in their home, local shops, and the streets of their residential neighborhood and revolves around their families and neighbors. Men's lives are centered in the fields and plaza, and their concerns revolve around questions of land, politics, and economics. Rayna Reiter's description of a village in southern France, for example, gives a sense of this fundamental separation in women's and men's social worlds:

> There is a sexual geography to the way people use space within the village as well as outside of it. . . . Public places like the village square, the cafes and the mayor's office are the domain of men, while private places such as houses and the back streets that connect them into residential neighborhoods belong to women. . . . Watching the village day after day, a coordinated choreography can be observed; not only do men and women use different space in different ways, but they use it at different times as well.[23]

Because women and men do different things in different places with different people, their talk differs. Women's talk is about people and takes place in small groups in private settings. Men's talk is less personal, more public, and often takes on the character of performance. For example, Silverman notes that talk is central to all in the Italian village of Montecastello, but that the conventional styles of women and men differ:

> It is men's talk in public that is most characteristic of the civil life. This kind of talk is developed as a skill, even an art of discourse, argument, and verbal play. . . . The best talk requires a minimum of five or six men, for there must be at least two or three participants to take turns at speaking while others form an audience. . . any topic can be picked up if it lends itself to a development of different aspects and opposing positions.[24]

In contrast, women's talk is not elaborated as performance and takes place in small groups as women work together or stroll the town:

> Generally women's talk takes more the form of a running commentary. The manner of presentation tends to be indirect, and exchanges often begin as if they were continuing an earlier conversation. . . . The subject matter is more personal and more individualized than the men's with less elevation of particular cases into generalizations. The favorite topics are the events of the female life-cycle—courtship, marriage, birth and child care. However, there is also detailed examination of an individual's behavior.[25]

Reiter notes that in a French village both the content and location of women's and men's talk differs:

> The sexes have a distinctly different relation to information and to behavior. Hidden behind curtains and closed doors, women speak only of their own realm. The topic of their conversation is almost always kinship. . . . The information men control is also distinctly different. Their topics of conversation at the cafe or when visiting other villages are usually impersonal. Men will discuss agriculture, politics, the weather or hunting, and will sometimes tell stories about one another. But they do not talk about families, discuss life crises, or retell stories that solidify information about dead or living relatives.[26]

Throughout the descriptions what stands out is that women talk in small groups or pairs of kin or neighbors. Through the overlapping ties of women to one another, a network is formed by which information moves. This talk occurs as women move through the villages shopping, as they wash clothes in community sites or get water from communal wells, and as they visit one another in their homes. And for the most part this talk is about people in the community.

Researchers have been especially interested in women's gossip because it is seen as an important source of social power for women in these communities. Researchers in southern Europe have seen women's gossip as an important mechanism for social control and for asserting social values[27], supporting the general anthropological view of the functions of gossip.[28] Gossip works as social control because of the importance of reputation in establishing one's social status within the villages. Through their evaluation of community members' behavior, women define what is and is not acceptable. Further, through wit and humor, women in gossip groups can transform people's image of a village member. Constance Cronin notes that in Sicily:

> There are women who function in the role of comedians or social satirists, always in an explicitly sexual context. They can make any subject and any person a figure of such hilarity, ridicule, and grotesqueness that the person will never again appear to be the same. The joking can be teasing and affectionate when applied to a person who is present, but it usually concerns someone who is not there and is strong, biting, and underneath all the laughter, bitter. . . .This entire complex of sexual joking and satire is a powerful covert strategy used only by women to give notice publicly that they are not always the innocent, ignorant, and put-upon creatures demanded by the culture. For while men do not participate in these sessions, they know of them, acknowledge the experts, and fear the day when they will be the subjects of these female dramas.[29]

In addition to making and breaking reputations, women can disrupt relationships within the village and generate conflict. Juliet duBoulay notes about a Greek village:

> The medium by which all these quarrels, accusations, counter-accusations, self-justifications, lies, and innuendos reach the community, is that of gossip.[30]

Because of its role in conflict and the constant tension between the desire for privacy and the desire to know about the actions of others, gossip is almost always condemned, but the condemnation itself makes clear its power in social life.

Women use the information they gather in talk to subvert male authority. Women are often recognized as manipulative and particularly skilled in "the technique of influencing decisions and controlling others without seeming to."[31] By presenting information to their husbands in ways previously agreed upon with other women, women can push their husbands to take the action women want. Talking about a Maltese village, Jeremy Boissevain comments:

> When her husband returns in the evening, his wife fills him in on the news and comments of the day while she gives him his tea. After

his tea he goes out into the square or to his club. There he discusses the news and gossip about which his wife has briefed him. He discusses these with men whose own wives have briefed them on the same matters. They use the arguments they first heard from their wives. These are similar because their wives have already discussed the issues. They are left to take the decisions, as is their right as holders of formal authority. But their wives by talking the issue out have already concluded what the decision should be, and briefed them accordingly.[32]

But it is clear that while divisions of the social world into separate men's and women's domains shape women's lives and words, the exact nature of women's power with words depends on the organization of the specific communities. The opportunity to gossip is a function of the organization of women's activities, just as whether or not men come together through their activities is a function of the specific organization of their activities. In the Portuguese villages described by Joyce Riegelhaupt, men work individually in the fields until late hours and rarely have time to talk[33]; while in some Greek and French villages, on the other hand, men spend hours talking in the cafes.[34] In Malta women gossip while shopping[35], but in some Greek villages shopping is done by men.[36] The type of information to which women have access differs from community to community. Again, in the Portuguese village, women's key resources are information and contacts with high-status people outside the village through selling homemade bread and working as domestic servants.[37] In most other communities, it is men, not women, who have such contacts. In the French village Reiter studied, for example, women leave the village only to see family and never interact with strangers.[38] The value of women's information also varies. In all cases women have greater knowledge of family and kinship relations and of people in general. However, when villages like the one studied by Reiter move from agricultural to industrial economies, the value of this information declines as kin ties become less important in the distribution of resources, and community members become less dependent on the village social structure.[39] Ironically, such a shift may free women's time for gossip.[40] Finally, the value of women's knowledge depends on their willingness to exploit it. In both Ernestine Friedl's village in Greece and Reiter's village in France women bring land to their families and in both cases land is inherited along kinship lines—an area of women's expertise. In the Greek village, women exercise their land rights through their talk, taking active part in decisions about land use, but in the French village women even deny knowing to what land they have rights and never assert their rights in conversations with men.[41]

Thus women's control of information, their ability to exchange it, and the people they can exchange it with vary and shape the purpose to which women can put their words and the benefits they can get from them in their interactions with other women or with men.

But even more important for understanding the way gossip and other forms of speaking fit into women's lives, it is essential to see that this web of words not only provides women channels for manipulation, it also binds them. As Harding writes:

> Each skill has a double edge, so that as it cuts for a woman, it cuts against her. If gossip provides a forum for a woman to influence the opinions and behavior of others, it also provides the others with a forum to influence her opinions and behavior. Gossip creates among those who participate in it a sense that there is no such thing as privacy. . . . This sense, if not the fact, of being under constant verbal surveillance restricts the behavior of women and helps keep them in their place.[42]

Secondly, a great deal of the power that women have is a negative power: to break reputations, to disrupt social relations, to cause conflict, and such power is devalued. Again, Harding writes:

> Gossip among women is not appreciated as a healthy process in Oroel. It is considered unhealthy and disruptive of the peace and order of the village. It is disdained by both men and women, and by the church. The tongues of women—and their thoughts about others as well—are dangerous, wicked, and sinful. The constant cultural campaign against women's gossip and certain changes in their work requirements are on the verge of making gossip among them an entirely underground activity, so swift and secret as to be socially invisible, if not impossible.[43]

Harding's analysis makes clear that gossip is not just talk about people's actions; it doesn't just grow out of the nature of women's social experience and the contexts in which they interact. It is also shaped by a wide range of cultural ideas about women and men, about power, about what is public and what is private. Women's gossip is condemned because:

> . . . power is not the cultural prerogative of women. . . . Gossip is dirty work in Oroel, not because it is so intrinsically, but because women do it.[44]

In understanding women's language and use of words we must not only look to their special position but also to the complex of cultural ideas that allow people to make sense of their experiences, to produce speech and interpret it. Even the model of domestic/public which is so important for understanding women's social position and use of words is part of a system of ideas for thinking about the social world.* In southern Europe there is a highly complex cultural system based on oppositions of public/private, honor/shame, male/female, which provides community members with an inclusive framework for interpreting experience and thinking about the sexes. The domestic domain here is not just the home, nor is it a neutral analytical construct but a conceptualization that is grounded in a specific cultural tradition that privatizes and spatializes it. This culturally specific concept of the domestic domain sets it in opposition to an equally culture-bound public domain, and associates the domestic domain with women.

CULTURAL DIMENSIONS OF WOMEN'S LANGUAGE USE

The centrality of cultural models in shaping men's and women's language use is particularly clear in two studies that have been done among American subcultures. In both cases, to understand male/female differences in language use, we must first understand people's ideas about women and men, about social life, and about the nature of speech itself.

To understand women's speech in the Afro-American community, Roger Abrahams examines basic assumptions in black culture about status, gender, and language.[45] He views women's speech in terms of "presentational strategies" for asserting and maintaining roles in interaction. Roles within Afro-American culture are subject to negotiation through verbal interaction and all members of the community, even those demanding serious respect, are open to role play in interaction. Women organize their presentations around the ideals of respectability. The essence of her negotiation of the role of "good woman" lies in a woman's "being both sweet and tough depending upon her capacity to define and reasonably manipulate the situation."[46] She "talks sweet" to those supporting her self-image—children and peers—but "talks smart" or "cold" to those who challenge it. Being respectable means being prepared to handle any type of behavior, good or bad. Respectability is not a static quality that characterizes a woman, but an ideal image that motivates her interactional

---

*See Rayna Rapp [formerly Reiter], "Review Essay: Anthropology," *Signs: Journal of Women in Culture and Society* 4 (1979): 479-513, for one discussion of the conceptual problems in the use of "domestic" and "public" in the analysis of women's social position. One frequent problem with such analyses is that the constructs of "public" and "domestic" which are used are not grounded in strictly logical models of social systems. Although conceived as neutral and universal, these constructs have actually been shaped by European cultural models of these domains. As Rapp points out, the development of the state and later industrialization led to a privatizing of the domestic and the family. The sharp contrast of public and private domains is particularly developed in the Mediterranean, but the tendency to privatize and spatialize the domestic is general to modern Western society. This cultural model has inadvertently been incorporated in many social analyses.

strategies, especially when that image is under attack. And respectability does come under attack. In Afro-American culture, social life is conceived as containing basic contradictions and conflicts which are dramatized in interaction. One of the most pervasive conflicts is the opposition of the sexes resulting from the independence of women and men from one another. In opposition to women's values of respectability are male values of reputation. While "home" is the domain of respectability, reputation rules in the "street." While women's power is based in the home, respect is earned by successfully confronting those who threaten it wherever one might be. To maintain respect, a woman must develop verbal styles and skills which allow her to monitor and order the behavior of others—children, men, other women—who challenge her control.

Women's speech gains power in part from economy—it is expected to be more restrained, less loud, less public, and less abandoned than men's. But particularly in interaction with other adults, it is also characterized by smartness and wit. "Talking smart" is essential both in dealing with men and with other women, to establish distance and make room for one's own manipulations. While "talking smart" is valued throughout the black community, Abrahams argues the need to maintain respect in the face of attack makes it especially important in women's speech. Gossip among women is a means of maintaining the ideal of the "good woman" through a constant commenting on behavior in terms of its adherence to or departure from ideals of respectability. Its purpose is to assert women's ideals and their surveillance of behavior, giving approval as well as disapproval. In fact, this approval seems marked by a form of "sweet talk" not found in women's other interactions.

Gerry Philipsen, in looking at men's speech in a white- and blue-collar neighborhood in Chicago, examines basic assumptions about speech and the opposition of men and women.[47] But the framework he finds for interpreting speech and its role in social life is very different from that of Afro-Americans. Rather than being seen as the means by which status and relationships are negotiated, speech is seen by men as having a highly restricted place in self-presentation. Talk is only seen as appropriate to being a man in interactions between peers and friends, those known and like oneself in age, sex, ethnicity, residence, and occupational status. In asymmetrical relationships speech itself is devalued and often seen as being in opposition to "being a man":

> When a man must assert power over or influence another person, speaking is disapproved as a dominant means of self-presentation and in such situations other means of expression are preferred, sometimes required, if the actor's male role enactment is to be credible to those who witness it.[48]

Philipsen discusses two cases in which men from outside the community used language to handle challenges rather than physical force and the crises created for community members in maintaining their evaluation of them as "real men." Philipsen's analysis suggests a conception of acceptable male behavior in

which speech has a very limited place. While conceptions of women and women's speech are not discussed, it is clear that a cultural system which restricts
the talk of men with women and children and which is based on a model of
power as force will have a major impact on the shaping of women's lives and the
context for women's speech, if in no other way than by the cultural and social
constraints it imposes on male-female interaction.

These studies show that the role of speech in presentation of self can vary
dramatically with different notions about language, status, and gender, which
interact with one another to create a framework in which speech is interpreted.
Philipsen's work also suggests that concepts of power may shape women's and
men's speech. Possible interactions of cultural assumptions about power,
language, and gender and their implications for shaping women's speech are
explored in three studies of African communities.

Working in a Malagasy community, Elinor Keenan found that men and
women were associated with very different styles of talk.[49] In everyday speech,
men are associated with an indirect style, called "speech that winds."[50] Winding
speech is associated with a non-confrontative style of interaction that is aimed
at avoiding affront to others. Men avoided ever confronting another person with
unpleasantness or disagreement. Women, on the other hand, are associated with
a direct style of speaking, that is seen as a source of conflict and as threatening
to social relations. Women are particularly associated with the direct expression
of anger. This direct speech of women is linked to women being emotional
and excitable, in contrast to the thoughtfulness of men.[51] Both men and
women see men's indirect speech as prefereable, and skill in "winding speech"
is highly valued. In fact, while this speech is preferred in everyday talk, it is
obligatory in the formal speechmaking that is the basis of political action.
This indirect and subtle form of speechmaking, in which real conflict is hidden
in disputes over speaking rules and in which elaborate statements of respect
and solidarity are mandatory, makes sense within an egalitarian social structure,
where one cannot force others to act. Speechmakers are the politically powerful
in this system and these speechmakers are men, since women are seen as lacking
the skill and control the role requires. While women are barred from positions
of authority, their directness in speech does give them a type of power. They
can bring conflict out into the open, so it can be resolved by men, and they can
deal with Europeans in the marketplace, where directness is the desired and
expected form.

In a study of speech and hierarchy among the Wolof of Senegal, Irvine
discusses a model of the relation between speech and power that is in sharp
contrast to that presented by Keenan.[52] The Wolof are organized into a sharply
stratified caste system based on a belief in the inherent and inherited quality of
nobles. This quality is manifested in reserve at all levels, from speech to biological functioning. Within this system, diffidence and even inarticulateness
preserve and protect the power of elite men by demonstrating their nobility.
The Wolof associate verbal fluency and skill with low status, and noble men
sometimes hire low status professional orators (*griots*) to speak for them in

public. Thus verbal skill provides no claim to political power and in fact is proof of one's inferior status. Within this system, the speech of noble men stands in marked contrast to that of both noble women and lower-status men.

The situation described by Sheila Dauer[53] and Peter Seitel[54] for the Buhaya of Tanzania is yet another way of putting together ideas of political power and language. Buhaya society is based on the superiority of aristocrats over commoners, and men over women. The skilled use of speech, especially metaphoric speech, is highly valued and associated with power. It is said to mark the speech of aristocrats rather than that of commoners, and the speech of men rather than that of women. The key cultural concept for thinking about speech is that of "knowing." Knowing is seen as the ability to control one's speech and social situations through speech, and it is manifested in the skilled use of proverbs. Both women and men place high value on being knowers. But women are in a double bind. While knowing and skilled use of proverbs for men is associated with having been a courtier, for women it was traditionally associated with being a slave. A women who displays too much verbal skill may be accused of having been a female slave, of having "taken the goats to pasture" (acting like a boy), of having been "late in learning to walk," or of being a prostitute.[55] The pressure of these accusations leads women to develop their own styles of proverb use, which are much more ambiguous than those used by males. While men use figurative language to reinforce a point already stated directly, women use figurative language to make their points indirectly. Among the Buhaya, while verbal skill gives status, the power that women can claim from speech is overriden by beliefs in sexual hierarchy.

These studies show that it is essential to understand cultural notions of power and language in order to understand women's speech. Power can be conceptualized in terms of persuasion, physical force, inherent quality, or control of material resources. Each conception of power structures relations between individuals in different ways, and each can incorporate notions of speech and gender differently. Skilled use of language may be a basis for power, merely a sign of power, or proof of powerlessness. Skilled speech may be judged in terms of creativity or careful following of elaborate rules. Women's speech can fit within such systems in a variety of ways which may be determined by concepts of gender and their relation to concepts of power and language. What these studies show is the complex way in which cultural notions frame women's speech in particular communities and the necessity of uncovering cultural ideas for understanding the value and power women's speech will have.

One of the most interesting areas for investigation that emerges from a focus on cultural concepts is the possibility that women and men hold different models of language use. Many ethnographers have clearly assumed over the years that the conceptions of reality they construct largely from discussions with men are shared by the rest of the population. Insofar as cultural symbols and conceptions articulate experience, this is a dangerous assumption. If women's experience is systematically different, then so too should be their interpretation and use of cultural ideas for understanding experience. This need not mean women have totally different conceptions of reality; it may be that women emphasize different parts of the cultural system or interpret the same basic cultural concepts differently than men. Some examples I think are useful.

Dauer, in her analysis of women's speech among the Buhaya, suggests that women have a "double consciousness" in which they see themselves through both their own and men's eyes.[56] Women, like men, evaluate speech in terms of the concept of "knowing," the ability to control speech and manipulate social situations with speech. Women know that men devalue women's speech and that they regard women as "nonknowers" in the use of figurative speech. But women's actual speech shows they use proverbs in even more indirect ways than men, and since indirection is a sign of control, this is a sign that women are "knowers." For example, women use figurative speech for insults. This form of insult has a double advantage: if the victim is offended, the women can deny that was her intent, and if the victim fails to understand the insult, then he has been doubly insulted by showing he is a "nonknower".* Both women and men see "knowers" as "people who guard their words," who know when to speak and when to listen. But women feel that men, because of their power, are rarely restrained in speaking, while all women must carefully guard their words because of their subordinate position. Finally, women see a basic hypocrisy in men praising other men for using proverbs in ways for which they criticize women. Because of their oppressed social-political position, women have developed their own ambiguous styles of language use. But these styles also represent a reinterpretation and reworking of the concept of "knowing." This reworking is made possible by the double perspective women have as both accepters and critics of the social system.

While Dauer presents a situation in which men and women use the same concepts for evaluating speech, although they interpret and manifest them differently, James Siegel presents a case in which women and men focus upon different elements within a shared cultural framework.[57] Members of each sex draw upon different sources of authority for their speech, resulting in very different speech patterns. For the Atjehnese of northern Sumatra, language is not just spoken language, but gestures and behavior as well. It is something possessed, something one "gets a fix on." Men believe they have authority from their rationality, generated by their prayers and chanting of the Koran, from "having God's language" and through reproducing it with their bodies. Their reason, men believe, gives them authority to speak, which they do seldom, feeling they can only speak when they have something of significance to say. They feel that must be substantive. As Siegel notes:

> The result is that it is usually portentous in tone but banal or absurd in content. Limiting oneself to saying only what is so limits one to the obvious or nearly obvious.[58]

---

*Dauer only discusses such cases for men, so I have used the masculine pronoun.

Women, on the other hand, talk all the time, for their authority to speak comes not from their prayers, but from freeing themselves from evil spirits (*djinn*) in curing rites and from recounting dreams. In doing so women believe they make themselves voices of the spirits and thus make the language their own. Through speaking, women move into control by transforming events. It is this process which is important, not the content of the speech which is in itself unimportant and usually trivial. While men and women share a set of ideas about language and religion, given their separate life experiences, they draw from this set differently, in such a way that the frequency and style of their talk varies greatly. As a result, speech is a resource for women in their constant struggles with their spouses, and it is not one for men.

Whether or not we ever find completely different conceptions between the sexes and at what point we label them as such is a complex question. Clearly, men and women in many societies focus upon different meanings of key cultural symbols and differently draw upon their cultural systems to understand their experience. At this point anthropologists are just beginning to explore the range of ideological and interpretive variation in communities, and generalizations cannot yet be made. However, it is clear that this situation of internal cultural variation has important consequences for the language use of women and men and the place of language in their lives.

This chapter shows some of the insights that an anthropological perspective can bring to our study of language and gender. Exploring the wider contexts of speech, whether women's social relationships and situations or the cultural ideas that women and men use for interpreting their experience, gives a far richer texture to our understanding of the role of language in women's lives than would otherwise be possible.

NOTES

1. Robin Lakoff, *Language and Woman's Place* (New York: Harper Colophon Books, 1975).
2. William M. O'Barr and Bowman K. Atkins, " 'Women's Language' or 'Powerless Language' ", in this volume.
3. Brenda Mann, "Bar Talk," in *Conformity and Conflict: Readings in Cultural Anthropology*, 2nd ed., ed. James P. Spradly and David W. McCurdy (Boston: Little, Brown & Co., 1974), pp. 101-11.
4. Anne Farber, "Language Choice and Sex Roles in Highland Guatemala" (paper presented at the American Anthropological Association Meetings, Mexico City, 1974).
5. Susan Gal, "Peasant Men Can't Get Wives: Language Change and Sex Roles in a Bilingual Community," *Language in Society* 7 (1978): 1-16.
6. In two parts of Tanzania, women use Swahili, the national language, among themselves but not with strangers. Sheila Dauer, "Language Choice and Sex Roles in Buhaya, in Process of Change," presented at the American Anthropological Meetings, San Francisco, 1975; William M. O'Barr, personal communication.
7. Karen Larsen, "Role-Playing and the Real Thing: Socialization and Standard Speech in Norway" (paper presented at the Ninth World Congress of Sociologists, Uppsala, Sweden, 1978).

8. Ibid., p. 7

9. Ibid.

10. Penelope Brown, "Why and How are Women More Polite?" in this volume.

11. Marjorie Goodwin, "Directive-Response Speech Sequences in Girls' and Boys' Task Activities," in this volume.

12. Daniel Maltz and Ruth Borker, "A Cultural Approach to Male/Female Miscommunication" (paper delivered at Pitzer College, 1979).

13. Susan Harding, "Women and Words in a Spanish Village," in *Toward an Anthropology of Women*, ed. Rayna Reiter (New York: Monthly Review Press, 1975).

14. James Faris, "The Dynamics of Verbal Exchange: A Newfoundland Example," *Anthropologica* 8 (1966): 235-48.

15. Marta Weigle, "Women as Verbal Artists: Reclaiming the Daughters of Enheduanna," *Frontiers: A Journal of Women Studies* 3 (1978): 1-9.

16. Constance Cronin, "Illusion and Reality in Sicily," in *Sexual Stratification: A Cross-Cultural View*, ed. Alice Schlegel (New York: Columbia University Press, 1977), pp. 67-93; Rayna Green, "Magnolias Grow in Dirt," *Southern Exposure* 4 (1977): 29-33.

17. Brown, this volume.

18. Cronin, "Illusion and Reality."

19. Inez Cardozo-Freeman, "Serpent Fears and Religious Motifs among Mexican Women," *Frontiers: A Journal of Women Studies* 3 (1978): 10-13; Sally McLendon, "Cultural Presuppositions and Assertion of Information in Eastern Pomo and Russian Narrative," in *Georgetown University Round Table on Languages and Linguistics 1977*, ed. Muriel Saville-Troike (Washington, D.C.: Georgetown University Press, 1977), p. 171.

20. Susan Kalčik, " ' . . . Like Ann's gynecologist or the time I was almost raped': Personal Narratives in Women's Rap Groups," *Journal of American Folklore* 88 (1975): 3-11.

21. See: Sally Yerkovich, "Gossiping as a Way of Speaking," *Journal of Communication* 27 (1977): 192-96 for a discussion of gossip as a way of speaking.

22. Jeremy Boissevain, "Some Notes on the Position of Women in Maltese Society," *Nord Nytt* 3 (1972): 195-213; Cronin; Juliet duBoulay, *Portrait of a Greek Mountain Village* (Oxford: Clarendon Press, 1974); Ernestine Friedl, "The Position of Women: Appearance and Reality," *Anthropological Quarterly* 40 (1967): 97-108; Harding 1975; Susan Harding, "Street Shouting and Shunning: Conflict Between Women in a Spanish Village," *Frontiers: A Journal of Women's Studies* 3 (1978): 14-18; Rayna Reiter, "Men and Women in the South of France: Public and Private Domains," in *Toward an Anthropology of Women*, ed. Rayna Reiter (New York: Monthly Review Press, 1975), pp. 252-82; Joyce F. Riegelhaupt, "Saloio Women: An Analysis of Informal and Formal Political and Economic Roles of Portuguese Peasant Women," *Anthropological Quarterly* 40 (1967): 109-26; Sydel Silverman, *Three Bells of Civilization: The Life of an Italian Hill* (New York: Columbia University Press).

23. Reiter, "Men and Women," pp. 256-57.

24. Silverman, *Three Bells*, p. 37.

25. Ibid., pp. 37-38.

26. Reiter, "Men and Women," pp. 264, 266.

27. Boissevain, "Some Notes"; Cronin, "Illusion and Reality"; duBoulay, "Portrait"; Silverman, *Three Bells*.

28. See especially: Max Gluckman, "Gossip and Scandal," *Current Anthropology* 4 (1963): 307-16; Max Gluckman, "Psychological, Sociological and Anthropological Explanations of Gossip," *Man: The Journal of the Royal Anthropological Institute* 3 (1968): 20-34; Bruce A. Cox, "What is Hopi Gossip About? Information Management and Hopi Factions," *Man: The Journal of the Royal Anthropological Institute* 5 (1970): 88-98; Robert Paine, "What is Gossip About? An Alternative Hypothesis," *Man: The Journal of the Royal Anthropological Institute* 2 (1967): 278-85; Peter Wilson, "Filcher of Good Names: An Enquiry into Anthropology and Gossip," *Man: The Journal of the Royal*

Anthropological Institute 9 (1974): 93-102.

29. Cronin, "Illusion and Reality", pp. 85-86.

30. duBoulay, "Portrait," p. 201.

31. Cronin, "Illusion and Reality," p. 77.

32. Boissevain, "Some Notes," p. 210.

33. Reigelhaupt, "Soloio Women."

34. Friedl, "The Position,"; Reiter, "Men and Women."

35. Boissevain, "Some Notes."

36. Friedl, "The Position."

37. Reigelhaupt, "Soloio Women."

38. Reiter, "Men and Women."

39. Ibid.

40. Boissevain, "Some Notes."

41. Friedl, "The Position,"; Reiter, "Men and Women."

42. Harding, "Women and Words," p. 307.

43. Ibid., p. 302.

44. Harding 1975, p. 303.

45. Roger Abrahams, "Negotiating Respect: Patterns of Presentation among Black Women," *Journal of American Folklore* 88(1975): 58-80; Roger Abrahams, *Talking Black* (Rowley, Mass.: Newbury House Publishers, 1976).

46. Abrahams, "Negotiating Respect," p. 62.

47. Gerry Philipsen, "Speaking 'Like a Man' in Teamsterville: Culture Patterns of Role Enactment in an Urban Neighborhood," *Quarterly Journal of Speech* 61(1975): 13-22.

48. Ibid., p. 15.

49. Elinor Keenan, "In's and Out's of Women's Speech," *Cambridge Anthropology* 1(1974): 61-70; Elinor Keenan, "Norm-makers, Norm-breakers: Uses of Speech by Men and Women in a Malagasy Community," in *Explorations in the Ethnography of Speaking*, ed. Richard Bauman and Joel Sherzer (Cambridge: Cambridge University Press, 1974), pp. 125-43. Nichols, this volume, also considers Keenan's study.

50. Keenan, "In's and Out's," p. 65.

51. Keenan, "In's and Out's," p. 67.

52. Judith T. Irvine, "Wolof Noun Classification: The Social Setting of Divergent Change," *Language in Society* 7(1978): 37-64.

53. Dauer, "Language Choice."

54. Peter Seitel, "Proverbs and the Structure of Metaphor among the Haya of Tanzania" (Ph.D. Thesis, University of Pennsylvania, 1972); Peter Seitel, "Haya Metaphors for Speech," *Language in Society* 3(1974): 51-67.

55. Seitel "Proverbs. . . ," cited in Weigle, p. 8.

56. Dauer, "Language Choice."

57. James T. Siegel, "Curing Rites, Dreams, and Domestic Politics in a Sumatran Society," *Glyph: John Hopkins Textual Studies* 3(1978): 18-31.

58. Ibid., p. 21.

3

TEXTUAL FEMINISM

Nelly Furman

In a short article entitled "The Art of Fiction" which is devoted to a review of E. M. Forster's book, *Aspects of the Novel*, Virginia Woolf deplores the lack of attention paid by literary critics to the question of language:

> Thus, though it is impossible to imagine a book on painting in which not a word should be said about the medium in which a painter works, a wise and brilliant book like Mr. Forster's can be written about fiction without saying more than a sentence or two about the medium in which a novelist works. Almost nothing is said about words.[1]

Later, in the same article, Woolf launches an attack against the critical establishment for its insistence on realistic representation:

> If the English critic were less domestic, less assiduous to protect the rights of what it pleases him to call life, the novelist might be bolder too. He might cut adrift from the eternal tea-table and the plausible and preposterous formulas which are supposed to represent the whole of our human adventure. But then the story might wobble; the plot might crumble; ruin might seize upon the characters. The novel, in short, might become a work of art.[2]

I wish to thank Caren Greenberg, Phil Lewis, Sandra Siegel and Laura Engelstein for their helpful comments.

45

Woolf's double-speared attack establishes an implicit relationship between critical assessment of a novel in terms of its true-to-life quality and the blindness of critics to the verbal medium which is the means of literary expression.

Mimetic or realistic criticism views literature as a representation of human life and, consequently, appreciates a work essentially for its historical or psychological veracity. One of the first and major thrusts of feminist criticism has been to study the "images" of women, to explain women's characterization, and to analyze the economic restrictions, social taboos, and cultural norms which, in specific historical contexts, govern women's behavior. In a second phase, feminist critics have convincingly argued that since it is largely the works of men which inform our literary standards, these reflect a male view of life. Thus, the neglect which has befallen many women writers can be attributed, in part at least, to our cultural biases which discount women's interests and perception of life, women's views of experience. In bringing forth the works which our literary prejudices have slighted, feminist historians of literature invest women writers with authorial power, bestowing on women's perspectives the authority hitherto reserved for men's views. Whether perceived as historical documents which can provide information regarding past or present social communities or appreciated as transcriptions of a female or male experience of life, such approaches still conceive of literature primarily as a mimetic art which reflects an outside social and psychological reality. Literature is still mostly valued for its referential function. Implicit in such approaches to literature, whether informed by a feminist perspective or not, is a conception of artistic expression as simply a secondary embellishment which is subordinate to informational content.

"Real art has the capacity to make us nervous. By reducing the work of art to its content and then interpreting *that*, one tames the work of art."[3] These words of Susan Sontag echo Woolf's complaint. For those who uphold the representational value of art, literature is conceptualized as a mirror of reality. However, this metaphorical mirror does not present a true likeness of human life to the reader's eyes, but only printed words, linguistic signs indicated by typographical characters arranged in an established order on a sheet of paper. From this perspective, literature is an artifact fashioned out of ink, paper, and language; rather than a mirror of life, literature is the scene of a verbal illusion. "Illusion" comes from the Latin *illudere* and means to mock, to play. Literature can delude us, for words—whether they evoke an outside reality or not—play with our perceptions and affect our understanding and pleasure. When literature is apprehended as a verbal art, its social or psychological relevance does not disappear, but it is simply found and revealed in language.

Selection of words and their combination are important to all forms of verbal communication, but they are the *raison d'être* of literary discourse. Literature probes the capabilities of language, making the choice and arrangements of words the major focus of interest and the fundamental message. This is what Roman Jacobson calls the poetic function of language: "Any attempt to reduce the sphere of poetic function to poetry or to confine poetry to poetic function would be a delusive oversimplification. Poetic function is not the sole function of verbal art but only its dominant, determining function, whereas in all other verbal activities it acts as a subsidiary, accessory constituent."[4]

Language is the very stuff of literature, yet, until recently, language was not the principal concern of the critical establishment.[5] Classical antiquity characterized literature as an imitative art which used language as a means for conveying a persuasive rendering of reality. For a long time thereafter the imitative nature of literature was not questioned, rather the topic of debate was which literary work rendered the most accurate view of reality. Not until the second half of the nineteenth century was the focus on the representational content of literature *effectively* challenged. Emancipated from the bonds of empirical reality, literature asserted itself as a self-reflexive, formal linquistic object which required new investigative methods. Indebted to Russian Formalism, American New Criticism, French structuralism, and semiotic practice, modern textual criticism makes the literary medium the focus of its interest.[6]

This is not to say that criticism paid no attention to language before modern times. On the contrary, linguistic features of literary expression have been studied since the days of Aristotle. The difference lies in the manner in which language is being apprehended. For example, formal features of language have traditionally been used for classification of literature: prose was the medium of fiction, verse the vehicle for poetry. Similarly, genres were characterized by different levels of style. The tragedy which portrayed the actions of kings and heroes had to be written in a "high" style befitting the rank and importance of its protagonists, whereas the "middle" or "low" style was deemed more appropriate to the plebian dramatic comedy. Furthermore, rhetorical devices have long been defined and categorized, and individual styles analyzed in terms of images, syntactic patterns, sonorities, and rhythms. However, in all of the examples mentioned above, language is seen as a stable corpus whose elements can easily be inventoried and classified.

In opposition to this static view of language, textual critics perceive language as a dynamic system. This view of language is rooted in the work of the Swiss linguist Ferdinand de Saussure, who distinguishes the individual uses of language from the system itself.[7] Language (*langue*) is defined as the code, the set of rules which allows verbal communication to take place, while speech (*parole*), be it written or oral, is an individual manifestation, the result of a personal interaction with the system. Another process of interaction takes place in the linguistic sign which is composed of two inseparable, yet distinct parts: the signified (*signifié*) and the signifier (*signifiant*). The signified encompasses the realm of referent and content; the signifier is the material transmitter which conveys sound and phonological resonances, visual reflections and typographical styles, and etymological traces as well as grammatical structures. *Female* and *woman*, for example, may refer to the same individual, yet because their cultural and symbolic connotations, their etymologies, their phonetic and graphic expressions are different, they take on different significances. The signifieds of the words *female* and *woman* exclude the masculine. The signifiers, on the other hand, seem to include the masculine: "fe-male" contains "male," and "wo-man" includes "man." *Female* comes from the Old French *femelle* and the Latin *femina*, neither of which connotes in any way the masculine sex. The "male" in "fe-male" is strictly a phonological and graphic phenomenon. Nonetheless for the English speaker, the word *female* appears a modification of "male." The etymology of the word *woman* [OE *wif*, woman, wife and *mann*, man, human being], however, does show that we speak from a patriarchy where "man" is the established standard against which others are measured. While *he* denotes the universal genus, *she* is simply defined by her social function as wife.

Roland Barthes reminds us that "it is language which teaches us the definition of man, not the reverse."[8] Since language is the place where the individual is apprehended as a social and historical being, language can also show us how woman is defined, understood, and appreciated in our culture. The signifier "wo-man" supports Simone de Beauvoir's contention in *The Second Sex*: "She is defined and differentiated with reference to man, and not he with reference to her; she is the incidental, the inessential as opposed to the essential. He is the Subject, he is the Absolute—she is the Other."[9]

Because content and referential meaning have been the main concerns of criticism, the substratum of significance created by linguistic expression has been largely disregarded. To ignore the signifier is to make reference the sole process of meaning, and to miss the crucial role played by the signifier in articulating and shaping signification. Yet, the signifier has most often gone unnoticed, seemingly transparent, as the invisible companion of the immediately acknowledged signified. Textual critics study the interaction of signifiers and the interplay between signifier and signified. These relationships constitute the signifying process. The object of textual criticism is not to demonstrate or consolidate a union between the linguistic conveyor and an apparent content; on the contrary, its aim is to explode the unity of the sign, to threaten the comfortable relationship between signifier and signified. By forcefully playing signifier against signified, the textual critic attempts to disturb the harmony of form and content.

Because textual criticism calls attention to the articulation of language and meaning, it can provide feminists with a useful methodological tool to expose the cultural components of the linguistic medium and debunk the myth of linguistic neutrality. As some of the articles in this volume exemplify, textual criticism can show how women appropriate gender-marked signs. Women's interaction with the linguistic system is a difficult and complex subject. If the question of the biological component in language acquisition is still hotly debated, the patently dissimilar socialization processes of the two sexes have now been well documented. Girls, for example, are often discouraged from repeating expressions readily used by boys. Hence, the use of gender-marked lexicons by men and women writers may take on a distinctive function in their texts, for what is a vapid expression in a man's world becomes under a woman's pen a willful transgression and a cause for scandal. Conversely, there is no reason to believe that, as readers, men and women impart identical connotations to words.

"The power of the fathers," writes Adrienne Rich "has been difficult to grasp because it permeates everything, even the language in which we try to describe it. It is diffuse and concrete; symbolic and literal, universal and expressed with local variations which obscure its universality."[10] Since meaning for the textual critic is no longer pre-established, words must constantly be redefined. The signifier, which is considered a form continuously in search of a meaning, resists permanence and closure, and thereby escapes universality. The concerns of the French feminist writer, Hélène Cixous, are akin to those expressed by Adrienne Rich; "Beware, my friend," Cixous warns us, "of the signifier that would take you back to the authority of a signified."[11] To refuse the authority of a signified means rejecting the status of defined object in favor of the dynamics of becoming, and privileging the freedom of process rather than the permanence of product.

Process, moreover, is itself the result of an interaction. In literature, both writer and reader interact with a linguistic medium. The relationship of writer and reader to the verbal medium creates a dynamic interchange, and the text is the locus and the product of that relationship. Text [from the Latin *textus*, fabric, structure, text; past participle of *texture*, to weave] is not merely a synonym for literary work or some portion of a work. It is more precisely a literary *passage*, that is to say, a place of transition, an area which either leads to something different or a space where change is occurring. Textual criticism presupposes that words imply and inform more than their referential meaning; consequently, it also presupposes the existence of a reader affected, to some degree, by this surplus of possibly meaningful signifiers.

Because it is the reader who perceives elements of a work as significant, the creative process which has traditionally been the sole prerogative of the author is now seen to be shared by the reader, and transferred in part to the reading process. Woolf already held this view: "What the reader has in common with the writer, though much more feebly [is] the desire to create."[12] Not only is the literary text a transmitter of explicit and implied cultural values, but the reader as well is a carrier of perceptual prejudices. It is the reader's acumen, expectations, and unconsciousness which invest the text with meaning. Perception and cognition are processes which involve an active agent and which are affected by the agent's psychology. Although the reader is an involved consumer, and an active participant in the making of the text, reading is not merely a kind of unrestricted exercise of self-expression, unbridled subjectivity. Rather, it is an awareness on the part of the reader that one's interaction with a literary work is circumscribed by one's sensitivity and culture, as well as the properties of the literary and critical discourses.

Recognizing the creativity of reading makes it possible to cast the question of women's relationship to literature in a new perspective which focuses on women as readers. Between reading and writing there exists a continuous alternating movement. Not only is the reader an acknowledged author of a new text, but the writer's work can also be construed as the product of a prior reading. Writing is an inscription within an existing literary code, either in the form of an appropriation or a rejection. To study women writers as readers is to analyze their interaction with the cultural system, and to determine how their texts propose a critique of the dominant patriarchal tenor of literary expression. The educational system fashions our reading habits; women, like men, are trained readers, but in so far as they are disaffected participants in the literary tradition, women's acculturation questions the whole of our literary practices. By examining women in the reading process, we could begin to elaborate a feminist poetics and see how literary works become meaningful for women.

In *A room of One's Own,* Woolf presents the following illustration of a woman's interaction with the linguistic system and inscription within the literary code. The narrator encourages women to write and to enter in numbers the realm of literary production from which they had hitherto been excluded because of social, educational, and economic restrictions. She is, however, acutely aware of the fact that the literary models available to women are, for the most part, man-made, and in her view ill-suited to a woman's sensitivity and experience. At the beginning of the book, the narrator declares that she will use the pronoun *I*: "only as a convenient term for somebody who has no real being [. . .] (call me Mary Beton, Mary Seton, Mary Carmichael or by any name you please—it is not a matter of importance)."[13] Much later in the book, the narrator discusses the overwhelming presence of the first pronoun in Mr. A's book: "One began to be tired of I. Not but what this I was a most respectable I; honest and logical; as hard as a nut, and polished for centuries by good teaching and good feeding. *I* respect and admire that I from the bottom of my heart."[14] In the last sentence, the opposition between the two signifiers *I*/ ↕ I calls attention to their differences. Mr. A's I represents a specific person designated by the initial of a name, that is to say, an individual psychological and historical being. Mr. A's I is a traditional, referential, first-person pronoun. The *I* assumed by the narrator of *A Room of One's Own* is divested of its usual meaning and function. It stands for a depersonalized identity, a pluralized *persona*; it is simply a functional agent of discourse—a speaking subject. The narrator's *I* and Mr. A's I convey different perceptions of the self and different experiences of life.

In and through language, one posits oneself as a subject, as an "ego" by saying I. The I is an empty signifier available to anyone. The mere use of I does not answer the question of who or what that I actually stands for. It is only by contrasting the narrator's *I* with Mr. A's I that differentiation becomes possible. The subject, as Emile Benveniste has shown, can only come into being as the articulation of a difference:

> Consciousness of self is only possible if it is experienced by contrast. I use I only when *I* am speaking to someone who will be a *you* in my address. It is this condition of dialogue that is constitutive of *person*, for it implies that reciprocally *I* becomes *you* in the address of the one who in his turn designates himself as *I* . . . . It is in a dialectic

reality that will incorporate the two terms and define them by mutual relationship that the linguistic basis of subjectivity is discovered.[15]

Mr. A's I is an easily recognizable personal "ego," in contrast to the narrator's *I* which is simply a linguistic construct. The depersonalization of the narrator is further underscored by the title of the book. In calling her feminist pamphlet *A Room of One's Own* rather than "a room of *her* own or *their* own," Woolf makes use of the psychological vacuity and nonreferentiality of the indefinite pronoun *one*. In order to assume an ideological content, Mr. A's I and the narrator's *I* must be put into relationship with a contextual meaning, be linked to a referent. Mr. A's I is characterized as an I "polished for centuries by good teaching and good feeding," and in Woolf's book, this polished, learned, and well-fed world is explicitly and exclusively a man's world. Mr. A's I is therefore a specifically gender-marked male subject, while the depersonalized narrator's *I* takes on, in the argument of the book, a female marking. As a differentiated subject, as other, the narrator's *I* is inscribed in Woolf's text as a woman's voice in a patriarchal literary tradition.[16]

"To read," as Jonathan Culler suggests, "is to participate in the play of the text, to locate zones of resistance and transparency, to isolate forms and determine their content and then to treat that content in turn as form with its own content, to follow in short, the interplay of surface and envelope."[17] The reading of *A Room of One's Own* sketched above is just a conjecture, of course. For it is I who put special emphasis on the narrator's reading of Mr. A's book, on the interaction between observer and observed, and projected onto this relationship my own feminist concerns, appropriating Woolf's text, speaking for her, and transforming her text into my own. Literary criticism, whatever its methodology or focus of interest, is an exercise in and of power; its speaker moves into a traditionally masculine role. Feminist criticism, in as much as it proposes to unmask the cultural biases of our literary system, cannot leave unquestioned the assumption of power inherent in our critical practices.

Textual criticism does not simply provide a change of cast whereby the reader is now recognized as having the last word instead of the author. One could argue that critics always had the last word, and that, in fact, literary history is but a catalogue which reflects the tastes and preferences of critics. For the feminist scholar, the importance of textual criticism resides in the implications of the switch to the power of the reader. In the last few years, literary criticism has undergone consciousness raising and introspection, and, like today's women, readers have come into their own with audible voices and distinguishable personae. The modern reader is aware that the self is a selective sifter that mediates everything with which it comes into contact. Reading is no longer just an attempt to decipher; it is simultaneously a gesture of self-inscription. By positing a reader as a subject engaged in a formal activity, textual criticism excludes the *disembodied* voice of some neutral, impartial, and absent speaker.

Reading and writing are activities pursued by socialized biological beings who inflect these activities, consciously or not, with their sex(uality) and cultural values. The perception of an object is defined, circumscribed, and delineated by the observer's abilities and limitations. In such a subjective viewpoint, as David Bleich indicates: "Knowledge is made by people, and not found."* Textual feminism implies a recognition of the fact that we speak, read, and write from a gender-marked place within our social and cultural context.

Because it is a subjective procedure, textual criticism mitigates the absoluteness of the third person and the power of truth which an impersonal, general statement readily conveys. A plurality of readers may generate a plurality of readings, and for each reader every reading also differs from the preceding one. Textual criticism accommodates the expression of differentiated perceptions and views, and because of this inherent pluralism, it avoids positing a universal truth. Furthermore, the reader is not a passive consumer, but an active producer of a new text. The reader's text is the medium which can give voice and visibility to a feminist literary consciousness. Whereas the *disembodied* voice of impartial criticism expresses its presumed neutrality through the transparency of expository prose, like a scientific or historical statement, the textual critic can mark her or his differentiated viewpoint not only in the inflection of the reading, but also through the very texture of the critical discourse.

For Roland Barthes, its foremost practitioner, textual criticism is ultimately a form of writing which puts into question the function and expression of critical discourse:

> A Theory of the Text cannot be satisfied by a metalinguistic exposition: the destruction of meta-language, or at least (since it may be necessary provisionally to resort to meta-language) its calling into doubt, is part of the theory itself: the discourse of the Text should itself be nothing other than text, research, textual activity, since the text is that *social* space which leaves no language safe, outside, nor any subject of the enunciation in position as judge, master, analyst, confessor, decoder. The theory of the Text can coincide only with a practice of writing.18

---

*An observer is a subject, and his means of perception define the essence of the object and even its existence to begin with. An object is circumscribed and delimited by a subject's motives, curiosities, and above all, his language. Under the subjective paradigm new truth is created by a new use of language and a new structure of thought. The establishment of new knowledge is the activity of the intellecting mind adapting itself to onto-genetic and phylogenetic developmental demands. Knowledge is made by people, not found." David Bleich, "The Subjective Paradigm in Science, Psychology, and Criticism," *New Literary History* 7 (Winter) 1976: 318-19. In the same issue, see also Norman N. Holland's reply to David Bleich, "The New Paradigm: Subjective or Transactive?" 335-46.

Literature and criticism are not separate entities; on the contrary, they reflect, sustain, imply one another. For textual criticism, which presupposes a subject exerting her or his creative power, the study of literature has been replaced by the study of writing. Literature, as defined by critical tradition, is an institution constituted by the history of genres and the biographies of authors; writing (*écriture*) is defined as an activity, a shared manner of expression. Writing is a practice which reflects a common view held, at a given time, of the function of literature and language. Writing is not merely a style, that is to say, an idiosyncratic use of language, rather it is a form functioning in a historical and social context.

For the textual critic, language plays an active, self-productive role in the creative process, and the critical text is often expressed in forms consistent with this principle. Neither expository nor descriptive, the modern critical text proposes itself as "writing," as a creative process. With its deliberate abuse of puns, anagrams, spoonerisms, diacritical signs, and syntactic displacements, the critical text calls attention to the creative process of the verbal medium. This is why a text cannot be translated, described, explained, or spoken for, without losing its status as text, as difference, as other. A text is unique, and cannot be told.

NOTES

1. Virginia Woolf, "The Art of Fiction", in *Collected Essays* (London: The Hogarth Press, 1966), II, p. 54.

2. Ibid., p. 55.

3. Susan Sontag, *Against Interpretation* (New York: Dell Publishing, Laurel Edition, 1969), p. 17.

4. Roman Jakobson, "Closing Statements: Linguistics and Poetics," in *Style in Language*, editor Thomas Sebeok, (Cambridge: MIT Press, 1960), p. 356.

5. For an examination of the functional differences between natural discourse and fictive discourse, see Barbara Herrnstein Smith, *On the Margins of Discourse. The Relation of Literature to Language* (Chicago: The University of Chicago Press, 1978).

6. For those without prior knowledge of contemporary criticism, a slim volume, *Structuralism and Semiotics* by Terence Hawkes (Berkeley and Los Angeles: University of California Press, 1977) provides the essential elements for understanding the change of perspective brought about by structuralist thought. It also provides an informative bibliography for further study.

7. For a clear and succinct assessment of Ferdinand de Saussure's work and its relation to structuralist and semiotic practice, see: Jonathon Culler, *Ferdinand De Saussure*, Penguin Modern Masters, ed. Frank Kermode (New York: Penguin Books, 1977), and Roland Barthes, *Elements of Semiology* a monograph appended to *Writing Degree Zero* (Boston: Beacon, 1970).

8. Roland Barthes, "To Write: An Intransitive Verb?" in *The Structuralist Controversy*, edited by Richard Macksey and Eugenio Donato (Baltimore: The John Hopkins University Press, 1972), p. 135.

9. Simone de Beauvoir, *The Second Sex* (New York: Bantam Books, 1961), p. xvi.

10. Adrienne Rich, *Of Woman Born: Motherhood as Experience and Institution* (New York: Bantam Books, 1977), p. 41.

11. Hélène Cixous, "The Laugh of the Medusa," *Signs, Journal of Women in Culture and Society*, 1 (Summer 1976): 892.

12. Virginia Woolf, "Phases of Fiction," in *Collected Essays* (London: The Hogarth Press, 1966), II, p. 57.

13. Virginia Woolf, *A Room of One's Own* (New York and Burlingame: Harcourt, Brace and World, A Harbinger Book, 1957), p. 4.

14. Ibid., p. 103-4. My italics.

15. Emile Benveniste, *Problems in General Linguistics,* translated by Mary Elizabeth Meek (Coral Gables, Florida: University of Miami Press, 1971), p. 224-25.

16. For a more complete analysis of the expression of feminist discourse in Virginia Woolf, see my article, *"A Room of One's Own:* Reading Absence," in *Women's Language and Style* (Akron: University of Akron Press, 1978), ed. Douglas Butturff and Edmund L. Epstein, p. 99-105.

17. Jonathan Culler, *Structuralist Poetics, Structuralism, Linguistics, and the Study of Literature* (Ithaca, N.Y.: Cornell University Press, Cornell Paperbacks, 1976), p. 259.

18. Roland Barthes, *Image-Music-Text*, essays selected and translated by Stephen Heath (New York: Hill and Wang, 1977), p. 164.

PART II

MEN'S POWER, WOMEN'S LANGUAGE

INTRODUCTION TO PART TWO

How does the power of men in society affect the use of language spoken to and used by women? To what extent are men's power and women's language interrelated? Each paper in Part II addresses and answers these central questions in different ways. Taken together, these essays refine our concept of power and help us go beyond a simplistic identification of "women's language" as "powerless language."

In "Proprietors of Language," Cheris Kramarae argues that the general social dominance of men gives men the wherewithal to legitimate particular linguistic uses and to coin terms that gain wide currency. Such institutions as the press, education, advertising, and local and national politics help establish and uphold this male linguistic "control." Kramarae also maintains, however, that such control can be exerted in social interactions even by men who are themselves dominated by "majority" social groups and thus lacking in institutionalized power. She suggests that the linguistic "proprietorship" of men has two important consequences: first, that women's and men's language use is differently evaluated, and second, that women lack adequate linguistic resources for making sense of their experience and for sharing that understanding of experience with others. Kramarae's second claim implies a more general thesis: namely, that our ways for talking about experience have considerable social and psychological import, that words have power to shape women's experience. As Kramarae shows, being able to establish the "propriety" of linguistic usages is a tremendous political resource that serves to maintain the social power of the "proprietors." Only if we recognize this, she argues, can we begin to understand why contemporary feminists are so concerned with linguistic conventions and why the changes in linguistic usage they propose have been so vigorously resisted.

In "The Psychology of the Generic Masculine," Wendy Martyna investigates the psychological reality for English speakers of the most hotly debated linguistic convention: the use of *he* for both generic (potentially non-sexed) as well as individual (male) reference. Martyna has designed and conducted a a variety of experiments to test empirically the psychological factors involved in use and interpretation of generic masculines. Her results suggest that women use generic masculines less, but are more likely to interpret them as nonsexed. Men, on the other hand, frequently attach sex-specific meaning to generic *he*, often reporting masculine imagery. For women, equating masculinity with humanity conflicts with their own sense of self-identity, and many resist the convention, whether or not they view themselves as "feminists." Martyna's data strongly suggest that the generic masculine convention does indeed have profound social and psychological consequences.

Terms of address have long been recognized as sensitive indexes of social relationships, especially in marking dimensions of power and solidarity. Drawing on a large corpus of actually observed uses, Nessa Wolfson and Joan Manes examine distribution of the three most common types of address forms received by women in service encounters (for example, from a store clerk). In "Don't 'Dear' Me," they demonstrate why addressing endearments to women in such situations denies them the status advantage generally accorded to the served by the server. The key factor is that endearments are not available to the woman being served, whereas in interactions between intimates, endearments are used by both parties to signal solidarity. As Wolfson and Manes show through detailed examination of particular cases, a switch in type of address during an ongoing interaction redefines the relationship and the relative status of participants in a given encounter.

In " 'Women's Language' or 'Powerless Language'?", William M. O'Barr and Bowman K. Atkins look at the language used by women. Starting with features that linguist Robin Lakoff has claimed typify "women's language," they analyze courtroom testimony from witnesses of both sexes. Although more women than men scored high on their "women's language"-index, social status rather than gender best predicted the use of such features as hedges (*I guess*) and respectful address forms (*sir*). O'Barr and Atkins suggest that what Lakoff classifies as "women's language" might be called "powerless language." This label is especially apt, for the observational studies establishing that such usage is typical of the socially powerless were followed by an experimental study showing that the so-called "women's language" style was ineffective in convincing "mock jurors." It is because of how it is heard rather than because of an inherent lack that the style itself contributes to "powerlessness." Since, as O'Barr and Atkins observe, women are over-represented among the socially powerless, they are more likely than men to suffer from use of "powerless language."

Many of the specific stylistic features of Lakoff's "women's language" (O'Barr and Atkins' "powerless language") also serve to express a general orientation toward politeness. In "How and Why are Women More Polite?" Penelope Brown sketches general theories of politeness and of the ways in which speakers pursue their goals through use of particular linguistic strategies. Applying these theories to analysis of speech in a small Mexican Indian village (where women are under direct male authority and where men control formal political institutions), she finds that these Indian women are indeed more polite in their speech than the men. She shows in detail how particular sorts of linguistic devices (exemplified by certain grammatical elements in the local Mayan Indian language) function in the expression of different types of politeness. Brown's strategic model of language use points to ways of establishing systematic and explicit links between linguistic usage and social realities, links mediated by women's (and men's) considered assessments of their situations and their needs. Thus, as Brown suggests, detailed analyses of language use may prove our best method for gaining a "woman's-eye" view of social structure in different communities.

There are no simple answers to the questions raised at the beginning of this discussion. But the studies in Part II advance our understanding of the subtle and varied interactions between social power, language, and gender; they also suggest methods and analytic frameworks for further investigations of how this interaction shapes women's and men's lives.

4
PROPRIETORS OF LANGUAGE

Cheris Kramarae

Women's speech has been described as polite, emotional, enthusiastic, gossipy, talkative, uncertain, dull, and chatty; men's speech, in contrast, as capable, direct, rational, illustrating a sense of humor, unfeeling, strong (in tone and word choice), and blunt. In recent years a great deal of research has attempted to translate such general stereotypes into specific linguistic terms so that "objective" measurements can be made to determine the nature and degree of sex differences in phonology, word choice, intonation, and syntax. While some differences have been found by these means, no evidence has emerged for many of the differences hypothesized on the basis of such stereotypes.[1]

To begin to explain the labels and the beliefs about women's and men's speech, we need to explore women's and men's different relationship to the means of expression, language itself—their different access to, different control over, and different involvement with the English code. By and large men have controlled the norms of use; and this control, in turn, has shaped the language system available for use by both sexes and has influenced the judgments made about the speech of women and men. Men have largely determined what is labeled, have defined the ordering and classifying system, and have in most instances created the words which are catalogued in our dictionaries and which are the medium of everyday speech. Thomas Hardy's heroine in *Far From the Madding Crowd* observes that "it is difficult for a woman to define her feelings in language which is chiefly made by men to express theirs."[2] Women have often had to fit their needs for self-expression to the vocabulary and thus the value-system of the other, custodian group. This different relationship to the language means that even similar speech by women and men might be perceived as being different.

It is not, of course, that women have played no role in the development of language systems. As Patricia Nichols documents (this volume), women are

58

sometimes in the vanguard of linguistic change. And, as the major sources of adult linguistic influence on young children, women have undoubtedly helped chart the course of many developments in language, although we still understand relatively little about this process. But in such public and self-conscious matters as the "legitimizing" of new words and meanings and establishing their general currency throughout the language community, it is men's influence that has predominated.

Women and men are believed and expected to have different behavior. "We *see* a man doing what we would ordinarily think of as feminine, sitting still, and manage to think of it as masculine because a man is doing it. Some people manage even to continue to think of men standing up when in fact they are sitting down," writes Mary Ellmann.[3] Similarly, what we hear will be affected by what we expect to hear, that is, what is "appropriate" for females and for males.

Language, its uses and powers, has been a foremost concern for feminists. In 1973 Mary Daly called attention to women's relationship to language.

> In a sexist world, symbol systems and conceptual apparatuses have been male creations. These do not reflect the experiences of women, but rather function to falsify our own self-images and experiences. . . . It is necessary to grasp the fundamental fact that women have had the power of naming stolen from us. We have not been free to name ourselves, the world, or god.[4]

Dale Spender thinks the power so basic that she writes of the Namer and the Named. Femininity, writes Spender, is not a symbol of women's making in the way that masculinity is a symbol of man's making.[5] Shirley Ardener, in fact, suggests that the gender division itself is basically of male construction, and that "physical differentiations (whether 'real' or 'socially perceived') are merely arbitrary markers which have been useful for setting up social oppositions."[6] Women's speech "exists" because men have labeled it.

A few men have mentioned the differing involvement women and men have with the organization of the language. For example, in 1922 the influential linguist Otto Jespersen wrote that "as a rule women are more conservative than men, and . . . they do nothing more than keep to the traditional language which they have learnt from their parents and hand on to their children, while innovations are due to the innovations of men."[7] Brian Foster in *The Changing English Language* deals at length with the way the British language has been influenced by American men: "In the mind of many a young Briton and his girl, American speech is the hall-mark of the tough guy and the he-man."[8] (Although Foster's book is almost entirely about male involvement in language change, he includes no explicit discussion of the exclusion of women.)

In his preface to *Dictionary of American Slang*, Stuart Flexner initially defines slang as "the body of words and expressions frequently used by or intelligible to a rather large portion of the general American public" although not considered good formal usage by most people. Slang is highly transitory, and it comprises at any given time about 10 percent of the words an average American knows. For Flexner, slang comes from the "imagination, self-confidence, and optimism of our people," and its creation and use represent Americans' intellectual, spiritual, and emotional restlessness and vitality. Thus, "by and large, the man who uses slang is a forceful, pleasing, acceptable person-ality." Furthermore, adds Flexner, "most American slang is created and used by males."[9] Many of the slang expressions become a part of standard usage in a continuous linguistic and social process from which women have been largely excluded. Women have been especially cautioned through at least 150 years of etiquette books to avoid the use of slang.[10]

Women are more likely to be isolated from each other or restricted to jobs which do not encourage or reward imagination, self-confidence, and optimism. Their homes, jobs, clothing, cars, and kitchen utensils are usually created and named by men. Or so it appears. It should be noted that one important factor here may be our scant documentation of women's actual contributions to material and linguistic culture. Inadequate histories of women's activities and relations to one another, coupled with prevalent assumptions of women's passivity and men's active creativity, may have obscured the real extent and nature of women's role in shaping our common heritage. Nonetheless, women and men do not have exactly the same heritage. The woman who would be a public speaker already violates norms, for there is "a trans-class prejudice against women as speakers at all." The limits to women's speaking rights seem to place women "in a special relation to language which becomes theirs as a consequence of being human, and at the same time not theirs as a consequence of being female."[11]

These restrictions are not, of course, new. In an essay first written in 1881—"Women and the Alphabet: Ought Women to Learn It?"—Thomas Higginson notes that women learn that it is proper for them to sing but indelicate to speak in public.[12] The stereotypes of "appropriate" verbal behavior for males and females are themselves restrictions on the idea that women could have something to contribute to the continuing creation of the English language. Certainly not all males are equally involved in the evolution of new words or in the setting of standards of usage. But, in general, it is men's and not women's interests, activities, and perceptions which have been recorded.

Evidence that the words and meanings of our general discussions are men's formations and more closely represent their and not women's experiences and perceptions comes from a variety of sources. In *Keywords*, Raymond Williams lists 155 words which he considers significant in formulating the way we see and discuss many of our "cultural experiences";[13] the first 12 entries suggest the types of concepts included—aesthetic, alienation, art, behavior, bourgeois, bureaucracy, capitalism, career, charity, city, civilization, and class. The publisher's book jacket presents Williams' work as showing "the complex interaction between the changed meanings of words, how these changes affect people's concepts and how people's concepts are once again changed by the changes." In his accounts of the evolution of certain words, Williams cites hundreds of people who were influential in forming, modifying, or redefining the meanings. Only a few of those hundreds mentioned are women; for instance, Jane Austen and Lady Bradshaugh are named under "Sensibility."

Williams' own preferences account for the material selected for his book, and his preferences may reflect a gender-biased interest. He also might very well have overlooked or underestimated women's influence in determining the formation and meaning of these and other "keywords." In any case, reviewers of Williams' book did not notice women's virtual absence and thus evidently found this representation of male dominance neither startling nor inaccurate.

Those who hold important positions in political and cultural institutions, from Washington, D.C., to Madison Avenue, have particular power to coin and to give wide circulation to new words or phrases.[14] Because they rarely occupy top positions, women are seldom involved in the promotion of new expressions which gain currency, yet women are nonetheless inevitably affected by new language. Many people have argued that our perception of social reality is shaped by our particular language; we will not see, hear, or think concepts except as our language allows. Whether or not language determines thought in any significant way, it seems plausible that language can at least *constrain* concept formation, and that gender-biased language may constrain the perception and expression of women, as well as men who do not conform to heterosexual male norms or are in other ways outside the "mainstream."

Women's experience when recorded has usually been recorded by men and through the medium of a language developed by men. About the resulting version of "reality," the women of the [British] feminist/philosophy writing collective ask:

> Is it possible that the language developed by one group in society within an oppressive relationship can simultaneously serve the purpose for the oppressed group?
> We would like to suggest that there is a problem both of concept formation within an existing male-constructed framework of thought and a problem of language use in developing and articulating an authentic understanding of the world and one's relationship to it.[15]

Betty Friedan in *The Feminine Mystique* talked of the problem, experienced by most housewives, which had no name; the lack of the name was, of course, one of the reasons the problem seemed so difficult to describe in 1963.[16] As Peter Berger and Thomas Luckmann write, "The subjective reality of something that is never talked about comes to be shaky."[17] It comes as no surprise then that feminists often suffer category confusion, " an inability to know how to classify things," for they suffer "a double ontological shock"—first the awareness that what is actually happening is quite different from what many others around them believe is happening, and second, their difficulty in categorizing what is really happening.[18]

Although there is little empirical study of how language helps us order our world, there is considerable reason to suppose that labels can help. First, having an "established" word means that there is no need for a personal narrative to explain the concept to others. Second, having a word legitimates the concept. Third, having a shared word helps establish a bond, a link with others for whom the concept is meaningful. An anecdotal illustration: one English woman described to a group of women a recurring frustrating experience. She and her husband both worked outside the home and would arrive home about the same time each evening. He would seldom do any kitchen work, saying, "I'd be glad to do it, but you do it so much better than I." She would go to the kitchen rather pleased at the compliment, but also rather upset and tired. She had some difficulty determining what was wrong, before eventually realizing that he was using flattery to keep her in her place. She said, "I need to be able to tell you—and to tell him—succinctly, in a word, what he is when he does this."[19] (A flatterpressor; or, more sonorously, *tyrannus adulatorius*?)

An essay by Jennifer Williams and Howard Giles suggests that Henri Tajfel's theory of intergroup behavior can be utilized to examine the *changing* relationship between women and men.[20] The Tajfel approach posits that our social identity, part of our self-concept, is derived from our knowledge of the social groups we belong to and the values we believe other groups hold. Tajfel is particularly interested in "inferior" groups—that is, groups which are negatively evaluated by many—and in the methods members of such groups employ to achieve a positive self-image.

Williams and Giles suggest that one strategy women are using today is to refuse to accept the negative definition of themselves that has been organized and perpetuated by men. Women concerned with language cull dictionaries, fiction, and conversations for the terms used to define women, in order to document the type and extent of the linguistic putdown of women.[21] While the old dictionaries remain a disturbingly accurate picture of the usage of many speakers, Ruth Todasco's introduction to an alternative dictionary, the *Feminist English Dictionary*, reminds us that "a general awareness of their sexism can weaken their authority," and thus promote the spread of ways of speaking that do not devalue women.[22] She argues that openly talking about words which have been men's property (for example, the many epithets for women) destroys some of their power.

In addition to pointing out and analyzing the manner in which women have been negatively defined by men, a number of women are also concerned to define themselves and their interests. Early in the contemporary women's liberation movement, many feminists began consciously developing a vocabulary to deal with their concerns. For example, a 1970 article in the *Long Island Press* lists 13 new expressions—including *sexist, male chauvinism, sexegration*—in use by feminists.[23]

Definition and redefinition have recently become the central concerns of many women who are investigating the interrelationships of people and their institutions from a variety of viewpoints. Mary Daly, feminist philosopher and theologian, writes that her book *Gyn/Ecology* is about "mind/spirit/body pollution inflicted through patriarchal myth and language" and about ways of creating new words and searching the rich etymology of old words such as *hag, harpy, crone, fury,* and *spinster.*[24] Similarly, in a panel discussion she spoke of the importance of overcoming "this inherited vocabulary of idiotology" in order to understand and break patriarchy. On the same panel, linguist Julia Penelope Stanley discussed the need to reclaim English in order to better serve women's purposes: "With language, I can claim aspects of myself that I've denied, express ideas that have been suppressed and tabooed for a long time . . . define my life as real, and I can act to change my life"; and poet Adrienne Rich talked about taboos, about what and where women, both black and white, have been forbidden to speak, and about women's recent "coming to language out of silence," naming themselves and their interests.[25]

As some recent research has shown, women in the past have been involved in at least some types of linguistic innovation.[26] We are now collecting the clues of such activity and building on our foremothers' language to create new modes of language use for ourselves. The impact this new writing and speaking will have is suggested by the interest which has been shown; *Gyn/Ecology* sold more than 10,000 copies in its first three weeks after publication.[27]

Additionally, women are not limiting their discussion to their own groups, but are asserting themselves in previously male-dominated spheres. They have pressured publishing companies into establishing guidelines for writers, suggesting new ways to avoid sexist terms. Feminists have published their own dictionaries challenging the views of language use codified by "standard" lexicographers. An entry in *A Woman's New World Dictionary* reads:

> MAN. [Generic] 1. An absurd assumption still accepted by some that both sexes are included when the word "man" is used. 2. A mis-statement of fact. 3. An egotistical male distortion, legitimized in the language, that "man" could/should represent both sexes. 4. A false hope. See WO/MAN.[28]

That standard dictionaries do not give an accurate picture of the actual usage and interpretation of so-called "generic masculines" by either women or men is clear from such empirical research as that of Wendy Martyna (this volume). Feminist groups are publishing their own journals, financing their own presses, and making public recommendations about how labeling should be changed. For example, in a *New York Times* essay, Ethel Strainchamps suggests that instead of discussing the alteration of the titles of women (for example, using *Ms.*), editors should, for once, consider that men might make an adjustment and begin to label themselves according to *their* marital history (perhaps *Master/Mister?*).[29]

Some women are also reconsidering and reevaluating structural and functional patterns of discourse. It has been argued that cooperation rather than competition is the prime pattern of communicative interaction within many women's groups.[30] Women's greater willingness to reach agreement and to avoid conflict has been traditionally evaluated as a weakness.[31] But today the "very 'male' pattern," that of vying with each other for individual attention, is being challenged, and the standards used by many men in evaluating both women and men are being forcefully questioned.[32]

As might be expected, women's challenges to male supremacy have brought strong reactions. The linguistic changes women advocate have, for example, often been redefined or put in a different context so that the meaning of the change is diminished or lost. For example, *chairperson* is used primarily to refer to females, while *chairman* is still used frequently to refer to males. So *chair-person*, proposed as a neutral term, has tended to become gender-specific.

Stanley argues that laughter is a strategy many men use to avoid consider-ing viewpoints that are inimical to their interpretation of reality. Analysis at the intergroup level suggests that laughter and ridicule can also be a defensive response through which a dominant group seeks to protect its threatened social identity. Especially in the early 1970s many columnists and writers of letters to editors played with the feminists' complaints about the so-called generic *man* and *he* by writing essays in which *person* was substituted for each *man* resulting in strings of sentences like the following: "It was interesting to see how a group with obviously persongled egos were able to personipulate an organization the size of ours into looking like a pack of fools. 'Chairperson' indeed!"[33]

Women who write for the public eye risk being considered "deviant" almost as much as those who adopt the "masculine" public speaking role. At the very least, their writing is seldom judged by the same criteria as men's. As many feminist critics have noted, women writers are often split off from "writers" and reviewed separately, with their sex and their marital status often prime considerations in the evaluation of their books. For example, the (London) *Sunday Times* reviewer concludes his comments on Erica Jong's novel *How to Save Your Own Life*, "It is not so much a case of Women's Lib as Women's Glib," and continues:

> So it was that when I took up *The Golden Honeycomb* I suffered some misgivings to find it was by another woman author, Kamala Markandaya, but my uneasiness quickly vanished, for soon after I began the book I realized I was reading a novelist of rare quality. Her insights are not prejudiced by her gender; her art is to report the truth and life of things.[34]

One suspects that in her historical saga she is not advocating changes threatening to the male reviewer.

Women who implicitly or explicitly recommend change in the relationship between women and men are often accused of intellectual deviancy. They are said, for example, to be making "childish war" on language, or to write "from a very subjective point of view."[35] One man suggested to the editors of the *Feminist English Dictionary* that they include a male adviser to provide an "objective view."[36] The Macmillan Publishing Company guidelines for more egalitarian standards in the representation of females and males in children's stories have been described as "a willful exercise in intellectual dishonesty."[37] The British feminist publishing house, Virago, is accused of "contemplating social follies and injustices from an arbitrarily feminist point of view which makes its literature not only non-serious but, worse, humourless."[38]

As Jessica Bernard, and Dot Griffiths and Esther Saraga, have noted, the kinds, extent, conclusions, and explanations of research on gender differences vary depending upon what issues are politically and socially useful for the dominant group at any particular time.[39] Seventeen members of Harvard's linquistics department replied to students asking for a ban on the use of *man* and masculine pronouns to refer to all people: "The fact that the masculine is the unmarked gender in English (or that the feminine is unmarked in the language of the Tunica Indians) is simply a feature of grammar. . . . There is really no cause for anxiety or pronoun-envy on the part of those seeking such changes."[40] Stefan Kanfer in a *Time* essay entitled "Sispeak: A Msguided Attempt to Change Herstory" warns that the women's liberation movement has "a touching, almost mystical trust in words" and sees in the feminist attack on words "only another social crime—one against the means and the hope of communication."[41] John Condon questions with paternal concern the wisdom of the women who are talking about male bias in language:

> Sometimes blaming language habits is a rhetorically effective way to alert us to and dramatize a social problem. But also, sometimes attempting to change some conventional habits is not very effective in changing the attitudes and behavior which are at fault. We must be careful that our efforts are not misguided and wasted.[42]

When women take steps to change the language structure and their own uses of language, they are in fact acting to change their status in society; they are challenging the legitimacy of the dominant group. By calling the challengers and their proposals for language change silly, unnatural, irrational, and simplistic, the dominant group tries to reaffirm its threatened social identity.

To return to our initial question: given that popular stereotypes of women's and men's speech bear little direct relation to the actualities of women's and men's ways of speaking, how can we explain their persistence?

An understanding of the strategies employed by women concerned with language use and structure, and a look at the types of responses by their critics, provide a means of interpreting the perceptions people have of women's and men's speech. The long tradition of male control of language, determining both the symbols which are developed and the norms for usage for women and men, means that women's speech will not be evaluated the same way as men's speech. Our understanding of what women say, of what men say, depends in part upon our understanding of the limits to what women do/should/can say and what men do/should/can say. Women's speech is not like men's speech even when the same words and grammatical constructions are used.

Recognition of traditional restrictions on women as language users can help explain the finding by several investigators of different labels for similar behavior. In a study involving the same child, identified for some observers as a boy and for some a girl, John Condry and Sandra Condry report that the child's crying was labeled "anger" if the infant was thought to be a boy, and "fear" if the infant was thought to be a girl.[43] D. W. Addington found that the changes in the tone of voice of males affect the evaluation of their personalities differently than do similar changes in female voices.[44] Meredith Gall et al. found that for women verbal fluency is negatively evaluated while for men it is positively evaluated.[45]

In an essay appropriately entitled "Truth Is a Linguistic Question," Dwight Bolinger suggests that linguists and others should show more concern not only with the way language is used—and with questions of appropriateness—but also with the way language *is*—and with questions of the fitness of language to the perceptions of speakers. Bolinger further adds:

> Women are taught their place . . . by the implicit lies that language tells about them. Now you can argue that a term is not a proposition; therefore merely having the words does not constitute a lie about anybody. . . . People may be liars but words are not. This argument has a familiar ring. We hear it every time Congress tries to pass legislation restricting the possessions of guns. . . . [However,] lots of casualties, some crippling ones, result from merely having weapons around.[46]

He suggests that students of language consider not only the meaning of the parts—the individual words and sentences—occurring in discourse, but also the meaning of the whole, the language code from which we draw. Of course, in actual social settings, meaning will be negotiated to some extent by the participants. But women will not be equal participants or successful negotiator's if the language code does not serve them equally. Dell Hymes begins a similar argument and suggests that women are "communicatively second-class citizens" because of the restrictions on what they may say, when and where they may say it, and what conceptions of themselves are presented in the English code.[47]

If successful, the feminist challenge to the myths of linguistic "propriety" will undermine the basis of any group's claim to "proprietorship" and thus will improve the chances for a class-free citizenry in the speech community.

NOTES

1. The above issues are discussed in detail in *The Sociology of the Languages of American Women*, ed. Betty Lou Dubois annd Isabel Crouch (San Antonio, Texas: Trinity University, 1976); Howard Giles, Philip M. Smith, and Jennifer A. Williams, "Women Speaking: The Voices of Perceived Androgyny and Feminism" (Paper presented at the International Conference on Sex-Role Stereotyping, at Cardiff, Wales, July 1977); Cheris Kramarae, "Folklinguistics," *Psychology Today* 8 (June 1974): 82-85; Cheris Kramarae, "Stereotypes of Women's Speech: The Word from Cartoons," *Journal of Popular Culture*

8 (1974): 622-38; Cheris Kramarae, "Perceptions of Female and Male Speech," *Language and Speech* 20 (April-June 1977): 151-61; Cheris Kramarae, "Women's and Men's Rating of Their Own and Ideal Speech," *Communication Quarterly* 26 (Spring 1978): 2-11; William Labov, *The Social Stratification of English in New York City* (Washington, D.C.: Center for Applied Linguistics, 1966); Robin Lakoff, "Language and Woman's Place," *Language in Society* 2 (1973): 45-79; Peter Trudgill, "Sex, Covert Prestige and Linguistic Change in the Urban British English of Norwich," *Language in Society* 1 (1972): 179-95.

2. One of the anonymous reviewers of this book drew attention to the Hardy quotation.

3. Mary Ellmann, *Thinking about Women* (New York: Harcourt Brace Jovanovich, 1968), p. 6.

4. Mary Daly, *Beyond God the Father: Towards a Philosophy of Women's Liberation* (Boston: Beacon Press, 1973), pp. 7-8.

5. Dale Spender, "The Namer and the Named," manuscript (University of London).

6. Shirley Ardener, "Introduction," *Perceiving Women*, ed. Shirley Ardener (London: Malaby Press, 1975), p. xviii.

7. Otto Jespersen, *Language: Its Nature, Development and Origin* (London: Allen & Unwin, 1922), p. 242.

8. Brian Foster, *The Changing English Language* (London: Macmillan, 1976), p. 14.

9. Stuart Flexner, "Preface," *Dictionary of American Slang*, eds. Harold Wentworth and Stuart Berg Flexner, 2nd supplemental ed. (New York: Thomas Y. Crowell, 1975), pp. vi, viii.

10. Cheris Kramarae, "Excessive Loquacity: Women's Speech as Represented in American Etiquette Books" (paper presented at the Speech Communication Association Summer Conference in Austin, Texas, July 1975).

11. Cora Kaplan, "Language Gender," *Papers on Patriarchy* (London: Women's Publishing Collective, 1976), pp. 28,29.

12. Thomas Wentworth Higginson, *Woman and the Alphabet* (Boston and New York: Houghton Miffin, 1900; reprinted ed. New York: Arno Press, 1972), p. 33.

13. Raymond Williams, *Keywords: A Vocabulary of Culture and Society* (New York: Oxford University Press, 1976), p. 13.

14. See the collection of essays ed. Hugh Rank, *Language and Public Policy* (Urbana, Ill.: National Council of Teachers of English, 1974).

15. feminist/philosophy writing collective, "Cutting through Phallic Morality," manuscript (London), n.p.

16. Betty Friedan, *The Feminine Mystique* (New York: Norton, 1963).

17. Peter Berger and Thomas Luckmann, *The Social Construction of Reality* (Harmondsworth, Middlesex, England: Penquin, 1975), p. 173.

18. Sandra Lee Bartky, "Toward a Phenomenology of Feminist Consciousness," in *Feminism and Philosophy*, ed. Mary Vetterling-Braggin, Frederick Elliston, and Jane English (Totowa, N.J.: Littlefield, Adams, 1977), p. 29.

19. This narration took place during a language-and-gender study group meeting in London, May 1977.

20. Jennifer Williams and Howard Giles, "The Changing Status of Women in Society: An Intergroup Perspective," in *Studies in Intergroup Behavior*, ed. Henri Tajfel (London: Academic Press, 1978). See also Henri Tajfel, "Social Identity and Intergroup Behavior," *Social Science Information* 13 (1974): 65-93.

21. This is the technique used by, for example, the Bristol [England] Women's Liberation Group, "Definitions," *Enough* (n.d.), pp. 23-24; the editors of the *Feminist English Dictionary: An Intelligent Woman's Guide to Dirty Words* (Chicago: Loop Center YWCA, 1973); Alleen Pace Nilsen, "Sexism as Shown through the English Vocabulary," in *Sexism and Language*, ed. Alleen Pace Nilsen, Haig Bosmajian, H. Lee Gershuny, and Julia P. Stanley (Urbana, Ill.: National Council of Teachers of English, 1977); Julia P. Stanley, "Paradigmatic Woman: The Prostitute," *Papers in Language Variation*, ed. David L. Shores

and Carol P. Hines (Birmingham: University of Alabama, Press, 1977): and Varda One, "Manglish," *Everywoman* 1 (31 July 1970).

22. Ruth Todasco, "Introduction," *Feminist English Dictionary*, p. iii.

23. Gay Pauley, "Women's Lib Lingo Replaces Girl Talk," *Long Island Press*, 21 November 1970, p. 8.

24. Mary Daly, *Gyn/Ecology* (Boston: Beacon Press, 1978), p. 9.

25. Mary Daly, in "The Transformation of Silence into Language and Action," *Sinister Wisdom*, 6 (Summer 1978): 9; Julia Penelope Stanley, p. 5; and other panel participants were Adrienne Rich, p. 21, Audre Lorde, and Judith McDaniel.

26. See the essay by Patricia Nichols in this volume.

27. Ann Marie Lipinski, "The Selling of Women Takes a Scholarly Twist in Publishing," *Chicago Tribune* (Lifestyle section), 21 January 1979, pp. 1, 4.

28. "A Woman's New World Dictionary," *A Paper of Joyful Noise for the Majority Sex* 2 (1973): 3.

29. Ethel Strainchamps, "Ethel Strainchamps Wrote This," *New York Times*, 4 October 1971, p. 39.

30. For example, Susan Kalčik, " ' . . . Like Ann's gynecologist or the time I was almost raped': Personal Narratives in Women's Rap Groups," *Journal of American Folklore* 88 (January-March 1975): 3-11.

31. See Alice H. Eagly, "Sex Differences in Influenceability," *Psychological Bulletin* 85: (1978): 86-116, for a review of some of the literature on "persuasibility."

32. "A Continuation of the Story of the Collective That Has No Name," *Ain't I a Woman* 1: (30 October 1970): 9.

33. Edmund Shimberg, Letter in the *APA Monitor*, October 1971, p. 9.

34. Ronald Harwood, "Confessions of a Trans-Sexual Lover," [London] *Sunday Times*, 1 May 1977, p. 41.

35. Jacques Barzun, "A Few Words on a Few Words," *The Columbia Forum* (Summer 1974): 18; "Bookshelf" [review of Carolyn Faulder, Christine Jackson, and Mary Lewis, *The Women's Directory*], [London] *Sunday Times*, 3 October 1976, p. 43.

36. Reported by Alice Klement, "Sex Life of Words Spelled Out," manuscript filed at the Women's Collection, Northwestern University Library, Evanston, Illinois.

37. James J. Kilpatrick, "And Some Are More Equal than Others." *The American Sociologist* 2 (May 1976): 85.

38. "Virago Salvo," *New Society* (27 January 1977): 164.

39. Jessie Bernard, *Sex Differences: An Overview*, MSS Module 26 (n.p.: MSS Modular Publications, 1973), pp. 1-18; Dot Griffiths and Esther Saraga, " ' . . . fundamentally suited to different social roles': Sex Differences in a Sexist Society," *Women, Biology and Ideology* (forthcoming).

40. Quoted in Casey Miller and Kate Swift, *Words and Women* (Garden City, N.Y.: Doubleday [Anchor], 1976), p. 76.

41. Stefan Kanfer, "Sispeak: A Misguided Attempt to Change Herstory," *Time*, 23 October 1972, p. 79.

42. John Condon, *Semantics and Communication*, 2nd ed. (New York: Macmillan, 1975), p. 68.

43. John Condry and Sandra Condry, "Sex Differences: A Study of the Eye of the Beholder," *Child Development* 47 (1976): 812-19.

44. D. W. Addington, "The Relationship of Selected Vocal Characteristics to Personality Perception," *Speech Monographs* 35 (1968): 492-503.

45. Meredith Gall, Amos Hobb, and Kenneth Craik, "Non-linguistic Factors in Oral Language Productivity," *Perceptual and Motor Skills* 29 (1969): 871-74.

46. Dwight Bolinger, "Truth Is a Linguistic Question," in *Language and Public Policy*, ed. Hugh Rank (Urbana, Ill.: National Council of Teachers of English, 1974), p. 164.

47. Dell Hymes, *Foundations in Sociolinguistics: An Ethnographic Approach* (Philadelphia: University of Pennsylvania Press, 1974), p. 205.

5
THE PSYCHOLOGY OF
THE GENERIC MASCULINE

Wendy Martyna

Words and their meanings — this is the subject I have chosen. Some of you, no doubt, will wonder at my choice; for the subject will strike you as odd and unimportant, even rather silly. . . . This is a most unfortunate attitude. For the fact is that words play an enormous part in our lives and are therefore deserving of the closest study. . . . They are matters of the profoundest ethical significance to every human being.

Aldous Huxley [1]

Words and their meanings are my subject as well. My justification echoes Huxley's, for the fact is that two words — *he* and *man* — "play an enormous part in our lives and are therefore deserving of the closest study." The feminist concern over sexist language is, essentially, a concern with sexist attitudes and behaviors. Sexist language is scrutinized not only as a reflection of sexism in society, but as a form of social behavior in itself, one which helps to create and maintain an atmosphere of inequality.

The question of the generic masculine has been a focus of this feminist concern. *He* and *man* have had to play two roles, conveying both specific references to males, and generic references to human beings. Increasing numbers of people have begun to urge that these terms be confined to their specific references.

The generic masculine is faulted on three counts. First, its *inequity*: the nonparallelism between the male and female terms. Thomas Paine's *Rights of Man* encompasses both male and human meaning; Mary Wollstonecraft's *Rights of Woman* can encompass female meaning alone. As the Association for Women in Psychology contends, "We should not countenance a language that refers to all humans as males."[2] Second, its *ambiguity*: the difficulty of determining

69

whether a particular use of *he* and *man* is meant to include or exclude females. Third, its *exclusiveness*: those instances in which the generic masculine clearly excludes a female interpretation (as in, "Automation is man's effort to make work so easy that women can do it all"). The National Institute of Education is among the many agencies that have adopted guidelines for avoiding *he* and *man* in order to counteract "the impression presently embedded in the English language that people in general are of the male gender."[3]

The case against the generic masculine is based on psychological assumptions about the ways in which *he* and *man* are used and understood. The intuitions of large numbers of language users are available to support these contentions of inequity, ambiguity, and exclusiveness. But the intuitions of others are available to argue against these claims—intuitions which suggest the generic masculine is neither unclear nor unfair. While differing opinions on equity are not open to empirical resolution, questions of clarity are. A growing body of research is exploring the use and understanding of the generic masculine, testing those psychological assumptions on which the arguments have been based. Unfortunately, much of the popular controversy surrounding the "he/man approach" to language has not taken this research into account and is instead characterized by a persistent misinterpretation of the claims of those who argue against the use of *he* and *man*.[4]

This chapter describes current research on the psychology of the generic masculine, suggesting that the psychological impact of *he* and *man* involves much more than what the Harvard linguistics faculty once termed "pronoun envy".[5]

My concern with these issues of clarity and equity led me to explore whether *he* is an adequate generic term, one that can refer to both females and males. I first examined our use, and then our understanding, of the generic masculine. Do we always use generic *he* to refer to a sex-unspecified person, or do we turn to alternatives, such as *they* and *he or she*, to convey generic reference? And when generic *he* is used, do we understand it in its generic or its specific sense?

To answer the first question, I designed a situation which elicited people's normal language use, and then asked them to reflect back on the pronouns they had just produced. Students completed sentence fragments which contained people in male-related roles ("When an engineer makes an error in calculation . . . "), female-related roles ("When a secretary first arrives at the office . . . "), and neutral roles ("When a teenager finishes high school . . . "); and I examined the pronouns they used in their sentence completions. If *he* is an adequate generic term, we would expect it to be used whenever a pronoun must be chosen without knowing the sex of the referent.

The sentence fragments of this type were accompanied by many others related to miscellaneous topics such as sports and weather, so that attention would be directed away from the repeated use of generic personal pronouns. After the elicitation experiment was over, students completed a questionnaire which asked them to reflect on how they had chosen the pronouns they used, and whether a particular image or idea came to mind as they chose a pronoun. Participants in this study included 400 students of all age levels, from kindergarten through college.

What pronouns did the students choose to express the generic meaning of the sentence fragments? Contrary to grammatical expectations, generic *he* was not the only generic term used to refer to the hypothetical person in the sentences. Both sentence type and sex of student were significant factors influencing the choice of pronoun. When the person was presumed male (as in, "When a police officer leaves the station . . . "), *he* was used 96 percent of the time. When the person was presumed female, *she* was used 87 percent of the time. For neutral sentences, *he* was the most frequent pronoun, but in 30 percent of the sentence completions, alternatives to *he* were chosen. These included *they, he or she*, and repetition of the sentence subject (as in, "When a human being grows old, the human being may feel sadness."). Table 5.1 illustrates the pattern of pronoun usage for both sexes, summarized across all age levels studied.

TABLE 5.1 Sentence Fragment Completions for All Participants (in percent)

	Male-related sentences	Female-related sentences	Neutral sentences
USE OF *HE*	96	7	65
USE OF *SHE*	0	87	5
USE OF ALTERNATIVES	4	6	30

Source: Original data

Our choice of pronoun is influenced not only by who we imagine we are talking about, but by whether we are female or male. Females used *he* less than did males, whether they were referring to hypothetical police officers, secretaries, or human beings. This sex difference appeared at all age levels studied—kindergarten through college. Among the college women, this avoidance of *he* was not attributable to a greater feminist awareness and concern with sexist language, since questioning revealed an equal number of male and female self-described feminists among the subjects (there were only two of each, among 40 subjects). Moreover, when asked what pronouns they used in everyday language, the college women did not report using fewer *he's* than did the men. Yet in an experimental situation which elicited their unselfconscious pronoun choices, they demonstrated this difference. For neutral sentences in particular, females used more alternatives to generic *he* than did the men. Again, this pattern was found among children as well as college women. (Since sociolinguistic studies have demonstrated that people often misreport their own language use, it seems likely that naturalist observations of spontaneous speech would tend to support the patterns found in the experimental data rather than those suggested by self-reports.)   Table 5.2 illustrates the contrasting pronoun usage of females and males in the fragment completion task.

TABLE 5.2   Sentence Fragment Completions for Male/Female Participants (in percent)

	Male-related sentences	Female-related sentences	Neutral sentences
	Males/Females	Males/Females	Males/Females
USE OF *HE*	97/95	9/6	74/56
USE OF *SHE*	0/0	84/90	2/8
USE OF ALTERNATIVES	3/5	7/4	24/36

Source: Original data

When questioned afterwards, both sexes reported receiving imagery of males as they chose pronouns for the male-related topics, and imagery of females for the female-related topics. The pronoun was picked to match the gender of image received, and thus seems to be a gender-specific rather than a generic term. A different pattern of imagery appears in response to the neutral sentence subjects. Among the college women and men, far fewer females than males reported any imagery at all for the neutral subjects (human being, person, teen-ager, and so on). While 60 percent of the men here reported imagery in this context, only 10 percent of the women did so. All of this imagery was male. Clearly, many of the women who used *he* did so without getting a particular image or idea. Instead, they selected *he* "automatically," "for lack of a better word," or because "I've been trained!" One woman explained, "It was sort of automatic, not that I got a particular image. You always use *he* if sex isn't specified." The men, however, selected *he* for such reasons as, "I pictured males, probably because I'm a male," and "I think of myself." Males may be generating a sex-specific use of *he*, one based on male imagery, while females are generating a truly generic *he*, one based on grammatical standards of correctness.

These patterns of usage reveal that *he* is far from adequate in covering generic ground. Instead of relying on the generic masculine to refer to the sex-unspecified person, we often turn to alternatives such as *she, they,* and *he or she,* depending on what sex we are, and what sex we imagine we are talking about. Why a shift to these alternatives—especially to a generic *she*—when *he* is supposed to be a clear generic referring expression? And what does this shift reveal about the actual meaning of *he* when it is the generic choice?

To explore that meaning, I studied the comprehension of the generic masculine as it appears in clearly generic contexts. Donald MacKay has found that when *he* appears as an isolated word, it is comprehended in its specific male rather than a generic human sense.[6] Asking people to judge which in a list of words were ambiguous, he discovered that no one rated *he* as an ambiguous word. All responded to *he* in its specifically male sense. But perhaps it is context that makes generic meaning clear. To find out, I presented people with complete sentences containing one of three generic pronouns (*he, they,* and *he or she*). Each sentence was followed by either a male or female picture, and people judged whether or not the picture applied to the sentence. If *he* is clearly comprehended in its generic sense, the female pictures should always be judged applicable to the sentences with generic *he*. If *he* is in fact ambiguous and often sex-exclusive, the female picture will sometimes be judged inapplicable to sentences with generic *he*.

Participants in this study included 72 students at Stanford University. They viewed the critical sentences among a large number of filler items related to miscellaneous topics, so that they were unaware that pronoun comprehension was being studied. Each critical sentence referred to a hypothetical neutral person ("When someone prepares for an exam, ---- must do some studying"). For all of these critical sentences, an 'apply' judgment was appropriate on the basis of sentence content, so that any 'not apply' judgments could only be attributed to the presumed mismatch between pronoun and sex of picture. Following the experiment, students were asked whether they had noticed *he* in the critical sentences, and whether the *he* had entered into their decision to respond 'apply' or 'not apply.'

If all three generic terms—*he, they,* and *he or she* — allowed a true generic inference to be drawn, both male and female pictures should seem applicable to the critical sentences. Yet nearly 20 percent of the students said a female picture did *not* apply to a sentence containing the generic *he*. To a sentence such as, "When someone listens to a record player, he will often sing along," equal numbers of male and female students reported that the female picture was inappropriate. Even in clearly generic context, *he* is open to both specific and generic interpretation. The ambiguity of *he* is such that not only do some students see it as specifically male, and others as a human referent, but the same students often reported contradictory judgments, deciding in one case that *he* includes *she*, and in another, that it does not.

Several features of this experiment make that 20 percent an underestimation of the extent to which *he* in a generic context typically excludes a female interpretation. Each sentence was cast in a hypothetical frame (referring to 'someone' or 'anyone'), and *he* appeared only once in each sentence. None of the filler sentences contained any pronouns, and there was thus no contrast between specific referring and generic usages of *he*. Our actual encounters with *he* rarely take place in generic contexts as clear as those devised for this study. In educational materials, for example, the sex-specific *he* appears five to ten times for every potentially dual-sex generic *he*.[7] In addition, generic *he* often appears in contexts that force a male interpretation onto supposedly neutral terminology. For example, one scientist describes a hypothetical researcher who produces a long list of publications, but little contribution to the enduring body of knowledge: "His true position is that of a potent-but-sterile intellectual rake, who leaves in his merry path a long train of ravished maidens, but no viable scientific offspring."[8] Such contexts leave little room for a generic interpretation. But even in a context explicitly designed to encourage a generic inference, the use of *he* allows a sex-exclusive inference to be drawn, and females to be excluded from the category of generic human beings.

Students were questioned following the experiment as to whether they had noticed the *he* in the critical sentences. More than half reported that they did not notice the *he*, but responded 'apply' on the basis of other features of the pictures. A significant sex difference appeared, with *he* noticed in 53 percent of the males' judgments, and only 37 percent of the females' judgments. A second study was therefore conducted which encouraged people to notice the *he* in the sentences. Rather than having the picture follow the sentence, I presented picture and sentence simultaneously, and students were told they would be answering questions about the items following the experiment. In this case, approximately 40 percent of the students reported that the female picture did *not* apply to the sentences with generic *he*—about twice the number in the previous study. Altering a few contextual factors so that the *he* was more readily noticed doubled the ambiguity and sex-exclusiveness of generic *he*. Had the experiment been designed to approximate the occurrences of *he* in everyday contexts, that percentage would undoubtedly have been even higher.

Even in clearly generic contexts, the generic masculine is open to an interpretation that excludes females. Whether that exclusion occurs 20 percent or 40 percent of the time, or whether in fact it occurs only once, the point is clear: the generic masculine fails to perform its generic duty adequately.

We have discovered clear sex differences in the way the generic masculine is used. Females use generic *he* less than males, regardless of antecedent and use alternatives to generic *he* more than males in response to neutral antecedents. In addition, we have seen that far less imagery is reported by college women than men in response to neutral subjects, and that the imagery that does occur is male in character for both sexes. Women thus tend to explain their generic usage in terms of grammatical standards, whereas men explain theirs as responses to male imagery.

Given that women and men use generic masculines differently, how do they comprehend them?

An additional study demonstrates that females are more likely than males to draw a generic interpretation from *he* and *man*.[9] Two hundred students, participating in a study on "the psychology of names," were asked to provide "a typical name" for each of 10 hypothetical people. Four of these ten were referred to as either *he, they,* or *he or she*, as in "someone who is always late to his classes." Sex of name chosen by the student was used to suggest patterns of pronoun comprehension. Both pronoun and sex of student were significant factors affecting comprehension of the generic masculine. When the pronoun used to describe a hypothetical "someone" was *he*, more male names were chosen than when it was *they* or *he or she*. In addition, males chose significantly more male names than did females, regardless of the pronoun used in the description. Just as males seem to base their use of *he* on sex-specific imagery, they tend to draw a sex-specific interpretation when *he* is used. Although women are unwilling to use the generic masculine to refer to themselves, they seem to make a special effort to draw generic interpretation from *he* and *man*, for to do otherwise means self-exclusion.

The consequences of a male-oriented language are significant for males as well as females. John Stuart Mill might have been speaking of the generic masculine when he asked us to imagine ". . . what it is to be a boy, to grow in the belief that without any merit or exertion of his own, by the mere fact of being born a male he is by right the superior of all of an entire half of the human race, including some whose real superiority he has hourly occasion to feel."[10] Alleen Pace Nilsen's work with young children suggests that a boy may have a much easier time learning the generic masculine than a girl. 'It's a very natural process for him to hear that every creature not obviously female is treated as masculine," she says, "and he has no reason to question the naturalness of the standard rule."[11] The earliest uses of pronouns are in reference to a specific individual ("my friend called and he invited me to a party") and allow only sex-specific interpretations. The young girl thus must eventually learn to apply the pronoun she first acquired in its specifically male contexts to herself, and moreover, must learn when and where and how to apply it. We know now that the generic masculine functions neither clearly nor fairly. What needs further exploration is the particular psychological consequences for both females and males who until now have had few options aside from *he* and *man* to convey generic reference.

Some would say that such consequences are minor, since ambiguity is common in our language and creates nothing more than mild confusion. The specific/generic ambiguities of *he* and *man*, however, lead to far more than confusion. Examinations of the "he/man approach" to language have focused on the social and psychological significance of the generic masculine usage.

Marguerite Ritchie has surveyed the legal implications of the generic masculine as it appears in Canadian law, concluding that its ambiguity has allowed either generic or specific interpretations to be drawn, depending on the judge's personal prejudices and the climate of the times. Her conclusion, based on an examination of several hundred years of relevant Canadian law: "Wherever any statute or regulation is drafted in terms of the male, a woman has no guarantee that it confers on her any rights at all."[12]

Susan Sontag has spoken of the intellectual implications of the generic masculine, viewing this aspect of grammar as "the ultimate arena of sexist brainwashing, [which] conceals the very existence of women—except in special situations."[13] Joan Huber notes the intellectual confusion caused by the generic masculine, citing a recent sociology text which notes, "The more education an individual attains, the better his occupation is likely to be, and the more money he is likely to earn." The statement is accurate only if the individual is a male, for unfortunately, women's educational level is not directly related to their occupation or income. Huber terms this kind of ambiguous usage "an exercise in doublethink [that] makes a muddle of sociological discourse."[14]

The possible psychological implications of *he* and *man* are often stressed by those who argue against the generic masculine. As the Association for Women in Psychology has said, "We do not know, but we can guess at the psychological costs of being a nonperson in one's own language. . . . to say that subtleties of language are trivial and thus can't affect us is to fall into the trap of psychological ignorance."[15] It is similarly shortsighted to claim that the subtleties of language have extensive psychological consequences, without attempting to assess those "psychological costs of being a nonperson in one's own language." In view of this, empirical substantiations of the claims of inequity have begun to appear. Most studies have focused on the impact of broad gender cues. Sandra Bem and Daryl Bem, for example, explored the effects of sex-biased wording in job advertisements. When sex-unbiased wording was used, far more women were willing to apply for male-related jobs.[16] In an early study, G. Milton altered the wording of math problems, and found that women's performance improved when the problems concerned female-related situations.[17] A. H. Stein and colleagues found that sex-labeling of a task influenced children's expectancy of success and valuing of attainment.[18] While there is ample data to suggest that the manipulation of such gender cues has psychological importance, we haven't yet assessed the particular contribution of the generic masculine to creating these cues. Although we don't know the precise role the generic masculine plays, the data we do have on the use and understanding of *he* and *man* suggest that role would be considerable.

Many resist the move toward a nonsexist language, seeing alternatives to the generic masculine as too troublesome to use. Columnist "Dear Abby," for example, feels that "writing he/she or him/her is a time-waster, and I for one would find it extremely burdensome." C. S. Lewis acknowledged the difficulty of language change and spoke of a "momentary aphasia" that can be produced from "prolonged thought *about* the words which we ordinarily use to think *with*." But in his view, this is to be welcomed. "It is well," he believed, "that we should become aware of what we are doing when we speak, of the ancient, fragile, and (well used) immensely potent instruments that words are."[19]

There is a growing trend toward nonsexist language in both official and informal usage, but the popular press still seems to treat the sexist language controversy with more satire than seriousness. Far from endorsing Lewis' view of words as "fragile" and "immensely potent instruments," the press often takes the [mistaken] view that language stands apart from the rest of society and that changing the language is therefore irrelevant to changing the society.

The belief that language is at most a reflection of social life is as prevalent among scholars as journalists. Linguist Robin Lakoff advanced a version of this "disease model" of sexist language, in which language is only a symptom of the underlying social disease of sexism. Even accepting this "disease model," one can argue, as does Virginia Valian in discussing Lakoff, that "while we are curing the disease, no overnight affair, we can use a little relief from the symptoms. Second, not only is reduction of suffering a good in itself, it often gives the patient the strength necessary to fight the disease more effectively."[20] But in addition, the disease model neglects the fact that sexist language is not only a reflection of societal sexism, but also a form of social behavior which creates and maintains an atmosphere of inequality. Changing the language is viewed by feminists not as a sufficient condition for changing society, but as one component of the attempt to alter sexist attitudes and behaviors. Robin Morgan refers to language as "that subtle Richter scale of attitudinal earthquakes,"[21] highlighting the eye-opening and ear-opening impact that nonsexist language can have. Yet language change is more than a consciousness-raising tactic. It is a step toward enhancing the self-concepts of those who have been excluded by sexist language forms and changing the views of those who view such exclusion as mere illusion. Mary Daly sees "the liberation of women as rooted in the liberation of language," and emphasizes the critical importance of a language that includes women explicitly, rather than implicitly or not at all.[22]

Mary Beard, writing in 1946, before this decade's attention to the "he/man" approach to language, saw the troublesome ambiguity of the generic masculine as a "problem [which is] really fundamental for precision in thought and its communication . . . it involves [our] judgments on everything human."[23] Then, there was no research to support her claims. Today, there is. And yet, the psychology of the generic masculine needs continued exploration, so that we may understand more fully the minds—and the behaviors—of those who use it, and who must respond to its use. How we refer to ourselves and one another has important implications for our intellectual clarity as well as our societal equity.

NOTES

1. Aldous Huxley, *Words and Their Meanings* (Los Angeles: Ward Ritchie Press, 1940).

2. Association for Women in Psychology, "Help Stamp Out Sexism: Change the Language!" *American Psychological Association Monitor* (November 1975).

3. National Institute of Education, *Guidelines for Assessment of Sex Bias and Sex Fairness in Career Interest Inventories* (Washington, D.C.: Department of Health, Education and Welfare, 1974).

4. Wendy Martyna, "Beyond the He/Man Approach: The Case For Language Change," *Signs: Journal of Women in Culture and Society* 5 (1980): 482-93.

5. *Harvard Crimson,* "Women Liberate Church Course," 11 November 1971.

6. Donald MacKay, "Birth of a Word" (Manuscript, UCLA, Department of Psychology, 1976).

7. Alma Graham, "The Making of a Non-sexist Dictionary," *MS.* 2 (December 1973): 12-16.

8. Paul Meehl, "Theory Testing in Physics: A Methodological Paradox," *Philosophy of Science* 34 (1967): 103-15.

9. Wendy Martyna, *"Using and Understanding the Generic Masculine: A Social-Psychological Approach to Language and the Sexes."* (Ph.D. diss., Stanford University, May 1978).

10. John Stuart Mill, *The Subjection of Women* (n.p., 1869).

11. Alleen Pace Nilsen, "Sexism in Children's Books and Elementary Teaching Materials," in *Sexism and Language*, ed. A. P. Nilsen et al. (Urbana, Ill.: National Council of Teachers of English, 1977).

12. Marguerite Ritchie, "Alice Through the Statutes," *McGill Law Journal* 21 (Winter 1975): 685-707.

13. Susan Sontag, "The Third World of Women," *Partisan Review* 40 (1973): 181-206.

14. Joan Huber, "On the Generic Use of Male Pronouns," *American Sociologist* 11 (1976):85-93.

15. Association for Women in Psychology, "Help Stamp out Sexism," November 1975.

16. Sandra L. Bem and Daryl J. Bem, "Does Sex-biased Job Advertising 'Aid and Abet' Sex Discrimination?" *Journal of Applied Social Psychology* 3 (1973):6-18.

17. G. Milton, "Sex Differences in Problem Solving as a Function of Role Appropriateness of Problem Context," *Psychological Reports* 5 (1959):705-8.

18. A. H. Stein, S. R. Pohly, and E. Mueller, "The Influence of Masculine, Feminine, and Neutral Tasks on Children's Achievement Behavior, Expectations of Success, and Attainment Values," *Child Development* 42 (1971);195-207.

19. C. S. Lewis, *Studies in Words* (London: Cambridge University Press, 1960).

20. Virginia Valian, "Linguistics and Feminism," in *Feminism and Philosophy*, ed. Mary Vetterling-Braggin, Frederick A. Elliston, and Jane English (Totowa, N.J.: Littlefield, Adams, 1977), pp. 154-66.

21. Robin Morgan, "Rights of Passage," *MS*, 4 (September 1975):74-78, 98-112.

22. Mary Daly, *Beyond God the Father: Toward a Philosophy of Women's Liberation* (Boston: Beacon, 1973).

23. Mary Beard, *Woman as Force inn History* (Collier Books, 1946).

6
"DON'T 'DEAR' ME!"

Nessa Wolfson
Joan Manes

The choice of a form of address is one of the ways in which speakers of American English may express and, indeed, influence their own status in relation to that of others. As Dell Hymes has pointed out:

> One value of terms, or modes, of address as a focus is that it makes so clear that the relation of linguistic form to social setting is not merely a matter of correlation. Persons choose among alternative modes of address, and have a knowledge of what the meaning of doing so may be that can be formally explicated.[1]

When a woman is addressed in a public situation the speaker has three major choices: to use the traditional respect form *ma'am*; to use a term of endearment (for example, *honey, dear*); to use no overt form of address whatever. There are other possibilities, of course. The addressee's name may be known to the speaker, and either first name or title plus last name (for example, Mrs. Jones) may be selected as the address form. In addition, there are terms such as *miss, ladies*, and *girl*, which are somewhat less frequent in occurrence. Our attention, however, will be focused on the three major choices mentioned above. For the sake of simplicity, we shall refer to all three as address forms and specifically to the lack of an overt form as the zero address form. This usage can be justified since, as we shall see below, the choice of no form at all, the zero form, can be in direct contrast to the choice of either *ma'am* or a term of endearment, and, therefore, the lack of an address form is often meaningful. While we shall not attempt to discuss in detail the address forms used to males in public situations, it should be noted that the major options seem to be zero

79

and *sir*. Terms of endearment are used on occasion, but they are not frequent.* Thus, in parallel situations, two forms of address exist for men and three for women. The third option, terms of endearment, is not simply a fill-in for zero. In cases where men are addressed as *sir*, women may be addressed as *dear* rather than by the apparently parallel term *ma'am*. We are thus faced with the question of what these three forms mean, when they are used, and how they contrast with one another. It is with these issues that we are concerned in this paper.

There has been a growing interest over the past few years in the way the use of language reflects women's status. All too many of the studies which focus on this issue have suffered from a lack of data from everyday conversational interactions, a problem which is not infrequent in studies of other aspects of language in society. However useful intuitions may be for suggesting hypotheses, it is only through empirical investigation that one may hope to ascertain the validity of one's suppositions.† For this reason, it was essential to observe and record data from everyday linguistic interactions; in no other way could we obtain the information needed to analyze the factors which might be involved in the choice of specific address forms.

Service encounters represent the major public speech situation in our society in which individuals, including total strangers, participate on a regular basis. Marilyn Merritt defines a service encounter as "an instance of face-to-face interaction between a server who is 'officially posted' in some service area and and a customer who is present in that service area, that interaction being oriented to the satisfaction of the customer's presumed desire for some service and the server's obligation to provide that service." We would like to expand this definition to include any encounter in which a service is performed for a fee or in expectation of such. This includes such interactions as those between a nurse and a patient or between a potential customer and a salesclerk over the telephone. Because nearly all of the adult population in our society is regularly involved in some sort of service encounter, these speech situations provide the researcher with a rich source of information about the way people address one another. Furthermore, the public nature of the service encounter makes it particularly amenable to observation by the researcher.

Observation of service encounters and of the forms of address occurring within them was carried out by means of three major techniques. The research-

---

*Our only examples of terms of endearment to men are of women addressing young men in their twenties, but our data on address to males are too limited, both in size (fewer than 90 encounters) and in scope, for us to make any definitive statements. Forms such as *Mack* and *Buster* do, of course, occur, and have been discussed in the literature (see Sally McConnell-Ginet, "Address Forms and Sexual Politics," in *Women's Language and Style*, eds. Douglas Butturff and Edmund L. Epstein [Akron: University of Akron Press, 1978], pp. 23-35). Such forms might appear to be the counterpart of terms of endearment used to women. However, our data include no examples whatever of these terms being used in such a way.

†We wish to express our deep indebtedness to Dell Hymes, who taught us the importance of empirical research.

ers, with the aid of a number of colleagues,* observed and recorded the forms of address used to them in a wide range of service encounters in which they participated. Address forms in transactions which occurred within the hearing of observers, but in which they did not themselves participate, were also carefully recorded. Finally, as a way of checking the data which had already been gathered, a systematic survey of responses to telephoned requests and inquiries was made. Using these three techniques, information on more than 800 interactions was recorded.† Over 80 percent of these are service encounters. The rest represent a variety of interactions between friends, acquaintances, co-workers, and strangers. Although our focus is on service encounters, these additional data were most helpful in clarifying points about the use and meaning of the address forms occurring in service encounters.

All three of the major address forms mentioned earlier occur quite frequently in service encounters. What is most significant, however, is the fact that each of the three can be shown to occur in functionally equivalent situations, to form, in effect, part of a paradigm. Indeed, as anyone who ever goes shopping can easily verify, the formulae:

(1) Can I help you, dear?

(2) Can I help you, ma'am?

(3) Can I help you?

are so much part of the traditional exchange that one hardly bothers to notice which has been said. The use of these forms in functionally equivalent ways is not limited by any means to such traditional formulae. When one of the researchers called shoe stores in the Philadelphia area to ask whether they carried girls' saddle shoes, she received, among others, the following responses:

(4) No, I'm positive we don't have them in stock.

(5) No, I can't help you, ma'am.

(6) I don't believe we have them here, hon.

It may seem counterintuitive that a respect form such as *ma'am* and a term of endearment such as *hon* or *dear* could occur in truly identical situations. To show that this is indeed the case, let us consider the following two exchanges, which occurred in two very similar delicatessens in the same suburb of Philadelphia. In each case the same customer was being served.

(7) A: Yeah, can I have four special hot dogs?

　　 B: Anything else, dear?

(8) A: I'd like a small sliced rye.

　　 B: Here you are ma'am. Anything else?

---

*Our thanks go to the following friends, colleagues, and students who so kindly contributed data for our study: Joan Atherton, Sharlene Brightly, Rebecca Driver, Edwin E. Erickson, Jenny Glusker, Daniele Godard, C. G. Holland, David Howell, Virginia Hymes, Terry Lewis, F. C. Miller, Gwendolyn Samuels, Neil Smith, Barry Taylor, Paula Vance, Stanley Walens, Stefani Walens, Lauren Wiener, Dan Wolfson, and Harvey Wolfson.

†The actual number is closer to 1,000, but we are excluding from consideration here data which contained only reference forms, no address forms.

The second example comes from a longer exchange which is discussed in more detail below (see example 28, p. 88).

Whenever two or more forms can occur within the same frame with no change in referential meaning, their differential usage is likely to carry social meaning. As John Gumperz says, speaking of the use of title plus last name, first name, or *boy* to an adult black man:

> Use of one term or another does not change the nature of the message as a form of address; but it does determine how the person addressed is to be treated, and to what social category he is to be assigned. Selection among such grammatically equivalent alternants thus serves social rather than linguistic purposes.[3]

What, then, are the social meanings associated with the choice of one of the three forms of address under discussion?

Ma'am is a conventional respect form for addressing women. It can occur in initiating a service encounter or at a later stage in the encounter, even if, as in examples 10 and 11, it did not occur in the initial utterance.

(9)   A: Yes, Ma'am, fill 'er?
       B: Yes, please, regular.
       A: Regular? Okay.
       A: (later) Ten twenty-five.
       B: Would you check the oil, please?
       A: You're a quart low, ma'am.
       A: (later) Eleven-fifty. (B hands him the money) Thank you, ma'am.

(10) A: What can I get you to drink before lunch?
       B: Nothing, thanks.
       A: Nothing at all, ma'am?
       B: No. thanks.

(11) A: Do you have shorts for him?
       B: Shorts? Everything I got is on that rack.
       A: Here?
       B: Yes, ma'am.

The first of these occurred in Charlottesville, Virginia; the third occurred in Philadelphia, Pennsylvania; the second occurred on a Delta Airlines flight between Philadelphia and New Orleans.

Although *ma'am* is used in both the northeast and the south, the frequency and distribution of the form show strong regional differences. If we consider all interactions in which either *ma'am* or some term of endearment was used, we find that in the south 68.5 percent of the speakers used *ma'am*, while only 31.5 percent used a term of endearment. Speakers in the northeast, on the other hand, used *ma'am* only 24.5 percent of the time and an endearment form 75.5 percent of the time. The difference is probably even greater than is indicated by these figures, since a fair amount of the southern, as opposed to the northeastern, data was collected by six women under 25, who might be expected by reason of age to receive more endearments. If their material is omitted from consideration, making the two sets of data more comparable, at least as regards the age of the researchers (who are often, though by no means necessarily, the addressees), the frequency of *ma'am* in the south rises to 83.1 percent and that of endearment terms drops proportionately to 16.9 percent. Other address forms, such as *miss, ladies* and proper names, do occur, but their frequency is too low to be statistically interesting. What is significant, however, is the very frequent occurrence of the zero address form, that is, of no overt address form whatsoever. Complete records of the interactions involving zero address were not consistently kept, and so comparisons between northeastern and southern use of this form can only be suggestive. In the Charlottesville, Virginia, data zero address is used in at least half of all service encounters. A small sample from the Philadelphia area suggests that its usage in the northeast may be even higher, around 75 percent, but the limited size of the sample (43 interactions) precludes our drawing any definite conclusions. When zero address is taken into account, the difference between the frequency of southern and northeastern use of *ma'am* is even more striking: 40 percent of all service encounters in the south involve the use of *ma'am* at least once;* only 7 percent of all such encounters in the northeast do so.

This regional difference is confirmed when we consider the sex and relative ages of the speaker and the addressee. In the south, all speakers, male and female, whether they were older, younger, or of the same age as the addressee, used *ma'am* more frequently than terms of endearment. In fact, only in the case of older women addressing younger women do we find a noticeable use of terms of endearment as opposed to *ma'am* (44 percent and 56 percent respectively).† In the northeast, on the other hand, only when the addressee was a relatively older woman did speakers (of either sex) use *ma'am* more frequently than terms of endearment. It seems, therefore, that in the south sex is a stronger influence than age: male service personnel, if they use an overt address form to a woman, use *ma'am* in almost every instance; relative age apparently influences the choice of form significantly only for female speakers who, if they are older than the addressee, fairly frequently select a term of endearment. In the northeast, on the other hand, relative age seems to be the more significant factor of the two: for both men and women, terms of endearment are more frequent than *ma'am* if the speaker is older than the addressee, and *ma'am* is more frequent if the speaker is younger. A more complete analysis of the interrelated effects of sex and age would require additional data to deal with

---

*Excluding the very few which exhibit forms of address other than zero, *ma'am*, or endearment terms, as mentioned above.

†Age should be understood to mean estimated age since neither the investigator nor, for that matter, the speaker can know the exact age of a stranger in a service encounter. Persons whose ages are estimated to be less than ten years apart are considered to be of equal age.

the fact that the absolute ages of both the speaker and the addressee may affect the choice of address form independently of their relative ages (for example, women over a certain age may tend to be addressed with a respect form no matter what their age relative to that of the speaker).* In addition, as we shall see below, both the respect form, *ma'am*, and terms of endearment may be used in a variety of ways, and it seems unlikely that such factors as age and sex act in the same way in all cases. Similar problems arise in the consideration of the effect of race on choice of address form, and since our data are much less comprehensive for blacks (both speakers and addressees) than for whites, we have left this question for later consideration.

Ma'am is not only found with much greater frequency in the south than in the northeast, it is also found in different contexts and with different meanings. Two southern uses of *ma'am* do not seem to occur at all in northeastern speech.† First, the single term *ma'am*, with rising intonation, can indicate that the speaker has not heard or understood what was said:

(12) A: Could you tell me how late you're open this evening?
    B: Ma'am?
    A: Could you tell me how late you're open this evening?
    B: Until 6.

This use is functionally equivalent to forms such as "pardon?" and "I'm sorry?" which occur in both regions:

(13) A: You're not open on Sundays?
    B: Pardon?
    A: You're not open on Sundays?
    B: No.

(14) A: Do you have rooms for tomorrow night?
    B: I'm sorry?
    A: I said, do you have rooms for tomorrow night?
    B: I can't hear you, ma'am.

Note that in 14 the address form *ma'am* was used in the second request for repetition, but not the southern construction, *ma'am*? The speaker was a hotel clerk in Philadelphia.

The second use of *ma'am* which is specific to the south is the phrase "yes, ma'am" which functions as a variant of "you're welcome":

(15) A: Could you tell me how late you're open this evening?
    B: Until nine.
    A: Thank you very much.
    B: Yes, ma'am.

---

*The same thing, of course, holds for sex of speaker and addressee, but since we are concerned in this chapter only with address to women, the problem does not arise.

†We are aware, of course, that people who migrate to a different area, and possibly their descendants, may continue to use the forms of their original dialects.

(16) A: Could you tell me how late you're open this evening?
      B: Until five-thirty.
      A: Thank you very much.
      B: You're welcome.

There also exists a regional difference in the range of extra linguistic contexts in which the form *ma'am* occurs. In the northeast, *ma'am* is heard almost exclusively in speech situations involving strangers.* In the south, on the other hand, certain uses of the form are perfectly appropriate to acquaintances and even intimates. For example, when a graduate student at the University of Virginia brought one of her professors a cup of coffee, the professor responded with "Thank you, ma'am." Similarly, a male colleague of one of the researchers, who is a good deal older than she is and who generally addresses her by first name or a diminutive, responds to direct questions from her with "yes, ma'am," or "no, ma'am." Even more striking to a transplanted northerner is the young man from South Carolina who, when his wife says something which he does not hear, questions her with, "Ma'am?"

The use of *ma'am* as an intrinsic part of certain polite formulae is so general in the south that it need not always convey respect. Even in a situation where the speaker was clearly annoyed at the addressee, who furthermore was not of such status as to command any expression of respect from him, the phrase "yes, ma'am" appeared three times:

(17) A: Mr. Jones?
      B: Yes, ma'am.
      A: I'm calling for John Smith, who's running in the Democratic
         primary next Tuesday.
      B: Yes, ma'am.
      A: May I ask what you think of Mr. Smith?
      B: I'll tell you, lady. I'm voting for Jim Brown.
      A: Well, thank you very much.
      B: Yes, ma'am.

Other speakers may express their annoyance by avoiding the polite address form, switching back to it when they feel their grievance is being attended to:

(18) A: Lady, I've spent all morning down here waiting.
      B: Did you put your yellow card in the box?
      A: Yeah.
      B: (looks in box and locates card) Did you want to get these filled
         out?
      A: Yes, ma'am.

In general, however, the use of *ma'am* does indicate that the addressee is either of higher status or older than the speaker. This is borne out by what at first glance appears to be an anomaly in the data. In a typical service en-

---

*Joking usage is one obvious exception.

counter, as has been pointed out by Roger Brown and Marguerite Ford,[4] the person performing the service is in a position of at least temporary subordination to the person for whom the service is being performed. We would thus expect that if the form *ma'am* is used at all it will be addressed to the customer, and, in general, our data support this expectation. Waiters, airline stewardesses, salesclerks at Army-Navy stores and at Fifth Avenue department stores, cashiers at supermarkets, all use *ma'am* to their female customers on occasion and do not receive it (or the comparable form *sir*).

There is one situation, however, in which the rule apparently breaks down entirely. Among the interactions recorded at the Albemarle County Department of Social Services, the Virginia Unemployment Commission,* and in the waiting room of a hospital out-patient clinic, there are fourteen in which the form *ma'am* appears; in seven cases a receptionist or clerk is addressing a patient or client, in the other seven the patient or client is addressing the clerk or receptionist. The problem is that a person applying for food stamps or unemployment insurance is not, like the customer in a department store or supermarket, buying anything from the person behind the counter; he or she is not a customer, but an applicant for assistance of some sort. Furthermore, the person waiting on the applicant may be seen as a professional. The status relationship is not the relatively clear-cut one of clerk and buyer, and this is evidenced in the fact that sometimes the clerk will use *ma'am* (or *sir*) and sometimes the applicant will do so. To some extent, the result seems to depend on whether the clerk or receptionist begins with the form *ma'am* or with a zero address form. If the latter, the client has the option of using *ma'am* and frequently does so:

(19) A: Yes, ma'am?
B: I had an appointment with . . .
(20) A: Have you been waited on?
B: Oh, yes, Ma'am.

Thus we can see that the use of the form *ma'am* is indeed tied to the relative positions of the participants in the verbal exchange. In most service encounters, if *ma'am* is used it will be addressed to the customer by the person performing the service. When status relations are ambiguous, however, either participant may feel it proper to address the other with a respect form.

Inherent in the use of any overt address form is the expression of the speaker's view of his or her relationship to the addressee. A speaker of American English, however, has the option of avoiding any such expression of relationship, since the use of address forms is not obligatory.† The use of zero address, while

---

*Our thanks to the people in these departments who kindly allowed various researchers to listen to and transcribe data from their interactions.

†In this respect, the norms governing the forms of address under discussion here parallel those governing the use of titles and proper names [See Roger Brown and Marguerite Ford, "Address in American English," in *Language in Culture and Society*, ed. Dell Hymes (New York: Harper & Row, 1964), p. 243.]

avoiding any implication of status difference, is not necessarily less polite than the use of *ma'am*. In fact, in phrases where *ma'am* often appears as part of a polite formula, its absence may be compensated for by the insertion of additional linguistic material, which lends politeness to the utterance but includes no overt address form. For example:

    (21) A: Are you open on Sunday?
            B: No, ma'am.
    (22) A: Are you open on Sunday?
            B: No, we're not.

Of course, whether using *ma'am* or a zero form, the speaker will often elaborate on the initial response. What is avoided is a simple, abrupt, *yes* or *no* with no elaboration. This is not to say that these never occur; we do find exchanges such as:

    (23) A: Hello, do you carry lawnmowers?
            B: No, I'm sorry, we don't.
            A: You don't?
            B: No.

Such responses are, however, quite infrequent, and the majority of them are in answer to a repeated request for the same information, as in example (23). Of close to 150 responses to yes/no questions on the telephone, only 26 consisted of a simple, unelaborated *yes* or *no*, and of these, only ten were in answer to an initial inquiry.

    The fact that terms of endearment appear in the same linguistic contexts as *ma'am* and zero places the three types of address forms in contrast. Since there is no difference in referential meaning, the selection of one form over another implies a difference in social meaning. Examining service interactions in which terms of endearment are used shows what social functions these terms serve. For some speakers, terms of endearment represent the standard form of address to all female customers. For example, a saleswoman in a small discount store in Philadelphia addressed a series of customers as *hon*:

    (24) You can tell better when it's on, hon.
    (25) We don't have a try-on room here, hon. You just have to slip it on.
    (26) Hon, look at this one. This is very nice—it wouldn't give you a heavy look at all.

At a gas station, again in Philadelphia, one (male) attendant addressed a woman with three different terms of endearment during a single interaction:

    (27) A: How much, honey?
              (Customer lets keys drop.)
            A: Butterfingers.
            A: (later) Five twenty-five, dear.
            B: Could you check the oil?
            A: (does so) It needs two quarts. That'll be five twenty-five.
            B: Could you put in the oil?
            A: I'm only kidding. If it needed oil I'd put it in.
              (Customer hands A the money.)
            A: Thanks, hon, have a nice day.

All our examples of this "indiscriminate" use were collected in the northeast. In gas station interactions in Charlottesville, Virginia, the researcher involved in the previous example is routinely addressed as *ma'am*, as in example (9) (p. 82). The contrast between these two gas station encounters does not lie only in the forms of address used. In example (27), in contrast to (9), the attendant does not limit himself to the routines necessary for the transaction of the business at hand. The interaction includes not only terms of endearment but also speech acts,[5] such as teasing and personal comments, which are typically restricted to speech situations involving intimates. Referring to the series of encounters at the discount store, we notice that here, too, the speaker combines a term of endearment with a personal comment, in this case an extremely personal one concerning the customer's weight problem.

Neither the use of terms of endearment in service encounters, nor their co-occurrence with "intimate" speech acts,* is limited to service personnel for whom these forms are a standard way of addressing female customers. In many cases, a speaker who routinely uses either zero or *ma'am* will switch to a term of endearment for a particular customer or within an encounter. Our data includes examples of such switching in both the south and the northeast. The following example typifies this switching to a term of endearment within an encounter:

(28) A: Can I help you, ma'am?
B: I'd like a small sliced rye.
A: Here you are, ma'am. Anything else?
B: Some herring in cream sauce, please.
A: How many do you want? One? Two? Three? Four? Five? Six?
B: (to friend: Two, Joan?) Two, please.
A: (big smile) Here you are, dear. You're a good friend.

The speaker here begins with what is apparently his standard address form, *ma'am*, and his utterances consist entirely of impersonal transactional routines. During the third exchange, however, he takes advantage of the customer's hesitation and starts joking about how many herring she wants; he also switches address forms and ends with the personal comment, "You're a good friend," Switching may also occur in telephone conversations, as this interchange shows:

(29) A: Does the doctor have office hours tonight?
B: Yes, he does. He has hours from 7 p.m.
A: From 7 until when?
B: From 7 until he's done, hon.

In this case, the speaker does not shift to a generally less impersonal speech mode; rather, she simply makes use of the term *hon* when answering what she aparently sees as an unnecessary, and possibly even foolish, question.

---

*By "intimate" here we mean typically used by such people as family members and close friends.

The use of different forms to different addresses is clearly exemplified by the behavior of a cashier at Woolworth's, as she addressed a series of customers and one of her co-workers:

(30) A: Come on over—ma'am, come on over here.

(31) A: Yes, they are, ma'am, you'll have to wait 'til they come in.

(32) A: What about a bag, ma'am?

(33) A: Oh, here, here, hon, here—got it?
      B: Oh, yeah.

(34) A: Do you want a separate receipt for this also, ma'am?

(35) A: They're three for a dollar.
      C: I'll take two more. And I'll show it to you, okay? I don't care what color.
      A: Do you have your receipt, hon?
      (later)
      C: Do you want me to bring it in? I don't want anyone to think I took it.
      A: That's all right, hon.

As we can see, *ma'am* is her standard form for addressing customers. In example (33), we see her using a term of endearment, *hon*, to address a much younger co-worker. In one instance, however, example 35, she used this same term to a customer, first in pointing out that the receipt needed to be corrected since the customer had changed her mind about how many plants to buy, and second, to reassure the customer that she would not be suspected of shoplifting. What is particularly interesting here is that the customer to whom the term of endearment was used was obviously a good deal older than the speaker.

An examination of all instances of terms of endearment in our data shows that, when such a term is other than the standard address form for that speaker, its use is generally triggered by something in the interaction which shows the customer to be somewhat less than totally competent. This may be anything from a slight hesitation to a major problem in the transaction. As we have also seen, whether the term of endearment is a standard address form in the service encounter or whether it is triggered by something in the interaction, it frequently co-occurs with speech acts, such as teasing, which are typical of interactions between intimates. This is not surprising, since terms of endearment themselves, of course, as their name implies, are regularly used between intimates.

There is one major difference between the way in which terms of endearment function in service encounters and the way in which they function among friends and family. In service encounters and, indeed, in other interactions between strangers, all the evidence points to the fact that terms of endearment may not be used reciprocally. This rule appears to be in direct contrast to that governing interactions between intimates, by which both parties are free to use these terms. There is, however, one important exception to the rule of reciprocity among intimates. Children do not have the right to address terms of endearment to adults, even their own parents. Adults, on the other hand, use these terms very freely to any and all children. It is not unreasonable to assume that social meanings associated with a term in one set of circumstances are carried over when the term is used similarly in other contexts. When address forms are used nonreciprocally, the implication is that the speaker and addressee are not equals.[6] These facts suggest that, along with any connotation of friendship involved in the use of terms of endearment in service encounters, goes the additional implication that the addressee is subordinate to the speaker in some way, just as a child is subordinate to an adult. This is supported by the fact that proper names in our own language, as well as pronouns in a number of Indo-European languages, have been shown to operate on the same pattern; the form which is exchanged by intimates is also the form used by superiors to subordinates in a nonreciprocal pattern which parallels usage by adults to children and often signifies condescension.[7] But how can a cashier at Woolworth's, younger than the customer to whom she is speaking, be regarded as the superior? Looking back at example 35, we recall that the customer had shown herself to be at a loss, and that the cashier was offering guidance and reassurance. In this instance, therefore, the customer is dependent and the cashier in control of the situation. For this reason, the cashier, instead of using the respect form *ma'am*, uses a term which indicates precisely the *lack* of need for any expression of respect. This meaning arises out of the contrast of this form with the respect form *ma'am* and the neutral zero form, combined with the fact that the speaker imposes on the addressee a form which implies intimacy or lack of social distance in a situation which does not allow reciprocal usage, a behavior normally associated with interactions with children.

In the situation just discussed, the customer had placed herself in a position of helplessness vis-a-vis the cashier. The use of terms of endearment in service encounters, however, is not limited to situations in which the customer shows any such lack of competence. A customer is, in fact, always dependent to some extent on the service personnel, since business cannot be transacted without their aid. On the other hand, by convention, any person performing a service for any other is assumed to be the subordinate. The service encounter thus involves a certain ambiguity with respect to power. It is this ambiguity which explains why we find, in one and the same situation, two terms with such opposite social meanings. It also explains why terms of endearment can be used even when the customer has given no overt sign of incompetence or helplessness, that is, why such terms can be used as a standard mode of address to female customers.

It is interesting that there are speakers who consistently address female customers as *hon, honey*, or *dear*, but use the respect form *sir* to their male customers. A waitress in a snack bar, for example, was heard to say to a woman:

(36) Honey, she just put this in.
and to a man:

(37) How about you, sir?

In a delicatessen, a young man behind the counter addressed a series of customers as follows:

(38) What else, dear?

(39) What else, hon?

(40) It's a little low, sir, is that okay?

(41) What else, dear?

(42) Can I help you, sir?

It should be noted that all three of the women were considerably older than he was.

Thus, male customers are routinely addressed by a respect form, *sir.* In contrast, female customers, who, except for their sex, are in exactly the same status relationship to the clerk, not only receive no sign of respect, but indeed receive a form which, as we have pointed out, implies specifically that no such sign of respect is needed. It might be argued that the speaker is using this form as a gesture of friendliness, and this may indeed be how the speaker views it. However, it must be remembered that this supposed friendliness is based on a term which, while implying intimacy, is nonreciprocal. As we have seen, this type of usage implies the subordinate and perhaps even childlike status of the addressee. Furthermore, it should be noted that the same speaker does not use a similar "friendly" form for male customers. It is true that this may not be entirely a personal choice on the part of the speaker; terms of endearment are used infrequently to males in service encounters and apparently never by other males. However, the speaker does choose to make a distinction between male and female customers, using the respect form only to men.

In sum, two of the three major address types occurring in service encounters can be and are used in absolutely parallel fashion to men and women. Both sexes may be addressed using the appropriate respect form, *ma'am* or *sir*, or both may be addressed by the zero form. The use of the third address type, terms of endearment, in a nonreciprocal pattern paralleling its use by adults to children, carries, as we have seen, the implication that the addressee is in some way subordinate to the speaker. It is extremely interesting that there are cases in which women are addressed by these "intimate" forms while men are not, but that we do not find the opposite occurring. It is perhaps this which so many women find irritating about the form *dear.**

NOTES

1. Dell Hymes, *Foundations in Sociolinguistics* (Philadelphia: University of Pennsylvania Press, 1974), p. 111.

---

*Long before this project was begun, one of the researchers angrily responded to a salesclerk, "Don't call me 'dear'!"

2. Marilyn Merritt, "On Questions Following Questions in Service Encounters," *Language in Society* 5 (1976): 321.

3. John Gumperz, "Sociolinguistics and Communication in Small Groups," in *Sociolinguistics*, ed. J. B. Pride and Janet Holmes (Harmondsworth: Penguin, 1972), p. 206. See also, in this regard, Susan Ervin-Tripp, "Sociolinguistics," in *Advances in the Sociology of Language I*, ed. Joshua Fishman (The Hague: Mouton, 1971), pp. 17-24.

4. Roger Brown and Marguerite Ford, "Address in American English," in *Language in Culture and Society*, ed. Dell Hymes (New York: Harper and Row, 1964), p. 236.

5. We are using this term as it is defined by Hymes. See Dell Hymes, "Models of the interaction of Language and Social Life," in *Directions in Sociolinguistics*, ed. John Gumperz and Dell Hymes (New York: Holt, Rinehart and Winston, 1972), pp. 56-57.

6. See Brown and Ford, "Address in American English," pp. 236-37.

7. See Roger Brown and Albert Gilman, "The Pronouns of Power and Solidarity," in *Readings in the Sociology of Language*, ed. Joshua Fishman (The Hague: Mouton, 1968), pp. 255, 266-67. See also Brown and Ford, "Address in American English," p. 239.

7
"WOMEN'S LANGUAGE" OR "POWERLESS LANGUAGE"?

William M. O'Barr
Bowman K. Atkins

INTRODUCTION

The understanding of language and sex in American culture has progressed far beyond Robin Lakoff's influential and provocative essays on "women's language" written only a few years ago.[1] The rapid development of knowledge in what had been so significantly an ignored and overlooked area owes much to both the development of sociolinguistic interest in general and to the woman's movement in particular. But as a recent review of anthropological studies about women pointed out, this interest has grown so quickly and studies proliferated so fast that there is frequently little or no cross-referencing of mutually suppor-tive studies and equally little attempt to reconcile conflicting interpretations of women's roles.[2] A similar critique of the literature on language and sex would no doubt reveal many of the same problems. But in one sense, these are not problems—they are marks of a rapidly developing field of inquiry, of vitality, and of saliency of the topic.

Our interest in language and sex was sharpened by Lakoff's essays. Indeed, her work was for us—as it was for many others—a jumping off point. But unlike some other studies, ours was not primarily an attempt to understand language and sex differences. Rather, the major goal of our recent research has been the study of language variation in a specific institutional context—the American trial courtroom—and sex-related differences were one of the kinds of variation which current sociolinguistic issues led us to consider. Our interest was further kindled by the discovery that trial practice manuals (how-to-do-it books by successful trial lawyers and law professors) often had special sections on how female witnesses behave differently from males and thus special kinds of treatment they require.

In this paper, we describe our study of how women (and men) talk in court. The research we report here is part of a 30-month study of language variation in trial courtrooms which has included both ethnographic and experimental components.* It is the thesis of this study that so-called "women's language" is in large part a language of powerlessness, a condition that can apply to men as well as women. That a complex of such features should have been called "women's language" in the first place reflects the generally powerless position of many women in American society, a point recognized but not developed extensively by Lakoff.[3] Careful examination in one institutional setting of the features which were identified as constituting "women's language" has shown clearly that such features are simply not patterned along sex lines. Moreover, the features do not, in a strict sense, constitute a *style* or *register* since there is not perfect co-variation.

This chapter proceeds as follows: first, it examines the phenomenon of "women's language" in the institutional context of a court of law; second, it shows that the features of "women's language" are not restricted to women and therefore suggests renaming the concept "powerless" language due to its close association with persons having low social power and often relatively little previous experience in the courtroom setting; third, it examines briefly some experimental studies which were conducted to answer the question of whether "powerless" language makes any difference in how mock jurors evaluate testimonies of witnesses; and finally, it calls for a refinement of our studies to distinguish powerless language features from others which may in fact be found primarily in women's speech.

HOW TO HANDLE WOMEN IN COURT— SOME ADVICE FROM LAWYERS

One of the means which we used in our study of courtroom language to identify specific language variables for detailed study was information provided to us in interviews with practicing lawyers. More useful, however, were *trial practice manuals*—books written by experienced lawyers which attempt to discuss systematically successful methods and tactics for conducting trials. Typically, little effort is devoted to teaching and developing trial practice skills in the course of a legal education. Rather it is expected that they will be acquired through personal experimentation, through watching and modeling

*The research reported here was supported by a National Science Foundation Law and Social Science Program Grant (No. GS-42742), William M. O'Barr, principal investigator. The authors wish to thank especially these other members of the research team for their advice and assistance: John Conley, Marilyn Endriss, Bonnie Erickson, Bruce Johnson, Debbie Mercer, Michael Porter, Lawrence Rosen, William Schmidheiser, and Laurens Walker. In addition, the cooperation of the Durham County, North Carolina, Superior Court is gratefully acknowledged.

one's behavior after successful senior lawyers, and through reading the advice contained in such manuals. Those who write trial practice manuals are experienced members of the legal profession who are reporting on both their own experiences and the generally accepted folklore within the profession. In all these situations, the basis for claims about what works or what does not tends to be the general success of those who give advice or serve as models—judged primarily by whether they win their cases most of the time.

One kind of advice which struck us in reading through several of these manuals was that pertaining to the special treatment which should be accorded women. The manuals which discuss special treatment for women tend to offer similar advice regarding female witnesses. Readers are instructed to behave generally the same toward women as men, but to note that, in certain matters or situations, women require some special considerations. Some of this advice includes the following:

1. *Be especially courteous to women.* ("Even when jurors share the cross-examiner's reaction that the female witness on the stand is dishonest or otherwise undeserving individually, at least some of the jurors are likely to think it improper for the attorney to decline to extend the courtesies customarily extended to women."[4]

2. *Avoid making women cry.* ("Jurors, along with others, may be inclined to forgive and forget transgressions under the influence of sympathy provoked by the genuine tears of a female witness." "A crying woman does your case no good."[5]

3. *Women behave differently from men and this can sometimes be used to advantage.* ("Women are contrary witnesses. They hate to say yes. . . . A woman's desire to avoid the obvious answer will lead her right into your real objective—contradicting the testimony of previous prosecution witnesses. Women, like children, are prone to exaggeration; they generally have poor memories as to previous fabrications and exaggerations. They also are stubborn. You will have difficulty trying to induce them to qualify their testimony. Rather, it might be easier to induce them to exaggerate and cause their testimony to appear incredible. An intelligent woman will very often be evasive. She will avoid making a direct answer to a damaging question. Keep after her until you get a direct answer—but always be the gentleman."[6]

These comments about women's behavior in court and their likely consequences in the trial process further raised our interest in studying the speech behavior of women in court. Having been told by Lakoff that women do speak differently from men, we interpreted these trial practice authors as saying that at least some of these differences can be consequential in the trial process. Thus, one of the kinds of variation which we sought to examine when we began to observe and tape record courtroom speech was patterns unique to either women or men. We did not know what we would find, so we started out by using Lakoff's discussion of "women's language" as a guide.

Briefly, what Lakoff had proposed was that women's speech varies from men's in several significant ways. Although she provides no firm listing of the major features of what she terms "women's language" (hereafter referred to in this paper as WL), we noted the following features, said to occur in high frequency among women, and used these as a baseline for our investigation of sex-related speech patterns in court.

1. *Hedges.* ("It's sort of hot in here."; "I'd kind of like to go."; "I guess . . ."; "It seems like . . ."; and so on.)

2. *(Super)polite forms.* ("I'd really appreciate it if . . ."; "Would you please open the door, if you don't mind?"; and so on.)

3. *Tag questions.* ("John is here, isn't he?" instead of "Is John here?"; and so on.)

4. *Speaking in italics.* (intonational emphasis equivalent to underlining words in written language; emphatic *so* or *very* and so on.)

5. *Empty adjectives.* (*divine; charming; cute; sweet; adorable; lovely;* and so on.)

6. *Hypercorrect grammar and pronounciation.* (bookish grammar; more formal enunciation.)

7. *Lack of a sense of humor.* (Women said to be poor joke tellers and to frequently "miss the point" in jokes told by men.)

8. *Direct quotations.* (use of direct quotations instead of paraphrases)

9. *Special lexicon.* (in domains like colors where words like *magenta, chartreuse,* and so on are typically used only by women)

10. *Question intonation in declarative contexts.* (For example, in response to the question, "When will dinner be ready?", an answer like "Around 6 o'clock?", as though seeking approval and asking whether that time will be okay)

WHAT WE FOUND

During the summer of 1974, we recorded over 150 hours of trials in a North Carolina superior criminal court. Although almost all of the lawyers we observed were males, the sex distribution of witnesses was more nearly equal. On looking for the speech patterns described by Lakoff, we quickly discovered some women who spoke in the described manner. The only major discrepancies between Lakoff's description and our findings were in features which the specific context of the courtroom rendered inappropriate, for example, *tag questions* (because witnesses typically answer rather than ask questions) and *joking* (because there is a little humor in a courtroom, we did not have occasion to observe the specifically female patterns of humor to which she referred).

In addition to our early finding that some women approximate the model described by Lakoff, we also were quick to note that there was considerable variation in the degree to which women exhibited these characteristics. Since our observations were limited to about ten weeks of trials during which we were able to observe a variety of cases in terms of offense (ranging from traffic cases, drug possession, robbery, manslaughter, to rape) and length (from a few hours to almost five days), we believe that our observations cover a reasonably good cross-section of the kinds of trials, and hence witnesses, handled by this type of court. Yet, ten weeks is not enough to produce a very large number of witnesses. Even in a single witness may spend several hours testifying. In addition, the court spends much time selecting jurors, hearing summation remarks, giving jury instructions, and handling administrative matters. Thus, when looking at patterns of how different women talk in court, we are in a better position to deal with the range of variation we observed than to attempt any precise frequency counts of persons falling into various categories. Thus, we will concentrate our efforts here on describing the range and complement this with some non-statistical impressions regarding frequency.

Our observations show a continuum of use of the features described by Lakoff.* We were initially at a loss to explain why some women should speak more or less as Lakoff had described and why others should use only a few of these features. We will deal with our interpretation of these findings later, but first let us examine some points along the continuum from high to low.

A. Mrs. W,† a witness in a case involving the death of her neighbor in an automobile accident, is an extreme example of a person speaking WL in her testimony. She used nearly every feature described by Lakoff and certainly all those which are appropriate in the court room context. Her speech contains a high frequency of *intensifiers* ("*very* close friends," "*quite* ill," and so on often with intonation emphasis); *hedges* (frequent use of "you know," "sort of like," "maybe just a little bit," "let's see," and so on); *empty adjectives* ("this *very* kind policeman"); and other similar features. The first example below is typical of her speech and shows the types of intensifiers and hedges she commonly uses.†† (To understand what her speech *might* be like without these features, example (2) is a rewritten version of her answers with the WL features eliminated.)

---

*Actually each feature should be treated as a separate continuum since there is not perfect co-variation. For convenience, we discuss the variation as a single continuum of possibilities. However, it should be kept in mind that a high frequency of occurrence of one particular feature may not necessarily be associated with a high frequency of another.

†Names have been changed and indicated by a letter only in order to preserve the anonymity of witnesses. However, the forms of address used in the court are retained.

††These examples are taken from both the direct and cross examinations of the witnesses, although Table 1 uses data only from direct examinations. Examples were chosen to point out clearly the differences in style. However, it must be noted that the cross examination is potentially a more powerless situation for the witness.

(1) L. State whether or not, Mrs. W., you were acquainted with or knew the late Mrs. E. D.

W. Quite well.

L. What was the nature of your acquaintance with her?

W. Well, we were, uh, very close friends. Uh, she was even sort of like a mother to me.

(2) L. State whether or not, Mrs. W., you were acquainted with or knew the late Mrs. E. D.

W. Yes, I did.

L. What was the nature of your acquaintance with her?

W. We were close friends. She was like a mother to me.

Table 7.1 summarizes the frequency of several features attributed to WL by Lakoff. Calculated as a ratio of WL forms for each answer, this witness's speech contains 1.14—among the highest incidences we observed.

B. The speech of Mrs. N, a witness in a case involving her father's arrest, shows fewer WL features. Her ratio of features for each answer drops to .84. Her testimony contains instances of both WL and a more assertive speech style. Frequently, her speech is punctuated with responses like: "He, see, he thought it was more-or-less me rather than the police officer." Yet it also contains many more straightforward and assertive passages than are found in A's speech. In example (3), for instance, Mrs. N is anything but passive. She turns questions back on the lawyer and even interrupts him. Example (4) illustrates the ambivalence of this speaker's style better. Note how she moves quickly to qualify—in WL—an otherwise assertive response.

(3) L. All right. I ask you if your husband hasn't beaten him up in the last week?

W. Yes, and do you know why?

L. Well, I . . .

W. Another gun episode.

L. Another gun episode?

W. Yessiree.

(4) L. You've had a controversy going with him for a long time, haven't you?

W. Ask why—I mean not because I'm just his daughter.

C. The speech of Dr. H, a pathologist who testifies as an expert witness, exhibits fewer features of WL than either of the other two women. Her speech contains the lowest incidence of WL features among the female witnesses whose speech we analyzed. Dr. H's ratio of WL features is .18 for each answer. Her responses tend to be straightforward, with little hesitancy, few hedges, a noticeable lack of intensifiers, and so on. (See Table 7.1.) Typical of her speech is

example (5) in which she explains some of her findings in a patho-
logical examination.

(5)   L.   And had the heart not been functioning, in other words,
    had the heart been stopped, there would have been no
    blood to have come from that region?

        W.   It may leak down depending on the position of the body
    after death. But the presence of blood in the alveoli
    indicates that some active respiratory action had to take
    place.

What all of this shows is the fact that some women speak in the way
Lakoff described, employing many features of WL, while others are far away
on the continuum of possible and appropriate styles for the courtroom. Before
discussing the reasons which may lie behind this variation in the language used
by women in court, we first examine an equally interesting finding which
emerged from our investigation of male speech in court.

We also found men who exhibit WL characteristics in their courtroom
testimony. To illustrate this, we examine the speech of three male witnesses
which varies along a continuum of high to low incidence of WL features.

    D.   Mr. W exhibits many but not all of Lakoff's WL features.* Some
of those which he does employ, like intensifiers, for example, occur
in especially high frequency—among the highest observed among
all speakers, whether male or female. His ratio of WL features for
each answer is 1.39, actually higher than individual A. Example (6),
while an extreme instance of Mr. W's use of WL features, does
illustrate the degree to which features attributed to women are in
fact present in high frequency in the speech of some men.

    (6)   L.   And you saw, you observed what?

        W.   Well, after I heard—I can't really, I can't definitely state
    whether the brakes or the lights came first, but I rotated
    my head slightly to the right, and looked directly behind
    Mr. Z., and I saw reflections of lights, and uh, very, very,
    very instantaneously after that, I heard a very, very loud
    explosion—from my standpoint of view it would have been
    an implosion because everything was forced outward, like
    this, like a grenade thrown into a room. And, uh, it was,
    it was terrifically loud.

    E.   Mr. N, more toward the low frequency end of the continuum of
male speakers, shows some WL features. His ratio of features for
each answer is .64, comparable to individual B. Example (7) shows
an instance of passages from the testimony of this speaker in which

---

*This speaker did not use some of the intonational features that we had noted among
women having high frequencies of WL features in their speech.

TABLE 7.1 Frequency Distribution of Women's Language Features[a] in the Speech of Six Witnesses in a Trial Courtroom

	Women			Men		
	A	B	C	D	E	F
Intensifiers[b]	16	0	0	21	2	1
Hedges[c]	19	2	3	2	5	0
Hesitation Forms[d]	52	20	13	26	27	11
W asks L questions[e]	2	0	0	0	0	0
Gestures[f]	2	0	0	0	0	0
Polite Forms[g]	9	0	2	2	0	1
Sir[h]	2	0	6	32	13	11
Quotes[i]	1	5	0	0	0	0

Total (all powerless forms)	103	27	85	24	47	24
# of Answers in Interview	90	32	61	136	73	52
Ratio (# powerless forms for each answer)	1.14	0.84	1.39	0.18	0.64	0.46

Notes: [a]The particular features chosen for inclusion in this table were selected because of their saliency and frequency of occurrence. Not included here are features of WL which either do not occur in court or ones which we had difficulty operationalizing and coding. *Based on direct examinations only.* [b]Forms which increase or emphasize the force of assertion such as *very, definitely, very definitely, surely, such a,* and so on. [c]Forms which reduce the force of assertion allowing for exceptions or avoiding rigid commitments such as *sort of, a little, kind of,* and so on. [d]Pause fillers such as *uh, um, ah,* and "meaningless" particles such as *oh, well, let's see, now, so, you see,* and so on. [e]Use of question intonation in response to lawyer's questions, including rising intonation in normally declarative contexts (for example, "thirty?, thirty-five?") and questions asked by witness of lawyer like "Which way do you go. . .?". [f]Spoken indications of direction such as *over there,* and so on. [g]Include *please, thank you,* and so on. Use of *sir* counted separately due to its high frequency. [h]Assumed to be an indication of more polite speech. [i]Not typically allowed in court under restrictions on hearsay which restrict the situations under which a witness may tell what someone else said.

Source: Original data

there are few WL features. Example (8), by comparison, shows the same hedging in a way characteristic of WL. His speech falls between the highest and lowest incidences of WL features we observed among males.

(7)   L.   After you looked back and saw the back of the ambulance, what did you do?

       W.   After I realized that my patient and my attendant were thrown from the vehicle, uh, which I assumed, I radioed in for help to the dispatcher, tell her that we had been in an accident and, uh, my patient and attendant were thrown from the vehicle and I didn't know the extent of their injury at the time, to hurry up and send help.

(8)   L.   Did you form any conclusion about what her problem was at the time you were there?

       W.   I felt that she had, uh, might have had a sort of heart attack.

F.   Officer G, among the males lowest in WL features, virtually lacks all features tabulated in Table 7.1 except for hesitancy and using *sir*. His ratio of WL forms for each answer is .46. Example (9) shows how this speaker handles the lack of certainty in a more authoriatative manner than by beginning his answer with "I guess . . .". His no-nonsense, straightforward manner is illustrated well by example (10), in which a technical answer is given in a style comparable to that of individual C.

(9)   L.   Approximately how many times have you testified in court?

       W.   It would only have to be a guess, but it's three or four, five, six hundred times. Probably more.

(10)   L.   You say that you found blood of group O?

       W.   The blood in the vial, in the layman's term, is positive, Rh positive. Technically referred to as a capital r, sub o, little r.

Taken together these findings suggest that the so-called "women's language" is neither characteristic of all women nor limited only to women. A similar continuum of WL features (high to low) is found among speakers of both sexes. These findings suggest that the sex of a speaker is insufficient to explain incidence of WL features, and that we must look elsewhere for an explanation of this variation.

Once we had realized that WL features were distributed in such a manner, we began to examine the data for other factors which might be associated with a high or low incidence of the features in question. First, we noted that we were able to find *more* women toward the high end of the continuum. Next, we noted that all the women who were aberrant (that is, who used relatively few WL features) had something in common—an unusually high social status. Like Dr. H, they were typically well-educated, professional women of middle-class background. A corresponding pattern was noted among the aberrant men (that is, those high in WL features). Like Mr. W, they tended to be men who held either subordinate, lower-status jobs or were unemployed. Housewives were high in WL features while middle-class males were low in these features. In addition to social status in the society at large, another factor associated with low incidence of WL is previous courtroom experience. Both individuals C and F testify frequently in court as expert witnesses, that is, as witnesses who testify on the basis of their professional expertise. However, it should be noted that not all persons who speak with few WL features have had extensive courtroom experience. The point we wish to emphasize is that a powerful position may derive from either social standing in the larger society and/or status accorded by the court. We carefully observed these patterns and found them to hold generally.* For some individuals whom we had observed in the courtroom, we analyzed their speech in detail in order to tabulate the frequency of the WL features as shown in Table 7.1. A little more about the background of the persons we have described will illustrate the sort of pattern we observed.

A is a married woman, about 55 years old, who is a housewife.

B is married, but younger, about 35 years old. From her testimony, there is no information that she works outside her home.

C is a pathologist in a local hospital. She is 35-40 years old. There is no indication from content of her responses or from the way she was addressed (always *Dr.*) of her marital status. She has testified in court as a pathologist on many occasions.

D is an ambulance attendant, rather inexperienced in his job, at which he has worked for less than 6 months. Age around 30. Marital status unknown.

E is D's supervisor. He drives the ambulance, supervises emergency treatment and gives instructions to D. He has worked at his job longer than D and has had more experience. Age about 30-35; marital status unknown.

F is an experienced member of the local police force. He has testified in court frequently. Age 35-40; marital status unknown.

"WOMEN'S LANGUAGE" OR "POWERLESS LANGUAGE"?

In the previous section, we presented data which indicate that the variation in WL features may be related more to social powerlessness than to sex. We have presented both observational data and some statistics to show that this style is not simply or even primarily a sex-related pattern. We did, however, find it related to sex in that more women tend to be high in WL features while

---

*We do not wish to make more of this pattern than our data are able to support, but we suggest that our grounds for these claims are at least as good as Lakoff's. Lakoff's basis for her description of features constituting WL are her own speech, speech of her friends and acquaintances, and patterns of use in the mass media.

more men tend to be low in these same features. The speech patterns of three men and three women were examined. For each sex, the individuals varied from social statuses with relatively low power to more power (for women: housewife to doctor; for men: subordinate job to one with a high degree of independence of action). Experience may also be an important factor, for those whom we observed speaking with few WL features seemed more comfortable in the court-room and with the content of their testimony. Associated with increasing shifts in social power and experience were corresponding decreases in frequency of WL features. These six cases were selected for detailed analysis because they were representative of the sorts of women and men who served as witnesses in the trials we observed in 1974. Based on this evidence, we would suggest that the phenomenon described by Lakoff would be better termed *powerless language*, a term which is more descriptive of the particular features involved, of the social status of those who speak in this manner, and one which does not link it unnecessarily to the sex of a speaker.

Further, we would suggest that the tendency for more women to speak powerless language and for men to speak less of it is due, at least in part, to the greater tendency of women to occupy relatively powerless social positions. What we have observed is a reflection in their speech behavior of their social status. Similarly, for men, a greater tendency to use the more powerful variant (which we will term *powerful language*) may be linked to the fact that men much more often tend to occupy relatively powerful positions in society.

SOME CONSEQUENCES OF USING POWERLESS LANGUAGE

Part of our study of courtroom language entailed experimental verifica-tion of hypotheses about the significance of particular forms of language used in court.[7] We conducted this part of our research by designing social psycho-logical experiments based on what we had actually observed in court. First, we located in the original tapes we had recorded in the courtroom a segment of testimony delivered by a witness in the powerless style. For this study, we chose the testimony given under direct examination by individual *A* described above. Her original testimony was used to generate the test materials needed for the experiment.

The original, powerless style testimony was edited slightly to make it more suitable for use in the experiment.* The testimony was then recorded

---

*This editing involved only minor changes in the testimony. Specifically, we changed the names, dates, and locations mentioned in the original testimony in order to fulfill our promise to the court that we would protect the privacy of those involved in the actual taped trials. In addition, we removed attorney objections and the testimony to which the objections were addressed. The removal of this material was prompted by our observa-tion in an early stage of the study that objections tended to divert attention from the relatively brief segment of testimony used in the experiment. We are currently studying the effect of objections as a style topic in its own right.

on audio tape with actors playing the parts of the lawyer and the witness. In this recreation of the testimony the actors strove to replicate as closely as possible the speech characteristics found in the original testimony. Another recording was then made using the same actors. In this second recording, however, most of the features which characterize the powerless style—the hedges, hesitation forms, intensifiers, and so on—were omitted from the witness' speech, producing an example of testimony given in the powerful style. It is important to note that the powerful and powerless experimental testimony differed only in characteristics related to the speech style used by the witness. In both samples of testimony exactly the same factual information was presented.

TABLE 7.2 Comparison of Linguistic Characteristics of the Four Experimental Tapes

	Female Witness		Male Witness	
	Powerful	Powerless	Powerful	Powerless
Hedges[a]	2	22	2	21
Hesitation forms	13	73	18	51
W asks L questions	2	5	2	6
Use of *sir* by W	0	3	0	4
Intensifiers	0	35	0	31
Running time of tape[b]	9:12	11:45	9:35	12:10

Notes: [a]For definitions, see Table 7.1. [b]Time given in minutes and seconds.
Source: Original data

The first two columns of Table 7.2 present the results of linguistic analyses of the two experimental testimony tapes described above. As may be seen from an examination of the table, the two testimony tapes differed markedly on each of the features which distinguish the two styles. Differences between powerful and powerless modes are illustrated by Example 1 (powerless original) and Example 2 (powerful rewrite) above.

The original testimony on which the experimental tapes were based was delivered by a female witness. To have conducted the experiment only with a female witness would have limited the conclusions to be drawn from the results. To assure that we would be able to determine whether any particular effects of the speech style factor were restricted to one sex of witness or the other, the process described above was followed using both a female and a male actor acting as the witness. The *four* tapes thus produced presented the same information. The differences consisted of a female witness speaking in either the powerful or the powerless style and a male witness speaking in either the powerful or the powerless style.

As may be seen from Table 7.2, for both witnesses the intended differences between powerful and powerless styles are presented in the tapes used in the experiments. It will be noted from Table 7.2 that the powerful versions of the testimony taped by the male and female actors are quite similar. The powerless tapes, however, contain some important differences between the male and female versions. In frequency of powerless characteristics, the male version has relatively fewer instances of the powerless features. It contains, for example, fewer hesitations and intensifiers than the female version. In general, the male powerless tape contains many elements of powerless language, but it is a less extreme variant of the style than that utilized by the original witness and replicated in the female experimental version. These differences between the male and female powerless version were intentionally programmed in making the experimental tapes because members of the research team were in agreement that a faithful replication of the original female witness's speech style and powerless mannerisms—although suitable for a female witness—were not within the normal range of acceptable male verbal usage.

Once the four experimental tapes had been produced, it was possible to proceed with the experimental test of the results of the two styles. Ninety-six undergraduate students at the University of North Carolina at Chapel Hill participated in the experiment.* The participants were scheduled to report to the experimental laboratory in groups of five to seven at a time. Upon arriving at the experiment, the participants were given written instructions describing the experiment. These instructions, also read aloud by the experimenter, explained that participants would hear a segment of testimony from an actual trial. The instructions then briefly outlined the details of the case and the major issues to be decided.

The case involved a collision between an automobile and an ambulance. The patient in the ambulance, already critically ill and en route to a hospital, died shortly after the collision. The experimental participants were told that the patient's family was suing the defendants (both the ambulance company and the driver of the automobile) to recover damages for the patient's death. The participants were also told that the witness under examination in the trial segment they would hear was a neighbor and friend who had accompanied the now-deceased patient in the ambulance and was therefore present during the collision. The participants were informed that they would be asked questions about their reactions to the testimony after listening to the trial segment. Note taking was not allowed.

The participant-jurors then listened to one of the four experimental tapes described above. After the participants had heard the testimony, the experi-

---

*Of the 96 participants, 46 were males and 50 were females. The experiment was later repeated at the University of New Hampshire with essentially similar findings.

menter distributed a questionnaire asking about the participants' reactions to the case and the individuals involved. The responses to these questions formed the basis of our statements below concerning the effects of the style in which testimony is delivered.

The average-rating-scale responses to each of five questions about the witness are shown in Table 7.3. For each of these questions, a rating of "+5" indicates a very strong positive response to the question, while a rating of "-5" indicates a strong negative response. The effects of the testimony style on impressions of the female witness may be seen by contrasting the first and second columns of the table. The results for the male witness are presented in the third and fourth columns of the table.

Statistical analyses confirm the patterns of testimony style influences seen in the table.* These analyses permit us to state with a generally high degree of certainty that, compared to those who heard the female witness give her testimony in the powerless style, those who heard her use the powerful style indicated that they believed the witness more (p<.01), found her more convincing (p < .06), and more trustworthy (p < .02). Obviously, the female witness made a much better impression when she used the powerful style than she used the powerless style.

The same pattern of results was found in the comparison of the powerful to the powerless style testimony with the male witness. Again the statistical analyses indicate with high certainty that participants who heard the powerful style testimony responded more favorably than those hearing the powerless style testimony to questions asking how much they believed the male witness (< .05), and how convincing they thought the witness was (p<.05). As was the case with the female witness, participants who heard the male witness testify in the powerful style thought the witness was more competent (p<.001), more intelligent (p < .005), and more trustworthy (p < .02) than did those who heard the witness testify in the powerless style. Thus, it is apparent from the results of the experiment that, for both male and female witnesses, the use of the powerless style produced consistently less favorable reactions to the witness than did the use of the powerful testimony style.

Although the results just presented are quite clear, we undertook a further investigation of testimony style effects in order to accumulate additional information relevant to the topic. Specifically, we sought to discover whether the powerful-powerless style distinction is of importance in contexts other than testimony delivered orally in court. To test the influence of style in another common mode of evidence presentation, we repeated the experiment described above using transcripts of testimony rather than tapes of spoken testimony. If this second experiment were to produce results similar to those described above,

---

*The significance of the results reported in this section was assessed by the appropriate multivariate or univariate analysis of variance technique. Only those differences that are reported to be significant should be regarded as "true" or real differences.

TABLE 7.3 Average Rating of Witness

	Female Witness		Male Witness	
	Powerful	Powerless	Powerful	Powerless
"How convincing in general was this witness?"	3.00[a]	1.65	3.52	2.09
"To what extent did you believe the witness was telling the truth?"	3.70	1.88	4.24	2.86
"To what extent do you feel that the witness was competent?"	2.61	0.85	2.44	0.18
"To what extent do you feel that the witness was intelligent?"	2.57	0.23	1.80	0.18
"To what extent do you feel that the witness was trustworthy?"	3.04	1.65	3.48	2.00

Note: [a]All differences are significant at $p < .05$ or less.
Source: Original data

there would be evidence that differences in reaction to powerful/powerless styles could not be said to be based solely on characteristics of spoken language, such as intonation.

The transcript experiment was begun by asking a free-lance court reporter to transcribe the four experimental tapes as she would for testimony given in court. The transcripts thus produced were given to 56 participants similar to those who took part in the first experiment.* With the exception of the fact that the participants read, rather than heard, the testimony, much the same method of experimentation was used as in the first study. The responses of the participants in the transcript experiment showed no major differences from those observed in the corresponding conditions of the tape experiment. Thus, the second experiment, in showing that the testimony style affected impressions of the witness in transcribed, as well as taped, testimony, provides striking evidence of the general importance of the powerful-powerless distinction in testimony style.

The two experiments described above demonstrate that the style in which testimony is delivered has strong effects on how favorably the witness is perceived, and by implication, suggest that these sorts of differences may play a consequential role in the legal process itself.

CONCLUSION

In this study, we have attempted to argue that our data from studying male-female language patterns in trial courtrooms suggest that Lakoff's concept of "woman's language" is in need of modification. Our findings show that, in one particular context at least, not all women exhibit a high frequency of WL features and that some men do. We have argued that instead of being primarily sex-linked, a high incidence of some or all of these features appears to be more closely related to social position in the larger society and/or the specific context of the courtroom. Hence, we have suggested a re-naming of the phenomenon as "powerless language". What has previously been referred to as "women's language" is perhaps better thought of as a composite of features of powerless language (which can but need not be a characteristic of the speech of either women or men) and of some other features which may be more restricted to women's domains.

Thus, Lakoff's discussion of "women's language" confounds at least two different patterns of variation. Although our title suggests a dichotomy between "women's language" and "powerless language," these two patterns undoubtedly interact. It could well be that to speak like the powerless is not only typical of women because of the all-too-frequent powerless social position of many American women, but is also part of the cultural meaning of speaking "like a

---

*Twenty-nine of the participants in the second experiment were female, while 27 were male.

woman." Gender meanings draw on other social meanings; analyses that focus on sex in isolation from the social positions of women and men can thus tell us little about the meaning of "women's language" in society and culture.

In addition to investigating language as a reflection of social position, we have also in this study attempted to consider how powerless language in particular might affect those situations in which it is found. We reported experimental research in which our major conclusion is that speakers using a high frequency of powerless features, whether they be male or female, tend to be judged as less convincing, less truthful, less competent, less intelligent, and less trustworthy. The major implication of these experimental findings is that using this type of language—for whatever reason—tends to feedback into the social situation. Powerless language may be a reflection of a powerless social situation, but it also would seem to reinforce such inferior status.

NOTES

1. Robin Lakoff, *Language and Woman's Place* (New York: Harper & Row, 1975).

2. Naomi Quinn, "Anthropological Studies of Women's Status," *Annual Review of Anthropology* 6 (1977):181-225.

3. Lakoff, *Language and Woman's Place*, pp. 7-8.

4. Robert E. Keeton, *Trial Tactics and Methods* (Boston: Little, Brown, 1973), p. 149.

5. Keeton, *Trial Tactics*, p. 149; F. Lee Bailey and Henry B. Rothblatt, *Successful Techniques for Criminal Trials* (Rochester, N.Y.: Lawyers Co-Operative Publishing Co., 1971), p. 190.

6. Bailey and Rothblatt, *Successful Techniques*, pp. 190-91.

7. Detailed descriptions of the experimental studies can be found in Allan E. Lind and William M. O'Barr, "The Social Significance of Speech in the Courtroom," in *Language and Social Psychology*, ed. Howard Giles and Robert St. Clair (Oxford: Basil Blackwell, 1979). The research on powerful versus powerless language summarized here is described in greater detail in Bonnie Erickson et al., "Speech Style and Impression Formation in a Court Setting: The Effects of 'Power' and 'Powerless' Speech," *Journal of Experimental Social Psychology* 14 (1978):266-79.

8

HOW AND WHY ARE WOMEN MORE POLITE: SOME EVIDENCE FROM A MAYAN COMMUNITY

Penelope Brown

INTRODUCTION

Two separate lines of linguistic inquiry in recent years have yielded results which suggest that women are "more polite" than men. On the one hand we have the observations by sociolinguists like William Labov and Peter Trudgill,[1] which claim that women typically "hypercorrect," that (in terms of particular phonological variables sensitive to social status and level of formality) women speak more formally, using a higher proportion of standard ("prestige") forms than men do in comparable situations.* The explanation Trudgill proffers for this phenomenon is that, since women tend to gain their status through how they *appear* (rather than through what they *do*—job or income), they try to secure their social status (and social connotations of refinement and sophistication) through signals of status in their speech.[2] By contrast, the tendency of men to actually *lower* the status level of their speech is seen as evidence that men have

This is a revised version of a paper delivered at the 74th Annual Meeting of the American Anthropological Association in San Francisco, December 1975. I am indebted to Gwen Awbery, Paul Meara, and Stephen Levinson for their helpful comments on the first draft.
*The examples originally observed for New York English involved phonological variables like whether or not one pronounces the *r* in words like *car*. The forms with the *r* pronounced differ from the *r*-less ("nonstandard") forms in social prestige—only the former is assumed by speakers to be "prestigious." The claim, then, boils down to this: women pronounce their words in accordance with the standard or "correct" forms more often than men do. This tendency for women to use more standard forms has by now been found repeatedly in research carried out in this paradigm, occurring in naturalistic settings as well as in the interview situations where it was originally observed [Trudgill, p.c.].

a "covert norm" of prestige that runs contrary to that assigning prestige to the standard forms.

To this claim that women generally speak in a more formal style than men, we may add an apparently related claim to be found in the work of Robin Lakoff. In *Language and Woman's Place*, Lakoff describes traits which she suggests are characteristic of "women's language" and which crosscut the grammar, occurring in the lexicon, in syntax, in phonology and prosodics; they build up to a "style" in which women express themselves hesitantly, tentatively, weakly, trivializingly, "politely." Asking why women speak in this style, Lakoff answers in terms of a psychological analysis of the nature of women's secondary status, that is, her sense of inferiority: women feel unsure of themselves (and hence are thus treated by others) because they have been taught to express themselves in "women's language," which abounds in markers of uncertainty.[3] This insecurity, it could be further argued, accounts as well for their propensity to use more standard forms in speaking.

Now intuitively it seems reasonable to predict that women in general will speak more formally and more politely, since women are culturally relegated to a secondary status relative to men and since a higher level of politeness is expected from inferiors to superiors. We might even predict that the internalization of inferior status would lead to a conventionalization of more polite forms in women's speech so that their speech would be more polite than men's even when addressed to equals or to inferiors. If we turn from English to Japanese, a language spoken in a culture where women's subordinate status is more overtly institutionalized, we do indeed find evidence that women are more polite in many situations.[4]

However, in opposition to such a sweeping generalization we find that in the Malagasy village studied by Elinor Keenan, women are considered to be *less* polite than men—that in fact women regularly and habitually violate the norms that both men and women say should govern speaking: norms favouring non-confrontation and indirectness in speech.[5] There is no suggestion that women are higher status than men in this Malagasy community; on the contrary, the way in which men obey the norms is seen by members of the society as support for and evidence of their superiority to women.

So the relationship between the status of women and the politeness or formality of their speech is by no means as simple and straightforward as has been assumed. The bulk of recent research on langauge and sex has focused on documenting differences between the speech of men and women in some respect for some sample, usually accompanied by the suggestion that differences in language usage are attributable to social differences in the position of women and men in the society. What is notably lacking, however, is a way of analyzing language usage so that the features differentiating the speech of men and women can be related in a precisely specifiable way to the social-structural pressures and constraints on their behavior.

Specifically, I have three basic complaints about the work on women's speech to date:

1) Linguistic features said to differentiate women's and men's speech have been treated as a collection of random linguistic facts. But the elements that make up any one of these putative "femine" styles are not just an odd collection; they make an internally coherent picture, they "go together" naturally. I suggest that this is because when women speak, they are following certain strategies, intending to do certain kinds of things, such as create rapport with the addressee, or flatter the addressee that her/his opinion is worth soliciting, or assure the addressee that no imposition is intended.

2) The sociological concepts utilized in studies of women's speech have been equally random and arbitrary. Women are seen as following certain "rules" or "norms" of linguistic behavior laid down by society, such as "Be polite" or "Speak correctly," with no sense of the rational choices that lie behind such rules.

3) There is no explicit connection drawn between the linguistic facts (traits of women's speech) and the sociological facts (the secondary position of women in society) in analyses to date.

This study, then, is in part a reaction against the behavioristic poverty of much sociolinguistic analysis, the view of people as truncated *homunculi sociologici* who do what they do because of the social slot in which they find themselves. What is missing from accounts of women's speech is an account of the choices being made and the reasons for the choices.

If we bring humans as rational actors into the picture, we come up with a set of connections between language usage and social categories which makes sense of the data. *Social networks* (the kinds of people with whom one interacts regularly) give the individuals involved in them certain *social motivations* (the goals and desires that motivate their actions), which in turn suggest certain *communicative strategies* as means to achieve those goals, and these in turn suggest certain *linguistic choices* which will effectively implement those communicative strategies. The linguistic choices then are seen to be not random with respect to the communicative strategies, and the coherence which relates the features of a style (such as a "feminine style") is explained. With such a model we can relate strategic use of language styles to sex roles and social relationships in a particular society, thereby connecting the linguistic facts with the sociopolitical system within which they occur.

To illustrate the power of a strategic analysis in explicating the contention that women are "more polite," I will examine the class of social motivations related to the preservation of face, to the general desire that members of a speech community attribute to one another, the desire that one's face be respected. If we assume that all (normal adult) interactants have face wants, then a number of strategies for satisfying these wants may be derived. Taken in reverse, an examination of samples of speech can reveal what politeness strategies are being followed by the speakers, and an account can then be given of what the speakers are trying to do. A formal model of politeness along these lines has been developed in detail by myself and Stephen Levinson. That model delineates the universal assumptions underlying polite usage in all languages, defining politeness as rational, strategic, face-oriented behavior and predicting the kinds of linguistic strategies which will be employed in particular circumstances. In this study the model is informally presented and applied to the analysis of the differences between women's and men's speech in Tenejapa, a community of Mayan Indians in Chiapas, Mexico. Finally, I suggest some implications of this approach for cross-linguistic studies of women's speech, and some hypotheses about in what senses and under what social conditions we do indeed find that women are more polite.*

A THEORY OF POLITENESS

What politeness essentially consists in is a special way of treating people, saying and doing things in such a way as to take into account the other person's feelings. On the whole that means that what one says politely will be less straightforward or more complicated than what one would say if one wasn't taking the other's feelings into account.

Two aspects of people's feelings seem to be involved. One arises when whatever one is now about to say may be unwelcome: the addressee may not want to hear that bit of news, or be reminded of that fact, or be asked to cooperate in that endeavor. A request, for example, or anything that requires a definite response directly imposes on the addressee. One way of being polite in such situations is to apologize for the imposition and to make it easy for the addressee to refuse to comply. So we try to give the most interactional leeway possible, and this, in one sense, is what it is to be polite.

Our long-term relations with people can also be important in taking their feelings into account. To maintain an ongoing relationship with others, one greets them on meeting in the street, inquires about their health and their family, expresses interest in their current goings-on and appreciation of the things they do and like and want.

These two ways of showing consideration for people's feelings can be related to a single notion: that of FACE. Two aspects of people's feelings enter into face: desires to not be imposed upon (negative face), and desires to be

---

*The analysis presented here is based on 15 months' fieldwork in Tenejapa, supported by National Science Foundation and National Institute of Mental Health grants. The data base for the linguistic analysis consists of tape-recorded natural conversations which were transcribed in the field with extensive annotations as to meanings and context provided by informants. The formal model relies or is presented in Penelope Brown and Stephen Levinson, "Universals of Language Usage: Politeness Phenomena," in *Questions and Politeness: Strategies in Social Interaction*, Cambridge Papers in Social Anthropology 8, ed. Esther Goody (Cambridge: Cambridge University Press, 1978), pp. 56-311.

liked, admired, ratified, related to positively (positive face).[6]   Both can be subsumed in the one notion of face because it seems that both are involved in the folk notion of "face loss."   If I walk past my neighbor on the street and pointedly fail to greet him, I offend his face; and if I barge into his house and demand to borrow his lawnmower with no hesitation or apology for intrusion (for example, "Give me your lawnmower; I want it") I equally offend his face.*   So blatantly and without apologies *imposing on* and blatantly and without apologies *ignoring* the people with whom one has social relationships are two basic ways of offending their faces.

Three factors seem to be involved in deciding whether or not to take the trouble to be polite:

1)   One tends to be more polite to people who are socially superior to oneself, or socially important: one's boss, the vicar, the doctor, the president.

2)   One also tends to be more polite to people one doesn't know, people who are somehow socially distant: strangers, persons from very different walks of life.

In the first situation politeness tends to go one way upwards (the superior is not so polite to an inferior), while in the second situation politeness tends to be symmetrically exchanged by both parties.

3)   A third factor is that kinds of acts in a society come ranked as more or less imposing, and hence more or less face threatening, and the more face threatening, the more polite one is likely to be.

These three factors appear to be the main determinants of the overall level of politeness a speaker will use.

Now given that politeness is about respecting the other's face, the way to incorporate politeness into the structure of one's utterance is to ensure that in the very act of threatening face, one disarms the threat by showing that one does indeed care about the other's face. *Positive politeness* aims to disarm threats to positive face.   Essentially approach-based, it treats the addressee as a member of an in-group, a friend, a person whose desires and personality traits are known and liked, suggesting that no negative evaluation of the addressee's face is meant despite any potentially face-threatening acts the speaker may be performing. Especially clear cases of positive politeness include expressions of interest in the addressee ("What magnificent roses you have, Mrs. Jones, where did you get them?"); exaggerated expressions of approval ("That's the most fabulous dress,

---

*This sentence illustrates the difficulties created in English when a sex-neutral noun such as *neighbor* is antecedent of a third-person singular pronoun. The generic *he* is retained here, despite feminist scruples, because the intended meaning requires its singularity: face inheres in individuals, not in groups.   Alternatives such as *she, they,* or *he/she* are either semantically less accurate, blatantly ungrammatical, or stylistically horrific (especially given five pronominal occurrences in rapid succession).   I await development in standard written English usage of a truly sex-neutral and singular pronoun for such third-person individual references.

[See other discussions of the generic masculine throughout this volume and especially in the chapter by Wendy Martyna, ed.]

Henrietta!"); use of in-group identity markers (slang, code-switching into the "we" code, in-group address forms and endearments, as in "Give me a hand with this, pal"); the seeking of agreement and avoidance of disagreement (using safe topics, such as the weather, and stressing similarity of point of view); joking; claiming reflexivity of goals (that I want what you want and you want what I want); claiming reciprocity (you help me and I'll help you); and the giving of gifts, in the form of goods, sympathy, understanding, and cooperation.

Strategies of *negative politeness*, on the other hand, are essentially avoidance-based, and consist in assurances that the speaker recognizes and respects the addressee's negative face and will not (or will only minimally) interfere with his or her freedom of action. The classic negative politeness strategies are characterized by self-effacement, formality, restraint, where potential threats to face are redressed with apologies for interfering or transgressing ("I'm terribly sorry to bother you, but I . . ."); with linguistic or non-linguistic deference ("Excuse me, sir . . ."); with hedges on the force of the speech act (using expressions like: *maybe, perhaps, possibly, if you please*) and questioning rather than asserting ("Could you do X for me?"); with impersonalizing mechanisms (for example, passives) that distance the act from both speaker and addressee; and with other softening mechanisms that give the addressee an "out" so that a compliant response is not coerced.

Evidence of such strategies in people's speech allows us to infer, given the appropriate supporting context, that they are attending to one another's face wants, they are "being polite." Presumably this is quantifiable: the more face-saving strategies in evidence, the more polite.

Such strategies in speech take time and effort. As such, they contrast with segments of speech where no face redress appears at all—where the speaker is expressing him/herself in the most direct, clear, unambiguous and concise way possible, following H. R. Grice's Maxims of Conversation[7] (for example, saying: "Give me five dollars now," meaning exactly that). Such *bald on record* expression involves a gain in clarity and efficiency, but runs whatever risk attends ignoring the addressee's face.*

---

*The motives for speaking baldly on record, as argued in detail in Brown and Levinson, "Politeness Phenomena" can be various: a speaker can choose not to minimize the face threat in cases of great urgency, or where there is channel noise sufficient to provoke a need for clarity and efficiency, or where the speaker's desire to satisfy the addressee's face is small (either because the speaker wants to be rude, or doesn't care about maintaining face), or where the act is primarily in the addressee's interest so that simply by *doing* the act the speaker conveys concern for the addressee, so no face redress is required. There are also special cases where bald on record usage is particularly designed to redress face threats; the most notable examples being offers, where the baldness of the form of expression can be a way of assuring the addressee that the latter may impose on the speaker and accept the offer. So the use of bald on record strategies in speaking may convey a variety of different states of mind in the speaker, and cannot necessarily be taken as evidence of rudeness, indifference, status superiority, or intimacy.

Since two of the three factors influencing level of politeness have to do with the social relationship between the interlocutors, and since relationships (except among lovers, and so on) tend to be relatively stable, particular stable levels of politeness will reflect particular relationships. So strategies are tied to relationships, and politeness level is relative to the expected level for that relationship. Now given that there are three variables, if this expected level makes a notable shift at some point in an interaction, there is always a potential ambiguity as to whether the extra politeness is indicating:

1) a sudden increase in the speaker's respect for the addressee (or his/her perceived lack of power vis-à-vis the addressee; this is unlikely except in special cases such as violent confrontation or initiation into office); *or*

2) a sudden increase in social distance from the addressee (which may be used to symbolically convey anger or disapproval; witness the switch to a formal mode of address or an out-group code when familiars become angry with one another); *or*

3) a change to highly face-threatening material.

But on the assumption that relationships tend to be relatively stable, minor fluctuations in politeness level can be attributed to the third variable. Given then a range of politeness level over a wide range of kinds of acts, we can infer degrees of social closeness and degrees of relative power in relationships. Thus, politeness strategies are a complicated but highly sensitive index in speech of kinds of social relationships. It is for this reason that they provide a useful tool for analysing the differences between the speech styles of men and women.

Under what conditions and in what situations do women actually use more polite expressions than men do in comparable situations? And why? If women are more polite than men, our theory suggests that women are either, 1) generally speaking to superiors, 2) generally speaking to socially distant persons, or 3) involved in more face-threatening acts, or have a higher assessment than men have of what counts as impositions. We may then look to the minutiae of utterances in context to distinguish the facts of women's speech from the images and stereotypes that seem to be the basis of many claims that women are "more polite." Let us now apply this approach to data from Tenejapa, to see what insights about the differences between men's and women's speech emerge.

THE TENEJAPAN CASE

Men and Women in Tenejapa: an Impressionistic Overview

Tenejapa is a Tzeltal (Mayan) municipio situated in the central highlands of Chiapas, Mexico, some 20 miles by precipitous dirt road from the town of San Cristóbal de las Casas. Following the ancient Mayan pattern, the Indians live in scattered hamlets and subsist largely by milpa agriculture. As a single corporate entity, Tenejapa has its own native civil-religious hierarchy, and Tenejapans have their own characteristic dialect of Tzeltal, their own Indian dress, and a strong sense of identity as Tenejapans, distinguishing them from the 16 other corporate communities of Tzeltal-speaking Indians and from the surrounding Tzotzil-speaking communities.

An outsider entering this community notices immediately the marked separation of the spheres of activity of women and men. Indeed, the sex-role division appears to be the most salient distinction between kinds of people in this relatively homogeneous egalitarian society.* Women's activities center in the home, focusing on cooking, food preparation, child-rearing, and weaving; men's work takes place primarily outside the home, in the fields, in the market, or in Tenejapa Center. Furthermore, antagonism between the sexes is institutionalized in a number of customs: men commonly beat their wives, marriage by capture is not uncommon (and is the terror of unmarried girls), and even courtship traditionally is initiated with a hostile act: the boy pelts the girl with orange peels, and she (in public) responds by pelting him with stones. On the symbolic level, women and men are seen as entirely different kinds of beings: men are "hot" like the sun, the sky, the day, while women are "cold" like the moon, the earth, the night.

The quality of interaction of women is likewise noticeably differentiated from that of men. Women appear to be highly deferent to men, but are extremely warm and supportive to other women. Thus, women are highly deferential and self-effacing in public; they walk behind the men on the trails, stepping aside to let men pass them if the men come up behind; they speak in a high pitch falsetto voice with kinesic humbling (hunched-over shoulders, avoidance of eye contact); in short, they give avoidance-type respect in the presence of men. By contrast when talking to women in the security of their homes, or even in public when in encounters with women not in the center of the public gaze, women are highly supportive and empathetic, stressing their closeness with many prosodic modifications and rapport-emphasizing expressions. In short, they emphasize commonality and appreciation of each other's personality.

Men, on the other hand, treat people in general in a much more matter-of-fact and businesslike manner. Their trail greetings are often short, even brusque, and their speech habitually lacks many of the elaborate mechanisms for stressing deference as well as for stressing solidarity that abound in women's speech.

From an impressionistic point of view, then, women's speech and demeanor appear to be elaborated for the extremes of both positive and negative politeness; men's speech and demeanor tend to be baldly on record to a much greater extent. The few notable exceptions to this general pattern have significant implications for the meaning of the general rule. The negative politeness pattern for women is modified somewhat by age—women become more assertive, less deferential, when they pass child-rearing age, when they become, as it

---

*Age is the other salient basis for differentiation, and hierarchy based on age is firmly institutionalized in ritual. But it does not have such a clear-cut effect on everyday interaction (except adult/child interaction) as sex does.

were, socially sexless.* The behavior of men is modified in two situations: when drunk, exaggerated positive politeness expression appears, with joking, back-slapping, and repeated assurances of solidarity. And in ritual contexts, when addressing the gods and saints, men's speech takes on many of the vocal and prosodic features that characterize women in daily interaction: exaggerated rhythmicity, falsetto, high trailing-off pitch contours.[8] But apart from these exceptions, we may take the initial impressionistic generalization as a working hypothesis: that relative to men's, women's speech is highly elaborated for both positive and negative politeness. Now how can we test such a hypothesis? How can we find an index of positive politeness and of negative politeness with which to measure the differences between men's and women's speech?

Being Polite in Tzeltal

Tzeltal has a built-in apparatus which is highly sensitive to nuances of social relations between speaker and hearer. There is a syntactically definable class of particles in Tzeltal which operate as adverbs on the highest performative verb, modifying the force of a speech act by expressing something about the speaker's attitude toward the act being performed (or toward the addressee). There are some 20 of these particles, and although the usage conditions for each one differ somewhat, what they basically do for any speech act is say, in effect, either "I maybe, perhaps, tentatively, in some respects, assert/request/promise/declare/, and so on" or "I emphatically, sincerely, really assert/request/promise/declare, and so on." So they may be classified crudely as strengtheners or weakeners of the force with which the speaker performs the speech act.

Some examples should clarify how the particles operate† :

Strengtheners—rhetorical assurances of sincerity or emphatic opinion:

(1) eh, haʔ čʼe.

Oh, so it is, *to be sure*! (emphatic agreement with the preceding utterance)

(2) weʔan me ȼ in čʼi.

Do eat, *then*! (polite emphatic offer of a meal)

---

*In fact for the elderly of both sexes, politeness level seems to be adjusted on the basis of the perceived power of the addressee, but sex no longer is a major element in assessing that power. Some old women are powerful, some old men are, and others of both sexes will tend to be more polite to such elders. But despite some differences in wealth, possessions, successfulness, luck, and so on (although such differences are culturally downplayed for fear of envy), women during their reproductive years all seem to be categorized as nonpowerful in relation to men; the fact of their femaleness overrides any advantages due to personal circumstances and requires them to behave interactionally as deferential to men.

†Tzeltal examples are glossed underneath in English, with explanations of the glosses following in brackets. The tzeltal transcription is roughly phonemic, where č represents the sound spelled in English *ch*, š corresponds to English *sh*, ȼ represents English *ts*, ʔ indicates a glottal stop, and ' indicates glottalization of the preceding consonant.

(3)   *melel* te ho?one, ma hk'an.
      Truly, as for me, I don't want it. (stresses the speaker's sincerity)

(4)   ya *naniš* stak ya šba? ȼ'us ?a.
      You *really* can go shut it (the door). (that is, 'I sincerely say, you can shut it'; a woman's politely eager acceptance of a visitor's offer to shut the door, with the particle stressing her appreciation)

(5)   bi lah *kati* yu?un ȼ'in, ?oč šan ta yakubeli ?
      Why *in the world* then has he gone and got drunk again?! (speaker's emphasis solicits audience sympathy)

Weakeners—performative hedges:

(6)   tal *me* kilat hwayuk.
      I've come *if I may* to see you for a night or so. (hedged request)

(7)   mač'a mene ȼ'i *bi* ?
      Who is that one, *do you suppose*? (avoids presuming that the addressee knows the answer)

(8)   *mak* bi yu?un me ma šp'ihube me sluse?
      Why doesn't that Lucy wisen up, *I wonder*? (softens the implied criticism)

(9)   ma *lah wan* ?ayuk ya?čon ?a?mutik.
      You don't *perhaps* have any chickens to sell, *it is said.* (hedged request to sell chickens, plus devolving of responsibility for the request onto third party)

(10) ha? *naš* ya hk'an hohk'obet ?a?wala ?ič.
      It's *just* that I want to ask you to sell a bit of chili. (minimizing the imposition involved in the request)

Although the meanings conveyed by these particles in context are extremely subtle and complex, in combination with intonation and prosodic patterns that themselves either emphasize or weaken, it is usually possible in particular cases to identify whether they are acting as speech act strengtheners or weakeners.

Now the point to stress here is that *any* particles or words or expressions in any language that do this kind of thing, that is, that modify the performative force of speech acts, are prime candidates for formulating polite utterances. This is because speech acts are intrinsically potent things, because they presuppose various things about the addressee (for example, that he/she doesn't know the truth of what is being asserted, or that he/she is able to carry out the order, or that he/she is willing to perform the act requested, and so on). Therefore, to hedge these acts is in general to be negatively polite, and to emphasize them (in many cases) is to be positively polite.*

It seems clear that the Tzeltal particles provide rich resources for performing strategies of positive politeness (which requires emphasizing one's apprecia-

---

*Of course, the validity of such a generalization depends on the semantics of the sentence in question. If a speaker emphasizes a speech act of criticizing or insulting the addressee, it is hardly positively polite. Yet if the addressee is known to agree with the speaker in a negative evaluation of a third party (or event), it may be a positively polite stressing of solidarity to emphasize that evaluation.

tion of, approval of, similarity with, the addressee) and of negative politeness (which requires hedging of one's encroachment on the addressee's territory, or softening the force with which one does face-threatening speech acts, or giving the addressee an "out" in interpreting what speech act is being done). So it might be reasonable to expect that a simple count of particle usage would provide a rough index of the extent of face-redress being employed in speech. On the basis of our above hypothesis about the differences between men's and women's speech in Tenejapa, we might predict that:

1. Women use more strengthening particles when speaking to women (more than to men, and more than men speaking to men);

2. Women use more weakening particles when speaking to men (more than to women, and more than men use to men); and

3. Women speaking to women use more particles, overall, than men to men.

If we compare the speech of male and female dyads, matched so as to neutralize status differences, familiarity (social distance) differences, and differences in the culturally rated face-threateningness of the material being discussed (the three factors which our theory claims form the basis for determining politeness levels), insofar as natural conversation data allow such matching,* it turns out that some such crude correlations do appear, differentiating the speech of women and men. But they appear only when the particle counts are corrected for the subtleties of the semantics, which vary depending upon a number of factors. For example, the topic under discussion is a crucial variable, for both men and women use many more hedging particles when talking about something for which they do not have firsthand knowledge; similarly, they use many more emphatic particles when giving value judgments about what they think or feel. But when such factors are minimized by choosing passages with (roughly) comparable topic valency, gross counts of particle usage do show interesting sex differences.

The results for a few samples are summarized in Tables 8.1, 8.2, and 8.3.†

---

*The difficulties of getting comparable data neutralizing face-threateningness (cultural rating of impositions) are considerable, since men and women have different concerns and hence tend to talk about different things and to perform different kinds of speech acts. It is even more difficult to find dyads equivalent in hierarchical status and in social distance for men and women, due to their different social structural loci. Getting comparable data is then a matter of matching as well as possible degrees of "more" and "less" on the scales of power, distance, and rating of imposition.

†The figures were computed on samples of approximately 1000 words each. The calculations were made of number of particles in relation to number of speech acts (roughly but not precisely equivalent to sentences) rather than simply to number of words because what is being assessed is the extent of speech-act modification, and speech acts can vary greatly in length. The counts were made of samples ranging from 74 speech acts (for one participant) to 236 speech acts (for one conversational chunk as a whole), and were adjusted to give the average number of 100 speech acts. I include these tables to indicate the nature of the differences found; a more thorough illustration would require breakdown into individual particles and extensive explanation. For further details, see Penelope Brown, "Language, Interaction, and Sex Roles in a Mayan Community: A Study of Politeness and the Position of Women" (Ph.D. Diss. University of California, Berkeley, 1979), chapter 4.

TABLE 8.1 Average Number of Particles for 100 Speech Acts: Same-sex Dyads

		Strengtheners	Weakeners	Total particles
Female dyads:				
3 girls (tape 17.1)		20.8	28.8	49.6
Tape 11	Mo	31.4	33.7	65.1
	Da	19.8	43.4	63.2
Tape 7	L	25.6	26.9	52.5
	S	23.1	26.9	50.0
Tape 7	M	33.2	48.1	81.2
	S	22.2	31.2	53.3
Mean		25.2	34.1	59.3
Male dyads:				
Tape 15.2	t	12.2	16.2	28.0
	M	20.0	17.5	39.5
2 'cousins' Tape 15.1		11.1	20.7	31.8
Mean		14.4	18.1	32.6

Source: Original data

To begin with the counts of particle usage in same-sex dyads, it can be seen from Table 8.1 that women do use more particles. That is, their speech is more elaborated than men's speech is for both positive-politeness emphasizing and negative-politeness hedging, as far as the use of particles is concerned, for on the order of half again to twice as many particles, both weakeners and strengtheners, appear in the female conversations. So our hypotheses about the speech of women to women as opposed to that of men to men appear to be supported by these passages, although of course we would need larger samples to ascertain statistical significance. The hypotheses for cross-sex dyads, however, are not confirmed in my counts. As Table 8.2 shows, there have appeared to be no clear-cut differences between men and women in terms of the number of particles they use when speaking to one another. That is, I have not found as predicted that women use more strengthening particles to women than to men,

TABLE 8.2 **Average Number of Particles for 100 Speech Acts:
Cross-sex Dyads**

	Strengtheners	Weakeners	Total particles
Women speaking to men:			
14.1 Mo (to So)	36.2	24.3	60.5
17.2 s (to h')	34.3	20.6	54.9
12.1 A (to Pr)	36.7	28.4	65.1
Mean	35.7	24.4	60.2
Men speaking to women:			
14.1 h' (to Mo)	19.2	31.0	50.5
17.2 h' (to s)	17.1	36.8	54.0
12.1 Pr (to A)	35.6	31.5	67.1
Mean	24.1	33.1	57.2

Source: Original data

nor that women use more weakening particles to men than to women. Indeed, in both these cases the data actually reverse the order expected. Table 8.2 shows women using more strengtheners to men than to women, and women using more weakeners to women than to men, although I hesitate to draw any broad conclusions from this very small sample. This result is at least partly due to the fact that natural conversation yields little of comparable semantics in the speech of cross-sex dyads in my data, so the comparability of samples is highly questionable.

However, the gross differences between women and men in same-sex dyads are very large, and even when sex of addressee is ignored and particle usage of women is compared with that of men (see Table 8.3), female speakers came out as using considerably more particles than male speakers. We may conclude, then, that despite the semantic/pragmatic difficulties in counting particles, they

TABLE 8.3 Summary Table of Particle Usage

	Strengtheners	Weakeners	Total particles
women to women	25.2	34.1	59.3
women to men	35.7	24.4	60.2
men to men	14.4	18.1	32.6
men to women	24.1	33.1	57.2
Totals regardless of sex of addressee:			
female speakers (n = 10)	28.3	31.2	59.5
male speakers (n = 6)	19.2	25.6	44.9

Source: Original data

do appear to offer a possible quantitative index to politeness strategies, albeit a very crude one.*

More revealing differences between the speech of men and women appear when we examine qualitative differences in their particle usage. To get a real understanding of the sex differences in verbal strategies, we must look at the characteristic feminine and masculine usages to which the particles are put. For women, irony, rhetorical questions, and negative assertions used to convey the opposite (positive) assertion, are characteristic usages. For example:

(11) *mak* yuʔ *wan* ma haʔuk yaʔwil!
  Lit: *Perhaps* because *maybe* it's not so, *as it were, you see.*
  Implicating: Isn't that just how it is!

(12) haʔ yuʔun ma ya *niš* šlah htakʼintik yuʔune, yakubeli.
  Lit: It's because our money *just* doesn't get used up because of drunkenness.
  Implicating: It *does* get used up!

---

*A word about the emic status of these particles is in order. Conscious awareness by Tzeltal speakers of the particles' functions as speech-act modifiers is limited to a very few which are recognized to operate as softeners of imperatives, for example, or are seen as being especially polite when tacked onto requests. But in most instances of usage the particles are very much in the background of awareness; while among the most frequently used words in Tzeltal, they do not lend themselves to introspection as to their meanings or uses. I was unable to elicit any definitions for the particles (and indeed, they tend to drop out in Tzeltal-speakers' speech to nonnative speakers of Tzeltal), although informants were able to compare sentences containing a particle with the same sentence minus the particle and make judgments about the relative politeness, implications, and so on, of the two versions. For further details see Brown, "Language, Interaction, 4 Sex Roles."

(13) yuʔ *bal* hoʔon ʔay ba ya hta tak'in?
    Lit: Because as for me, *is there* anywhere I'll come up with money?
    Implicating: Of course not!

(14) *bi yuʔun ñiš* ʔay šaʔnaʔ *sȼ'isel* ʔek ʔa ?
    Lit: *Just why would* you know how to sew?
    Implicating: Of course you wouldn't.

Ironies and ironic rhetorical questions are used to stress feelings and attitudes; by asserting the opposite of what one feels or thinks, one stresses the shared assumptions about such feelings between speaker and addressee, the shared views that make such ironies interpretable. In this way they are positive-politeness strategies, emphasizing in-group feelings and attitudes. In my data, women spend more time talking about feelings and attitudes toward events than do men, hence the ironies.*

Another positively polite feature of particle usage among women is the extensive use of the diminutive ʔ*ala* as a marker of small talk. This particle, usually glossed as 'a little', appears repeatedly in conversations between women where little or no new information is being conveyed, but the purpose of speaking is to stress their shared interests and feelings. This passage, for example, comes from a conversation between an elderly woman and her visiting married daughter:

(15) Da: ʔay binti ya k*ala* pas šane, šon yuʔun, nail to hoy ta koral k*ala* mut.
        There is something else I'll *a-little* do, I said to myself, *first* I'll gather together my-*little* chickens in an enclosure.
    Mo: la wan ʔaʔhoy ta koral ʔaʔw*ala* mut.
        You perhaps put your-*little* chickens into an enclosure!
    Da: la. haʔin ya sloʔlaben k*ala* k'ale.
        I did. It's because they eat my-*little* cornfield up for me (if I don't confine them).
    Mo: ya sloʔ ta me yaš ʔ*ala* č'iise.
        They eat (it) if it *a-little* grows up (big enough).
    Da: ʔ*ala* lawaltikiš!
        It's *a-little* grown already!

The subject to which the diminutivizing ʔ*ala* is applied moves from what Da' is going to do, to her chickens, to her cornfield, to the size to which the corn grows; the function of ʔ*ala* here is to stress the emotional bond between Mo and Da in engaging in this conversation, not to literally describe Da's actions, corn,

---

*Again, the propensity to ironic humor is recognized by Tenejapans to be a characteristic of women's speech—that is, they recognize that women are prone to this "lying" (that is, literally false) form of expressing themselves in casual speech—but the role of the particles in producing these ironic utterances is (as far as I could ascertain) completely opaque to them.

chickens, and so on.* This emphasizing usage of ʔ*ala* is a trait of women's speech; men consider it to be femine and "soppy," although men certainly use the particle for other reasons, for example, to minimize an imposition, as in a negatively polite request:

> (16) ya hkˈan k*ala* kˈinal, ya hpas k*ala* na.
>
> I want my-*little* bit of land, to make my-*little* house (there).
>
> (as when a son asks his father for his share of land)

or to minimize the implications of what one is doing:

> (17) yas ʔ*ala* yakubon hoʔtikike.
>
> We are $\left\{ \begin{array}{l} \text{sort of} \\ \text{a little bit} \\ \text{merely} \end{array} \right\}$ getting drunk.

I even have one example on tape where a man proliferates the use of ʔ*ala* in one utterance in a way apparently similar to the women's usage:

> (18) maʔyuk, ya naš hkˈan, wokol kˈopta, ʔay sȼˈisben y*ala* hun k*ala* čˈin kerem, ʔay lah haȼem y*ala* hun.
>
> It's nothing, I just want to please ask if she would sew up for me the *little* book of my *little* small boy, his *little* book is ripped, he says.

But as the gloss indicates, the ʔ*ala*s here are functioning as negative politeness, to minimize what is actually an unusually humiliating request—since the man is asking his sister to do what his wife should have done, thereby revealing a serious domestic breach. So the ʔ*ala*s are making a plea for sympathy, perhaps, but their main function here is to minimize an awkward request, and they certainly are not oriented to stressing shared attitudes and values as the ʔ*ala*s in (15) are doing.

On the negative-politeness side, women also have some characteristic usages. Thus it appears that while both men and women use hedging particles in cases of genuine doubt, only women use them even in utterances where there is no doubt, where in fact only the speaker herself can know the truth of the proposition, for example, hedging on one's own feelings:

> (19) ya niš hmel koʔtantik yuʔun ȼˈin *mak.*
>
> I just really am sad then because of it, *perhaps.*
>
> (20) čahp niš me koʔtan ta melel yuʔun ȼˈi *bi.*
>
> My heart is just really terrible (that is, miserable) because of it then, *isn't it.*

Here the hedges in combination with emphatic expression of the speaker's feelings serve purely negative-politeness functions; the woman appears to think it an imposition to express her feelings strongly to the addressee—or rather, she

---

*ʔ*ala*, in fact, cannot be used to mean literally small in size; there is a different word (čˈ*in*) for the description of size. The two can be used together to convey both affect and size, as in (18), k*ala* čˈ*in kerem,* 'my-*little* small boy'.

appears to feel it is necessary to act as if she were thus hesitant. As a form of understatement these hedges can even make the assertion more exclamatory, by implying the necessity to suppress the full expression of one's outrage. For example:

(21) *puersa* kʼešlal ȼʼin *mak!*

She's *really* embarrassed then *maybe!* (Compare English: She's really a bit upset!)

As for the men, they too have characteristically sex-typed usages of the particles. One of the most noticeable occurs with the particle *melel*, which is a sincerity emphasizer usually glossed as 'truly' or 'really'. This particle abounds in male public speaking or any male speaking with the aim of political persuasion. For example:

(22) *melel* haʔ lek tey naš ya šʔainon hoʔtik, *melel* mukʼul parahe yilel ta baʔayon hoʔtik.

Really, it's good if we just stay there, *really*, ours is a big village.

(23) ma me štun ta me yaʔwakʼik tey ʔa te sna maestro tey ʔa, *melel* ma me štun.

It's no good if you put the teacher's house there, *really* it's no good.

In a heated attempt at persuasion, *melel* and other sincerity emphasizers can occur in virtually every sentence for several minutes of discourse. Another markedly male feature of such public speaking is the liberal interpolation of Spanish words into the stream of speech. Men tend to publicly flaunt their knowledge of Spanish; women, in contrast, tend to hide their knowledge and pretend to understand Spanish less well than in fact is the case. In male public speaking one also hears three Spanish-derived words used like the Tzeltal emphatic particles: to stress the strength of the speaker's commitment to what he is saying. These are *meru, puru,* and *bun*:

(24) *meru melel* ya kil!

That's really true, (as) I see it!

(25) *melel* lom bol te promotor, *puru* baȼʼilkʼop ya yakʼ ta nopel, *puru* lom bolik.

The teacher is really stupid, he teaches nothing but Tzeltal, he's really (that is, purely, completely) stupid.

(26) lom spas kʼop, *bun* lom šcukawan, te maestro.

He fights very much, *boy does he ever* jail people a lot, that teacher.

This kind of particle-like use of Spanish-derived expressions appears to be restricted to male speech.

Speech and Style in Tzeltal

I hope to have demonstrated that the speech of men and women in Tzeltal differs in systematic ways. First of all, it differs in terms of how many particles members of each sex tend to use, thus establishing frequency of speech-act modifiers as a promising index of the complex verbal strategies that speakers are employing.* We may conclude that such quantitative comparisons are useful as a rough guide to what is going on at the strategic level, although they will not replace the painstaking comparison of individual strategies employed in speech. Theoretically it should be possible to quantify underlying intentions such as strategies and count them up, but a methodology that would allow us to do that in any rigorous way is still in its infancy.[9] While one could count up Tzeltal ironies, it would be much more difficult to isolate all the instances of positive-politeness strategies in a passage, quantify their relative strength of face redress, add them up, and compare the speech of women and men on this basis.[10] If we were to attempt such an enterprise for Tzeltal, we would need an inventory of the kinds of politeness strategies (in addition to the use of particles to modify performative force) available in the Tzeltal repertoire. An inventory of the conventionalized linguistic resources for positive politeness, available potentially to both women and men, would include the following: the emphatic particles (as illustrated above, and including a number of others); exaggerated empathetic intonation and prosodic patterns; negative questions ("Won't you eat now?") as offers which presuppose an affirmative reply; repeats and other ways of stressing interest and agreement; irony and rhetorical questions as ways of stressing shared point of view; use of directly quoted conversation; diminutives and in-group address forms; expressions like 'you know' (*ya'wa'y*) and 'you see' (*ya'wil*) which claim shared knowledge; joking (which also presupposes shared knowledge and values); and the Tzeltal inclusive-*we* used to mean 'I' or 'you', pretending that the speech act is for the common weal.

Linguistic realization of negative politeness strategies in Tzeltal include performative hedges; indirect speech acts; pessimistic formulation of requests and offers ('You wouldn't have any chickens to sell'); minimization of impositions ('a little', 'for a moment', 'just', 'merely', 'only'); deference (including ritually falsetto high pitch and other forms of symbolic self-minimization); and depersonalizing and deresponsibilizing mechanisms which imply that the speaker is not taking responsibility for the force of this particular speech act.

Although both sexes have access to these resources, the usage of men and women differs systematically both in terms of which strategies they choose to use and how much effort they put into face redress, whether positive or negative. The results of comparing male and female use of these strategies (nonquantitatively, so far) supports the two claims I have made on the basis of simple particle

---

*Eleanor H. Jordan, "Language-Female and Feminine," in *Proceedings of a U.S.-Japan Sociolinguistics Meetings*, ed. Bates Hoffer (San Antonio, Texas: Trinity University, 1974) pp. 57-71, provides some evidence for this conclusion from another language: she claims that in Japanese, the most statistically significant sources of evidence for deciding whether a sample of speech was produced by a male or a female speaker come from the area of politeness, formality levels, and sentence particles.

counts: (a) that women use the extremes of positive and of negative politeness, while men speak much more matter-of-factly, and (b) that women have characteristically feminine strategies of positive politeness and negative politeness so that what might be called "feminine styles" can be isolated. Similarly, there are usages characteristic of men, especially sexy joking (*ʔišta kʼop*) and the preaching/declaiming style discussed above, which define kinds of typical "masculine style."

In labeling these systematic patterns of language usage "styles," however, a clarification is in order. "Style" is frequently used to label surface-structural features of language with no reference to why particular stylistic features go together or what is the reason for using them, rather than others, in a given instance. I am claiming rather that there is a coherence among the features of positive politeness, and among those of negative politeness, at the strategic level. The features of positive politeness all contribute to the aim of a positively polite conversational style: to stress in-group knowledge, shared attitudes and values, appreciation of the addressee, and so on; and the features of negative politeness contribute to the aim of distancing, non-imposing, that defines negative politeness. It is the employment of strategies that generates surface-structural features that can be called "style." If linguistic form differs in two styles it is because language is being used for different ends. This argument has significant implications for sociolinguistic theory, for the claim is that only by probing below the surface and identifying the strategies that actors are pursuing when they speak can we see how the linguistic minutiae of utterances are related to the plans of human actors. And only thus can we claim that there is a deep, intrinsic relationship between language usage and social facts.

Ethos and social context

We may conclude that women are, overall, more polite than men in Tenejapan society. That is, the general quality of interaction between women, their interactional ethos, is more polite than that for the men, as measured by the particles and other strategies in usage. It remains to integrate these linguistic facts with the social context that gives rise to them, in order to explain the basis for the patterns that are observable.

This result contradicts our initial impressionistic hypothesis, that women are positively polite to women and negatively polite to men. Rather, the data suggest that women are overall more sensitive to possibly face-threatening material in their speech, and hence use negative politeness to women as well as men, and are more sensitive to positive face wants and hence use positive politeness to men as well as women. We may reformulate our hypothesis in these terms, therefore, which may perhaps be made clearer by recourse to schematic representation in the form of a graph. Imagining that we may quantify the level of politeness by indexing number and quality of politeness strategies used,[11] the vertical axis in Figure 8.1 indicates that women overall employ a higher level of politeness than men. The horizontal axis shows that there is greater variation in politeness usage between women from moment to moment; men are, in comparison, relatively stable over time in the amount of face redress encoded in their speech. Recalling that according to our theory there are three reasons for increasing face redress in speech, Figure 8.1 indicates that women are speak - ing as if the social power of addressee and social distance between interlocutors are higher overall than they are for men, and therefore their overall politeness level is higher. In comparison, men are speaking in a relatively familiar manner, treating each other as though power and social distance were both very low. The social weighting of seriousness of impositions, based on the potential face-threateningness of acts, varies to account for the variations in politeness level in each sex's speech over time, severely for women, mildly for men. Thus I am suggesting that women are more sensitive from moment to moment to the

FIGURE 8.1: Politeness in Women's and Men's Styles: Schematic Representation

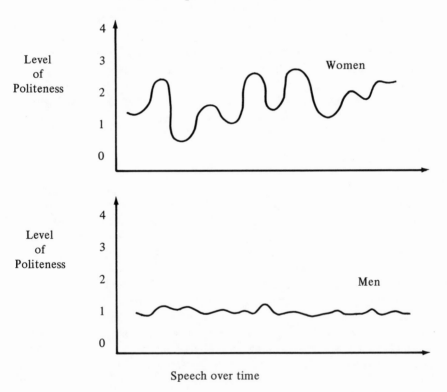

Speech over time

potential face-threateningness of what they are saying and modify their speech accordingly.

Ethnographic support for this interpretation comes from three salient facts of Tenejapan life. The first is that women are vulnerable to men in this society where wives, sisters, and daughters are likely to be beaten if there are threats to their reputation, and women are vulnerable to women as possible sources for slights on their reputations. Secondly, in speech to women, a higher level of politeness may be due to the fact that residence is generally patrilocal, so that women marry into their husband's family's household. For this reason there is likely to be a somewhat greater social distance between the women than between the men of a household. Thirdly, women treat some kinds of speech acts more cautiously than men; the vulnerability of women means that more acts, as well as certain particular acts (such as talking to an unrelated male at all), are defined as face-threatening. This also motivates the particular strategies that women choose, most obviously the ubiquitous expression denying knowledge or responsibility: *maškil* ('I don't know'), which is used conventionally as a self-protective device.

As for men, it may simply be the case that they have a higher evaluation of wants that conflict with face wants—for example, those supporting a goal of communicative efficiency which conflicts with the elaboration of face-redressive strategies.* One other possible factor is a process akin to Gregory Bateson's "schismogenesis"[12]: it is possible that men are stressing their brusqueness as a sign of tough masculinity, and women their polite graciousness as a display of feminine (contrasting to masculine) values. This parallels Trudgill's suggestion that middle-class men in England use linguistic forms typical of working-class usage as a way of stressing their masculinity, whereas women tend to hypercorrect, using forms typical of persons of a higher social class.[13]

The negative politeness between women is a surprising result in the light of our initial predictions, and implies that there is not a dichotomizing of the social world into men vs. women, with the former receiving negative politeness and the latter positive politeness, but that overall women are paying more attention to face redress than men are. This would parallel the suggestion of Peter Trudgill, for British English and Roger Shuy for American English, that women show greater sensitivity to the socially diagnostic features of their language, so that they use a higher percentage of valued (standard) forms.[14] Women, in this

---

*This conclusion disagrees with the position taken in my earlier paper, where the politeness theory was developed (Penelope Brown and Stephen Levinson, "Universals in Language Usage: Politeness Phenomena," in *Questions and Politeness: Strategies in Social Interaction*, Cambridge Papers in Social Anthropology 8, ed. Esther Goody [Cambridge: University Press, 1978], pp. 56-311.) There we took the position that extrinsic weighting of events was not an element in the evaluation of politeness strategies.

view, maintain a degree of "normativeness" over men in English. Tenejapan women, then, appear to be like English women in this respect.*

We still need some explanation of cross-sex relations in Tenejapa. Although certain social forces make women vulnerable, there are several reasons why women are not totally powerless in the society. Women make a considerable economic contribution to the household; they help with work in the fields and are solely responsible for food preparation, raising of small domestic animals, child rearing, and weaving. In Tenejapa it is frequently said by young women that they "don't want to marry." They fear separation from their natal families, husbands' physical power over wives, and the embarrassment or shame of illness and physical deterioration due to childbirth. In fact there seems to be no opprobrium attached to unmarried women (*tektom ?an¢etik*); there were six such adult women in the hamlet in which I worked, living with parents or siblings. Men, on the other hand, all want to be married, for they cannot get along without a woman to cook for them. This may be one reason for the relative courtesy with which men treat women in this society.

A second important fact is that Tenejapan culture interactionally downplays differences in status and power. Fear of envy and witchcraft provides a powerful motive for minimizing differentials in wealth and status. Political positions (cargos) are rotated annually or triannually; men are coerced into taking them on and the ritual accoutrements of a cargo are very expensive, so that anyone with accumulated wealth is more than likely to be forced into spending it on a cargo position. There is an ideology of complementarity in sex roles: the overseeing gods are called *me?tiktatik*, ('mother-father'), and cargos all involve a complementary female role requiring ritual food preparation and prayers. So women are seen as indispensable to the order of things, not simply in their reproductive function but in maintaining and guarding the society in a role parallel to that of men. The egalitarian ethos and downplaying of wealth and power differentials mean that women (indeed, all adult members of the household) generally take a major role in decision making at the domestic level.

While these facts mitigate the status differences between the two sexes, that there remains a power/status difference between men and women is indisputable. Physically—men beat women, women do not beat husbands or fathers or brothers. Interactionally—husbands routinely give wives direct bald on record imperatives: 'Cook that meal,' for example. However, I never heard a woman give her husband a direct order of that sort. In public, women give men (especially unrelated males) marked interactional deference; the reverse is not the case. Politically—men hold the positions that are prestigious and publicly visible,

---

*While comparisons of phonological standardness and use of politeness strategies are not necessarily one to one, they seem to be both aiming at the common goal—social approval.

and it is men who make the decisions affecting the community as a whole. Women's role in decision making, while very important domestically, is from a society's-eye view more or less invisible.

CONCLUSIONS

What then can we learn about women from looking at language? In the past linguists came up with descriptions of code differences between the speech of men and women in some exotic languages,[15] but there was no claim of the relevance of these descriptions to languages where such code differences were lacking, and no attempt to relate the existence of code differences between the sexes to social-structural facts about the societies wherein such languages were operative. In recent years sexism in language has been enthusiastically examined and well documented,[16] especially with reference to semantics and to the asymmetry of lexical items for men and women. There is also considerable evidence that women are particularly sensitive to nuances of social categories and to levels of formality.[17] But the area that has been most disappointing has been the attempt to show how the ways in which women choose to express themselves reveal truths about their social relationships and their social status in the society. I have argued here that a prerequisite to such an inquiry is an adequate theory of the relationship between language usage and social relationships, and I have offered the present sketch of a strategic analysis of language usage to suggest a means to pursuing relatively subtle indications of the position of women in society. The approach has several advantages which should be stressed.

The analysis of communicative strategies provides an intervening variable allowing us to relate language and society in a direct and motivated way, rather than simply to correlate them. The ethos of women, in this view, is tied to culture and social structure via strategies for behavior. By linking behavior to social structure we are thereby enabled to ask the question *why* do women talk the way they do in this society and what social-structural pressures and constraints are molding their behavior?

Another important feature of analysis in terms of communicative strategies is that it allows us to work from the point of view of the speakers themselves. Through looking at the strategies women are pursuing in their speech, we can get a woman's-eye view of her networks of relationships, who she esteems, who she looks down on, and who she feels intimate with. This is a distinct step forward from the prevailing methodology in sociolinguistics, which provides correlations between linguistic and social facts which may have no reality for the speakers themselves.

Furthermore, the link between behavior and social structure also provide a basis for predictions about when and where and under what conditions women's speech will take on certain characteristics—of positive as opposed to negative politeness, or of high overall politeness in both domains as opposed to low levels overall, for example. It allows us to predict universals in linguistic usage based on universals in the position of women cross-culturally; to the extent that women occupy similar social-structural loci with similar social-structural constraints on behavior, women will behave similarly at the strategic level. Thus we would not expect linguistic similarities between West African women or high-caste Indian women and Tenejapan women, the former having apparently much more structural power. But we can predict similarities between language usage of Tenejapan women and other peasant women in egalitarian small-scale societies with similar social-structural features. I would suggest two hypotheses which could fruitfully be tested in further cross-cultural research:

1. Deference (and, in general, negative politeness) prevails if and where people are in a position of vulnerability or inferiority in a society. Hence women in an inferior, less powerful position than men will be likely to use more negative politeness. However if women are so far inferior as to have no face at all (like children, or beggars, or slaves, who in many societies are treated as having no face), the particular strategies of negative politeness they use will be different than in societies where women are accorded some social esteem.*

2. Positive politeness prevails if and when social networks involve multiplex relationships, that is, members have many-sided relationships with each person they interact with regularly, so that each relationship involves the whole person, or a large part of his/her person.[18] In many societies like Tenejapa, where men dominate the public sphere of life and women stick largely to the domestic sphere,[19] it seems likely that female relationships will be relatively multi-stranded, male ones relatively single-stranded. And where these conditions prevail, positive politeness should be strongly elaborated in women's speech.

NOTES

1. William Labov, *Sociolinguistic Patterns* (Philadelphia: University of Pennsylvania Press, 1974) chapters 8 and 9; Peter Trudgill, *Sociolinguistics* (London: Penquin, 1974)

---

*Some evidence for this prediction comes from Indian data: beggars and low-caste members (Harijans) use highly honorific titles to superiors, but otherwise their requests are often made baldly. Thus you hear things like: 'Give us a little cent, oh Lord-God'. (Brown and Levinson, "Politeness Phenomena;" Stephen Levinson, "Social Deixis in a Tamil Village" [Ph.D. diss., University of California, Berkeley, 1977]). This may also be the explanation of Keenan's Malagasy data, where women are said to be *less* polite than men. Her data are from a stratified society of people who were formerly slaves, and now have a monopoly on "high" forms of speech used in politics. The forthrightness of women is socially useful for reprimanding people, for efficiency in bargaining, and so on. And there is some suggestion that women when speaking to women are highly positively polite (Keenan, personal communication).

chapter 5; Peter Trudgill, "Sex, Covert Prestige, and Linguistic Change in the Urban British English of Norwich," in *Language and Sex: Difference and Dominance*, ed. Barrie Thorne and Nancy Henley (Rowley, Mass.: Newbury House, 1975).

2. Trudgill, "Sex, Covert Prestige and Linguistics Change," pp. 91-92.

3. Critiques of this work have been both theoretical and empirical; see for example Betty Dubois and Isabel Crouch, "The Question of Tags in Women's Speech: They Don't Really Use More of Them, Do They?" *Language in Society* 4 (1975):289-94; Penelope Brown, "Women and Politeness: A New Perspective on Language and Society," *Reviews in Anthropology* 3 (1976):240-49; and Philip M. Smith, "Sex Markers in Speech," in *Social Markers in Speech*, ed. Ulaus R. Scherer and Howard Giles (Cambridge: Cambridge University Press, 1979), pp. 271-85.

4. Samuel Martin, "Speech Levels in Japan and Korea," in *Language in Culture and Society*, ed. Dell Hymes (New York: Harper & Row, 1964), pp. 407-15; Roy Andrew Miller, *The Japanese Language* (Chicago: University of Chicago Press, 1967); Tazuko Yamanaka Uyeno, "A Study of Japanese Modality: A Performative Analysis of Sentence Particles" (Ph.D. diss. University of Michigan, 1971); Eleanor H. Jorden, "Language–Female and Feminine," in *Proceedings of a U.S.-Japan Sociolinguistics Meeting*, ed. Bates Hoffer (San Antonio: Trinity University, 1974), pp. 57-71.

5. Elinor O. Keenan, "Norm-Makers, Norm-Breakers: Uses of Speech by Men and Women in a Malagasy Community," in *Explorations in the Ethnography of Speaking*, ed. Richard Bauman and Joel Sherzer (Cambridge: Cambridge University Press, 1974), pp. 125-43.

6. The notions and labels for positive and negative face derive from Durkheim's positive and negative rites (Emile Durkheim, *The Elementary Forms of the Religious Life* [London: George, Allen & Unwin, 1915]), partially via Goffman (Erving Goffman, *Interaction Ritual* (Chicago: Aldine, 1967); also *Relations in Public* (New York: Harper & Row, 1972).

7. H. P. Grice, "Logic in Conversation," in *Syntax and Semantics, Volume 3,* ed. Peter Cole and Jerry Morgan (New York: Academic Press, 1975), pp. 41-58.

8. Cf. Brian Stross, "Tzeltal Conceptions of Power," in *The Anthropology of Power,* ed. Raymond D. Fogelson and Richard N. Adams (New York: Academic Press, 1977), pp. 271-85.

9. Brown and Levinson, "Politeness Phenomena," 1978.

10. I know of one study that has attempted to do this for English (Susan B. Shimanoff, "Investigating Politeness," in *Discourse Across Time and Space*, Southern California Occasional Papers in Linguistics No. 5, ed. Elinor Keenan and Tina L. Bennett [Los Angeles: University of Southern California Department of Linguistics, 1977], pp. 213-41.), but the methodological problems were substantial and she found no clear differences between the speech of the two sexes.

11. Brown and Levinson, "Politeness Phenomena," 1978.

12. Gregory Bateson, *Naven* (Stanford, Calif.: Stanford University Press, 1958.)

13. Trudgill, "Sex, Covert Prestige and Liguistic Change," 1975.

14. Ibid.; Roger Shuy, *Sociolinguistic Research at the Center for Applied Linguistics: The Correlation of Language and Sex*, Georgetown Monographs in Language and Linguistics (Washington, D.C.: Georgetown University Press, 1974).

15. Mary Haas, "Men's and Women's Speech in Koasati," in *Language in Culture and Society*, ed. Dell Hymes (New York: Harper & Row, 1964), pp. 228-33; Edward Sapir, "Male and Female Forms of Speech in Yana;' 1929, reprinted in *Selected Writings of Edward Sapir*, ed. David G. Mandelbaum (Berkeley: University of California Press).

16. Compare, for example, Casey Miller and Kate Swift, *Words and Women* (Garden City, N.Y.: Anchor, 1977); Barrie Thorne and Nancy Henley, eds. *Language and Sex: Difference and Dominance* (Rowley, Mass.: Newbury House, 1975); Mary Ritchie Key, *Male/Female Language* (Metuchen, N.J.: Scarecrow Press, 1975); Robin Lakoff, *Language and Woman's Place* (New York: Harper & Row, 1975), and a great deal of as yet unpublished material.

17. Labov, *Sociolinguistic Patterns*; Trudgill, "Sex, Covert Prestige and Linguistic Change;" Shuy, "Correlation of Language and Sex." See also evidence for South Indian Tamil in Levinson, "Social Deixis."

18. Cf. Elizabeth Bott, *Family and Social Network* (New York: Free Press, 1957).

19. Michelle Rosaldo, "Women, Culture and Society: A Theoretical Overview," in *Women in Culture and Society* ed. Michelle Rosaldo and Louise Lamphere (Stanford: Stanford University Press, 1975), pp. 17-42.

PART III

LANGUAGE IN WOMEN'S LIVES

INTRODUCTION TO PART THREE

To see how language functions in women's lives, we must examine carefully the interplay between women's experience of language and various features of the contexts in which that experience is situated. The essays in Part III examine a multiplicity of contextual factors affecting and affected by language, taking account of such diverse considerations as education, economic activities, membership in social groups, physical environment, political ideologies, and historical period. The papers are not unified by topic or method, by theoretical orientation or conceptual framework. Rather, each elaborates selected details from the indefinitely various tapestries woven by the complex patternings of women's language in a range of times and places, activities and situations.

In Part II, the question of the implications of men's power was developed and some of its complexities demonstrated through attention to the varied details of language use in different social contexts. As those papers showed, even the ubiquitous contextual feature of "male dominance" is by no means everywhere identical. Without examining the specificities of relationships between the sexes in different settings, we couldn't begin to understand the sexual politics of language. Additionally, as Penelope Brown's discussion of women's politeness to other women showed, there are important features of language in women's lives that are simply not explained by male dominance. The intricacies of the interaction of women's lives and language will not emerge from consideration of a universalized Woman: we need many accounts of specific sociocultural and verbal features of particular women's distinctive experiences, that is, women-centered "ethnographies of language use." Only a composite of portraits can help us see alternatives to the inadequate theories of women's relation to language that are suggested by the modes of explanation we inherit from scholarly traditions preoccupied with language in a "man's world."

Patricia Nichols argues that ignoring the particularities of women's experience—assuming as universal what are either sexist stereotypes or context-bound generalizations about women—has led linguists to inadequate accounts of women's participation in language change.

In "Women in their Speech Communities," Patricia Nichols draws sociolinguistic profiles of women from three different "minority" groups, each of which is in contact with a more dominant social group that has a language history distinct from its own. She argues that the profiles of women and men differ in each community, but that the precise nature of the contrast between female and male speakers depends on the particular roles and activities of women (and men) in their own community. The methodological moral she draws: sociolinguists studying language variation and change cannot rely on standard sociological classifications of speakers but must use rich ethnographic descriptions of the speech communities they study.

Social psychologist Howard Giles and his colleagues Philip Smith, Caroline Browne, Sarah Whiteman, and Jennifer Williams report experimental investigations of the role of speech styles—for example, the use of a regional rather than a "standard" British accent—in contributing to "first impressions" of women. A question of major interest for the listeners (British undergraduates of both sexes) on first meeting a woman was her attitude toward feminist issues. "Women's Speech: The Voice of Feminism?" explores the relationship between speech style and political consciousness in a follow-up to an earlier study that found women attach more social and psychological significance to a woman's accent than men do.

Anthropologist Marjorie Goodwin's analysis of girls' and boys' directives (for example, requests and commands) in play groups in a black, working-class community in Philadelphia supports the earlier claim by Cheris Kramarae of a "cooperative" speech style among females, although, as Goodwin points out, these girls have well-honed "competitive" linguistic skills as well. "Directive-Response Speech Sequences in Girls' and Boys' Task Activities" offers empirical support for the frequently advanced but seldom clearly articulated thesis that females create their own distinctive forms of social structure. Goodwin also shows how, for each sex, speech constructs social forms and structures social relations.

In "Anger and the Politics of Naming," Naomi Scheman develops a provocative philosophical analysis of the interplay between our socially shaped linguistic resources and the social construction of individual consciousness. Scheman considers arguments about how experience is to be named—"that's not really 'anger' "; she examines as well the situated social and political processes that refine the ways we apply the names available to us—for example, changing what "counts" as anger in the historical context of contemporary feminism. More conventional accounts of our ways of speaking of emotions treat them as pre-existing "things." Scheman proposes to replace this view of emotions as "things"—that is, as "leaves in the stream of consciousness"—by an account of consciousness of our emotions as constructed and negotiated through linguistic, social, and political processes.

It is the metaphoric process as a means through which a woman inscribes herself in a given setting that concerns Annette Kolodny in "Honing a Habitable Languagescape: Women's Images for on the New World Frontiers." She looks at the ways eighteenth century women arriving at the Western frontier wrote of their new environment. Kolodny argues that these frontier women domesticated their new surroundings, not only through direct contact with the land itself—planting seeds from the gardens of the cultivated homeland left behind—but also through coming to articulate views of their surroundings in familiar and "domesticated" figures of speech that helped conceptually transform the remote pioneering settlements into tolerable homes.

In "The Silence is Broken" Josephine Donovan describes the ideological, sociological, economic, and educational factors that excluded most women from European literature throughout medieval and early modern periods. European women's ignorance of classical canons of language use and their restriction to the domestic sphere were, however, to prove an asset rather than a handicap in their acquiring the skills needed to write successful novels. Already familiar with writing of the minutiae of daily life from their considerable experience as letter writers, they found in the novel a genre in which they could make use of their expertise. As Donovan shows, women's writing skills and experience have played an important role in their contribution to the modern novel. Literature, however, involves not only writing but, just as crucially reading, and both processes are examined in Part IV.

9
WOMEN IN THEIR
SPEECH COMMUNITIES

Patricia C. Nichols

Many words have been spent on the subject of "women's speech." Perhaps because women are so readily identifiable as a group it is assumed that women speak as a group. Women's experiences have much in common throughout the world, to be sure. And it is possible that we may identify certain common patterns in women's lives and in women's speech. But women are members first and foremost of their own small speech communities, and it is in the daily context of their lives as speaking members of a larger group that their language must be examined. Without this contextual grounding, we are doomed to repeat the stereotypic nonsense of past generations about the language use of women.

What is a *speech community*? It is not necessarily the same as a political entity or an ethnic grouping. It is defined by the shared communicative process of a group, whose members may or may not have frequent face-to-face contact with each other. One definition which has been offered is: "a community sharing rules for the conduct and interpretation of speech, and rules for the interpretation of at least one linguistic variety."[1] It is not enough to speak the same language or dialect; the rules of use must be shared also. Two English speakers may utter the same string of words; one may mean the string to be interpreted as a command, while the other may understand it as a simple statement of fact. On the other hand, speakers may share rules for use, but speak entirely different languages. Certain countries of eastern Europe, for example, are said to share norms for greetings, topics of conversations, and the conduct

This paper has benefited greatly from discussions with Barrie Thorne and Pamela Tiedt.

140

of conversations, although different languages are spoken. In the working definition of *speech community* used here, both the language variety and the norms for its use must be shared by all members of the community, though it is not necessary that they all speak the same in similar speech situations.

A major new approach to the study of language and sex has recently developed within the discipline of linguistics. Variously called *sociolinguistics* or the *sociology of language*, this paradigm recognizes language variability as playing an essential role in language change. An early conference defined the task of the sociolinguist thus: "to show the systematic covariance of linguistic structure and social structure—and perhaps even to show a causal relationship in one direction or the other."[2] The sociolinguistic tradition has from the beginning taken linguistic diversity to be a subject worthy of study, in and of itself. Variable language use is taken to be a potential source of insight about processes of language change, rather than in need of "regularizing" or simply a matter of "performance" and thereby unworthy of study. Using data from spoken language, often recorded by electronic means, contemporary socio- linguists study the language varieties used by several social groups within a larger speech community. Often the variable language use of a single speaker in different speech situations or styles is studied as well.

The growing body of studies on the language use of women in a variety of settings and cultural groups provides convincing evidence that differences will exist in the speech of men and women in every social group.[3] From other perspectives, sociologists and anthropologists have observed that men and women have different roles and life experiences within their social groups all over the world, though these experiences and roles may differ from society to society. Dell Hymes, from his long-standing concern with language in use, has pointed out that differences in the social situations which are available to some speakers, and not to others, lead inevitably to inequality among speakers.[4] Simply to document that men and women speak differently in every known society, while an important starting point, is not enough, however. We need now to formulate hypotheses about the connection between the kinds of life experiences available to women and the kinds of language use they will exhibit.

Sociolinguistic respect for and interest in variation in linguistic structures as they are used by different segments of a social group must be combined with an ethnographic concern with language as it is used in specific contexts within the speech community. Ethnography is "any rigorous attempt to account for people's behavior in terms of their relations with those around them in differing situations."[5] An ethnographic approach to language use sees it as behavior occurring within social and cultural contexts that are systematically linked to one another. It grounds the analysis of language use in the realities of the lives of individuals within particular social-cultural systems and requires that language use be understood in terms of speakers' positions within those systems.

While sociolinguistic studies select representative speakers from a variety of social classes and ethnic groups and elicit speech from the same speakers using a variety of styles, what such studies often fail to note are the parameters of the particular speech community and the life experiences available to members of that community which might influence language use. Part of this failure stems from the discipline of sociology, since the sociolinguists have relied on measures of social classification developed within sociology for describing the speech community. There is increasing evidence that these measures are not adequate for sociology itself, and they are patently inadequate for use in studies of language variation. First and foremost, the family unit is arbitrarily taken to be the primary social unit in all systems of social stratification used within sociology. Second, the occupation of the head of this family unit is used as the major index of social class, and all members of the family unit are assigned to the same social class. As early as 1964, Walter Watson and Ernest Barth discussed the inaccurate classifications of women which result within sociology from such practices. More recently, Marie R. Haug has shown that in many marital pairs where both partners work, wives' occupational and educational levels exceed that of their husbands, especially at the lower end of the occupational scale.[6] In Haug's analysis, the use of one of the major indexes of social position had led to misclassification of about one-third of all families. Haug proposes a measure of social class which would take the highest level attained by either spouse as that of the entire family. This proposal, however, does not address the larger question of whether or not the family unit is the social unit of primary importance of linguists. In particular, it does not address the question of how to classify women who live outside family units for all or part of their lives. Is women's language use related to familial position on the social scale or more fundamentally to their life experiences—at school and on the job, as well as within the family unit?

I suggest that the conflicting findings of many sociolinguistic studies about language and sex roles are related, at least in part, to this failure to consider women's life experiences as members of their speech community. By relating women's language use only to their membership in family units, linguists have missed important facets of their interaction with the wider community. Particularly in the industrialized societies where most of the sociolinguistic studies have been conducted, these interactions can be rich and varied, over time and geographic space.

THREE STUDIES OF WOMEN IN THEIR COMMUNITIES

Three recent studies have combined the sociolinguistic respect for variability with the ethnographic appreciation of contextual factors which may affect language use. They are described here as examples of the direction in which we must move for adequate descriptions of the ways in which sex role can interact with language use.

Elinor Keenan discusses the speech of men and women in a small village in contemporary Madagascar in terms of "norm-makers" and "norm-breakers."[7]

Indirectness is considered to be the community norm in speaking, and men are skilled in the avoidance of confrontation. Women, on the other hand, are more straightforward, especially in the expression of anger or criticism. Other wives openly express critical feelings which their husbands hold toward another party but cannot appropriately express in public. Criticism or anger voiced by a woman is not considered as shocking as it would be if it came from a man. The majority of bargaining encounters in the markets are conducted by women, with men selling items which typically have a more or less fixed price. The directness characteristic of women's speech among these Malagasy people is more in tune with the speech use of Europeans than is the indirectness of men's speech. As European languages and customs are introduced in urban contexts and in the schools, the language use of the entire community is changing to some extent toward that previously characteristic only of the women. This change is particularly noticeable in commercial settings. In other settings the older norms are still honored, particularly in public social situations within the community itself.

Susan Gal has studied a community in Austria which is bilingual in Hungarian and German.[8] In this community, the economic base is gradually changing from one based on a farming economy to one based on industrial jobs held in urban centers outside the community. Hungarian is the language used to conduct the daily affairs of the community; German is associated with the wider world in which industrial jobs are to be found. Women are consistently choosing to speak German in this setting, as they choose both jobs and mates in industrial centers outside their peasant village. In contrast, men who choose to remain in the village and engage in a farming life maintain Hungarian as their primary language. In terms of community speech norms, women are displaying innovative linguistic behavior.

My own study of a small speech community in rural South Carolina indicates something of the complex role which sex-related choice can play in linguistic change as a community moves from a pre-industrial to an industrial economy.[9] On a river island in an area which was heavily populated in the 1700s by West African slaves, the language now spoken comprises a continuum ranging from an English-related creole known as Gullah at one extreme to a regional variety of standard English at the other. In between these extremes a dialect of English known as Black English Vernacular is found. This dialect shares features with dialects spoken by blacks in other parts of the United States, as described by William Labov and colleagues, and by Walt Wolfram and Ralph Fasold.[10] Within this coastal South Carolina speech community of some two hundred members, all of whom are black, the transition from a creole to a dialect of English can be observed in the speech of members of the same family. The speech of the entire community is changing in the direction of a standard variety of English.

A quantitative study of three morphosyntactic features in the speech of men and women in three different age groups indicates that young and middle-

aged women are changing most rapidly toward a variety of standard English.*
In the oldest age group in this community, men and women speak much the
same, using more of the older creole features than any other group except the
youngest group of men. Young men between the ages of 15 and 25 use more
creole features in their speech than any other group of adults in this community.

While these facts are interesting in and of themselves, they tell us little
about the meaning of these differences unless we know something of the experiences available to members of the community. Residents of the community all
belong to the three or four major families which have owned land on the island
since it became possible for blacks to buy land there in the late 1800s; though
there are now some differences in income level, there are no major divisions in
social status. Originally, the major economic base of the island was the
communal growing of rice, supplemented by individual gardens, hunting, and
fishing. The tasks involved in the rice crop were divided according to both sex
and age. Because transportation to the mainland was a long and tedious trip by
rowboat over several miles of river, the community was largely self-contained
and had little interaction with the mainland population on a daily basis. A few
male members took jobs off the island for extended periods of time, returning
to help with the rice harvest at a certain time of the year. With the increasing
availability of motorized transportation after World War II, jobs could be taken
closer to home by commuting daily via motor boat and automobile. Both men
and women now work off the island at some time in their lives. Island children
have been transported daily to mainland schools for the past decade. All of the
islanders now have contact with some portion of the mainland population on
a regular basis, but the nature of this contact is different for men and women.
The jobs held by men are usually in the construction industry, often in situations
where several islanders work together. No special spoken or written language
skills are required in these jobs. Up until the past ten years, most island women
held jobs as domestic workers, either in private households or in motels which
operate during the summer in a nearby resort town. Recently women have been
obtaining jobs as sales clerks, an occupation requiring use of a fairly standard
variety of spoken English as well as some writing skills. One woman has worked
as mail carrier on the mainland, and a few have left the island entirely to work
as school teachers in mainland schools. Young men can make more money within
the construction industry than they can as school teachers, and none of the

---

*These morphosyntactic features were the pre-infinitival complementizer *fE* [fə],
the third person singular pronouns *ee* [i] and *Em* [əm], and the static-locative preposition
to [tu], as illustrated in the following sentences:
(1)   I come *fE* get my coat.
       'I came to get my coat.'
(2)   And *ee* was foggy, and they couldn't see.
       'And it was foggy, and they couldn't see.'
(3)   Can we stay *to* the table?
       'Can we stay at the table?'

men attend college except to obtain some technical training from the two-year vocational colleges in the region. Several of the women in the youngest age group have attended either college or secretarial school.

On the island itself, men and women participate in speech situations according to patterns which have long existed in the community. Generally, men are the primary public speakers. The Sunday church service is the major weekly social event on the island and is attended by most of the residents. Women teach the two children's Bible-study classes, while the adult class is taught either by a (male) deacon or by the oldest and most respected woman in the community. The women attending seldom comment during this class, although they are present and free to speak if they wish. In the church service itself, the head deacon typically opens the service and conducts the rituals prior to the sermon, which is given by an ordained minister from the mainland once a month. Women participate primarily through the musical portion of the service; they conduct and comprise most of the choir. General observations to be made about the language characteristic of this major community social event are that it ranges across the entire linguistic continuum found in the community, but that men are the primary speakers throughout.

In homes men are also the primary speakers in mixed company, unless a woman is the oldest living member of a given household. Women typically talk freely among themselves, but an older woman will limit her participation in the conversation when her husband enters the room. Age seems to be at least as important a factor as sex in determining who will occupy the most conversational space in a given interchange. In homes where an older woman is the senior member of the household, her opinions are deferred to when family decisions are made, and she generally speaks more than other family members in mixed groups. In homes where both a male and a female of approximately the same age reside, the male speaks more than the female in mixed company. Children are typically quiet in the presence of adults and often spend hours listening to adult conversations without interrupting. The oral tradition valued by the entire community is handed down by the older inhabitants of the island, often in the form of stories told to these children.

In school the picture of language use is complex. School-age children interact with each other daily on their boat rides to the mainland and in after-school games on the island. Boys and girls play together until about the age of ten. After ten the activities of the boys and girls become segregated by sex, with girls helping with the inside chores and boys with the outside. The language of island girls and boys begins to show differences, with the boys continuing to use many creole features and the girls moving rapidly toward a variety of standard English. Island girls typically do well in school and are often at the top of their class. Island boys usually experience some difficulty with academic subjects, though they are good athletes and generally well liked by their mainland peers. Most boys are excellent story tellers and excel in activities requiring oral language skills—provided a standard variety of English is not required. Island girls perform better than their male peers in activities requiring writing and reading skills in

TABLE 9.1 Percentage of Creole and Nonstandard Varients[a] Used by Sex and Age Groups

	Speaker	PREPOSITION		PRONOUNS		COMPLEMENTIZER		Overall c/ns	Sex Groups c/ns
		%	N	%	N	%	N	%	%
MAINLAND (old)	1f	100	(7)	39	(87)	66	(12)	68	f 73
	2f	90	(20)	79	(101)	65	(26)	78	-------
	3m	70	(10)	15	(103)	20	(5)	35	m 34
	4m	50	(4)	47	(15)	0	(3)	32	
	old adults							53%	
ISLAND (old)	5f	57	(7)	14	(50)	43	(7)	38	f 31
	6f	67	(6)	3	(68)	0	(7)	23	-------
	7m	70	(10)	23	(96)	11	(28)	35	m 37
	8m	70	(10)	39	(66)	6	(30)	39	
	old adults							34%	

146

ISLAND		% (N)	% (N)	% (N)	%	
middle	9f	0 (1)	0 (19)	0 (7)	0	
	10f	25 (4)	0 (48)	0 (7)	8	f 4
	11m	30 (10)	14 (125)	0 (24)	15	
	12m	86 (7)	6 (49)	0 (11)	31	m 23
	middle adults				8%	
young	13f	100 (2)	0 (5)	0 (3)	33	
	14f	0 (15)	0 (114)	0 (36)	0	f 17
	15m	100 (4)	40 (5)	17 (12)	52	
	16m	100 (1)	8 (66)	17 (12)	42	m 47
	young adults				32%	

[a]N = number of possible occurrences. f = female speaker. m = male speaker.

This table of data will also appear in two other articles discussing different aspects of my research: "Variation among Gullah Speakers in Rural South Carolina: Implications for Education," in *Proceedings of the Fifth Annual Conference on New Ways of Analyzing Variation in English* (Washington, D.C.: Georgetown University Press, forthcoming) and "Linguistic Options and Choices for Black Women in the Rural South," in *Language and Sex II* ed. Nancy Henley, Barrie Thorne, and Cheris Kramarae (Rowley, Mass.: Newbury House, forthcoming).

standard English, though they are inexperienced story tellers and must be coaxed into telling a story in front of a group.

Comparative data were obtained on the speech of older men and women in a nearby mainland community and are summarized in Table 9.1. In a group where few older adults had an opportunity to attend school and most were consequently illiterate, the occupational opportunities were far more limited for all adults than for those in the island community. The differences in life experiences and communication networks are reflected in the greater use of standard English features by men in this less-educated mainland group. Women here worked as domestic laborers and as seasonal farm workers on large plantations in the area. Men held laboring jobs on these plantations or unskilled factory jobs in nearby towns. In this group older men typically had traveled more than the women they lived with, and consequently had a wider communication network. Older mainland men used about the same number of creole features in their speech as the older island group described above, while the mainland women in their age group used more creole features than any other speakers in either community. In the contexts of these two adjacent social groups, women are more innovative than men in the island group and more conservative than men in the mainland group. In both of these groups, the differences in speech are related to differences in available occupational and educational experiences for each sex and the communication networks associated with these life experiences.

In three widely dispersed speech communities—a village off the east coast of Africa, a village in central Europe, and a rural community in the southern United States—women exhibit a wide range of linguistic behavior in terms of the norms of their communities. In the Malagasay community on Madagascar, women maintain their directness of speech as outside European influences reinforce that portion of the speech community's repertoire. In terms of this context, women here exhibit conservative linguistic behavior. In the Austrian community, women are adopting German as their primary language as they choose an urban-oriented, rather than peasant, life. Men, who remain in the village in greater numbers than women, retain the older farm-associated Hungarian language. In this context, women exhibit innovative linguistic behavior. In rural South Carolina, women in two black communities are exhibiting both innovative and conservative behavior. In one community, as educational and occupational opportunities expand to include situations requiring the use of a standard variety of English, young and middle-aged women are abandoning creole forms more rapidly than men. In another community, where both education and job choices are severely limited, older women maintain the creole forms characteristic of the speech community to a greater extent than any other group of speakers. In all three studies, women are found to speak differently than men in their communities in ways that are significant for the groups as a whole. These differences interact with ongoing language change, but women's role in language change is unique for each group.

That men and women will speak differently in at least some portion of the linguistic repertoire of a speech community has been well documented in a variety of geographic and cultural settings. Where the life experiences of men and women are more nearly similar, will their respective linguistic behaviors also be more similar? This question is the kind that studies of language and women's lives must address in the immediate future if we are to make any sense of the linguistic differences we are describing.[11]

Language can operate as a door—one which either opens to new experiences or which closes off a wide range of human interaction. What kind of door language is for women will depend upon the unique experiences available to them within particular speech communities.

NOTES

1. Dell Hymes, "Models of the Interaction of Language and Social Life," in *Directions in Sociolinguistics*, ed. John Gumperz and Dell Hymes (New York: Holt, Rinehart and Winston), p. 54.

2. William Bright, ed., *Sociolinguistics: Proceedings of the UCLA Sociolinguistics Conference, 1964* (The Hague: Mouton, 1971), p. 11.

3. See especially the discussion in Mary Ritchie Key, *Male/Female Language* (Metuchen, N.J.: Scarecrow Press, 1975); the annotated bibliography and original studies in Barrie Thorne and Nancy Henley, eds., *Language and Sex: Difference and Dominance* (Rowley, Mass.: Newbury House, 1975); and the summaries of unpublished research in Pamela Tiedt and Sharon Veach, eds., *Women and Language News* (Stanford, Cal.: Stanford University Department of Linguistics, 1977).

4. Dell Hymes, "On the Origins and Foundations of Inequality Among Speakers," *Daedalus* 102.3 (1973):59-86.

5. R. P. McDermott, "Social Relations as Contexts for Learning in School," *Harvard Educational Review* 47 (1977), p. 200.

6. Walter Watson and Ernest Barth, "Questionable Assumptions in the Theory of Social Stratification," *Pacific Sociological Review* 7 (1964):10-16; Marie R. Haug, "Social Class Measurement and Women's Occupational Roles," *Social Forces* 52 (1973):86-98.

7. Elinor Keenan, "Norm-Makers, Norm-Breakers: Uses of Speech by Men and Women in a Malagasy Community," in Richard Bauman and Joel Sherzer, eds., *Explorations in the Ethnography of Speaking* (Cambridge: Cambridge University Press, 1974) pp. 125-43.

8. Susan Gal, "Peasant Men Can't Get Wives: Language Change and Sex Roles in a Bilingual Community," *Language in Society* 7 (1978): 1-16.

9. Patricia Nichols, "Black Women in the Rural South: Conservative and Innovative," in Betty Lou Dubois and Isabel Crouch, eds., *The Sociology of the Languages of American Women: Papers in Southwest English IV* (San Antonio: Trinity University, 1976) pp. 103-14.; Patricia Nichols, "Linguistic Change in Gullah: Sex, Age and Mobility" (Ph.D. diss., Stanford University, 1976).

10. William Lobov, Malcah Yaeger, and Richard Steiner, *A Quantitative Study of Sound Change in Progress* (Philadelphia: U.S. Regional Survey, 1972); Walt Wolfram and Ralph Fasold, *The Study of Social Dialects in American English* (Englewood Cliffs, N.J.: Prentice-Hall, 1974).

11. See Susan Ervin-Tripp, "What Do Women Sociolinguists Want?: Prospects for a Research Field," in Dubois and Crouch, eds., *Sociology of the Languages of American Women, Op. cit.*, pp. 3-16.

10
WOMEN'S SPEECH:
THE VOICE OF FEMINISM

Howard Giles
Philip Smith
Caroline Browne
Sarah Whiteman
Jennifer Williams

When we form first impressions of strangers, we do so on the basis of a large number of interacting cues such as dress style, physical appearance, and so on. Speech style—how rather than what is said—is one such cue. Our aims in this research are to begin determining the salience of a woman's speech style in forming impressions and to interpret our findings within the context of a current theory of the development of interpersonal relations.[1]

Charles R. Berger and Richard J. Calabrese argue that when two strangers meet for the first time their "uncertainty" levels are high in the sense that they are initially doubtful about the alternative behaviors and beliefs the other is likely to manifest or hold and, consequently, are uncertain themselves as to how to behave appropriately. According to this view, acquaintanceship is concerned with reducing such uncertainty so that a decision can be made about the likelihood of future interactions. In order to reduce uncertainty in first encounters, interactants need to elaborate a basis for predicting the other's behaviors and attitudes; predictions that Berger and Calabrese call "proactive attributions". Speech style has been shown cross-culturally to be used in the formation of proactive attributions.[2] For example, in many social contexts, we not only predict the likely background and attributes of individuals from their regional accents (a socially meaningful aspect of speech style in Britain), but also modify our behavior toward them accordingly. Given that the majority of research on speech style has highlighted reactions to male speakers, the question remains as to how people use regional accent and other features of speech style as a means of making proactive attributions when encountering *women* for the first time.

As a first step in exploring this issue we, together with Olwen Elyan and Richard Bourhis,[3] devised a study using the matched-guise technique[4] which required 76 Bristol students to listen to and rate a series of people we had tape recorded reading a standard passage of prose. The stimulus voices on this tape included those prepared by two bidialectal, middle-class women who were able to read the same passage realistically in both a standard accent and in their local Lancashire accents. They read the passage in both guises attempting to maintain the same speech rate, paralinguistic features, and impression of temperament throughout. Other voices, both male and female, both Standard and local accents were recorded for inclusion on the tape in order to disguise the fact that some of the speakers appeared twice. The voices were then randomly arranged to create the stimulus tape. The study was introduced to listeners in what has now become a standard fashion. They were told by a female investigator that we were interested in determining whether people can infer characteristics from others on the basis of just listening to their voices; a task analogous to listening to unseen speakers on the radio. No mention was made, of course, of our interest in regional accent or women. Each voice was listened to and rated separately on 25 rating scales chosen on the basis of current research on voice evaluation, sex-trait stereotyping, and sex-role ideology, with subjects unaware that in some cases individual voices occurred with different accents.

Statistical analyses showed that listeners considered the Standard speakers to be significantly higher (all $p_s < .01$) in self-esteem, to be clearer, more fluent, intelligent, self-confident, adventurous, independent, feminine, and less weak than the regional accented women. In addition Standard speakers were more likely to be perceived to have a job that was well paid and prestigious and have an egalitarian relationship with their spouses in the home, but less likely to have children than the Northern-accented speakers. At the same time regional speakers were perceived to be more sincere and likeable, and less aggressive and egotistical than their Standard-accented counterparts. Accent of speaker interacted significantly with sex of listener on six of the scales ($p_s < .01$), a result found to be due to female listeners polarizing the differences between the ratings of the Standard and Northern speakers indicated in the main effects above.

In summary, Standard-accented women were upgraded in terms of competence and communicative skills but downgraded in terms of social attractiveness and personal integrity relative to regional accented females; these data were in line with the stereotypes associated previously with male speakers. Standard-accented women were expected to bear fewer children, to create a more egalitarian relationship with their husbands, and they were seen to be masculine in their sex traits, both positive and negative,[5] while at the same time they were also rated higher on femininity as such than Northern-accented females. The data suggest a stereotyped picture of Standard-accented women as highly competent, articulate, lacking in warmth, masculine in certain ways and yet feminine, and espousing egalitarian ideals between the sexes. Interestingly, this profile is highlighted more by women listeners than by men.

At first sight, the results may seem contradictory in the sense that Standard-accented women are seen as both highly masculine on certain traits and yet definitely high on the femininity scale as well. Given recent research on psychological androgyny,[6] it is not surprising that people may be able to *perceive* both masculine and feminine qualities in the behavior of others. Tentatively, then, one could label the female Standard accent as a "perceived voice of androgyny."[7]

The study has suggested that accent could well be an important basis for stereotyped proactive attributions about the probable behaviors and attitudes that women manifest and hold. Regional accent is, however, only one, albeit important, aspect of a woman's speech style that may be a potential source for making first impressions; there may be many others. Yet, rather than move limply from one linguistic feature to another and try to determine its social meaning for listeners, we decided it would be more illuminating to attempt another approach suggested by the Berger and Calabrese model, namely, to investigate what people are most concerned with reducing uncertainty about when meeting women for the first time. In an informal pilot study, we asked students of both sexes what characteristics they would be looking for initially when meeting a young woman casually for the first time. One feature mentioned by almost everybody was the extent to which the target female was affiliated with feminist ideals. This appeared to both sexes to be quite an important factor to be able to predict in these times of a changing relationship between the sexes. The question then arose as to whether speech style cues are or could be used to reduce uncertainty about a woman's feminist stance.

With this in mind we designed a study to determine whether listeners perceive differences in the speech of "feminist" and "nonfeminist" women, and whether these differences are evaluatively meaningful. Twenty-four female undergraduates were interviewed and tape recorded in their own homes by a female investigator. After the interview, which was concerned with discussing a so-called "trivial" topic (clothing and fashion) and a more "serious" topic (Margaret Thatcher as the possible next Prime Minister of Britain), the informants were administered the "Attitudes Towards Women" (ATW) scale.[8] A low score on this scale indicates that the informant generally accepts the inferior role of women in relation to men whereas a high score reflects a great deal of dissatisfaction with the unequal treatment of women in society. Sixteen of these women scored low, and these will be referred to as the "nonfeminist" group, while eight scored relatively high, and these will be referred to as the "feminist" group. A further eight were subsequently interviewed who were known to be actively involved in the local women's movement; they scored no differently from the other so-called "feminist" women on the ATW scale. The inclusion of this subgroup was not only to increase the size of the feminist group interviewed, but also to investigate a possible relationship between active commitment to the women's movement and women's speech. In other words if differences were perceived between the speech styles of feminist and nonfeminist women, would they be accentuated in the eight who were active members of the movement? The interviewer told the informants that she was interested in eliciting their views on topics of current interest, and no mention was made of our concern with speech style or with feminism.

From each of the 32 interviews, the first 30 seconds of the informant's speech on each of the two topics discussed were edited out. These 64 extracts were then randomly placed onto a stimulus tape which was played to 16, linguistically untrained male and female students who were asked to rate each extract on a number of speech-related and personality scales chosen on the basis of previous research. Each scale was submitted to statistical analysis by means of appropriate three-way analysis of variance with the factors of feminist group, sex of listener, and topic discussed. The results showed that, irrespective of topic, feminist speakers were rated as significantly more profeminist**, as having a higher lucidity of argument** and as seeming more intelligent* and sincere*. Nonfeminist speakers were rated as sounding more frivolous**, superficial* and as having more standard accents*. No important effects emerged for sex of listener or topic discussed, and no interactions appear worthy of mention. Within the feminist group of speakers another set of statistical analyses showed significant differences between the two subgroups. The "committed" feminist speakers (those active in the women's movement) were rated as more lucid**, confident**, intelligent**, likeable* and sincere**, but less monotonous* and superficial** than the "uncommitted" feminist speakers.

These findings suggest the importance of speech style in mediating between social attitudes and social perception. The speech and perceived personalities of feminist and nonfeminist speakers are seen to differ (at least among British college women) in interesting ways, as are indeed those of the committed and uncommitted subgroups. The picture of the feminist speaker emerges as a lucid, intelligent person, confident and sincere in what she is saying, and as we would expect, perceived to be profeminist. In contrast, the nonfeminist speaker sounds more superficial and frivolous even when talking about politics. It is interesting to note that the nonfeminist speakers were also judged to have more standard accents. The differences between the committed and uncommitted feminists seem of the same order as well, in that the more committed to a liberationist viewpoint a woman is, the more accentuated the profile becomes.

This study, however, involved the recording of *spontaneous* speech and hence any differences arising from the analysis might be due simply to the content of what was said rather than to the speech style. From listening to the tapes, this did not seem to us to be the case. Nevertheless, we repeated the study but this time using content-controlled material with a larger group of listeners. Another 26 female students were recorded reading a 40-second neutral passage of prose (on humor) which they rated subsequently as neither masculine- nor feminine-oriented, pro- nor anti-feminist, and that they considered to be interesting and not difficult to read. No mention was made at this stage of our concern with feminism. Having read the passage, speakers were administered the ATW scale. The five highest scorers were to comprise the "feminist" and

---

*p<.05; **p<.01

the five lowest scorers the "nonfeminist" speakers. Forty linguistically unsophisticated male and female students listened to these voices randomly arranged on a stimulus tape and rated them on more or less the same scales as previously.

Statistical analyses of the ratings showed that differences were perceived between feminist and nonfeminist women reading the same passage. In this task, feminist speakers were perceived to be less fluent** and standard accented**, lower in pitch*, less precisely enunciated*, more masculine* and less feminine-sounding* than the nonfeminist speakers. Once again, sex of listener had no perceptible effect on evaluations and no interactions emerged between sex of listener and feminist/nonfeminist speaker. In this formal reading context, as opposed to the spontaneous speech task, the voice of feminism appeared to be at a social disadvantage in the sense that such speakers were rated as *less* intelligent** than the nonfeminist women. It does seem then that even when the content of what is said is controlled for, male and female listeners can still detect differences in the speech styles of feminist and nonfeminist women.

The differences emerging from these studies suggest that feminists have a more assertive, nonstandard, "masculine-sounding" speech style than nonfeminists. Indeed, previous research on marital decision making is in line with this perspective. Sibilla Hershey and Emmay Werner[9] analyzed recorded interviews with "liberated" and "unliberated" couples; the former were chosen on the basis of the wives' participation in a university women's liberation group. Among the liberated families, the wives were found more often to speak last and speak for longer than their husbands where just the opposite pattern was found in so-called unliberated families. It may well be that women who question the legitimacy and stability of the subordinate role ascribed to females in society reflect this not only in their ideological beliefs and social actions but in their speech styles as well. Adopting an intergroup analysis of male-female relations, Jennifer A. Williams and Howard Giles[10] have suggested that one of the strategies used by some feminists in pursuit of a change in women's status is that of assimilating toward what is held to be typical of the dominant group in attitudes, values, and behavior in an attempt to secure equality and a reasonable share of its social power. As with other modes of group assimilation, for example, ethnicity and classs, this may also be manifest linguistically in the adoption of the power group's stereotypic speech style, leading the feminists' vocal presentation to be heard as "masculine-sounding." This process may be mediated by the feminists' knowledge of socially undesirable speech stereotypes associated with women, which leads to their divergence away from the "Kind, correct but unimportant" appraisal to a more assertive self-presentation through speech style.[11]

Further support for the interpretation that certain feminists may be attempting to adopt the more positively valued stereotype of male speech behaviorally in their speech styles comes from a recent study we conducted with Jane Byrne. Despite the "verbose" stereotype often associated with female speech, a number of studies have shown that males are verbally more productive than females on a wide range of topics and under many different conditions.[12] We found that 20 female students scoring high on the ATW scale spoke at greater length (34.5 percent more) and with a faster speech rate (16 percent faster) when being interviewed by a woman on a number of emotively neutral topics than 20 students scoring significantly lower on the ATW ($p_s < .05$). In other words, the feminist students again seemed more "male-like" in their speech characteristics than their nonfeminist counterparts. It seems important to stress however that feminism is not a monolithic movement and that feminists who have different views of male-female relations and advocate different social policies and actions from those in our study might well show very different speech styles than those reported in this chapter.

Two other plausible interpretations besides the above "assimilationist" one can be offered. First, it may be that the speech style characterizing feminist women is in actual fact that associated with females who are committed to *some* issue whether it be environmental pollution, child-health care, anti-abortionism, or whatever. Rather than the "voice of feminism", we might have the "voice of commitment." Second, it could be that feminist and nonfeminist views are simply components of two larger sociopolitical belief structures such as, for example, liberalism/radicalism and conservatism, respectively. In such a case, we would expect the same speech style differences described above to distinguish between other ideological dimensions—perhaps even among men. Therefore, rather than the voice of feminism, we might have uncovered the "voice of liberalism." These issues are obviously worthy of empirical attention, and it would be valuable in future research to determine how the feminist voice (as well as perhaps its concomitant nonverbal behavior patterns) is perceived by others across a wider range of speech, personality, and social attributes. In addition, it is essential to complement our investigations of listeners' subjective impressions of feminist and nonfeminist voices with detailed objective, linguistic, and acoustical analyses.

We have tried to make women a proper subject of first impressions in their own right rather than as an adjunct to males. In this vein, we have suggested that, on the basis of admittedly exploratory data, a woman's voice can provide her interactants with a rich source of data from which to make proactive attributions about her background, personality, and social attitudes. It seems possible that on the basis of voice cues alone, people will make inferences about a woman's psychological androgyny and her feminist perspective. Obviously, it needs to be determined how these proactive attributions are translated into behavioral responses by different types of interactants in different situations and how these are responded to in return by women.

NOTES

1. Charles R. Berger and Richard J. Calabrese, "Some Explorations in Initial Inter-action and Beyond: Toward a Developmental Theory," *Human Communications Research* 1 (1975):99-112; also Charles Berger, "Beyond Initial Interaction: Uncertainty, Under-standing, and the Development of Interpersonal Relationships," in *Language and Social Psychology*, ed. Howard Giles and Robert St. Clair (Oxford: Blackwell, 1979), pp. 122-44.

2. See Howard Giles and Peter F. Powesland, *Speech Style and Social Evaluation*, (London: Academic Press, 1975); and Giles and St. Clair, *Language and Social Psychology*, 1979.

3. Alwen Elyan et al., "R.P.-Female Accented Speech: The Voice of Androgyny?" in *Sociolinguistic Patterns of British English* (London: Arnold, 1978), pp. 122-31.

4. Wallace E. Lambert, "The Social Psychology of Bilingualism," *Journal of Social Issues* 23 (1967):91-109.

5. John E. Williams, et al., "Sex-trait Stereotypes in England, Ireland, and the United States," *British Journal of Social & Clinical Psychology* 16 (1977):303-9.

6. Sandra Bem, "The Measurement of Psychological Androgyny," *Journal of Con-sulting & Clinical Psychology* 42 (1974):155-62; and Sandra Bem, "Sex Role Adaptability: One Consequence of Psychological Androgyny," *Journal of Personality & Social Psychology* 31 (1975):634-43.

7. See Also Howard Giles and Patricia Marsh, "Perceived Masculinity and Accented Speech," *Language Sciences* 1 (1979): in press.

8. Janet T. Spence, Robert Helmreich, and Joy A. Stapp, "A Short Version of the Attitudes Towards Women Scale," *Bulletin of the Psychonomic Society* 2 (1973):219-20.

9. Sibilla Hershey and Emmay Werner, "Dominance and Marital Decision-Making in Women's Liberation and Non-women's Liberation Families," *Family Process* 14 (1975): 223-33.

10. Jennifer A. Williams and Howard Giles, "The Changing Status of Women in Society: An Intergroup Perspective," in *Differentiation Between Social Groups: Studies in the Social Psychology of Intergroup Relations*, ed. H. Tajfel (London: Academic Press, 1978), pp. 431-36.

11. Cheris Kramarae, "Women's Speech: Separate But Unequal?" *Quarterly Journal of Speech* 60 (1974):14-24.

12. Marion Wood, "The Influence of Sex and Knowledge of Communication Effec-tiveness on Spontaneous Speech," *Word* 22 (1966):112-37; Michael Argyle, Mark Cook, and Mansur Lalljee, "The Effects of Visibility on Interaction in a Dyad," *Human Relations* 21 (1968):3-17; Marjorie Swacker, "The Sex of the Speaker as a Sociolinguistic Variable," in *Language and Sex: Difference and Dominance*, ed. Barrie Thorne and Nancy Henley (Rowley, Mass.: Newbury House, 1975), pp. 76-83.

11
DIRECTIVE-RESPONSE SPEECH SEQUENCES IN GIRLS' AND BOYS' TASK ACTIVITIES

Marjorie Harness Goodwin

INTRODUCTION

Both girls and boys in our society have access to the same general language system, but detailed study of the talk they produce shows systematic differences in how the sexes put that common system to work. In this paper, I focus on speech transactions involved in coordinating a group project, comparing spontaneous speech from boys and girls who live on the same Philadelphia Street. I examine in some detail the structure of directives—speech acts that try to get another to do something—and the responses to them, looking at directive-response sequence that occurred during an episode of boys' making sling shots and during an episode of girls' making rings from bottle rims. The

The fieldwork constituting the basis of this study was made possible by a National Institute of Mental Health research grant (19216-01), administered through the Center for Urban Ethnography, University of Pennsylvania. Data are transcribed according to the system developed by Gail Jefferson and described in Harvey Sacks, Emanuel Schegloff, and Gail Jefferson "A Simplest Systematics for the Organization of Turn-Taking for Conversation," *Language* 50 (1974):731-33. Punctuation symbols refer to intonation changes rather than grammatical structure. A period is used for falling intonation, a question mark for rising intonation, and a comma for falling rising intonation. Such intonations are described in Richard Gunter, *Sentences in Dialog* (Columbia, S.C.: Hornbeans Press, 1974). Data were collected in a variety of natural settings: on front steps, on a lightly traveled tree-lined street where the children lived, in back yards, and in city parks. I attempted to interact with the children as little as possible, being more interested in what they said to each other than in what they might have to say to an adult. A Sony TC-110 tape recorder with built-in microphone was used to make recordings.

materials analyzed come from conversations of a group of black, working-class children, ages eight through thirteen, whom I recorded for a year and a half as they went about their natural play activities.

ORGANIZATION OF A TASK AMONG BOYS

Making sling shots is a pastime which could be organized in a variety of different ways. The sling shot is an individual instrument, and, in theory, play with it could be construed as an individual activity in which all participants fend for themselves, the only preparation being that each have a sling shot and an adequate supply of "slings" to shoot. Among the boys I observed, however, the activity of making slings became organized into a competition between two separate teams with a hierarchical organization of participants on each team. (Such an organization is not unlike that characteristic of football or basketball, popular games among boys of this age.) The sling shot fight itself was preceded by an extended period during which, not only were weapons and slings prepared, but the organization of the group was also negotiated. All of the elements in this process, such as where the preparation would occur, who would provide materials, who had rights to materials, the allocation of necessary tools, the spatial organization of participants, when the activity was to move from stage to stage, and so on, became the focus for status negotiations between participants.

A typical way that one party attempted to display or establish his position with respect to another party was by making directives in the form of explicit commands to that party. In the sling shot session I will examine, Michael and Huey, who are brothers, became the "leaders" of two opposing teams. Preparation for the sling shot fight took place at their house. The following provides examples of ways in which Michael and Huey issued directives to those on their teams and the responses to them.

(1) Michael: Gimme the pliers!
     Poochie: ((gives pliers to Michael))
(2) Michael: *All* right. *Gi*mme some rubber bands.
     Chopper: ((giving rubber bands to Michael)) Oh.
(3) Michael: *All* right. Give me your *h*anger Tokay.
     Tokay: ((Gives hanger to Michael))
                  ((Raymond starts to come into Michael's space))
(4) Michael: Man don't come down *in* here where I *am*.
     Raymond: ((goes back up steps))
(5) Michael: *Gi*mme your other hangers. I'm a *b*end them *a*ll.
     Chopper: ((gives Michael his hangers))
(6) Michael: Give me that man. After this after you chop em give em to me.
     Chopper: ((gives Michael his cut-off piece of hanger.))
                  ((Poochie moves up the steps to where Huey is seated.))

(7) Huey: Get off my *st*eps.
     Poochie: ((moves down))
                    ((Chopper moves up the steps to where Huey is seated.))
(8) Huey: Get a*way* from here Gitty.
     Chopper: ((moves))

Michael and Huey construct their moves in the imperative form as explicit commands rather than as hints or suggestions, thus opting for non-"mitigated" or relatively "aggravated"* directive forms.   In the cases above, compliance followed each imperative.

Frequently, however, next moves   to commands are responses which constitute refusal to perform what the directive requires.   Explicit refusals contrast with explanations of failure to comply that refer to task-relevant conditions related to the context of the directive, for example, the addressee's inability to carry out what is demanded. Refusals may take the form of statements that the person addressed does not want to perform the action in question or insults or criticisms of the speaker's right to deliver the command.

(9)   Nettie: Go down there now.
      Nate: I don't *feel* like it.
(10) Juju: Terry would you go hurry up and get it!
      Terry: No. I'm not goin in there. I don't *f*eel like it.
                     ((requesting hangers))
(11) Huey: *Gi*mme the *things*.
      Chopper: You sh:ut up you big lips.
(12) Juju: Terry go and get your pick.
      Terry: What pick, I'm not goin in the house now.
(13) Michael: Get *out* of here Huey.
      Huey: I'm not gettin out of *no*where.
(14) Chopper: Get *outa* here you *w*ench. You better get *out*a here.
      Pam: No! You don't tell *me* to get out.

Return actions such as those in examples 9-14 not only show that the imperative is a form of first pair part which need not be accepted by the addressee but also interpret prior moves as ritually insulting. Refusing a directive constitutes a challenge on the respondent's part to the (implicit) claims of the party issuing the command. Recipient does not have to obey the command of the speaker and either party can format his talk to the other in a relatively

---

*William Labov and David Fanshel, *Therapeutic Discourse: Psychotherapy as Conversation* (New York: Academic Press, 1977). In discussing mitigation and aggravation Labov and Fanshel have stated that references to needs of the activity or abilities of the recipient are generally mitigating, while references to rights of the speaker or obligations of the recipient are aggravating.

aggravated or a mitigated form. From such a perspective, cases such as examples 1-8, in which aggravated commands are indeed obeyed, become more interesting.

In such cases, the actions of both participants ratify a claim by one party to be able to do something ritually offensive to the other with the other's acceptance of the offense. A view of the parties as having asymmetrical rights and duties with respect to each other is thus collaboratively displayed. Aggravation in the directive thus not only functions ritually but also constitutes part of the currency through which status and leadership are negotiated. Viewed in this way, alternative forms of giving a directive are not merely stylistic variants of a speech act but crucial elements of the process through which the social organization of the group is achieved and displayed.

The wording of the directive frequently indicates an implicit comparison between speaker and hearer. In some cases an explicit contrast between speaker and hearer is provided in the directive itself. For example:

(15) Michael: Man don't come down *in* here where I *am*.

In other cases a comparison between speaker and hearer is provided in a statement appended to the directive giving a reason for why it should be performed. For example:

(16) Michael: Ma:n back out.=I don't *need* y'all *in* here I keep *t*ellin ya.
(17) Michael: PL:IERS. I WANT THE PLIERS!
(18) Michael: GIMME THE WIRE:.
                    . . . . .
      Michael: *L*ook man.=I want the wire cutters right *n*ow.
(19) Michael: Man: I told you it kind a crowded around here. Now I can't *st*and it.

Actions which refer to the speaker's desires rather than to the requirements of the situation at hand are among the most aggravated forms of directives.* In other cases of aggravated directives, the degraded position of the recipient, rather than the needs of the speaker is highlighted. For example in (3) and (5), Michael, the boy assuming the leadership of the group, uses the adjective *your* to precede the object asked for, explicitly indicating that he is making claims over resources that rightfully belong to someone else.

---

*Catherine Garvey, "Requests and Responses in Children's Speech," *Journal of Child Language* 2 (1976):41-63; Susan Ervin-Tripp, "Is Sybil There? The Structure of American English Directives," *Language in Society* 5 (1976):25-66. Garvey notes that the most aggravated forms of "adjuncts" to a request (statements appended to a request giving a reason for why it should be performed) are subjective expressions of a need or desire on the speaker's part. Likewise Ervin-Tripp has stated that directives which are "need statements" are as baldly stated as the imperative form.

Having examined some of the consequences that follow from constructing the directive in an aggravated form I will now briefly examine the types of next moves that follow more mitigated forms. For comparability with examples 1-8 I will focus on cases in which the action requested in the directive is not performed. If the first pair part is expressed in a mitigated way, for example, as a question or a request for information, then the refusal also tends to be mitigated; for example, the refuser might provide an account for why the requested action cannot be done:

		((practicing dancing))
(20)	Terry:	Come on Maria. *C*an't you show us the steps.
	Maria:	I don't know em that good.
		((wanting to borrow Vanessa's yoyo))
(21)	Johnny:	Can I hold it for a minute,
	Vanessa:	That isn't mine. It's Eddie *F*oster's.
		((requesting pliers while making slings))
(22)	Chopper:	Could I hold yours now Poochie?
	Poochie:	No. I didn't even get five yet.

Thus the format of the first pair part is characteristically implicative for the format of the second pair part. In examples 9-15 aggravated directives receive aggravated responses. In examples 20-22 mitigated directives, in these cases, receive mitigated responses.

A contrasting situation was found in a previous set of examples. In examples 1-8 the addressee of an aggravated command does not produce an aggravated counter, but rather complies with the command. In this situation, we can recognize that special interactive work is being done because a readily available alternative has not been selected. This is also the case in examples 23-26, in which a mitigated directive gets an aggravated reply:

(23)	Tokay:	Can I have some hangers?
	Michael:	Put that thing back.
(24)	Bruce:	Can me and Robert play if Robert be on Huey's team?
	Michael:	IT'S ALREADY TOO MANY OF US.
(25)	Chopper:	We gonna go up here?
	Michael:	We gonna make it right *h*ere. *I* ain't goin all the way down there to make some.
(26)	Tokay:	Anybody wanna buy any rubber bands?
	Michael:	Put em in your pocket. Cuz you gonna pop em.

Requests for information are responded to, not as in 20-22 with accounts for refusing the command, but instead with counters and direct contradictions. It can be observed that in this particular group the person who produces asymmetrically aggravated directives and responses is Michael; and his actions here would indeed seem to be substantial elements in the process through which his position as "leader" in the group is interactively achieved. Michael's ability to violate with impunity the sequencing conventions that others follow is shown in other ways as well:

(27) Robby: May *I* be on your side Poochie?
     Michael: YOU WASN'T ON *MY* SIDE *BA*BY,
(28) Chopper: I don't want to play in the same place. You Poochie?
     Michael: No I wanna play back up *there*.

Not only does Michael respond to requests for information, mitigated forms of directives, in an aggravated fashion, but, moreover, he responds to requests explicitly addressed to *other* parties, usurping their turns.

Michael's position in the group is thus displayed and validated in a number of different ways: through issuing direct commands while receiving indirect requests, through contradicting proposals and requests of others, while expecting and getting compliance to his own, and through usurping the turn space of others. Direct (or aggravated) and indirect (or mitigated) forms are not randomly distributed. Rather, they function as complementary moves in the social process through which differences in the actions the participants may perform toward each other are collaboratively displayed and sustained.

It is important to realize that the hierarchy is not just reflected by the patterns of talk, but is actually achieved through the use of such speech resources as the directive and its possible responses. The following is a more extended piece of talk which occurred at the beginning of the day the boys were making sling shots.

                 ((Chopper with an armload of hangers joins the boys seated
                 on his steps))
(29) 1 Chopper: *M*ichael. My mom came and *c*atch me,
      2 Poochie: Ca//tch you,
      3 Michael: Catch you for what.
      4 Chopper: I had all- *I* had the hangers I had all
      5   under my shirt.= *She* said ((snicker))
      6   knh knh Come h*e*re.
      7 Poochie: ⌊eh heh
      8 Poochie: Ah hah hah! She *caught* chu,
      9 Chopper: *Y*eah,
     10 Michael: ⌐*AH*:: *AH*:: *Ah*:::
     11 Poochie: ⌊Then she said you could have em,
     12   (0.4)
     13 Chopper: No I- I got *these* from down sch:ool.
     14 Michael: *WO*::::,
     15 Nate: ⌐I wish someone would come give me a fen.
     16 Poochie: ⌊Need wire cutters.
     17 Michael: You got your chance.

18 Nate: Who got the wire cutters.
19 Poochie: Michael.
20 Nate: Who got the wire cutters.
21 Poochie: *Mi*chael.
22 Chopper: *Mi*chael, Michael supposed to be makin em at
23   *my* house.
24 Michael: I'm gonna go up my house. Go get some more hangers.
25 Chopper: You gonna make some more slings?
26   (1.3)
27 Michael: Alright. We gonna make some slings. Come on.
28 Poochie: *W*ait-a-minute.=*W*ait-a-minute. What's the matter
29   with my hand.
30 Chopper: Y'all I have the scissors.
31 Tokay: Chopper can *I* have one,
32 Chopper: I can't//cuz I need them for slings.
33 Michael: Heck *no* boy.=*He* givin them to *m*:e.
34   *I*'m goin to my house so go *ge*t it.
35 Poochie: ((whining)) You always play (   )
36 Michael: *N*o:. I'm going to my *h*ouse. Come o:n.

At the beginning of this fragment in lines 1-13 Chopper attempts to make use of a particular conversational structure, the organization of a story[1] in order to argue his position. Line 1 of example 29 contains Chopper's offer to tell a story. In lines 2 and 3 Michael and Poochie respond to Chopper's request to tell a story, thus permitting him to proceed with the telling, and Chopper continues in line 4.

With his elaboration in Line 4 Chopper argues that his story is about to come to its climax. He has produced what can be called an "orientation,"[2] in line 1, and then gives "complicating action" in lines 4, 5, and 6, and a beginning "evaluation" of the story in lines 5 and 6, as revealed through his laughter. Laughter by a story teller is frequently a paralinguistic cue that a "laughable" is forthcoming.[3] And the story teller's laughter here does generate subsequent laughter from Poochie (line 7).

Chopper, however, does not provide the resolution or climax. One of his recipients, Poochie, makes a guess as to what the next move in the story is ("She caught chu, in line 8). However, this is still not a laughable event and in response to Poochie's guess, Chopper provides only a minimal answer and does not elaborate the story further. A puzzle is posed by Chopper's story: structurally, what the humor and the climax of the story consist of and, from the content viewpoint, how Chopper eventually got the hangers. The story concerns how a figure of authority, Chopper's mother, caught him with hangers. The content of a story such as this would normally generate a "so what?" response, in that being caught by one's mother in a forbidden act is hardly a "tellable" event (and much less a laughable one). Though being the victor in an interactive game with an adult constitutes a "tellable," being the loser in such an encounter does not.

When Chopper fails to elaborate further, Poochie makes a second guess that would explain how he now has the hangers ("Then she said you could have em,") in line 11. Note that Michael continues to laugh but does not co-participate in the elaboration of the events of Chopper's story. After Poochie's guess a pause occurs (line 12) for the first time in the story and then (line 13) Chopper's narrative is revealed to be not a story about how he tricked his mother in the past, but rather an event in which his current recipients are tricked in the present by making assumptions about both the event and its telling, which he, with a display of naive innocence, undercuts. Chopper's success at one-upmanship is acknowledged by Michael's "WO.:.::.," (line 14).

This trick could not have been done by Chopper alone, but required the collaboration and co-participation of his recipients. By making detailed guesses about ensuing scenes and the structure of the events being described, Poochie demonstrates and displays to his co-participants his understanding of what Chopper is saying including, in line 11, his assumption that the hangers in the story are the hangers Chopper is carrying. Michael, however, (line 10) restricts his participation in the event to laughter and thus does not display to the others present that he had made the same assumptions. Rather, he lets Poochie be the "goat."

Chopper at this point is thus in an advantageous position. He has outwitted one of the present participants, and, in addition, he is in possession of valuable resources for a game activity; he has hangers for making sling shots. In lines 22 and 23 it can be seen that Chopper had anticipated that sling shot making would occur at his house ("Michael supposed to be making em at *my* house.") However, it is Michael rather than Chopper who, seconds later, (lines 24 on) gains control over the activities which occur during the afternoon. Michael (line 24) ignores Chopper's pleas that the activity should occur where the boys are seated; he states instead that sling shot making will take place at his house and orders that others get their supplies for the activity.

The particular distribution of speech actions in this fragment subsequently shows Michael making use of aggravated actions and others using more mitigated forms. Through these acts he thus displays his position as a person who has the right to make demands of others while others display their obligation of deference to him.

Through his speech actions, Michael gains control both of the allocation of resources and of the location of the activity. Example 29 shows a negotiation for the position of authority in the encounter. Despite the fact that Chopper has the resources necessary for the activity about to begin and has succeeded in making Poochie look "one down" for having bought into a trick, sling shot making does not occur on his property. Instead, Michael is successful in arranging for the play to occur as he wants it: in his yard and under his direction.

This fragment thus provides some indication of how social hierarchy can result through an emergent process of negotiation, at least within structures such as this peer group of children, where hierarchies are fluid rather than fixed. (With the present group activities of comparison do not lead to a single ranking of all the members of the group. Rather each comparison is situated within a particular activity, and a party who is ranked low in one activity may rank very high in another.) Types of speech actions are not merely correlated with forms of social organization. Rather, these actions, their sequencing, and other linguistic and conversational phenomena as well, constitute tools with which social structure can be built.

THE ORGANIZATION OF A TASK AMONG GIRLS

The decisions faced by girls in the manufacture of their objects are not significantly different from those faced by boys. Both must work out procedures for obtaining the necessary resources and for actually performing relevant tasks in the manufacturing process. Thus, in making rings the girls must decide where they will get the bottles necessary to make the rings, how many bottles are needed, who should break the bottles, how precisely the rims of bottles should be broken over metal manhole covers or other rough surfaces so that a nearly perfect "cut" is achieved, how used bottles should be disposed of, and how the rings should be decorated.

Among the boys the coordinating of such tasks is handled through hierarchical organization. This type of organization is uncommon in girls' games generally, and in accomplishing a task activity even among four- and five-year-old girls, all participate jointly in decision making with minimal negotiation of status. The process is both reflected in and achieved through the selection of syntactic formats for the production of directives which stand in opposition to those selected by the boys.

The following are a set of directives typically found among the girls:

		((Girls are looking for bottles.))
(30)	Sharon:	Let's go around Subs and Suds.
	Pam:	Let's ask her "Do you have any bottles."
		((Girls are looking for bottles.))
(31)	Terry:	Let's go. There may be some more on Sixty Ninth Street.
	Sharon:	Come on. Let's turn back y'all so we can safe keep em. Come on. Let's go find some.
		((Talking about bottles girls are picking out of the trash can))
(32)	Terry:	Hey y'all. Let's use these first and then come back and get the rest cuz it's too *m*any of em.
		((Planning strategy to keep ring making secret))
(33)	Sharon:	If the boys try to follow us here let's tell em- let's act just like we don't even know. ·h Just say "N:o". You know,
		((Planning how to get quantities of bottles))
(34)	Terry:	Hey let's go in there and ask do they have some *c*ases.
		((Planning to look at rings))

(35) Sharon: Come on y'all. Let's go on the steps and see-
                      ((Planning what to do with broken bottles from which rings
                      were made))
(36) Terry: Let's move *these* out *first*.
                      ((Looking for bottles))
(37) Pam: Okay. Let's go in the other *two* trashes.

The term "gonna" with a plural subject can also be used to format an action
close to a suggestion, a joint plan.

(38) Sharon: We gonna paint em and stuff.
(39) Sharon: We gonna- we gonna decorate them all up.
(40) Sharon: We gonna make a *whole* display of rings.

     Whereas boys' directives typically constitute commands that an action
should be undertaken at the time the imperative is issued, girls' directives are
constructed as suggestions for action in the future. The form *let's*, almost never
used by the boys, includes both speaker and hearer as potential agents of the
action to be performed. The syntactic forms utilized by the boys, on the other
hand, always differentiate speaker and hearer. One party is either ordering
another to do something, or alternatively, requesting action from some other
party. *Let's* signals a proposal rather than either a command or a request and
as such shows neither special deference toward the other party (as a request
does) nor claims about special rights over the other (as a command does).
     Another syntactic form that can be utilized to format the directive as a
suggestion also uses the plural subject, but uses the modal verb *can* or *could* with
the verb form:

                    ((Discussing how best to break bottle rims))
(41) Sharon: We *could* use a sewer.
(42) Pam: We could go around lookin for more bottles.
(43) Sharon: Uh we could um, (2.4) shel*lac* em.
                      ((Discussing keeping the activity of finding bottles secret
                      from boys))
(44) Terry: We can *l*imp back so nobody know where we *g*ettin them
                      from.

In some cases the overt tentativeness of the modal is further intensified through
the use of terms such as *maybe*:

(45) Terry: Maybe we can slice them like that.
                      ((Discussing obtaining bottles))
(46) Sharon: Hey maybe to*m*orrow we can come up here and see if they
                      got some *m*ore.

Finally, and less frequently, girls' suggestions for future action may use the form "we gotta":

((As girls prepare to make glass rings))
(47) Pam: We gotta do em on the ground.
(48) Pam: We gotta find some more bottles.
(49) Pam: We gotta wash these off.

Though *gotta* has a more nearly imperative force than the other terms examined thus far, the girls use it so that both speaker and hearer figure as agents in the proposed action. Thus, it does not construct a command, as would happen, for example, if only the hearer were the subject of the utterance. Consider the last set of examples with *we* changed to *you*.

(47a) You gotta do em on the ground.
(48a) You gotta find some more bottles.
(49a) You gotta wash these off.

Actions 47a through 49a resemble commands. What might appear to be a change in the structure of the utterance, a shift in the person of the pronoun, creates strong differences in meaning. The utterances with *we* treat the reasons for performing the action as coming out of the requirements of the task at hand, while utterances constructed with *you* index obligations of the recipient.

Directives with *gotta* may also contain an account providing explicit reasons for why an action should be undertaken. Characteristically, such accounts consider the benefits which would accrue to all members of the group:

(50) Sharon: Pam you know what we could do, (0.5) We gotta *clean* em first. We gotta *clean* em.
Pam: Huh,
Sharon: We gotta *clean* em first. //You know,
Pam: I know.
→ ⌈Cuz they got germs.
Sharon: →⌊Wash em and stuff cuz just in case they got germs on em.
⌈And then you clean em,
Pam: ⌊I got some pictures.
(3.5)
Sharon: Clean em, and then we *clean* em and we gotta be careful with em before we get the glass cutters.
→ You know we gotta be careful with em cuz it cuts easy.

This type of account contrasts with the accounts accompanying boys' commands, which state personal desires rather than deal with requirements of the current activity.

It was noted earlier that asymmetry among the boys was displayed not only in the format of particular directives, but also in the differential usage of both directives and responses to them. In the girls' group, however, proposals for certain courses of action can be made by many different participants, and the girls generally agree to the suggestions of others. For example:

(51) Sharon: We gonna paint 'em and stuff.
     Terry: Yep.
(52) Sharon: Hey maybe tomorrow we can come up here and see if they got some more.
     Terry: =Yep.
(53) Terry: Hey let's go in there and ask do they have some cases.
     Sharon: Yep. Okay? Yep. Let's go and ask them.
(54) Sharon: You can get people to cut this though,
     Pam: Yep.
(55) Terry: Hey y'all. Let's- let's use these first and then come back and get the rest cuz it's too many of us.
     Sharon: That's *right*.
     Terry: We can limp back so nobody knows where we gettin them from.
                    (0.8)
     Sharon: That's right.
     Terry: And w- a-d wash our hands. And wash your hands when you get *fin*ish now.
     Sharon: If the boys try to follow us we don't know. Okay?
     Terry: Yep.
(56) Terry: Wanna sweep em out?
     Sharon: Yeah.
     Pam: Okay.

Boys and girls thus construct directives in quite different ways. Boys' directives are formatted as imperatives, or requests (for example, 23-26), but girls phrase theirs as proposals for future activity and frequently mitigate even these proposals with a term such as *maybe*. Girls tend to leave the time at which the action being proposed should be performed somewhat open, while a boy states that he wants an action completed *right now*. Syntactically, the directives of the boys differentiate speaker from hearer. (This is perhaps illustrated most dramatically in examples 16, 18, and 19.) Among the girls, however, the party issuing the directive is usually included as one of the agents in the action to be performed. The usage of alternative asymmetrical forms for the directive, such as the request and the command, is differentially distributed among members of the boys' group but not in the girls', where most directives indicate symmetrical relationships.

Although girls do not characteristically respond to directives in ways which show one party superior to another, they do counter proposals for action (see examples 10, 12, 14). Argumentation is as common an activity in the girls' group as it is among boys or in mixed groups. The following is an example of a directive/encounter sequence:

(57) 1 Pam: ((on reaching a city creek))
                Y'all gonna walk in it?
     2 Nettie: Walk in it, You know where that water come from? The toilet.
     3 Pam: So, I'm a walk in it in my dirty feet. I'm a walk in it
     4   and I don't care if it do come.=You could // easy wash your feet.
     5 Nettie: ((to investigator)) Gonna walk us across? Yeah I'll show y'all where you can come.

Here, as we saw in example 29, negotiations can occur with regard to issuing and responding to directives. The directive initially posed by Pam is countered by Nettie (line 2); Pam then counters Nettie's opposition move in response (line 3). During Pam's turn (line 4), Nettie interrupts to reinstate Pam's initial directive and issue a second directive regarding where to step in the creek. Upon completion of this fragment, each of the major parties to the conversation has both given a directive and countered the other's action.

The form of the argumentation, however, has not attempted to affirm the relatively superiority of one party with respect to the other. The directives in lines 1 and 4 are requests for information, and in line 5 the directive is framed as a proposal using a modal verb. Moreover the counters do not refuse prior actions; instead they provide first (line 2), an argument against the appropriateness of the suggested action and second (line 3), an argument against the consequentiality of the suggested action. The directive/counter sequences do not result in the formation of a hierarchy, in that counters to proposals are themselves considered counterable, and a proposal initiated by one party may be reinstated subsequently by another.

Though direct commands have not appeared in the data of girls' conversation presented here, they are utilized by girls, even those as young as four years, in several different situations: responding to prior offenses of age-mates, being teacher or mother while playing school or house, telling younger siblings what to do, and ridiculing ostracized girls. Bald commands, however, are talked about as being special forms when they are issued among status equals.

(58) Pam: I s'd *I* said "you c'd *roll* your eyes all you *want* to. Cuz I'm *t*ellin you. (0.5) *T*ellin- I'm not *ask*in you." And I ain't say no plea:se *ei*ther.

Though boys seldom discuss the form of their commands, girls, when wanting to characterize someone as having been particularly bold, cite instances of the usage of direct commands. Giving direct commands is taken to be an action which displays offensive character for girls though it is such commonplace verbal behavior among boys as to not even be considered remarkable.

GIRLS' COMPETENCE WITH AGGRAVATED FORMS

Two focal ideas that have emerged from work on women's speech are that women are more polite[4] and that in cross-sex situations women are dominated by men.[5] By emphasizing the selective use of language to construct an egalitarian social structure the preceding analysis might seem to be compatible with such ideas. It should therefore be emphasized that the girls being studied not only have full competence with aggravated forms of action but systematically use them in appropriate circumstances—for example, while responding to prior offenses of age-mates, whether male or female (see examples 59 and 60), telling younger siblings what to do (examples 61 and 62), being mother or teacher while playing house or school (example 63 and 64), or ridiculing ostracized girls (example 65):

		((Chuckie starts drinking water from Terry's spout))
(59)	Terry:	You act so greedy. Go *home* if you want some water.
		((Boy from neighborhood steps on Nettie's lawn))
(60)	Nettie:	Get out the way offa that- get off that *lawn!*
(61)	Sharon:	Run to Mommy.
		((Delin pulls down the hood of her jacket))
(62)	Terry:	*Don't* put that down. Put that back *up!* It's sup*po*sed to be that way.
(63)	Deniecey:	Give me my *baby.*
(64)	Sharon:	Now go over there and get your paper, ·h And I want *every*body over here, to act like grow:n men and grown women.
(65)	Pam:	Better go in the house!

Girls' ability in the use of aggravated forms is perhaps most clearly demonstrated in cross-sex argumentative situations, such as the following:

		((Nettie is sitting on top of Johnny))
(66)	Johnny:	Get off!
	Nettie:	I wasn't never *on.*
	Johnny:	Girl why don't you get off!
	Nettie:	No! If I had- if e- heh- he he heh!
	Johnny:	Get off! Get off or // I'll hit you with my thing!
	Nettie:	Cindy smack him. You'se a mother. Stop. I'm a- I- I hate to do something nasty in front of y'all. But if he hit me again,
	Michael:	eh heh!
	Nettie:	I'm not playin *ei*ther. Just hit me again.=Hear?

(67) Eddie: ((singing)) You didn't have to go to school today, *d*id you.

     Terry: Yes we *did* have to go to school today.

     Eddie: ((singing)) No you *did*n't have to go to school (1.0) was on strike.

     Terry: ((falsetto)) We had our school today! The strike is *off* you dummy.

     Eddie: *Uh* uh. The strike- // the strike came *on*.

     Terry: The strike is // *off*.

     Eddie: The strike ca//me on today.

     Terry: I don't wanna hear it. I don't wanna hear it. ((Juju is eating a banana))

(68) Nettie: ((chanting)) Monkey, Monkey eat // bananas.

     Juju: So, when Mommy buys them when Mommy *y*ou eat them.

     Nettie: Mommy don't hardly buy no- bananas in her— hardly. (0.4) And // I don't eat no- buy bananas.

     Juju: Well when she *do* buy em you eat em.

In cross-sex situations girls are just as skillful at countering another party as boys. Not only can this ability be observed in ordinary argumentative situations; the effectiveness with which girls can maintain their positions is perhaps most vividly seen in elaborated argumentative exchanges built on counters such as sounding (a speech event so far reported on only for boys).[6] The following are fragments from a more extended ritual insult sequence:

(68) Nettie: Okay. One day- (0.2) *my broth*er was spendin the night with chu, ˙h And // the next mornin he got up,

     Michael: °I don't wanna hear about it. Your brother // ain't *n*ever been in *my* house.

     Nettie: THE NEXT TIME HE GOT UP, ˙h heh He was gonna brush his teeth so the roach tri(h)ed ta(h) bru(h)sh hi(h)s!

     Michael: °Don't swag. An if he was up there If the roach was tryin ta *brush* it he musta brought it up there with him.

(69) Nettie: And one *more* thing! One day(h) (0.2) I went in your hou- *I* was gonna walk in the door for two sets // a roaches. One roach here (0.2) and one roach here. THE ONE RIGHT HERE,=

     Michael: Oh you tryin ta *sell* em for him.

     Nettie: THE ONE RIGHT HERE W- THE ONE RIGHT HERE WAS UP HERE SAYIN'- THE ONE RIGHT here was up here sayin', (0.2) "*Peo*ple movin ou:t" (0.2) And the one right here was sayin' (0.2) "*Peo*ple movin in," Why? Be:cause of the color of their ski(hh)n.

     Michael: You understand their language. You must be *one* of em. You understand their language cuz you *one* of em.

     Nettie: I(h) know(h) you(h) ar(hh)re! You was *b*orn from the *r*oach family.

172 / *Women and Language in Literature and Society*

Thus, the fact that with each other the girls structure their talk in particular ways does not in any way mean that 1) they lack the ability to organize their talk in alternative more aggravated ways, 2) that they are less skillful than boys in that type of talk, or 3) that they are at a disadvantage to boys. Indeed the observation that the girls not only have access to but also make use of aggravated forms only heightens our appreciation of the fact that the structures of talk they use among themselves constitute not a limited repertoire or a kind of "restricted code," but rather systematic procedures through which a particular type of social organization can be created.

CONCLUSION

The social organization of girls and boys differs in terms of the ways in which activities are coordinated. Differences in girls' and boys' social organization may be seen in the syntax and sequencing of directive-response pairs used in task-related activities. Variation in syntactic forms is also found in a range of other language activities not investigated in this paper. Girls and boys, for example, use different types of accusations. Boys make their accusations directly, in forms such as "Boy you broke my skate board." Girls, by way of contrast, frame their accusations as reports about offenses heard from an intermediary.[7]

Boys and girls also differ in the ways they make comparisons among group members. Boys boast openly about their achievements in the presence of others. Such behavior occurs rarely in the girls' group; girls talk about their appearance and relationships. Although boys' critiques of others' bragging, as well as insults, occur generally in the presence of the person discussed, criticisms of girls who "show off" occur more frequently in the absence of the target of conversation.

As a result of talk about absent parties considerable tension can occur in the girls' group. The non-hierarchical framework of the girls provides a fertile ground for rather intricate processes of alliance formation between equals against some other party.* Gossip events may lead to ridicule in song, elaborated confrontations constructed through accusations and insults taking place over several days, and even, on occasion, the ostracism of a girl from the group for periods as long as one-and-a-half months. Boys, by way of contrast, deal more directly and expediently with their grievances and seldom does a dispute extend longer than a few minutes. Although boys who are insulted may elect to leave the group for short periods of time they are never excluded from the play group or subject to public taunting. The content and timing of criticisms as well as

---

*Fredrik Barth, *Political Leadership Among Swat Pathans* (New York: Athlone Press, 1959). As anyone who has read Barth's description of egalitarian relationships among the Swat Pathans is aware, the absence of hierarchy does not guarantee peacefulness, cooperation, or absence of tensions. For a description of a speech event among the girls in which considerable jockeying for position and formation of alliances occurs see Marjorie H. Goodwin, "Conversational Practices in a Peer Group of Urban Black Children" (Ph.D. diss. University of Pennsylvania, 1978, pp. 424-639).

the speech events in which they occur differ for boys and girls. While girls do not establish a rank ordering of their members during task-oriented activities as boys do, the coalitions between equals that they do form can lead to characteristic tensions and realignments within the social group.

The present study argues that sex differences in language use do not emerge only when men and women deal with each other, the situation which has formed the basis for most investigations of language and women's place, but are apparent in the ordinary ways of "doing things with words" used in single-sex groups. Different approaches of girls and boys to talk in similar activities are not only indicative but also constitutive of characteristically different social organizations.

In this paper I have investigated directive-response sequences occurring within the single-sex clusters in which a particular group of children spend most of their time outside the classroom and away from home. The group for which these sequences were observed has been described in terms of a specific set of criteria: urban, black, working-class children ages eight through thirteen. This does not mean, however, that these features are necessarily the defining characteristics of the phenomena being described.[8] It seems, in fact, quite likely that structures and processes of the sort described in this paper would be found in many different groups.

NOTES

1. See Harvey Sacks, "Analysis of the Course of a Joke's Telling in Conversation," in *Explorations in the Ethnography of Speaking*, ed. Richard Bauman and Joel Sherzer (London: Cambridge University Press, 1974), pp. 337-53.

2. See William Labov, "The Transformation of Experience in Narrative Syntax," in *Language in the Inner City: Studies in the Black English Vernacular* (Philadelphia: University of Pennsylvania Press, 1972), pp. 354-96.

3. See Gail Jefferson, "Notes on the Sequential Organization of Laughter in Conversation: Onset Sensitivity in Invitations to Laugh" (Paper presented at the 73rd Annual Meeting of the American Anthropological Association, Mexico City, 1974).

4. See Robin Lakoff, *Language and Woman's Place* (New York: Harper & Row, 1975); and Penelope Brown, "Women and Politeness: A New Perspective on Language and Society," *Reviews in Anthropology* 3 (1976):240-49.

5. See Candace West, "Against Our Will: Male Interruptions of Females in Cross-Sex Conversation," in *Language, Sex, and Gender: Does la Difference Make a Difference?* ed. Judith Oransanu, Marian K. Slater, and Leonore Loeb Adler, Annals of the New York Academy of Sciences 327 (1979):81-100.

6. See Roger Abrahams, *Deep Down in the Jungle: Negro Folklore from the Streets of Philadelphia* (New York: Athlone Press, 1959); William Labov, "Rules for Ritual Insults," in *Language in the Inner City: Studies in the Black English Vernacular* (Philadelphia: University of Pennsylvania Press, 1972); and James Leary, "White Ritual Insults," in *Play and Culture: 1978 Proceedings of the Anthropological Society for the Study of Play*, ed. Helen B. Schwartzman (West Point, N.Y.: Leisure Press, 1979), pp. 125-38.

7. See Marjorie H. Goodwin (in press), "He-Said-She-Said: Formal Cultural Procedures for the Construction of a Gossip Dispute Activity," *American Ethnologist*.

8. See Emanuel Schegloff and Harvey Sacks, "Opening Up Closings," *Semiotica* 8 (1973):229-92.

12
ANGER AND THE POLITICS OF NAMING

Naomi Scheman

> "As interworked systems of constru-
> able signs . . ., culture is not a power,
> something to which social events, behaviors,
> institutions, or processes can be causally
> attributed; it is a context, something within
> which they can be intelligibly described."
> — Clifford Geertz[1]

To discover what we are feeling (our emotions) is not necessarily or usually
to discover some new feelings (pang, *frisson*, wave, or whatever); rather, it is
to discover what all of that means, how it fits in with who we are and what we are
up to. It is to put a name to a mass of rather disparate stuff, to situate the
otherwise inchoate "inner" in a social world, to join (introspectible) feeling and
behavior in a significant way, to note a meaningful pattern.

The long history of this paper has implicated, beyond my ability to disentangle
their contributions, many members of the Canadian and American Societies for Women in
Philosophy and the Canadian Research Institute for the Advancement of Women. I am
grateful for the criticism, the ideas, the support, and the entanglement. Burton Dreben
and David Hills were particularly helpful with the penultimate version, which appeared in
my doctoral dissertation "Depsychologizing Psychology: Essays Against Individualism in
the Philosophy of Mind" (Harvard, 1978). Sally McConnell-Ginet was an encouraging and
insightful editor, particularly when it came to recasting the essay in a more intelligible form.
The preparation of the final version was managed, with the most tactful bullying, by Eta
Schneiderman, to whose stylistic sensibilities and clearheadedness this paper owes whatever
clarity it may have.

The ways we have for doing this, our vocabulary of the emotions, are given socially: the patterns to be found are various but not infinite and not wholly in our individual power to change. Societies categorize at least some of the emotions in at least slightly different ways. They find different conjunctions of feeling and behavior significant, and the significance can change over time.*

On an individual level poetry and novels can change the ways we read ourselves—not just tell us we have been in love, but enable us to be by showing us what it would mean for *that* to be love (perhaps homosexual love, or non-spectacular, quiet attachment).† This enabling is not just freeing us to feel in the future but, equally importantly, showing us how to read the past.

In addition, changes can be seen as political and ideological. As we change our beliefs and opinions about, for instance, the existence and nature of sexual oppression, we can come to change the ways in which we interpret our own feelings and behavior.

In this paper I will examine three different sorts of changes that can occur in the case of anger. One is *becoming angry*, the second is *discovering that one has been angry*, and the third is *changing what counts as being angry*. While the first is (philosophically) uncontroversial, the second and (especially) the third pose difficulties for the traditional picture of mind and language, a picture which stands opposed to the view I have just outlined. After sketching the traditional picture, I will elaborate the alternative model as a way of giving a better account of what we are learning through the practices of the women's movement, in particular through the experiences of the creation and the discovery of anger in consciousness-raising groups.

THE TRADITIONAL PICTURE

The traditional picture of mind comes from Descartes: on the surface of the stream of consciousness float leaves that are our sensations, thoughts, and feelings, each unmistakably labeled.††

Freud has modified this picture: not all the leaves float on the surface. Some leaves, by the force of the directional flow of the stream (the ego), have been thrust to the bottom and covered with silt (repression). Because they are

---

*See Denis DeRougemont, *Love in the Western World* (New York, N.Y.: Pantheon, 1956). Also Virginia Woolf, *Night and Day* (New York, N.Y.: Harcourt Brace Jovanovitch, 1948), for a discussion of whether intense and obsessive feelings are to count as love for two sensible, "modern" people.

†In his portrayal of Oscar Wilde, Vincent Price tells of an easy friendship with a younger boy and the awesome sweet pain of discovering, after a blithely obtuse parting, left in a railway car with the other boy's tears on his face and his kiss on his lips, that *that* had been love. Not a new feeling, caused by the parting, but the old one, revealed and interpreted by it.

††Descartes (and Freud, see below) are of course more subtle than my impressionistic account, but I do not think the subtlety affects my argument.

there, they disturb in gross or subtle ways the flow of water over them and thus the behavior of the leaves still on the surface (neuroses, parapraxes, dreams, and so on). In order to free the leaves and hence to free ourselves from the disturbances they cause while hidden, we need to uncover them. We can do this by interpreting the clues we gather from the eddies and whirlpools they create (psychoanalysis).

The heart of the traditional picture is this: when we talk about the emotions, conscious or unconscious, we are talking about some particular mental or physical state that is "in" us (or that we are in) that makes what we are saying true. The anger, the joy, the love, the grief are supposed to have been there all along, awaiting discovery and naming. It is this picture I want to argue against through a consideration of the three ways in which our emotions and our knowledge of them can change.

BECOMING ANGRY

The first sort of change is this: as women come to believe that it is neither natural nor inevitable that they stay at home and experience most of the world at one remove, that their sacrifices of goals and dreams and freedom were not in their real interest, they often become angry. Their lives could be a whole lot better than they are, and someone or something is to blame. The object of their blame and anger varies from the closeness and specificity of a husband to the political generality of society and social institutions.

We can question whether the anger these women feel is justifiable, and if so what its appropriate objects are. We can even question whether emotions are the sorts of things that can be justifiable or appropriate at all. However, the claim that people *do* become angry in this way appears uncontroversial.

The traditional picture of mind can account for becoming angry by explaining how changes in leaves in or beneath the stream engender new ones. To give such an account strains only my metaphor, but the account itself is strained when we turn to the second and third sorts of changes.

DISCOVERING THAT ONE HAS BEEN ANGRY

To begin with, we need a clear and detailed account of what is meant to have happened when someone is said to have discovered that she was angry. Alice belongs to a consciousness-raising group—When she first joined she was generally satisfied with her life. But she became gradually more aware of those times when she felt depressed, or pressured and harried, as though her time were not her own. However, she didn't believe her time ought to be her own, so in addition she felt guilty. She would sometimes snap at her husband or children, or cry without quite knowing why, and then put her "moodiness" down to various *causes*, such as her neuroses or her menstrual cycle. She didn't think she had any *reason* to feel this way; she never took the bad feelings as justified or reasonable; she didn't identify with them; they came over her and needed to be overcome.

Within the group Alice's feelings are responded to differently. She is encouraged to acknowledge and to express them in a safe environment, in which she has little fear that her feelings will disappoint, disillusion, hurt, or anger those around her. Furthermore, there is a growing shared sense, not only of the reality, but of the legitimacy and, finally, the justifiability of Alice's feelings.

We must distinguish here among the reality, the legitimacy, and the justifiability of feelings. One can acknowledge the reality of an emotion while believing that it is in some way illegitimate. And to acknowledge that one's feelings are legitimate—sincere, not self-deceptive—is not necessarily to take those feelings to be justifiable. They may, no matter how deeply or fully felt, be irrational, unfounded, needlessly self- or other-destructive.

It is likely that the other women in the group will urge Alice to acknowledge the reality of her depression and guilt, but to deny the legitimacy of those feelings. This denial amounts to the claim that she is in some way feeling something that she is unable to face. The guilt and depression are a response to and a cover for those other feelings, notably feelings of anger. Alice is urged to recognize her anger as legitimate and justifiable in this situation.

If Alice comes to this recognition, we may describe her as having discovered that she had been angry, though she hadn't previously recognized it. She would, in fact, have denied it if she were asked: "Why *should* I be angry?" It is significant that a denial that one is angry often takes the form of a denial that one would be justified in being angry. Thus one's discovery of anger can often occur not from focusing on one's feelings but from a political redescription of one's situation.

If we accept the plausibility of the notion that Alice can discover that without knowing it she had been angry, we may initially be tempted by the analogy of the submerged leaves. We may think that the anger must have been there all along, to make Alice's anger not just a politically helpful fiction. But we cannot, of course, actually produce her past anger to satisfy the critic who says we manipulated Alice into a suspiciously revisionist rewriting of history. Even if she is now clearly and straightforwardly angry, couldn't it be that she just *became* so? It's *yesterday's* anger we need here, and there seems no way of laying our hands on that.

Not only would no newly discovered leaf provide conclusive evidence of past anger, but it may be that there is no particular item of our mental life left to be discovered. What is primarily keeping us as women from acknowledging our anger is an inability to interpret our feelings and behavior in the proper political perspective. At least three different aspects of sexist ideology help prevent our synthesizing the pieces and naming the puzzle of our feelings.

One is the myth about the emotions, women's emotions in particular, that tells us they are irrational or non-rational storms. They sweep over us and are wholly personal, quite possibly hormonal. The emotions that fit with this picture tend to be diffuse, like moods, or episodic and undirected. They don't, in any event, *mean* anything. Thus we have outbursts of anger aimed at children, the weather, or a piece of balky machinery. We often feel there's something not quite right about the anger; it's out of proportion, and, especially if aimed at children, feels unfair and wrong. Instead of encouraging us to interpret these outbursts, the myth makes us feel guilty for having succumbed.

A second feature of our lives that keeps us from putting the pieces together is our own insecurity. The central cases of anger are judgmental, a way of feeling that someone (or some group) has acted badly. In order to be straight forwardly angry, one standardly has to trust one's own reactions and take oneself to be in a position to judge.* That can be very hard to do from a position of dependency, where one's welfare and happiness depend on pleasing others. Even outside of marriage women are expected to be uncritical and unchallenging, and it can be very threatening to step back from this network of expectations.

A third thing keeping us from seeing ourselves as angry is the picture we are likely to have of what the good life for a woman consists in. Anger is "object-hungry": if there is no one and nothing to be angry at, it will be harder to see oneself as really angry. If the life one has is just what one has expected would be most satisfying and fulfilling, and if one's sacrifices are seen merely as the transcending of childish dreams, then it will be hard to find anyone or anything to be properly angry at. It is similarly hard to be properly angry if one thinks one's life as a woman is "natural," ordained by biology. The limitations that flow socially from one's being a woman are seen as on a par with those that flow from physical or biological factors.†

It is, of course, possible to be irrationally angry at a situation that is as one thinks it should be or that no one is to blame for. We may find ourselves angry and wonder why; it seems so uncalled for and childish. But the difference between someone who is irrationally angry and someone who is not may not be a difference in what they *feel* so much as a difference in what sorts of feelings, under what sorts of circumstances they are ready to take as anger. When we judge that people are right to deny the name of anger to their irrational reac-

---

*Not, of course, that all anger is so explicitly judgmental or sees itself so clearly in the right. But although people can be angry while knowing they have no good reason to be, those who find it difficult to acknowledge anger are often helped by coming to see that it would be justifiable for them to feel it.

†Freud is often mistakenly seen as holding this view ("anatomy is destiny"), but his actual view, although more subtle, serves the same ends. He is well aware both of the social origin of the norms of femininity and of their mutilating effects, but it is perhaps the clearest evidence of the deep pessimism of his later life that he saw the alternative to such socialization (and to the corresponding socialization of men) as barbarism: the situation may be awful, but there is nothing to blame but civilization itself, a barely more appropriate object of anger than biology.

tions, we are often judging that their situation, unlike Alice's, does not really call for anger.

But those who do take those reactions as anger may not be mistaken. Having noted this point, we are faced with the complex relationship between being angry and taking ourselves to be. If we take ourselves to be angry, whether justifiably or not, our anger changes. We begin to see things differently, as it were *through* the anger; it colors our world, both inner and outer. We find, because we are looking for them, more reason for our anger and more feelings we can take as anger, which we may before have labeled differently or not have noticed. Our feelings, judgments, and behavior become organized around the fact of our anger.[2]

Or we can resist this. We can either let our feelings and our behavior remain uninterpreted or search for some other meaning. We can be mistaken in doing this. Thus, to discover that we have been angry is to correct an earlier interpretation. But we are never simply mistaken, the way others can be about us. We can be confused, but we cannot be "merely or wholly wrong."[3] If we are confused about our emotions, those emotions themselves are confused.

We can recognize this difference between how I see my emotions and how others see them and go on to ask why this difference exists. One point is clear. If I fail to interpret my feelings and behavior as anger, they are likely to be both odd and erratic, and therefore less coherent and predictable than you would expect of someone who was angry straightforwardly. The patterns we pick out when we name the emotions have to do with the needs of social life: seeing people as angry is connected with a complex set of expectations of them, and their not seeing themselves in the same way affects the validity of those expectations.

In the light of these observations, the theory of privileged access (the philosophical view that we are each the ultimate authority about our own emotions) can be seen less as a fact of epistemology than as a piece of social theory—a clue to what we care about in our interpretations of people. That we are inclined not to notice this, in part because of the emotions-as-inner-states picture of mind, is typical of the workings of an ideology: matters of political choice come to seem matters of unchangeable fact. We think that emotions just *are* particular states of individuals, specifiable independently of social context.

The individualism that characterizes this view of the mind and the emotions is historically nonaccidental. It fits with the essentially atomistic view of persons underlying liberal economic and political structures, of agents entering the marketplace freely with already formed motivations and desires. We treat each other as psychologically detachable units and regard ourselves as the owners of ourselves. We are both the legal and the epistemic authorities. Since the view about psychological predicates (such as *is angry*) that I am urging is that they pick out socially significant patterns, ways of organizing feeling and behavior in accordance with particular social needs, it would be expected that in a society like ours primacy would be given to first-person perception. We care most about our own view of ourselves since we are the ones who are allowed to determine how we are to be taken as feeling: privileged access functions as a sort of property right.

I may think, and you may disagree, that you are angry at me, or in love with me, but are afraid to admit it even to yourself. That may seem to me to be the clearest sense to be made of the confusing ways you feel and the strange ways you act. And I may, insofar as I can, treat you as someone who is angry at (or in love with) me, thus making our relationship to a certain extent what it would be if you acknowledged these things. But are you *really* angry or in love? There may be no answer to this; what you are is confused and conflicted: you haven't settled yet on a clear way to be. There is no reason to think that under the muddle is a clear fact, a leaf beneath the silt.

Now why do you get to do the settling? What is wrong with my taking you to be some way you don't take yourself? What I want to suggest is not that I am any less likely than you to be right, but that I haven't got the right: I am an intruder, failing to respect your privileged access to yourself.[4] It is certainly true that we take people to have these sorts of rights to their own(ed) feelings; we may think they are wrong, but we do not normally have the right to treat them according to our conception of them rather than their own. People can confer on others the right to interpret their feelings, or can lose their right to do it themselves, by being declared insane, which means, among other things, that one's own view of oneself is not the one the rest of us have to respect.

Less extremely, this right is unequally distributed. Adults, for example, often tell children what they are and are not feeling, and what those feelings mean ("You're just overtired"). And the interpretation of women's feelings and behavior is often appropriated by others, by husbands or lovers or by various psychological "experts." Autonomy in this regard is less an individual achievement than a socially recognized right, and, as such, people with social power tend to have more of it.

But, as with other sorts of property rights, we can recognize and seek to change an inequality of distribution while working ultimately for more fundamental changes. We can, that is, explore the possibility of allowing our emotions to be fully and openly social constructions, rather than needling, as we do now, to acquire and keep to ourselves the final authority about them.

Consider, for example, the interaction of feeling and perception in a consciousness-raising group. A frequently remarked feature of such groups is that each woman's ability to recognize and change her situation depends on the others' doing the same. Part of why this is important lies in how it is that one is being seen and responded to. Although it is true that women are taught to be overly dependent on our reflections in the eyes of others, it is a serious mistake to conclude from this that we ought not to care about or attend to how others see us. We need to be selective about whose views we care about and why and about how people's views are distorted and manipulative. But to attempt to cease to care is to adopt an asocial, individualistic picture of people that it has been one of the important goals of feminism to deny. The serious question posed by the experience of such groups is how to characterize the connections between how we really are and how we are seen. This question is at once normative and descriptive.

There are many such connections apparent in the workings of a consciousness-raising group: that between being listened to and taken seriously and the development of self-respect, or between being genuinely sympathetic and having one's expressions of sympathy acknowledged.[5] Here I want to focus on the relevance of these considerations to the discovery of anger.

For example, when Alice finds herself snapping at the children or complaining to her husband, she is apt to feel like some sort of monster for not being made happy by her life. The crystallization of her feelings will be impeded in part by her unwillingness to face the sort of person she thinks she would be were she really angry. But in the group, women she has grown to know and to like confess to similar feelings. As the other women realize that they are angry, Alice's certainty that they are not monsters will make it easier for her to accept that she is angry too.

Shifting notions of normality function like this: as it becomes more expected that children will be angry at their parents, it becomes easier for people to interpret a lot of darkly baffling feeling and seemingly perverse behavior.

Conversely, R. D. Laing draws our attention to the ways in which family members can invalidate each other's experiences.[6] A powerful family mythology about what someone ought to be feeling can override otherwise much more plausible readings by warping her interpretations, leading her to focus on or to ignore certain aspects of her feeling and behavior. One reason this can happen is that feelings don't bear their meanings on their faces: we need to learn socially what they add up to. We interpret our reactions and our behavior in the light of this family mythology, so when, as happens in a consciousness-raising group, it is challenged and undermined, we are apt to see our lives and our emotions differently.

The bestowing or the withholding of a name can be personally and politically explosive. To see that some state of affairs counts as oppression or exploitation, or that one's own feelings count as dissatisfaction or anger is already to change the nature of that situation or those feelings.

CHANGING WHAT COUNTS AS BEING ANGRY

We inherited from Freud, whether he intended it or not, a way of accounting for the discovery of anger. There is supposed to be a particular state people are in when they are angry, a state that can be either conscious or unconscious. Unconscious anger is the same sort of thing as conscious anger, just as a submerged leaf is the same sort of thing as an unsubmerged leaf: it is supposed to be obvious that whatever is repressed is *anger*. What Freud is supposed to have discovered is that emotions, intentions, beliefs are not necessarily conscious; just those things can be hidden from us.

To put the matter this way is to represent Freud as holding a sophisticated version of the view of emotions as inner states. Most of the time this is how he represents himself. By demonstrating that the processes that characterize our conscious lives also appear in unconscious forms, Freud claims to be taking the sort of insight into feeling and behavior we receive from poets, novelists, playwrights and both extending it and making it scientific (ultimately neurophysiological).

Freud defines "psychical acts" as those that "have a sense." In showing that, for example, parapraxes, dreams, and neuroses have a sense, that is, "meaning, intention, purpose and position in a continuous psychical context" rather than arising "immediately from somatic, organic and material influences," he takes himself to be making "a quite considerable extension to the world of psychical phenomena and [to] have won for psychology phenomena which were not reckoned earlier as belonging to it."[7]

This description of Freud's achievement is, I think, apt, but it admits of two divergent interpretations, one that fits with the emotions-as-inner-states view and one that fits with my alternative. Under the first interpretation there is a mechanism of the mind, a set of basic processes, that produces all the contents of consciousness and all intentional behavior. On this view Freud takes himself to have discovered convincing evidence for the claim that many pieces of behavior we had been taking as caused by a distinct sort of physical mechanism are in fact caused by an underlying and hidden extension of the mechanism of the mind and by underlying states essentially like their conscious counterparts (which cause pieces of straightforwardly intentional behavior). It is in terms of this (as yet only programmatically specified) mechanism of the mind that unconscious intentions, motivations, and beliefs are identified. Psychoanalysis uncovers evidence for the causal structure of this mechanism, and thus for the unconscious states and processes that can be recognized by their roles in it. This is a natural way of taking what Freud means when he says that to have sense is to have a "place in a continuous psychical context."

But there is another, I think more plausible, interpretation, which neither relies on nor supports the view of emotions as inner states. We could take what Freud marshals as *evidence* (parapraxes and dreams and what people spontaneously say about them, the behavior of children, neurotic symptoms) as itself significant, as constituting a meaningful pattern of mental occurrences and behavior, without the postulation of ghostly entities and a ghostly mechanism holding it all together.

Consider the following picture: we have some pieces of intentional behavior, say, my shouting at and then walking out on someone I take to have wronged me. We also have a number of relevant beliefs (in particular, that he has wronged me and that he could have avoided it) and some conscious feelings.

The traditional picture tells us that these fit together causally. The focal point is the feeling (one of the feelings?), which is the anger, caused by (my beliefs about) his behavior, and in turn causing mine.[8] When we turn from the conscious case to the case of a parapraxis or a piece of neurotic behavior or a dream, we are supposed to see the causal chain clearly enough for us to infer the existence of the central, apparently missing piece: the emotion itself. So, for example, we infer the existence of my repressed anger as caused by my belief (perhaps itself repressed, a complication) that I have been somehow avoidably wronged and as causing my otherwise inexplicable behavior or symptoms.

The problem here is not with the convincingness of the analogy between the conscious and the unconscious cases but with the initial picture of how the feelings, beliefs, and behavior fit together when the whole affair is conscious. Simply, there is no justification for identifying the anger with the feeling, because most of the time there is no one feeling (sometimes there are none; sometimes there are many, possibly conflicting), and there is most certainly no *sort* of feeling characteristic of anger (it can feel like almost anything, from exhilarating to crushing to nothing at all). Nor is there any real reason to infer that behind it all is some identifiable, peculiar state that is the anger and causes the behavior *and* the feelings.

What makes the whole affair a case of someone's being angry is how it is as a whole similar, in ways we particularly care about, to other cases. The similarity is not inferred similarity of mechanism but conferred similarity of meaning. There is no particular state, conscious or unconscious, mental or physical, that will by itself settle the question of whether someone is angry. In order to settle this question, we need to learn more about the person's behavior, feelings, circumstances, and we need to know how to interpret what we learn.

I have argued that by extending the range of phenomena we can see as meaningful Freud has given us an alternative way of thinking about our psychic lives. We can speak of unconscious motivations, emotions, and so on, just as we speak of conscious ones: as ways of interpreting feelings and behavior that are complex and otherwise inchoate (despite whatever causal links science may uncover). Thus Freud has led us to expand the range of cases that count as cases of anger, not just in the sense that we can now point to some we couldn't have pointed to before (as biologists increased our repertoire of organisms by discovering the existence of many invisible to the naked eye), but by changing our notions of what it is to be angry. Although unconscious anger is anger in just the same sense as conscious anger is, to see that this is so is not so much to uncover some new datum as to learn to see the old data differently. Freud's insight leads us away from focusing on the nature of the emotion itself as some identifiable thing, toward looking at the meaning of feelings and behavior seen in historical and interpersonal context.

SPECULATIONS ON THE EMOTIONS, POLITICS, AND THE POWER OF NAMING

I have suggested that to account for the phenomenon of discovering that someone has been angry it is necessary to change the sorts of patterned situations that are seen as significant. Even people not otherwise sympathetic to psychoanalysis are now inclined to identify emotions by their place in an individual's history, not just by how they feel. What I want to consider now is the possibility that we can come to name and classify emotions differently for reasons that are not just individually historical—a sort of "political psychoanalysis."

One thing that led us to see unconscious anger as genuine anger was that we saw someone's feelings and behavior as hanging together coherently and pointing in a certain direction. And we came to see this by seeing a stretch of her life as a whole: the judgment that she was angry embodied not just a claim about her present state but facts about the past and expectations about the future. We can come to a similar realization about a group—that it has a history, an organized present, a probable future. And coming to see this can lead us to think differently about the feelings and behavior of individual members of that group.

Consider women and anger. Part of what makes it true that a woman is angry today is that her vague and unfocused feelings are apt to crystallize in the future as she becomes clearer about the nature of sexism and its role in her life.

We identify her feelings and behavior today as unstraightforwardly angry partly with reference to this possible future, their natural one. Calling this future course "natural" means here that the political beliefs she comes to have are *true*, and her not having had them previously can be explained as part of the distorting effect of a false ideology. The requirement that the future course be in this sense natural supports one of the central points of this essay—that substantive political considerations are prior to the correct identification, even to the identity, of the emotions.*

But this future course has become at all likely only quite recently. Although, of course, having feminism in the air has a great deal to do with how people (introspectively) feel, there is another, subtler difference. I want to suggest that previously someone who felt like a woman today who is unstraightforwardly angry would not have been considered, and *would not have been*, angry. There was then neither the likelihood of future crystallization nor any way of thinking that would have made it appropriate to gather together some odd jumble of feeling and behavior and call it "anger." The

---

*This point about naturalness needs both clarification and defense. Both are beyond the scope of this paper and, at the moment, of its author.

meaning that the jumble has for us today is the product of social change; it has acquired a way to organize itself and grow.

We can look back and say of someone then that she was angry because it enables us to explain more of what was going on. But it doesn't follow that it would have been correct to say it of her then: what counts as anger has changed. We have given a meaning to what previously had none; it had none because there was no future for it within the social, political, and economic reality of earlier times. We can see confused and obscure anger today as anger by seeing it as embryonic, as a state that would become straightforward anger were certain social pressures, false beliefs, and internalized fears removed. But the corresponding feelings and behavior of women in the past were not leading anywhere, not for most women in their lifetime anyway, and so there was no reason to see them as meaning anything; they didn't count as anger because they lacked even the potential social significance such feelings and behavior have today.

In the light of this claim I think we can make sense of the defensiveness and belligerence of critics of consciousness-raising groups. If there is the connection I have been suggesting between politics and the discovery and even the nature of anger, then emotions become much more threatening than they would be were they simply inner states. Anger could on that view lead people to act in ways we might reasonably fear, but it wouldn't be intimately bound up with collective political action.

We can thus make sense of the current craze for psychological individualism: "you just feel what you feel; get in touch with what's really there inside of you." It is no accident that such a view is flourishing. It functions as a reaction to and a damper on the sorts of personal and political changes central to feminism, making the sort of discovery of anger I have been discussing impossible. As long as only you can really know what's going on in your own head, the odds are fairly high you never will.

Another, more intellectually serious way in which consciousness-raising groups are criticized is that they are seen as manipulative of the feelings of the women in them, that people come to feel (or to think they feel) what the group deems proper. If I am right and there actually is something like this going on, it is important to acknowledge, define, and ultimately defend it, rather than simply accept the terms in which the criticism is couched and try to refute it. Some groups undoubtedly are manipulative in a way any disinterested person would recognize and deplore—I'm not concerned with them here. But the idea that there is a context in which you can simply "get in touch with your feelings," free from the influence of other people or of political concerns, is a dangerous myth.

The idea that I am the way I am no matter what anyone else thinks is not politically neutral. To take this position is to stifle the possibility of particular sorts of political change. But it's also to blind ourselves to the truth that we are in many deep and important ways what others take or at least allow us to be. Whether or not we are really angry, beneath the confusion and the pain, depends in part on particular social processes, which will give or fail to give our feelings the possibility of definition.

The structure that consciousness-raising groups provide for the interpretation of feelings and behavior is overtly political; it should be immediately obvious that one is presented with a particular way of making sense of one's experience, a way intimately linked with certain controversial political views. Consciousness-raising groups are not, however, unique in this respect. What they are is unusually honest: the political framework is explicit (though often vague) and openly argued for. The alternative is not "a clear space in which to get your head together" but a hidden political framework that pretends not to be one and hence is spared the bother (and the risk) of argument.

APOLOGIA

In this paper I have attempted to identify a source of discomfort, a project that makes complete sense only to those whose discomfort it is. I have gone on to suggest how we might construct an alternative framework, a project that is likely to seem simply perverse to someone committed to the old one.

We experience this discomfort as feminists when we realize that our experiences are leading us to think differently about people and human relationships, while the only concepts available to think with are suited to forms of social organization shown to be outmoded by those very experiences. Forms of practice such as consciousness-raising groups can lead us to a fundamental revision of the conceptual structures in terms of which we name our experiences. We can, in particular, question the underlying individualism of the traditional picture of mind.

It would be satisfying to think I could marshal arguments sufficiently cogent to convince any (rational) reader: philosophers are supposed to aim at that, not just preach to the converted. But there's another kind of philosophical task: to bring to light, clarify, and explain the nature and sources of dimly perceived contradictions in or between our concepts and our social practice. Such contradictions may have been there all along, but their presence causes particular trouble when social practice is changing. One doesn't choose here between explaining the world and changing it; rather one explains (and perhaps facilitates) the changes by changing the explanations.

NOTES

1. Clifford Geertz, *The Interpretation of Cultures* (New York: Basic Books, 1973) p. 25.
2. For a similar view in the context of a different sort of theory, see Ronald DeSousa, "The Rationality of Emotions," *Dialogue: Canadian Philosophical Review* and in *Explaining*

Emotions, ed. Amelie Ockensberg Rorty (Berkeley and Los Angeles: University of California Press, 1980).

3. Stuart Hampshire, "Sincerity and Singlemindedness," *Freedom of Mind and Other Essays* (Princeton, N.J.: Princeton University Press, 1971), p. 237. My discussion here owes much to his, although his does not extend beyond the limits of the individual.

4. For an interesting discussion of the nature and importance of our consideration of other people's self-conceptions, see Victoria Spelman, "Treating Persons as Persons," *Ethics*, LXXXVIII (1978):150-61.

5. For a discussion of this and related issues, see my "On the Conditions of Sympathy," *The Monist* (1979) 320-30.

6. R. D. Laing and Aron Esterson, *Sanity, Madness and the Family* (New York: Basic Books, 1965).

7. Sigmund Freud, *Introductory Lectures on Psychoanalysis*, ed. James Strachey and Angela Richards, Pelican Freud Library, Vol. I (Harmondsworth, Middlesex: Penquin Books, 1976), pp. 87-88.

8. For a criticism of this point similar to mine but from a slightly different angle, see J. L. Austin, "Other Minds," *Philosophical Papers* ed. J. O. Urmson and G. J. Warnock, (Oxford: Oxford University Press, 1961), esp. p. 77.

13

HONING A HABITABLE LANGUAGESCAPE: WOMEN'S IMAGES FOR THE NEW WORLD FRONTIERS

Annette Kolodny

"Even in Paradise the Wicked would be miserable," complained Cornelia Greene in a letter to cousins in 1800. For her, Cumberland Island, off the coast of Georgia, to which her family had so optimistically removed during the turbulent years of revolution, had never been any kind of paradise. Each August brought seasonal discomforts, and this year again, her "family . . . taken with the Fever & Ague—myself excepted," she must act as nurse. "How strange are things distributed." she muses: "Those that would be satisfied to see every thing here perfect, have ill health." She herself, she makes clear, had never been so disposed: "We that have never expected to find any thing extraordinary & never saw any thing very pleasing [about this place]—am the most blessed." When, further, she notes wryly that "the climate at least wants gratitude to its advocates," she offers tacit recognition of the inevitably disappointing encounter between exaggerated human expectations and Georgia realities.[1]

That Cornelia Greene could so easily dismiss the paradisal associations, however, does not mask the fact that for over a hundred years others had been lured to Georgia by the very power of that fantasy-laden language. Indeed, those who first helped to settle Georgia perceived themselves "Invited to possess this

Research for this study was conducted under the generous auspices of a Ford Foundation Fellowship for the Study of Women in Society; it was completed with help from the Central University Research Fund of the University of New Hampshire. I wish here to thank the staff of the Southern Historical Collection at the University of North Carolina Library, Chapel Hill, for their patience and intelligence; and Verna and C. Hugh Holman, also of Chapel Hill, without whose caring this work would never have been so pleasurably begun. For her help in suggesting relevant primary source materials and in providing valuable historical information, I am most grateful to Mary Beth Norton.

promised land . . . laid out as an *Earthly Paradise*." In documents published in Charles Town, South Carolina in 1741, and again in London in 1742, many of those so enticed bitterly complained that they had found, not a "Spot of Earth uncurst," as had been promised, but, instead, poor weather and *"Land . . .* of *Four* Sorts; *Pine Barren, Oak Land, Swamp* and *Marsh*." Insisting upon an original credulity "void of all Suspicion of Artifice or Design," the disgruntled settlers were actually acknowledging the fact that the successful "selling" of the New World had been, at least in part, an evocation of fantasy-laden imagery which promised itself as daily reality—thus encouraging them to "feed our Wishes into Realities."[2]

Even more than the possible end to toil and poverty or the call to high and heroic adventure, the most potent element inhering in that imagery was the blatantly psychosexual promise of possessing a *"Paradise* with all her Virgin Beauties."[3] It was, as I have argued elsewhere, a verbal accommodation which permitted recurrent physical accommodations to alien and often hostile terrains.[4] For, while brief entry into unknown territories may prove momentarily exciting or even exhilirating, to be forced to accept the unfamiliar and unknown as daily experience challenges sanity itself. To avoid the heart of that particular darkness, ever since Columbus,[5] male adventurers to the New World have projected upon it a metaphorical complex which represented for them all forms of comfort, protection, nurture, and, at the same time, guaranteed them both possession and mastery: almost inevitably, then, exploiting a gender prediliction already available in most Indo-European languages, the landscape became an experiential analogue of the human feminine. Historically, sustaining that fantasy appears to have been both useful and societally adaptive, bringing successive generations of immigrants to strange shores and then propelling them across a vast uncharted terrain.

As with the female imagery at its core, it was as well an infinitely adaptable and malleable fantasy; so that, when the demands of a fledgling nation called for something other than the passive appreciation which Paradise implied, the virginal Eden of the promotional tracts was replaced by a femininity which now required, or even invited, mastery and alteration. For David Humphreys, sometime poet, soldier, and landscape engineer, the transformation of the American wilderness at the end of the eighteenth century seemed to suggest a projection of masculine force over a nature which, "once rustic and rude, now embellished and adorned, appears the loveliest captive that ever befell to the lot of a conqueror!"[6] In 1822 Timothy Dwight, president of Yale, applauded a less brutal, but no less erotic, transformation: "Where nature, stripped of her fringe and her foliage, is now naked and deformed, she will suddenly exchange the dishabille; and be ornamented by culture with her richest attire."[7]

The same challenge of accommodation, of course, applied also to women. Ann Bradstreet recorded that her "heart rose" as she looked out, for the first time, upon the rugged New England coastline; and Eliza Burgwin, after spending most of her life with her mother's relatives in England, experienced the return to her father's North Carolina plantation in the 1790s as a journey through an unrelentingly menacing terrain.

> The road was so narrow & thro' a pine forrest, We thought we were in a *lane* & expressed to the driver a dread of "Wild Beasts"—emerging from the woods; he, perfectly astonish'd, ask'd "What sort'o Wild Beastees Missus?"[8]

Her own exaggerated wording, coupled with the driver's reply, tells us not so much about the areas outside her father's holdings as about the quality of the young girl's imaginative responses. In fact, as her memoir later makes clear, with "no neighbors within visiting walking distance" and "afraid to ride thro' the woods alone," Eliza Burgwin was to suffer an almost intolerable sense of confinement and isolation within her father's carefully manicured plantation gardens. For her, the "greatest relief in this solitude" was contact with the familiar: "writing to, & receiving letters from England."[9]

Not even the fact that the Burgwin grounds included "extensive, & beautifully laid out" gardens in the English style mitigated her sense of "exile" and isolation.[10] This suggests that one's comfort on any landscape may be related not only to its familiarity but, as well, to one's own ability to put a personal stamp upon it. For this, Eliza (and her mother before her) had arrived too late in America. Frances Ann Tasker Carter, of an earlier generation, had known quite well "that to live in the Country, and take no pleasure at all in Groves, Fields, or Meadows; nor in Cattle, Horses, & domestic Poultry, would be a manner of life too tedious to endure." Wife to Robert Carter III and mistress of his extensive Nomini Hall plantation in tidewater Virginia, she did much more than merely "take pleasure" in these activities; clearly, she superintended many of them and, on occasion, even had her say in the design of the whole. As her children's tutor recorded in his 1773-74 diary, "Mrs. Carter told the Colonel [her husband] that he must not think her settled . . . til he made her a park and stock'd it."[11]

Intrinsic to the meaningfulness of Mrs. Carter's command, as it was to David Humphreys' and Timothy Dwight's approbation of civilization's use and "improvement" of nature's resources, is their prior confidence in having accurately known, and hence assessed, their landscape. The more successful the verbal identification—that is, the greater the correlation or congruence between the shape of the psycholinguistic projection and that of the actual phenomenon— the greater the success of the intended activity based upon it will be. In other words in order to easily put one's stamp on a landscape, one must first have a comfortable, or at least usable, linguistic tool for *knowing* that landscape. (Verbs denoting "to know" and "to name," after all, have often been confused and even thought to have common ancestral roots.) Consequently, insofar as women entered a landscape which had already been appropriated, both physically and verbally, by the males who had preceded them, they were challenged not merely to find viable experiential projections of their own but, at the same time, to counter those discomforting imagings—and their attendant landscapes— in which they could not easily function. It should be no surprise, then, that in reconceiving the New World garden for their own purposes, women generally steered clear of the male adventurers' images of a feminine domain literally requiring the services of a human *husbandman*.

In the 1660s, Ann Bradstreet's tactic was to insist upon a creation suffi- cient unto itself, making of the sun and the earth a completed marriage pair. Paraphrased directly from Psalms (XIX, 11. 4-6), the fifth stanza of her much anthologized "Contemplations" apotheosizes the sun as "a bridegroom" which "in the darksome womb of fruitful nature dive[s]."[12] Although in some ways her lines counter the general Puritan wariness of ascribing sexual or sensual dimensions to the New World landscapes, their overall impact is to edit man out of any direct participation in the fructifying dynamic. Man might thus appre- ciate God's creation and act as its steward, but he was not to be seduced by it. An even greater reticence marks the diaries and letters of later colonial women, both north and south, as they avoided not only the imagery of Paradise but any hint of its associated feminine qualities as well. By 1800, Cornelia Greene—that wry and sardonic voice with which this study opened—was typical in her refusal to recognize any female activity in her garden beyond her own: her October letter to cousins on Jamaica gives an account of "two Young Citron trees which *I nursed* with much care but something—I know not what—pulled them up" (my emphasis).[13]

Coincident to this gradual (and probably largely unconscious) editing of male linguistic response was a developing assertion, by women settlers, of their rights to own and to help design the landscape as they deemed appropriate. Although it had not always been the case, by the end of the seventeenth cen- tury, generally, women who were single or widowed could hold property anywhere in the colonies. And even married women could, in a technical sense, claim ownership—though, legally, their husbands held complete control of all property and could dispose of it at any time without their wives' consent. By the eighteenth century, it was not unusual for fathers to bequeath land to their daughters as well as to their sons, though this hardly became the rule, and land, for the most part, remained under male title.* As with Eliza Lucas, for example, it was more probably the exigencies of colonial life that determined women's increasing impact on the landscape than changing legal codes or liberalized

---

*In this connection it may be worth noting that the disgruntled Georgia protestors listed as second among "the REAL Causes of the Ruin and Desolation of the Colony," "The Restricting the Tenure of Lands . . . [and] cutting off Daughters" from the right to inherit land from their fathers, in Pat. Tailfer et al., "A True and Historical Narrative . . . ," p. 79. Originally planned simply as a military outpost, Georgia had initially excluded women from title to land; pressures such as these, however, soon forced a change in that policy.

attitudes toward women's roles. With her father repeatedly absent on military campaigns and her mother incapacitated by illness, the young girl had little choice but to take over her father's extensive Wappoo plantation near Charleston.* The memorable result, of course, was her experimental cultivation of indigo, that plant that eventually provided a staple crop for South Carolina.

From Eliza's letterbook, it is clear that her father remains a beloved, if distant, presence in her life and that it is through his aid and encouragement that she first began her experiments with various crops at Wappoo. In July 1740, for example, her letterbook records that she "Wrote my Father a very long letter on his plantation affairs and. . . . On the pains I had taken to bring the Indigo, Ginger, Cotton and Lucerne and Casada to perfection, and had greater hopes from the Indigo (if I could have the seed earlier next year from the West India's) than any of the rest of the things I had tryd."[14] Only 17 at this point, and still rather tentatively acting the role of proprietor, Eliza sees all plantation affairs as still her father's and depends upon him for suggestions and supplies of seeds. But two years later, feeling perhaps more comfortable with the success of her management, she asserts a clear independence of her father's direction and confides in a letter to her friend, Mary Bartlett, "I am now making a large plantation of Oaks which I look upon as my own property, whether my father gives me the land or not." She perceives herself in this endeavor as "busey in providing for Posterity" and explains to her correspondent that she looks ahead "many years hence when oaks are more valueable than they are now—which you know they will be when we come to build fleets."[15]

That planting which is done for business or profit, however, is carefully distinguished in her letters from the smaller planting done for pleasure—her "garden" activities, as she more usually terms it. Here, she cultivates flowers and ornamental shrubs sent her from abroad or attempts to domesticate local flora which she discovers in the woods. As she explained in a 1740 letter to her former friend and teacher in England, one Mrs. Boddicott, her well-furnished library "(for my papa has left me most of his books). . . . my Musick and the Garden, which I am very fond of," comprise the recreational counter to those hours "not imployed in business,"[16] with her reading often enough suggestively shaping her responses to the terrain around her.

If Virgil's *Ecloques* provided many an Enlightenment reader, but especially so in America, with ready models for reconstituting golden age pastoral bliss, one must assume from her letter on the subject that, as far as Eliza Lucas was

---

*In 1738 Colonel George Lucas of the British Army moved his ailing wife and his two daughters, the 15-year-old Eliza and her younger sister, Polly, from England to the Carolina plantation that his father had owned for at least a quarter of a century. The next year, 1739, Colonel Lucas resumed military duties in Antigua; from then until his death in 1747, Lucas remained assigned to military duties abroad and never saw Carolina again.

concerned, his *Georgics* were of more interest since they could be read also as a gardening manual. Again writing to Mary Bartlett, she admits

> I have got no further than the first volume of Virgil but was mosst agreeably disappointed to find my self instructed in agriculture as well as entertained by his charming penn; for I am pursuaded tho' he wrote in and for Italy, it will in many instances suit Carolina. I had never perused those books before and imagined I should imediately enter upon battles, storms and tempest that puts one in a maze and makes one shudder while one reads. But the calm and pleasing diction of pastoral and gardening agreeably presented themselves.[17]

This reading is particularly apt, she continues, because it comports so nicely with "this charming season of the year." (An undated entry, the letter was probably written in late April or early May 1742.) Though she excuses herself for lacking "the fine soft language of our poet to paint it properly," her attempt to portray for her friend "the beauties of pure nature unassisted by art" nonetheless employs a rather careful selection of devices from among the several competing pastoral dictions available to any writer of this period. Self-consciously ornate, the language is less Biblical and Paradisal than it is a compound of elements from Virgillian and Renaissance pastoral romance schema:

> The majestick pine imperceptably puts on a fresher green; the young mirtle joyning its fragrance to that of the Jessamin of golden hue perfumes all the woods and regales the rural wander[er] with its sweets; the daiseys, the honysuckles and a thousand nameless beauties of the woods invite you to partake the pleasures the country affords.[18]

As with Bradstreet's lines, the natural world evoked here is animate, almost sentient. The youthful renewal described demands no human agents, but only invites their passive appreciation. Were the scene specifically gendered, it would approach that traditional southern pastoral of filial homage before an all-giving, wholly delight-filled (often virginal) mother;[19] but it is this element precisely which is missing.

On the only other occasion in which she indulges a fully elaborated pastoral diction—with which she was obviously well acquainted through her reading—the young girl carefully ignores the sexual suggestiveness of the physical design she describes and permits only the explicit joining of hands between the goddess of gardens and orchards and the goddess of grains and fertility: thus, "the smiling fields dressed in Vivid green" suggests the rather sisterly locus where "Ceres and Pomona joyn hand in hand to crown the hospitable board." What provokes this, for her, unusual usage is a 1743 visit to "Goose-Creek, St Johns, etc. . . . in which are several very handsome Gentlemens Seats." "Crow-field, Mr. Wm. Middletons seat," which she details at some length, appears typical of that southern yearning to stylize, through the design of physical space, the latent psychological components of pastoral diction; artificially contrived landscapes thereby became a means of manipulating a viewer's mood or sensibilities.[20]   Though Eliza Lucas never remarks upon it, "the fruitful Vine mantleing up the wall loading with delicious Clusters," the "spacious bason in the midst of a large green," or the "charming spott where is a large fish pond with a mount rising out of the middle . . . and upon it is a roman temple," all suggest the inherently sexual element in both classical and renaissance pastoral. Hardly unimpressed by these elaborate contrivances, she nevertheless does little more than describe them and, instead, emphasizes that "what immediately struck my rural taste" were not the artificial manipulations of sense and sensibility but, rather, "a thicket of young tall live oaks where a variety of Airry Chorristers pour forth their melody."[21]   Happy enough to admire others' attempts to relocate Arcadia in America, she herself apparently never had it in mind for her own acres.

Eliza Lucas' characteristic eighteenth-century attempts to make of her landscape a living emblem were, by contrast, far more modest. In the spring of 1742 she contemplated a Cedar grove (usually associated with gloom or contemplation) in which "to connect . . . the solemnity (not the solidity) of summer or autumn with the cheerfulness and pleasures of spring, for it shall be filled with all kinds of flowers, as well wild as Garden flowers, with seats of Camomoil and here and there a fruit tree—oranges, nectrons, Plumbs, &c.,"[22] Like the letters of so many other women from the colonial and early Republican period, both north and south, Eliza Lucas' show her busily engaged in domesticating native flowers and herbs and exchanging cuttings, seedlings, and overripe fruit (for their seeds) with her correspondents. It is, in fact, the most recurrent subject matter marking generations of American women's letters and diary entries. And even where the intention was not a grove, but a more modest garden, the effect was the same: "Do not forget my ripe fruit which I intreated you to send me" implored Cornelia Greene to her cousins in 1800, because "any flower or fruit which you can share & send to me would be a great acquisition to our country as well as a gift of highest prize."[23]

If the men persisted in discovering—and then despoiling—Paradise, the women (it appears) all along knew the garden needed tending. The picture handed down to us of Frances Ann Tasker Carter, for example, shows a woman not only concerned with, but wholly knowledgeable about the gardens under her care. In February she ordered "the Gardener to sew Lettice, & plant Peas . . . in the Garden" and, as her childrens' tutor recorded in his diary, she took great pride in "shew[ing] me her Apricot-Grafts; Asparagus Beds &c." One December, walking in one of the many gardens surrounding the main house, the tutor recalled that he "began to ask her some questions upon a Row of small slips—To all which she made polite and full answers; As we walked along she would move the Ground at the Root of some plant; or prop up with small stickes the bended *scions*."[24]

Because the exclusive and continual cultivation of tobacco, the main staple crop of the great tidewater Virginia plantations, depletes the soil in seven to ten years (forcing upon the planters the acquisition and cultivation of ever yet more acreage),[25] only such unusually extensive holdings as those of the Carters could properly be expected to maintain the family in its accustomed luxury for more than another generation or so. Daughters from families with smaller land holdings in the area would marry men who were already eyeing the western lands eagerly. The Revolution gave new impetus to land speculation in Tennessee and Kentucky, and Virginia planters were among the first to consider relocating to more fertile fields; during the last third of the eighteenth century, for example, both George Washington and Patrick Henry were leading figures in the western land speculations.[26] By the beginning of the nineteenth century, as Everett Dick has pointed out, along the eastern seaboard, "particularly in the Piedmont region, the land was wearing out. With Kentucky competition, tobacco prices fell, but ever rising cotton prices lured the planter to the new cotton West."[27] Once again, that lure combined, as it had since the first explorations and settlements, the promise of both economic betterment and inherently fantasy-laden delights. Among those who first crossed the Appalachian Mountains, Thomas Hanson noted in his journal that "all the land that we passed over today is like a paradise it is so good and beautiful."[28] For the male imagination, then, the depletion of eastern lands meant only that paradise would have to be relocated anew to the west.

But as women had earlier denied the image in the east, so too they were to avoid it in their contacts with the western frontiers. One early traveler to the Ohio River Valley, delighted at her discovery of "a clear beautifull stream" in the mountains, "shaded with evergreens," was careful to qualify the scene's potential associations in her journal entry: "I cou'd not but figure to my self that this must be the Lethe tho the fields were not Elysium."[29] Thus, the manuscript diary of Elizabeth House Trist of Virginia provides a highly suggestive source for understanding the linguistic attitudes through which the comfortable daughters of the plantation south were to accommodate themselves to an unchartered wilderness. Wife of Nicholas Trist of Virginia, who was himself then engaged in scouting for possible land claims in the western territories, Elizabeth Trist kept a diary from December 26, 1783, through July 1st, 1784, recording a trip from Philadelphia to the frontier outposts of Carlisle and Pittsburgh and thence down the Ohio and Mississippi Rivers to meet up with her husband at Natchez.*

The landscapes with which she expresses herself as most comfortable are those within which she can either detect or project the signs of settlement, or those which elicit from her the eighteenth century's aesthetic penchant for

---

*Elizabeth Trist was a very early visitor to this area. An American colony did not really settle there until 1792, and even this was a crude settlement, located mainly on the Tensaw River and also above Natchez, Mississippi, where Americans mingled with Spanish, French, and British, living in the rudest log cabins and eking out a livelihood from the cultivation of indigo and the making of tar. Significant settlement began with the opening decades of the nineteenth century. For further information, see Everett Dick, *The Dixie Frontier*, p. 54

charming vistas. "If the country which is mountainous was cleared it wou'd be
beyond description beautifull," she writes of the area outside Pittsburgh. And,
after "an excursion over the Monongahala . . . about 10 miles from Pittsburgh," she notes, "here and there a farm wou'd present itself to our view with
a few acres around it cleared, but the country is yet in a very rude state or else
it wou'd afford many beautiful prospects."[30] In this, she is echoing not only
the political sentiments of Jeffersonian agrarianism but, as well, a general
eighteenth-century blindness to the beauty of *any* densely wooded and unculti-
vated landscape. By 1757, when Thomas Godfrey complained in letters to friends
in Philadelphia of the rude woods surrounding Fort Henry and, a year later,
turned his vexations to rhymed couplets, such attitudes had already become a
literary commonplace:

> Here no enchanting prospects yield delight,
> But darksome forests intercept the sight.[31]

David Humphrey's solution to his own similar distress was a virtual call to arms:

> Let the keen adze the stubborn live-oak wound—
> And anvills shrill, with stronger strokes resound.[32]

Apparently unable (or perhaps unwilling?) to even imaginatively call forth any
analogous transformation of the scene, Trist's response to finding herself in the
woods is to feel "oppress'd with so much wood towering above me in every
direction and such a continuance of it." Discomfited by that "very confined
prospect," she is thus a prototype neither for the Daniel Boones nor the Natty
Bumppos who sought out nature's most intimate embraces; nor does she
prefigure, like Thomas Godfrey, David Humphreys, and Timothy Dwight, the
assertive "improvements" of a westering nation. Instead, as she recorded in her
diary, "I began at last to conceit myself Attlass with the whole world upon my
shoulders. My spirits were condenc'd to nothing; my head began to ache and I
returned to town quite sick."[33]

In short, for Trist, any settlement, even the rudest, was to be preferred to
the stifling oppression of those dense and darkened woodlands that bore no
human markings. Even when she comes upon what "looks like a garden" in the
wilderness, with "a number of beautiful flowers and shrubs . . . [and] several
wild vegetables," she maintains, "I would give the preference to those that are
cultivated"; she then proceeds to catalogue those wild herbs which American
women, by this time, had made familiars in their home gardens: "Wild
Asparagus, Indian Hemp, shepherd sproats, lambs quarters, &cc."[34]

Accompanied only by a business associate of her husband's and a single
woman servant, Trist takes the difficult horseback traveling through treacherous
winter snows with surprising aplomb, never omitting comment, when she can, on
the "many delightful prospects" afforded by the countryside through which she
rides. From Philadelphia to Pittsburgh, her journey takes her through mountain

passes of breathtaking beauty and close to areas which are already identified with historical events. Trist misses neither, noting down Revolutionary War battle sites, forts from the French and Indian Wars and, always, giving some description of the local geography. Two days out of Carlisle, Pennsylvania, she notes "a very pretty creek that arises in the mountains and discharges itself into the Susquehanna," followed by the comment that "that country in the last war was the frontier." By 1784, however, "the account of former sufferings being continually harrassed by the Indians," provides only a subject of entertaining conversation from a pioneer couple now in their eighties who "have lived to see an end to them." Living happily with their son and his "house full of children," the family and their sitution together represent for Elizabeth Trist "a true picture of rural felicity."[35]

Until the spring thaws sufficiently melted the ice floes along the Ohio and Mississippi rivers, thus enabling her to continue her journey by boat, Trist spent the long winter—from January 9, through May 20th, 1784—in Pittsburgh. Her diary entries, during her last days in this fledgling frontier community, suggest that while the woods oppressed and entrapped her, the settlements upon their edges left her with a fear of yet another kind of isolation. "Upon the whole I like the situation of Pittsburgh mightily," she notes in a May entry, "and was there good Society I shou'd be contented to end my days in the Western country." Her final Pittsburgh entry is somewhat less sanguine, making clear that however attractive the countryside may have been, it was human society she required.*

As the Ohio takes her into the Mississippi and thence into more and more desolate and unsettled areas, her diary confirms her need for evidence of the human community, especially in terms of opened spaces. On June 17, 1784, she noted that "we pass'd two Glades the only clear land I have seen except where some person had been living." With navigation slowed by inclement weather, headwinds, and the sheer difficulty of maneuvering the treacherous river channels; and with almost every day rendered uncomfortable by gnats, mosquitoes, and diminishing stocks of food, Trist strives, in her daily jottings, to adjust the river and her increasingly distressful experience of it into some kind of verbally and experientially meaningful paradigm. What she finally designs is an image of the river that expresses her own bewilderment and discomfort, her growing sense of being where she does not belong.

> I have various ideas about this river. Some times conceit I am got to the far end of the world or rather that it is the last of Gods creation and the seventh day came before it was quite finish'd. At other times I fancy there has been some great revolution in nature and this great body of water has found a passage where it was not intended

---

*Trist's entry for May 20, 1784, reveals that had it not been for the occasional social events of the winter months, she "shou'd certainly have been very miserable" (pp. 11-12).

and tore up all before it. . . . Alltogether its appearance is awful and
Melancholy and sometimes terrific. (June 18th, 1784)

Again and again she records "violent headaches" and complains, "I can hardly
keep my self alive." "I am every day more anxious to be at the end of my
journey or voyage," she writes on June 28th.

But the end of her journey was not a happy one. Arriving at Natchez in
early July, she learned that her husband had died five months earlier, while she
was still in Pittsburgh. "The characteristic American gesture in the face of
adversity," suggests Richard Slotkin in his mammoth and provocative study,
Regeneration Through Violence, "is . . . immersion in the native element, the
wilderness, as the solution to all problems, the balm to all wounds of the soul,
the restorative for failing fortunes."[36] Slotkin's conclusions derive from a
wealth of materials mainly by men, however, and, as Trist's dairy entries make
abundantly clear, for women at this period the wilderness offered no such refuge.
Its woods had entrapped her in almost claustrophobic oppression, giving her
violent headaches; in all, the untamed frontier had too often deprived her of
the human community, and now it had taken from her what she most loved: her
little dog presumably eaten by crocodiles during the river passage and now her
husband dead while engaged in land speculations in the western territories.
Trist's response is not to immerse herself in the threatening element but, instead,
to return to her comfortable Virginia plantation, "Birdwood," where she lived
out the rest of her days.

To understand why, in spite of her appreciation for its beauties, Trist
found the frontier so threatening, while at the same time she could call the
ancient pioneer couple an emblem of "rural felicity" and even momentarily
contemplate a potential contentment at the prospect of ending her "days in the
Western country," we must first understand the pattern of her accommodation
to the landscape with which she was most familiar. Her later letters, written
from Virginia, perhaps provide the clue. In 1801, in a friendly letter to her
neighbor and then-President Jefferson, Trist describes a recent "dreadful hail
storm" from which "the Sky lights at Monticello I hear has not escaped." Her
own dwelling, happily, has "experienced no damage except the blowing down
of a few pannel of fence." What has saved it, she emphasizes, is neither its
grandeur nor its size, but instead its very humility: "I expected that our Cabbin
wou'd have been carried off by the Wind, but its humility not its strength
preserved it."[37] The facts of her social situation, however, belie the rhetoric
of her description. Both born and married into comfortable and well-connected
business and planting families, Elizabeth House Trist may not have enjoyed
the most luxurious dwelling in Virginia, but her home was far from what even
then would have been labeled merely a "Cabbin."

An analogous rhetorical ploy appears in a letter of 1762, written by Eliza
Lucas (now the widow of Charles Pinckney) to friends outside of London. Her
husband's death having precipitated her return to their estates in America, after
several years in England, Eliza described her home at the extensive Belmont
plantation on the Cooper River as "a little hovel." However ill-managed the

estates had been during her own and her husband's absence abroad, the gracious mansion at Belmont was hardly a "hovel." The context of the usage, however, suggests that the widow Pinckney was attempting to experience herself within a highly stylized, limited "middle landscape"—not unlike the one which Elizabeth Trist was to adopt some years later. Sharing with her corrrespondent a mutual pleasure in gardening, Mrs. Pickney goes on to call it "an innocent and delightful amusement." And it is in describing her own gardening activities that Belmont is reduced to a "hovel":

> I have a little hovel about 5 miles from town, quite in a forrest where I find much amusement 4 or 5 months in the year, and where I have room enough to exercise my Genius that way. . . . I am my self head gardener, and I believe work much harder than most principal ones do.

Except for the limited time allotted (she need be there only "4 or 5 months in the year"), the impression evoked by these lines is of a woman situated, under rather humble circumstances, upon a landscape neither wholly urban nor wild, but poised precariously between the two ("about 5 mile from town, quite in a forrest"); it is sufficiently circumscribed in extent to be called a garden and to permit a lone woman "to exercise my Genius" upon it. "We found it in [such] ruins when we arrived from England," she continues, "that I have had a wood to clear."[38] Again, the exaggeration is pointed: for while she is, in actuality, only clearing away the overgrowth of several years' neglect of already carefully manicured grounds, she prefers the more humble usage of a woman clearing a garden for herself in the midst of a somewhat-less-than-wild landscape.

It would appear, then, that what Leo Marx and others have termed "the middle landscape"—that is, that band of small but prospering farms and grazing lands newly wrested from the wilderness—suggested a design to which these women might easily accommodate themselves. Politically, of course, it implied the basis of democracy itself, in Jefferson's vision of a nation of small yeoman farmers. Imaginatively, it restored, on a real-world geography, classical pastoral's most cherished dreams of harmony and reconciliation. Indeed, as Marx so succinctly put it, "In the egalitarian social climate of America the pastoral ideal, instead of being contained by the literary design, spills over into thinking about real life."[39]

So compelling—or perhaps necessary—was this "spillage" that Trist, for one, applied certain components of its vocabulary with equal assurance not only to the ancient pioneer couple as "a true picture of rural felicity," but as well to her "Birdwood" plantation if Virginia. "Had we a more convenient establishment," she boasted in her letter to Jefferson, "as it is, I don't know that I wou'd exchange with any of you in the Grand City." After all, she explains, her "grain is flourishing," she and her family "have few temptations to extravagance," and, all in all, "we . . . enjoy good health and of course appetites to relish our homely fare."[40]

From this later perspective, the language of Trist's 1783-84 diary appears, at least in part, an attempt to project upon and elicit from the western frontier those images and associative patterns which had served her so well in Virginia. Whenever possible, Trist saw in the frontier landscapes the beginnings of Jeffersonian agrarianism and delighted in finding, even in the wild places, hints of the cultivated kitchen herb gardens that might one day replace them. Thus, the pioneer couple became a familiar eighteenth-century emblem of "rural felicity," the wilderness took on at least minimal civilized associations through the historical events with which it might be invested, and Trist herself, even if only momentarily, could contemplate ending her "days in the Western country." If, in fact, there was some possibility that she would be asked to relocate here, then she would transport to these alien realms a languagescape of accommodation—as so many women after her were to carry with them seeds and cuttings from more familiar landscapes.

Indeed, the two are not unrelated. For, by the term *languagescape* I intend an elaboration of Leo Marx's perception that, in America, pastoral had always represented not merely the classical "symbolic structure of thought and feeling," but, rather, "a landscape of mind in which the movement in physical space corresponds to a movement in consciousness."[41] In other words, in order for her to function effectively—be it in Virginia or in Pennsylvania—Elizabeth Trist required the intercession of a meaningful relational paradigm in and through which she might be usefully and comfortably located on either terrain. Since for Trist, as for other women, massive physical alteration of plantation and frontier alike seemed beyond personal possibility, the alternative was a fantasy projection honed not by force but by the transforming power of language: a languagescape. Where the quality of relation implied by the paradigm was experientially feasible, the women enjoyed all manner of rural felicities. Where, as in the dense woods, that metaphorical relationship broke down, like Trist, unable to wield "the keen adze" and thereby alter the landscape accordingly, many early pioneer women experienced themselves "condenc'd to nothing" and, when they could (again like Trist), they "returned to town."

The theoretical premise underpinning these observations applies equally, of course, to both men and women; that is, that our social actions or so-called "real-world" activity takes its form and acquires meaning in and through the paradigms in the actor's heads.[42] And, more specifically, that the "knowing" of, and hence meaningfilled activity upon, any landscape relates intimately to that relational, meaningmaking, and transformative device in language usually called metaphor. To understand the different accommodations made by men and women to the New World frontiers, then, is not to distinguish between these psycholinguistic processes themselves but, rather, to identify the different paradigms employed distinctively by each sex in those processes. Or, to put it still another way, we need to identify the distinctive metaphorical complexes exploited by each sex for naming and, thereby, knowing the landscape.

From the material offered here, it is not clear that women shared any particular single paradigm by which they might appropriate the landscape as their own; what is clear, however, is that they *were* appropriating it—if only in limited ways—and that at least the beginnings of several potentially interrelated patterns may be discerned. If men felt themselves offered a new-found Paradise, for example, women apparently preferred one of their own cultivation. Elizabeth Trist's delighted discovery of flowers and herbs growing wild, we recall, was qualified by its construction as a simile: not a fortuitously found Eden, but only "*like* a garden;" and her preferences were for those plants which she probably already grew at home. For Trist, as for Cornelia Greene, there was to be no rediscovered Eden, nor any fortuitously found Paradise in the New World.*

But then the young women educated in eighteenth-century England and America had never been trained to perceive "paradise" as a geographical terrain; for them, the word resonated with other meanings entirely. With a critical eye for "Popular Education" "in this *enlighten'd* age" of mid-nineteenth-century America, Eliza Carolina Burgwin (now Mrs. George C. Clitherall) wistfully recalled her own education, as a young girl in England, into the attitudes of pious domestic sentimentalism marking the previous century:

> The Education of females was very differently conducted in those times to what it is now. Providence in unerring wisdom has appointed to each Sex, their various duties in their various stations. . . . To man's more vigorous frame & intellect, Manual labor, and scientific pursuits were appropriated; whilst the office of gentle Woman, was *to render Home a Paradise*, by the strict enactment of her several domestic duties. (my emphasis)[43]

It was a familiar phrasing, signifying the sexual division of labor deemed appropriate even by those comparatively progressive teachers like Susanna Rowson, who taught her girls that it was their duty to create a "paradise at home."[44] The point here is not only that paradise implied different spheres of activity for men and for women, but it imaged qualitatively different spaces for those activities, also. For men it was a potential linguistic tool, with all its concomitant associations, for appropriating the vast extent of the new and unknown continent to human use (and, eventually, abuse). For women, it was from the first a term that denoted domesticity and the limited habitation of home. If the men altered the landscape to make it comply with their dreams of the pleasures, the bounty, and the receptivity of paradisal realms, the women patched guilts and embroidered bed hangings with brightly colored flowers and cultivated a nearby garden plot in order "to render Home a Paradise."

---

*Marx's discussion of Robert Beverley of Virginia, in *The Machine in the Garden*, p. 87, pinpoints "the distinction between two garden metaphors," one a wild, pre-lapserian Eden, the other cultivated and man-made. As Marx persuasively argues, pp. 84-85, the confusion and ambiguities in those competing schema plagued the initial settlement of Virginia. My point here is that the women appear to have avoided that ambiguity in their writings, having come down solidly for the cultivated and woman-made from the eighteenth century onwards.

An analogous delimitation of the potential sphere of activity also defines the ways in which women picked and chose among the available conventional pastoral dictions. For psychological reason too obvious to require analysis, women did not easily identify themselves (like Crevecoeur) as literal husbandmen to a virgin soil, nor (like Natty Bumppo) describe themselves seduced by the embracingly intimate enclosures of the dense forests. But this alone is not sufficient explanation for why their writings generally lacked expressions of passion or elation at their ability to alter or master the various New World landscapes. Nor does it explain why those women who *did* own or manage vast plantations might contemplate planting a grove, stocking a park, or designing a garden, but never (in the materials available) sought to contrive for themselves any full-blown Arcadia. Their decided preference for evoking an ungendered semi-rural terrain of humble yeoman farms suggests that, within this language-scape only, could they conceive a comprehensible realm of meaningful roles and activities for themselves. Here, within a confined—but already semi-civilized—space they might appropriately act as *gardener*, "an Innocent and delightful amusement," as Eliza Lucas Pinckney described it, or as *nurse* to "two Young Citron trees"; home, women's traditionally appropriate (and thus comfortable) sphere of activity, might thereby be projected out of doors and provide, in however limited a way, a means of accommodation to landscapes otherwise impervious to women's presence.

That this was neither a simple nor, by the end of the eighteenth century, a wholly successful process, the Elizabeth House Trist frontier diary makes clear. But it was, nonetheless, a necessary process—and one that would have to be accelerated in the next century as women crossed the Alleghenies in increasing numbers, taking with them not only cuttings and seeds from the gardens left behind but, more important still, the challenge to devise new symbolic solutions to the contradictions and disorders implied by the almost exclusive male mastery of the American languagescape. To survive, women needed to readjust and recast alternative relational paradigms for "the fairest, frutefullest, and pleasauntest [land] of all the worlde,"[45] and, finally, to assert their right to a language-scape of their own.

NOTES

1. Cornelia Greene, Cumberland Island, Georgia, to Margaret Cowper, Baron Hill Plantation, Rio Bueno, Jamaica, August 6, 1800, in Mackay-Stiles Papers, the Southern Historical Collection, University of North Caolina Library, Chapel Hill.

2. Pat. Tailfer, Hugh Anderson, Da. Douglas, and others, "A True and Historical Narrative of the Colony of Georgia, in America, From the First Settlement thereof until this present Period" (Charles Town, South Carolina, 1741), p. 18; p. x; p. 18; p. viii, in *Tracts and Other Papers, Relating Principally to the Origin, Settlement, And Progress of the Colonies in North America, From The Discovery Of The Country To The Year 1776*, comp. Peter Force (Washington, D.C., 1836), Vol. I. Henceforth cited as *Force's Tracts*; the various pamphlets and papers compiled here are individually paginated.

3. Robert Mountgomry, "A Discourse Concerning the design'd Establishment of a

New Colony to the South of Carolina, in the Most delightful Country of the Universe" (London, 1717), p. 6, in *Force's Tracts*, I.

4. See Annette Kolodny, *The Lay of the Land, Metaphor as Experience and History in American Life and Letters* (Chapel Hill: University of North Carolina Press, 1975), esp. p. 147.

5. Ibid. p. 11. See also John Seelye, *Prophetic Waters, The River in Early American Life and Literature* (New York: Oxford University Press, 1977), p. 11, for a similar interpretation of Columbus' letters; and Christopher Columbus, *Select Documents Illustrating the Four Voyages of Columbus*, trans. and ed. Cecil Jane (London: Hakluyt Society, 1930), Vol. I, p. 12.

6. David Humphreys, *A Poem on Industry* (Philadelphia, 1794), p. 20; quoted and analyzed in Cecilia Tichi's excellent "The American Revolution and the New Earth," *Early American Literature* 11, 2 (Fall 1976):206.

7. Timothy Dwight, *Travels in New England and New-York* (New Haven, 1822), Vol. II, pp. 140-41; again, see Tichi, p. 206.

8. Eliza Carolina (Burgwin) Clitherall Books, Typed Vol. I: Mss. vol. 4, typed p. 30, in "Eliza Clitherall Diary (1751-1860)," 17 mss. vols., the Southern Historical Collection, University of North Carolina Library, Chapel Hill. Notes here refer to Vol. I of the library's typescript, which comprises vols. 1-6 of the original manuscript diaries; this typescript is divided into separate sections, following the original diaries, each individually paged.

9. "Clitherall Diary," Typed Vol. I: Mss. vol. 4, typed p. 37.

10. "Clitherall Diary," Typed Vol. I:Mss. vol. 4, typed p. 31; p. 38.

11. Philip Vickers Fithian, *Journal and Letters of Philip Vickers Fithian, 1773-1744: A Plantation Tutor of the Old Dominion*, ed. Hunter Dickinson Farish (Williamsburg, Va.: Colonial Williamsburg, Inc., and Princeton, N.J.: Princeton University Press, 1943), p. 42; p. 59.

12. Ann Bradstreet, "Contemplations," orig. publ. posthumously in *Several Poems Compiled with Great Variety of Wit and Learning, Full of Delight* (Boston, 1678).

13. Greene to Cowper, October 10, 1800, in Mackay-Stiles Papers.

14. Eliza Lucas Pinckney, *The Letterbook of Eliza Lucas Pinckney, 1739-1762*, ed. Elise Pinckney (Chapel Hill: University of North Carolina Press, 1972), p. 8; according to n. 8, "Lucerne is an alfalfa. 'Casada' is probably *cassava*, a plant with a fleshy rootstock which was cultivated in the tropics where it was a staple food."

15. Ibid. p. 38; n. 52 explains that "the live oak was valued in shipbuilding."

16. Ibid., p. 7.

17. Ibid., pp. 35-36.

18. Ibid., p. 36.

19. Discussed in Annette Kolodny, *The Lay of the Land*, pp. 115-32; see also my " 'Stript, shorne and made deformed': Images on the Southern Landscape," *South Atlantic Quarterly* 75, 1 (Winter 1976): pp. 55-73.

20. See John Dixon Hunt, *The Figure in the Landscape: Poetry, Painting, and Gardening during the Eighteenth Century* (Baltimore: Johns Hopkins University Press, 1976).

21. Pinckney, *The Letterbook*, pp. 60-61.

22. Ibid., p. 36.

23. Greene to Cowper, October 10, 1800, in Mackay-Stiles Papers.

24. Fithian, p. 85; p. 105; p. 58.

25. See Fithian's indictment of local agricultural methods as "slovenly, without any regard to continue their Land in heart, for future Crops," p. 118.

26. See Everett Dick, *The Dixie Frontier: A Social History of the Southern Frontier from the First Transmontane Beginnings to the Civil War* (New York: Alfred A. Knopf, Inc.; rpt. Capricorn Books, 1964), p. 8.

27. Ibid., p. 53.

28. Quoted in Dick, *Dixie Frontier*, p. 3.

204 / Women and Language in Literature and Society

29. "Elizabeth House Trist Diary," in Mrs. Nicholas Trist Papers, the Southern Historical Collection, University of North Carolina Library, Chapel Hill, Typescript, p. 4. The 23-page typescript is divided into two sections: the first 12 pages are a running narrative, and the typescript here is paged; the last 11 pages, unpaged, are separately dated entries in the manner of a daily journal. Subsequent footnotes will refer only to page numbers from the first section; dated entries will be indicated in the text.

30. Trist, p. 10; p. 11.

31. Thomas Godfrey, *Juvenile Poems* (Philadelphia, 1765), p. 20; also quoted in Howard Mumford Jones, *O Strange New World, American Culture: The Formative Years* (London: Chatto and Windus, 1965), p. 356.

32. Humphreys, *A Poem on Industry*, p. 7.

33. Trist, p. 11.

34. Trist, p. 10.

35. Trist, p. 2.

36. Richard Slotkin *Regeneration Through Violence: The Mythology of the American Frontier, 1600-1860* (Middletown, Ct.: Wesleyan University Press, 1973), p. 267.

37. Elizabeth House Trist to (President) Thomas Jefferson, June 13, 1801, in Nicholas Philip Trist Papers, the Southern Historical Collection, University of North Carolina Library, Chaptel Hill.

38. Pinckney, *The Letterbook*, p. 185.

39. Leo Marx, *The Machine in the Garden: Technology and the Pastoral Ideal in America* (New York: Oxford University Press, 1964), p. 130.

40. Trist to Jefferson, June 13, 1801, in Nicholas Philip Trist Papers.

41. Leo Marx, "Pastoral Ideals and City Troubles," *Journal of General Education* 20, 4 (January 1969): 263.

42. See Victor Turner, *Dramas, Fields, and Metaphors: Symbolic Action in Human Society* (Ithaca: Cornell University Press, 1974), p. 13; this is also the controlling thesis of my *The Lay of the Land*, esp. pp. 148-60.

43. "Clitherall Diary," Typed Vol. I: Mss. vol. 3, typed p. 15; p. 14.

44. Susanna Rowson, "Rights of Women" in *Miscellaneous Poems* (Boston: Gilbert and Dean, 1804), p. 100. For evidence that this poem was composed earlier than its publication date and contained much of Mrs. Rowson's pedagogical theory, see Dorothy Weil, *In Defense of Women: Susanna Rowson (1762-1824)* (University Park: Pennsylvania State University Press, 1976), p. 49.

45. Richard Hakluyt, "Discourse of Western Planting . . . 1584," in *The Original Writings and Correspondence of the Two Richard Hakluyts*, ed. E. G. R. Taylor, 2d ser. (London: Hakluyt Society, 1935), Vol. 77, p. 222.

14

THE SILENCE IS BROKEN

Josephine Donovan

Had she been born in 1827, Dorothy Osborne would have written
novels; had she been born in 1527, she would never have written at
all. but she was born in 1627, and at that date though writing books
was ridiculous for a woman there was nothing unseemingly in writing
a letter. And so by degrees the silence is broken . . .
                                                      —Virginia Woolf [1]

Had Shakespeare had a sister of equal genius, she would not have written
masterpieces. In all likelihood, as Virginia Woolf pointed out in *A Room of
One's Own*, she would never have written a line. Yet roughly two centuries
later women were creating masterworks of prose fiction. Indeed, women so
dominated the early history of the novel that it was thought to be a "female
thing."[2] My interest here is to examine some of the possible explanations for
women's rapid move from relative literary obscurity into the limelight of literary
production, an abrupt shift accomplished in a few hundred years.

Let us begin with Shakespeare's hypothetical sister: we know that she
would have been denied access to training in the Latin rhetorical tradition,
which at this time was a *sine qua non* for the construction of critically acceptable *oeuvres*. However "small" Shakespeare's Latin is claimed to be, and however "lesse" his Greek, he nevertheless was thoroughly initiated into that
tradition. T. W. Baldwin has exhaustively demonstrated the extent of Shakespeare's classical education by examining the Grammar School curriculum to
which young males of the period were exposed.[3] While there is no record of
which school Shakespeare attended, or if he attended any school, there is overwhelming evidence of such training in the plays themselves. Shakespeare was, in
short, exposed to the Latin rhetorical patterns of such authors as Cato, Terence,
Ovid, Virgil, Horace and Seneca, as well as to the classic ancient authorities

on rhetoric such as the author of the *Ad Herennium*, Cicero, and Quintilian. With a few minor exceptions most of the major English writers up to the eighteenth century (that is, up to Defoe and Richardson) received a similar training. Shakespeare's sister, however, would have been denied access to this tradition for girls were not permitted into the Latin schools.

Walter J. Ong characterized the Latin schooling system, as it developed through the Middle Ages, as a male initiation rite. In an article entitled "Latin Language Study As A Renaissance Puberty Rite," Ong notes how from roughly 500 to 700 A.D. Latin no longer functioned as a vernacular spoken language. Instead a split occurred between spoken Latin, which eventually developed into the modern romance languages, and written Latin, or what Ong calls Learned Latin.

> Learned Latin, which moved only in artificially controlled channels *through the male world of the schools*, was no longer anyone's mother tonque, in a quite literal sense. Although from the sixth or eighth century to the nineteenth Latin was spoken by millions of persons, *it was never used by mothers cooing to their children.*[4]

Latin had become a male, public language, which existed only within the academic institutions. Women could only learn vernaculars and for centuries were denied access to the world of formal, public communication (including literature). As Ong notes, until the nineteenth century learning Latin meant entrance into the male educated elite. Latin had become a *"sex-linked language, a kind of badge of masculine identity."*[5]

> Under these circumstances learning Latin took on the characteristics of a puberty rite, a *rite de passage* or initiation rite: it involved isolation from the family, *the achievement of identity in a totally male group* (the school), the learning of a body of relatively abstract tribal lore inaccessible to those outside the group. . . . The Latin world was a man's world.[6]

Intellectual education for women was scanty at best until the nineteenth century. Eileen Power notes that while there may have been some attendance by girls at elementary schools up through the fifteenth century, this practice, especially in England, was not widespread. Nor was the curriculum extensive.[7] While women of the middle class were often literate in the vernacular, it is only among the aristocracy or indeed in courtly circles that an occasional woman received a formal, classical education.

It is true, however, that treatises favoring the education of women began appearing with some regularity from the early Renaissance on. Christine de Pisan (1364-1430), for example, issued her treatise on the education of women in the early fifteenth century. Renaissance humanists such as More, Erasmus, and Vives also favored education for women, but none of them really conceived of female education as being truly equal to the male. For, as Diane Valeri Bayne points out, while they

> take exception to the contemporary beliefs by asserting women's capability for learning, [they] were traditional in judging the domestic role as the only one which women, educated or not, were suited to play. Thus, the curriculum suggested by Vives for girls is considerably less than that recommended for boys.[8]

In her *Doctrine for the Lady of the Renaissance* Ruth Kelso also emphasizes that the education for women—even of the leisure class—was primarily designed to make them entertaining wives and good mothers.[9]

Nevertheless, education of women of the courtly class at least became an ideal in the Renaissance. And in rare cases where women were highly educated they did in fact produce works of literature which were considered critically acceptable. One good example is Louise Labé (1526?-1566), a poet of the "School of Lyons," whose father decided to educate her "à la mode italienne," which meant a regimen almost equal to male education, including training in Latin and Greek.[10] Her sonnet sequence, still considered a significant classic of French literature, was modeled upon Petrarch's but is rhetorically considerably less artificial than his, with fewer elaborate conceits and with a more direct, fresh, and therefore seemingly more authentic description of experience.[11]

In England the situation was similar to that on the continent. As Myra Reynolds notes,

> Learning was a kind of high-class individual accomplishment purely for home consumption. . . . [It] belonged only to the daughters of the nobility or of the very rich. Even within these bounds it was sporadic.*

The importance of training in Latin rhetoric eventually diminished as a result of philosophical shifts that occurred in the sixteenth and seventeenth centuries. The gradual and highly complex transition from the classical-medieval world-view to the modern involved among other things an increasing de-emphasis

---

*Myra Reynolds, *The Learned Lady in England 1650-1760* (Boston: Houghton Mifflin, 1920), p. 427. Indeed, those rare pieces of secular literature created by women before the late seventeenth century were written by women of the upper or courtly class, as, for example, in England, Lady Elizabeth Tanfield Carey (1585-1639) or Lady Mary Sidney Wroth, the Countess of Montgomery (fl. 1621). For other examples, see *The Female Spectator, English Women Writers before 1800*, ed. Mary R. Mahl and Helene Koon (Old Westbury: The Feminist Press, 1977).

One study shows that even in the nineteenth century only 20 percent of women writers had any sort of formal schooling. See Elaine Showalter, *A Literature of Their Own* (Princeton: Princeton University Press, 1977), pp. 40-41.

upon "looking to the ancients" for models in form and style. At the same time there developed an increasing focus upon the self and the powers of the individual imagination as the source of aesthetic truth.

The novel could only emerge after this philosophical groundwork had been laid. Only in a post-Cartesian world would a form like the novel have legitimacy. This is because the novel asserts the value of the experience of one individual. The experiential details of everyday life have become legitimate sources of verification (as opposed to citations gleaned from Latin *auctores*).

Pointing to Descartes' determination "to accept nothing on trust," Ian Watt notes in his study of the novel that the *Discourse on Method* (1637) paved the way for "the modern assumption whereby the pursuit of truth is conceived of as a wholly individual matter, *logically independent of the tradition of past thought . . .".*[12]

> The novel is the form of literature which most fully reflects this individualistic and innovating reorientation. Previous literary forms had reflected the general tendency of their cultures to make conformity to traditional practice the major test of truth: . . . the merits of the author's treatment were judged largely according to a view of literary decorum derived from the accepted models in the genre. This literary traditionalism was first and most fully challenged by the novel, whose primary criterion was truth to individual experience. . . .[13]

The epistemological shift toward empirical observation and induction that occurred in the seventeenth century thus provided a philosophical justification for the new genre.

From the beginning there had been an association of women with the sentimental novel, both as readers and as writers. As Michael Danahy suggests, this association relied upon stereotypes of what is the feminine.* In France, it stemmed from the assumption that women are authorities on love, an emotion that played a central role in the French novelistic tradition.[14] In England too vast numbers of sentimental novels were written and read by women, especially in the eighteenth century.[15]

Mrs. Eliza Haywood, one of the most popular of these sentimental novelists of the early eighteenth century, explained why as a writer she was drawn to the new form:

> But as I am a Woman, and consequently depriv'd of those Advantages of Education which the other Sex enjoy, I cannot . . . ima-

---

*Michael Danahy, "Le roman est-il chose femelle?" p. 91. Danahy also suggests, however, that the novel was more accessible to women than other forms of literature such as drama where "social and moral prohibitions" tended to exclude them, or even poetry, rooted as it was in oral and religious traditions which were preeminently male (p. 93).

gine it in my Power to soar to any Subject higher than that which
Nature is not negligent to teach us.
Love is a topick which I believe few are ignorant of; there requires
no aids of Learning. . . . [16]

Haywood's statement suggests that it was a lack of education rather than any
particular affinity with sentiment that led women to dwell upon feeling in their
fiction.

But there is another reason why women writers should have gravitated to
the novel. It was a new form, not known in antiquity. Therefore, there were
really no classical models nor critical rules that one would have to know in
order to practice its writing. As early as 1594 Torquato Tasso remarked how
women favored new forms (in this case, the heroic romance) and defended them
against the classicists.[17]

To be sure there were attempts to appropriate classical models for the
novel. Dr. Johnson called it a "comedy of romance," thus returning to an
Aristotelian genre, the comedy. Henry Fielding called the novel "a comic epic
in prose," thus returning to another Aristotelian genre, the epic. But these
attempts were strained, and ultimately unsuccessful. Critical judgments on the
novel could not be rooted in ancient authority.

The novel broke with classical doctrine in another important way. It
violated the concept of the separation of styles. For, according to classical
rhetorical doctrine the domestic world was not considered appropriate matter
for serious or "high" literary attention. Comedy was the form appropriate for
the everyday "bourgeois" world (women's world) and the style appropriate for
comedy was the low style.

The novel, therefore, according to classical doctrine, could not be considered an important, "high" work of literature, because it dealt with common,
everyday matters and in the "plain style." The persistence of this prejudice
against the novel may be seen in an observation made by LeSage in 1715 regarding the literary taste of his epoch with its marked preference for classical genres.

At that time they read almost nothing but serious pieces. Comedies
were scorned. They thought the best comedy or the brightest, most
ingenious novel a feeble production unworthy of praise. Whereas the
slightest serious work—an ode, an eclogue, a sonnet—was considered
the highest effort of the human spirit.*

Ironically, this attitude kept male writers of the educated elite from
appropriating the novel as "theirs." This meant that even though critically

---

*As cited in Georges May, *Le Dilemme du roman au XVIIIe siècle*, p. 6 (my translation). The sonnet is not, of course, a classical genre, but it was nevertheless by this time
considered "high" literature.

disparaged, it was nevertheless a genre which women and other cultural outsiders (less well-educated men) were free to use.

The freedom which the novelist enjoyed meant that s/he could borrow or invent techniques taken from everyday life (which was of course the primary source for the subject matter of the novel, as well). A good example of an important novelistic technique which did not have a classical antecedent is the epistolary convention. As Mme de Staël remarked: "the ancients would never have thought of giving their fiction such a form [because it] always presupposes more sentiment than action."[18]

This technique developed in part from what had become a popular feminine pastime in the late seventeenth century, "amateur" letter writing.[19] While the familiar letter was a classical genre, the prototype of which was Cicero's *Epistulae ad Familiares* (still a model for schoolboys in the seventeenth century), the form had been considerably bowdlerized by a series of letter-writing manuals written in the 1600s. These provided correspondents with models of letters and style to be used in stock situations.[20] Because of these models it was no longer necessary to receive formal rhetorical training in order to write acceptable, if informal, prose.

Samuel Richardson, one of the earliest English novelists, had in fact been commissioned by two booksellers to compose a letter-writing manual. This apparently gave him the idea of using the epistolary convention in *Pamela* (1740). He eventually published the manual as *Letters Written To and For Particular Friends* in 1741. Richardson himself was not formally educated. Ellen Moers suggests that it was probably his own status as a cultural outsider that led him to identify with women as a class.[21] This status might also explain his willingness to use a nontraditional style and genre. For, as Watt points out, the use of the letter-writing style permitted Richardson to "break with the traditional decorums of prose,"[22] a move which may have been a conscious and deliberate one on Richardson's part.

> There is at least a strong suggestion in *Clarissa* that he regarded his own literary style style as infinitely superior to those of the classically educated. . . . Anna Howe [a character in *Clarissa*] tells us that '*mere* scholars' too often 'spangle over their productions with *metaphors*; they rumble into *bombast*: the *sublime* with them, lying in *words* and not in sentiment'; while others 'sinking into the classical pits, there poke and scramble about never seeking to show genius of their own.'[23]

Pamela itself became a model for the "familiar" style—a mode emulated by Fanny Burney, the first important female novelist in England, in her first novel, *Evelina* (1778). Burney has Evelina's mentor enjoin her against writing letters which are "correct, nicely grammatical, and run in smooth periods." Rather he urges her to "dash away, whatever comes uppermost. . . ."[24] Jane Austen also used the epistolary convention in *Eleanor and Marianne*, a precursor of her first published novel, *Sense and Sensibility*.

Many of the English women prose writers of the seventeenth century are known for their correspondence. The first English woman whose letters were preserved and eventually published was Lady Brilliana Harley (1600-1643). Other notable female letter-writers of the period include: Margaret Lucas Cavendish, the Duchess of Newcastle (1624-1674), Katherine Fowler Philips (1631-1664), Dorothy Osborne (Temple) (1627-1695), Aphra Behn (1640-1689) (known primarily for her plays and novels), and somewhat later, Lady Mary Wortley Montagu (1689-1762). Of these only Cavendish's works were substantially published in her lifetime.* Most of the others were not published until the nineteenth century.

The unseemliness of a woman daring to publish in the seventeenth century is signaled to us in the dismay expressed by Katherine Philips when an unauthorized edition to her poems was published in 1664:

> To me . . . who never writ any line in my life with any inten-
> tion to have it printed. . . . This is a most cruel accident, and
> hath made so proportionate an impression upon me, that really it
> hath cost me a sharp fit of sickness since I heard it.[25]

The Duchess of Newcastle, however, was considerably less coy on the subject of publication than the others. "All I desire," she is said to have remarked, "is fame."[26] This is undoubtedly one of the reasons she was dubbed "Mad Madge" by her contemporaries.

The other major secular prose writing done by English women in the seventeenth century was the autobiography or memoir. Here again we see a transitional genre, one that is fundamentally private or family-oriented, but which provides an experience in writing that is not far removed from the experience of writing a novel. The earliest novels, those of Defoe, for example, follow an essentially autobiographical pattern:

> [Defoe's] total subordination of the plot to the pattern of the
> autobiographical memoir is as defiant an assertion of the primacy
> of individual experience in the novel as Descartes' *cogito ergo sum*
> was in philosophy.[27]

The earliest extant autobiography in English was written by a woman, Margery Kempe (ca. 1373). Since she was illiterate, this work was dictated. Women writers of the seventeenth century who produced memoirs and auto-biographies include: Alice Thornton (1627-1707); the Duchess of Newcastle;

---

*Cavendish's letters were probably written for publication; indeed, they were probably fictitious, as Delores Palomo demonstrated in her paper, "Margaret Cavendish and the Letter Essay," presented at the Modern Language Association convention, 1977. Cavendish did not, however, follow the Ciceronian epistolary form but rather pioneered the informal epistolary essay.

Mary Boyle, Countess of Warwick (1624-1678); Lucy Apsley, Mrs. Hutchinson (1620- ?); Ann Harrison, Lady Fanshawe (1625-1680); Martha, Lady Giffard (1639-1722), and Mary De la Riviere Manley (1663-1724).

Women had in letter-writing, and the autobiography or memoir, genres which were not subject to critical censure, because they were not published. The emergence of the novel, in part from these semi-private genres, gave women a nontraditional form with which to work and relieved them of the fear of not living up to classical doctrine. By the mid-eighteenth century even critics were no longer judging according to classical rules. As Fielding remarked, critics were permitted to practice "without knowing one word of the ancient laws."[28]

The demise of classical authority was encouraged by the gradual replacement of literary patrons by capitalist booksellers as the primary source of remuneration for writers. Booksellers who themselves had little or no classical training and who were interested primarily in marketing to a large audience were not concerned about classical doctrine. They were in fact quite willing to pander to a reading public that was by the turn of the seventeenth century predominately female. The market was such that a periodical completely devoted to women's interests appeared in 1692, the *Ladies Mercury*. Booksellers also quickly discerned the "profitable connection between women and sentimental-epistolary fiction,"[29] the other genre dominated by women writers in the eighteenth century.

The breakdown of classical control over literature and the emergence of a nontraditional genre like the novel were therefore developments favorable to an out-group like women. No longer could educational conditions force them to automatic literary exile, for they, as well as any male, had access to the experiential details of daily life and therefore access to resources of legitimate literary expression.

Women were in fact in an ideal situation—the center of the family—to observe the everyday details of domestic life which became prime matter for the English "indoor" novel. And, since by the end of the century it was no longer expected that this "matter" be conveyed through a Ciceronian medium, through the "grand style," women could write in a vernacular close to the style in which they spoke without fear of critical chastisement.

There is considerable debate as to the exact reasons for the transition to the "plain style," and indeed as to when it occurred. The authority on the subject, Morris Croll, viewed the change as a "battle" that occurred during the late sixteenth and seventeenth centuries out of which the "plain style" emerged "triumphant." On one side of the battle lines were the traditionalists who favored a Ciceronian or "grand" or "Asiatic" style.[30] John Lily's *Euphues* and Sidney's *Arcadia* exemplify this style. On the other side were the anti-Ciceronians, Montaigne, Bacon, who adopted a more conversational, less artificial form of rhetoric. Croll thus dated the emergence of the new "modern" style at 1600.

Croll's views have been disputed by R. F. Jones who maintained that the term "anti-Ciceronian" is a misnomer, as it implies a reversion to the anti-Ciceronian authors of antiquity, namely Seneca and Tacitus, as models; instead, he asserted, the proponents of the plain style were in fact primarily under the influence of the new scientific epistemology, the Baconian "new philosophy," and were not looking to the ancients for models.[31] Jones dated the triumph of the new style at around 1660.

From our perspective the Jones date seems the more credible. For it is only around the time of the Restoration that women writers (specifically Margaret Cavendish and Dorothy Osborne) began to write in a consciously plain style. Margaret Cavendish's biographer notes a stylistic transition in her works from the fancifully original style of her early work to the "flatter, cautious . . . ordinary"[32] prose of her later writing (late 1660s to early 1670s).

While her style had never been Latinate and her preference had always been for "the natural and most usual way of speaking,"[33] she was nevertheless directly affected by the growing predisposition among scientific writers toward a simple style. Thomas Sprat had articulated this tendency in 1667 when he called for the use of a plain simple prose in scientific treatises in his *History of the Royal Society*.

One feature of the new style was the "loose period." It stands opposed to the Ciceronian rounded period, which implied a closed, "circular" or syllogistic logic, congenial to a worldview which rested upon a closed system of verities, and therefore upon a closed circle of initiates or cultural insiders. This was the design of all ancient and medieval societies, which were rigidly class-structured and which rested upon an educated elite of males. The "loose period," on the other hand, attempted

> to express . . . the order in which an idea presents itself when it is first experienced. It begins, therefore, without premeditation, stating its idea in the first form that occurs; the second member is determined by the situation in which the mind finds itself after the first has been spoken; and so on throughout the period. Each member being an emergency of the situation.[34]

Such a stylistic method implies an inductive, empiric logic, appropriate to seventeenth century European society, which had shifted toward the experientially verifiable and away from received premises as the source of truth. It also implies a spontaneous, unpracticed quality, which when valued, obviates the necessity for formal rhetorical training. Again, women as cultural outsiders stood to benefit from this kind of stylistic shift. For in the epistolary style, as in the loose period, "everything was subordinated to the aim of expressing the ideas passing in the mind at the moment of writing."[35] That the "dashaway" epistolary style with its "breathless, disorganized 'artless' informality"[36] became identified as a female style is not surprising.

Margaret Cavendish, interestingly enough, anticipated the rationale for the "artless" style nearly a century before it found expression in Richardson's novels. A collection of her poems published in 1653 included this critical prescription:

> Give me the style that Nature frames, not art,
> For art doth seem to take the pedant's part;
> And what seems noble, which is easy, free,
> Not to be bound with o'er-nice pedantry.[37]

While it would not be wholly accurate to assume a continuing tradition among women writers of a less artificial rhetoric than male writers, there are nevertheless several critical statements made by women writers over the centuries which suggest at least a preference for the *genus humile.* This preference may well have been the result of women's historical lack of access to formal training in rhetoric.*

We find, for example, that a woman named "Jane Anger" (presumably a pseudonym) wrote a feminist critique of John Lily in 1589.† In this tract Anger gave strong criticism of the artificial, Euphuistic style of her opponent's work, asserting that it was characteristically male.

> The desire that every man has to show his true vein in writing is unspeakable, and their minds are so carried away with the manner, as no care at all is had of the matter. They run so into rhetoric as often times they overrun the bounds of their own wits and go they know not whither.[38]

Less than a century later Dorothy Osborne (Temple) also urged the adoption of the plain style, and disdained artificial circumlocution. Significantly, her comments came in defense of letter-writing, a predominantly feminine genre which provided women with a useful apprenticeship in "amateur" writing before it was acceptable for them to be professional writers.

> All letters, methinks, should be free and easy as one's discourse; not studied like an oration, nor made up of hard words like a charm. 'Tis an admirable thing to see how some people will labour to find out terms that may obscure a plain sense, like a

---

*Indeed, it has been suggested that the entire tradition of English prose was initiated by two women (Margery Kempe and Julian of Norwich) because they were not comfortable with Latin composition. See Robert Karl Stone, "Middle English Prose Style: Margery Kempe and Julian of Norwich" (Ph.D. diss. Univ. of Illinois, 1962). pp. 2-3.

†Helen Andrews Kahin suggests that the work in question is Lily's *Euphues his Censure to Philautus*, which includes much misogynist material. See her "Jane Anger and John Lily," *Modern Language Quarterly* 8 (March 1947): 31-35.

gentleman I knew, who would never say 'the weather grew cold,' but that 'winter begins to salute us.' I have no patience for such coxcombs, and cannot blame an old uncle of mine that threw the standish at his man's head because he writ a letter for him where instead of saying . . . 'that he would have writ himself, but that he had gout in his hand' he said 'that the gout would not permit him to put pen to paper'. . . . 39

At about the same time the Duchess of Newcastle attempted to deflect critical censure of her style in her Preface to the *Sociable Letters* (published in 1664). She attributes her lapses to a lack of education, but asserts that the style or "wordative part" is not important; what matters is the content.

> They may say some Words are not Exactly Placed, which I confess to be very likely, and not only in that, but in all the rest of my Works there may be such Errors, for I was not Bred in an University, or a Free-School, to learn the Art of Words; neither do I take it for a Disparagement of my Works, to have the Forms, Terms, Words, Numbers, or Rhymes found fault with . . . for I leave the Formal, or Wordative part to Fools, and the Material or Sensitive part to Wise men.*

A century later we find Mary Wollstonecraft in her introduction to *A Vindication of the Rights of Women* (1792) consciously rejecting Ciceronian rhetoric, opting again for the plain style which she feels is appropriate to a work which urges that women be seen as rational agents rather than foppish supernumeraries.

> I shall disdain to cull my phrases or polish my style. I aim at being useful, and sincerity will render me unaffected; for wishing rather to persuade by the force of my argument than dazzle by the

---

*Margaret Cavendish, "The Preface," *CCXI Sociable Letters* (London: William Wilson, 1664; reprint ed. Menston: The Scholar Press, 1969). Significantly, the Duchess also rejects the heroic or gallant epistolary style, which had become somewhat faddish—especially in France.

> These Letters are an Intimation of a Personal Visitation and Conversation, which I think is Better (I am sure more profitable) than those Conversations that are an Imitation of Romancial Letters, which are but Empty Words, and Vain Compliments (Preface).

(See also Letters XXI, LXXXI).

See *The Novel in Letters*, ed. Würzbach, for a selection of romantic epistles of the period. The prototype of this genre was the *Lettres portugaises* (1667), allegedly written by a nun to her lover. The romanesque mode seems to have been established in France (with La Calprenède's and Mlle. de Scudery's mid-century novels setting the fashion). Before and during the Restoration the heroic romance crossed the channel; its influence can be seen in writers like Aphra Behn and Mary Manley.

elegance of my language, I shall not waste my time in rounding periods, or in fabricating the turgid bombast of artificial feelings. . . . I shall try to avoid . . . flowery diction. . . .[40]

A number of very specific historical developments explain why women were unable to compete in the construction of literary masterworks until the nineteenth century. Shakespeare's sister would have been denied access to Latin rhetorical training and hence to the symbolic tools with which to create public art. Only when the Latin influence had weakened, when serious prose was being written in the vernaculars, in a nontraditional form, and only after the rhetoric of the home and of the forum had once again merged could women hope to have equal access to the means of literary creation.

Since women had been excluded from the educated elites until this time and since their premises had never been included in the closed circle of knowledge that dominated Western culture for centuries, it is not surprising that few women produced cultural works. However, once epistemological assumptions had shifted so as to allow a literary legitimacy to nontraditional modes, and new conceptions of reality, women were in a position to put forth their own works of literature.

In the mid-seventeenth century women writers like Dorothy Osborne and Margaret Cavendish are at a kind of intermediate stage. They are writing in semiprivate genres, but they *are* writing—in the vernacular and for the most part in the plain style which is beginning to "triumph"—perhaps indeed because of them. From 1660 to 1800 women wrote more than one-third of the published works of prose fiction in English.* By the end of the eighteenth century women novelists predominated; they were writing "the better novels" of the time.†

From the first English women who began to appropriate the means of literary production for themselves, Osborne and Cavendish, to Jane Austen stretches a little more than a century. Three to four generations of women writers learning to master the trade passed between. But without their prac-

---

The New Cambridge Bibliography of English Literature, 2 (1660-1800), ed. George Watson (Cambridge: University Press, 1971), col. 975-1014, lists approximately 760 entries of "minor fiction." Of these 265 works, or approximately 35 percent of the total, were written by women. Many other authors are anonymous; these may well have been women. By the end of the eighteenth century at least half the entries are works by women. The total number of entries (760) represents a selection of roughly one-fifth the total published prose fiction of the period 1660-1800. A majority of the 760 entries in the *New Cambridge Bibliography* are sentimental novels in the epistolary mode.

†Harrison Steeves, *Before Jane Austen*, pp. 330, 362. Of the standard histories of the early novel only Steeves gives serious attention to the emergence of the female novelists. Other works consulted and not mentioned elsewhere include Arnold Kettle, *An Introduction to the English Novel* Vol. I; 2nd ed. (London: Hutchinson & Co., 1967); Walter Allen, *The English Novel, A Short Critical History* (New York: Dutton, 1955); Edward Wagenknecht, *Cavalcade of the Novel* (New York: Holt, Rinehart & Winston, 1954).

tice, without their having taken advantage of women's newly achieved access to the materials of the trade, we might never have had a Jane Austen, a Charlotte Brontë, a George Eliot, or indeed, a Virginia Woolf.

NOTES

1. Virginia Woolf, "Dorothy Osborne's *Letters,*" *Collected Essays* (London: Chatto & Windus, 1967), 3:60.
2. To borrow from Michael Danahy's recent article on the subject, "Le roman est-il chose femelle?" *Poetique* 25 (1976):85-106.
3. T. W. Baldwin, *William Shakespere's Small Latine & Lesse Greeke* (Urbana: University of Illinois, 1944). See especially Vol. I, ch. 22-30; Vol. 2, ch. 31-50.
4. Walter J. Ong, S. J., *The Presence of the Word* (New Haven: Yale University Press, 1967), pp. 250-51 (my emphasis). I would like to acknowledge Barbara Nauer who suggested this and other readings to me and who encouraged me to write an earlier version of this article.
5. Ibid., p. 250 (my emphasis).
6. Ibid., p. 251 (my emphasis).
7. Eileen Power, *Medieval Women* (Cambridge: Cambridge University Press, 1975), p. 84.
8. Diane Valeri Bayne, "Richard Hyrde and the More Circle," *Moreana* 12, no. 45 (Feb 1975):13.
9. Ruth Kelso, *Doctrine for the Lady of the Renaissance* (Urbana: University of Illinois Press, 1956). See especially ch. 4, "Studies."
10. Dorothy O'Connor, *Louise Labé, sa vie et son oeuvre* (Paris: Les presses francaises, 1926), p. 54.
11. I have detailed the evidence for this assertion in "The Love Sonnets of Louise Labé," unpub. article. See below for further discussion of women's inclination toward a less artificial rhetoric.
12. Ian Watt, *The Rise of the Novel, Studies in Defoe, Richardson and Fielding* (Berkeley: University of California Press, 1957), p. 13 (my emphasis).
13. Ibid., p. 13.
14. See Georges May, *Le Dilemme du roman au XVIIIe siècle* (New Haven: Yale University Press, 1963), especially ch. 8, "Féminisme et roman," for a discussion of the French connection between women and the novel.
15. See Harrison Steeves, *Before Jane Austen, The Shaping of the English Novel in the Eighteenth Century* (New York: Holt, Rinehart & Winston, 1965), pp. 161-62, and below, note 49.
16. Dedication to *The Fatal Secret* (1724), as cited in Robert Adams Day, *Told in Letters, Epistolary Fiction Before Richardson* (Ann Arbor: University of Michigan, 1966), p. 81.
17. Torquato Tasso, "Discourses on the Heroic Poem," *Literary Criticism From Plato to Dryden*, ed. Allan H. Gilbert (Detroit: Wayne University Press, 1962), p. 465.
18. As cited in Watt, *The Rise of the Novel*, p. 176.
19. Ibid., p. 193.
20. Nathalie Wurzbach, ed., *The Novel in Letters* (London: Routledge & Kegan Paul, 1969), pp. xiii-xiv. See also Day, ch. 4.
21. Ellen Moers, *Literary Women* (Garden City: Doubleday, 1977), p. 175. Frederick R. Karl, *The Adversary Literature: The English Novel in the Eighteenth Century, A Study in Genre* (New York: Farrar, Strauss & Giroux, 1974) also notes this identification, p. 130, n. 1.
22. Watt, *The Rise of the Novel* p. 194.
23. Ibid., p. 194.

24. Moers, *Literary Women*, p. 97.

25. As cited in Reynolds, *The Learned Lady in England*, p. 58.

26. As cited in Woolf, "The Duchess of Newcastle," *Collected Essays*, 3:51.

27. Watt, *The Rise of the Novel*, p. 15.

28. Ibid., p. 58.

29. Day, *Told in Letters*, p. 76.

30. Morris Croll, *Style, Rhetoric and Rhythm, Essays*, ed. J. Max Patrick, Robert O. Evans, John M. Wallace, and R. J. Schoek (Princeton: Princeton University Press, 1966), p. 68.

31. Jones' views are summarized in Robert Adolph, *The Rise of Modern Prose Style* (Cambridge: MIT Press, 1968), pp. 4-5; 19-20.

32. Douglas Grant, *Margaret the First* (Toronto: University of Toronto Press, 1957), p. 211.

33. *Natural Pictures*, p. c5^V, as cited in Grant, p. 210.

34. Croll, *Style, Rhetoric and Rhythm*, p. 224.

35. Watt, *The Rise of the Novel*, p. 194.

36. Moers, *Literary Women*, p. 97.

37. As cited in Grant, *Margaret the First*, p. 127.

38. Jane Anger, "Protection for Women," *by a Woman writt*, ed. Joan Goulianos (Indianapolis: Bobbs-Merrill, 1973), p. 24.

39. *The Love Letters of Dorothy Osborne to Sir William Temple*, ed. Israel Hollancz (London: De La More Press, 1903), p. 146.

40. Mary Wollstonecraft, *A Vindication of the Rights of Women* (Baltimore: Penguin, 1975), p. 82.

PART IV

READING
WOMEN WRITING

INTRODUCTION TO PART FOUR

As writers and as readers, we interact with a linguistic medium and a literary tradition. The processes of these interactions and the products they create must be approached from a variety of methodological and theoretical viewpoints. From literary history to textual analysis, from investigation of authorial viewpoint to the expression of a reading practice, each perspective brings new questions into focus and enlarges the context of inquiry into women and literature.

Women first learned to write about their experiences and about themselves in diaries and letters. Working with unpublished letters and diaries, Annette Kolodny showed in "Honing a Habitable Languagescape," Part III, how women made the new land theirs by describing it in familiar, often "domestic" metaphors. While pioneering women created a habitable environment for themselves by domesticating their surroundings through the descriptive process, educated English women were appropriating for themselves a corner of the literary world by writing novels. As Josephine Donovan explained in "The Silence is Broken," the novel, which deals with everyday problems, often borrows materials and narrative techniques used in private correspondence. Since letter writing was a popular activity for upper-class women, they found prose fiction a comfortable mode of expression.

In Part II, Penelope Brown discussed how women's strategies for speaking can generate what is culturally perceived as a "feminine style." A similar point in the literary context is illustrated by Bonnie Costello's study of "The 'Feminine' Language of Marianne Moore," which opens Part IV. Marianne Moore adopted and adapted traits and values often called "feminine" as effective stylistic and formal tools. In her poems as Costello shows, Moore deliberately (mis)uses these so-called feminine characteristics to transform their meaning and function.

In "The Construction of Ambiguity in *The Awakening*: A Linguistic Analysis," Paula Treichler argues that Kate Chopin's alternating of passive and active syntactic structures helps articulate and realize her protagonist's struggle for self-definition. The skillfully crafted narrative discourse of Chopin's novel reflects and undermines in its linguistic patterns our view of Edna Pontellier's changing awareness, playing language against life, metaphor against reality.

The novel, as Donovan suggested, is a genre in whose development women have played a substantial role, whereas autobiography, particularly as it evolved in France, is a literary genre marked from the beginning by a male viewpoint. Rousseau defined autobiography as candid self-expression yet, as Nancy Miller shows in "Women's Autobiography in France," such women authors as George Sand, Daniel Stern, and Colette faced a double-bind in dealing with the auto-biographical mode, whose generic conventions conflicted with social constraints on women's expected candor. Since Rousseau and Colette did not write their autobiographies according to the same rules or customs, they should not be read in the same way. Miller proposes that women's autobiographies be read as modulated by their fictions. In the last article of Part IV we find an inversion of intertextual procedure: Gayatri Spivak reads Virginia Woolf's biography into her novel *To the Lighthouse*.

Talk about sex and sexual talk impart different conceptions of power and pleasure. Using Diderot's novel, *Indiscreet Jewels*, and Nancy Friday's *My Secret Garden*, Jane Gallop in "Snatches of Conversation" discusses the assumptions and ambiguities at work in the *Hite Report*. Diderot's novel articulates the relation between objective and public knowledge (the goal of science) and power (control), whereas Nancy Friday's fiction of a woman's sexual fantasies provides the model of subjective and private expression. Hite's book itself consists of two parts, a scientific study and a selection of individual responses to a question-naire, thus accommodating both scientific research and feminist demands for self-expression. Hite's theory of an efficient auto-erotic female sexuality is reflected in the economy of scientific reporting, whereas the expansiveness of personal confidences elicit the pleasures of intersubjective sexual relations. Yet, whether described with the detachment of an outside observer or evoked in the fervor of recollection, both types of discourse convey sexual excitement.

Literary criticism implies values and ideologies, draws on cultural assump-tions about women and men. By reexamining the controversy surrounding the authorship of the seventeenth century masterpiece known as the *Portuguese Letters*, Peggy Kamuf in "Writing Like a Woman" points out the biases embedded in critical judgments. Commenting on the denial of a possible female origin for a deliberately crafted work and on the obsessive concern with the question of origin and authorship, Kamuf explains how such critical concepts (re)inforce and (re)produce cultural values.

In "Reading Reading: Echo's Abduction of Language," Caren Greenberg applies to traditional forms of critical inquiry the grid of the Oedipal myth which has, since Freud, served as an allegory of male sexuality, and thereby suggests that psychosexual desire feeds into critical procedure. Viewing reading as repetition "with a difference" and literature as dynamic textuality, she proposes the Echo myth as one model for a differentia and potentially feminist reading practice.

Gayatri Spivak's essay, "Unmaking and Making in *To The Lighthouse*," is an example of textual feminist practice and of an "echoic" reading. *To the Lighthouse*, Spivak suggests, could be construed as an allegory of reading where Mr. Ramsay (philosopher/theorist) and Lily Briscoe (artist/practitioner) are each involved in the production of a text: Mrs. Ramsay. As an attempt to portray Mrs. Ramsay, the structure of the novel parallels that of the grammatical construction "Mrs. Ramsay is _____." Yet to fill in the blank, whether with words or on a canvas, is to objectify Mrs. Ramsay through predication. By imposing a sexual reading on the grammatical structure "Subject-Copula-Predicate," Spivak sets the process of textuality into motion. The copula and its suggestive cognates (copulation, coupling) become the articulators of and the place of gestation for her textual activity. As a place of gestation, the copula acquires a womb-like function and a female marking. Through mediation of the copula, Spivak's reading presents itself as a new form of discourse that joins the integrates both Mr. Ramsay's theoretical approach and Lily Briscoe's artistic rendering.

As Part IV demonstrates, interpretive processes themselves carry cultural values. In the social as well as in the literary domain, language articulates and conveys meaning as part of a wider system of conventions and concepts. Because textual analysis tries to show how an element becomes meaningful and is understood, its procedures can be applied to any kind of discourse: from scientific treatises or historical and philosophical essays to gossip and teasing. Understanding how meaning is created can help us recognize the power of (mis)interpretation to form and transform women's lives.

15
THE "FEMININE" LANGUAGE
OF MARIANNE MOORE

Bonnie Costello

Several critics of Marianne Moore's poetry have remarked, directly or indirectly, on its "feminine" quality, although it is sometimes difficult to decide just what they mean by this. T. S. Eliot, for instance, concludes his 1923 essay on Moore with a statement he either seems to feel is self-explanatory or hasn't really examined: "And there is one final, and 'magnificent' compliment: Miss Moore's poetry is as 'feminine' as Christina Rossetti's, one never forgets that it is written by a woman; but with both one never thinks of this as anything but a positive virtue."[1] What can he have in mind? Is it the "restraint" and "humility" that Randall Jarrell talks about in his essay on Moore, entitled "Her Shield"?[2] Is it the ladylike quality, the "chastity" of taste (a term rarely applied to men that R. P. Blackmur saw as both the virtue and defect of her work?[3] Or perhaps Eliot was thinking of Moore's preoccupation with surfaces and objects of sense experience (especially trivial experience) which he and others have praised as her "genuineness" while they have distinguished genuineness from "greatness".[4] Men write out of primitive or heroic occasions, women write out of everyday occasions. In his essay about Edna Saint Vincent Millay, "The Poet as Woman," John Crowe Ransom distinguishes Moore for having less "deficiency of masculinity," that is, (and he is explicit about this) "intellectual interest" than other women writers.[5] Yet we feel a reserve of prejudice influencing his view of her, even when his purpose is to applaud, as in "On Being Modern with Distinction."[6] Woman's love, he says in the Millay essay, is a fixation to natural sense objects (woman can't transcend mundane experience). Woman's love is devoted (she has no self). Man has lapsed, since childhood, from natural feelings, and his mind thus grows apart from woman's (woman remains childish). Woman does not go to the office (she has the leisure to be idle and cultivate her tenderness). Woman is set in her "famous attitudes" (woman's mind is full of clichés and household truisms). These assumptions appear, under a gauze of affection, throughout criticism of Moore's poetry. Roy Harvey Pearce begins by praising Moore's modesty and ease, but his parenthetical criticism make him sound a little insincere in wishing William Carlos Williams, Conrad Aiken, and E. E. Cummings had Moore's female virtue.[7]

Surprisingly, in her staunchly feminist argument, Suzanne Juhasz agrees with the men, both in the way they read the poems and in how they evaluate them. Rather than reexamining the male standards she assumes them a priori. Rather than consider the possible complexity of Moore's predilections and the original strength of her verse, Juhasz accepts past interpretations and simply seeks to explain how Moore's social and historical situation might cause her to "retreat" into the "lesser" qualities of "spinsterly" writing for self-protection. Because she is looking for something else (confessional poetry), Juhasz completely misses the distinctiveness of Moore's inventions. To Juhasz, insofar as Moore's stylistic devices are "feminine" they are defenses.[8]

Moore's art does display much of the taste and manners, the "vanity" as well as the "nobler virtue" our society ascribes to women. She is a lover of ornamental surfaces; she is fascinated with fashion and wrote several articles on the subject;[9] she is "gossipy" and chatty, passing on bits of hearsay and borrowed phrases; she is a collector of knickknacks, her poems are like overstuffed cupboards, full of irrelevancies and distractions. Moore's life reflected the same tendencies and tastes. Her scrapbooks and library are full of literature on women's dress, interior design, jewelry, ornamental art. Her letters go on for paragraphs describing someone's living room, a new coat, a cat she is caring for.[10] But somehow, when she is describing a friend's hat or a clay bird someone gave her, these particulars seem more important as *occasions* for imaginative response than for their conventional value.

Moore's critics have tended to identify her "feminine" qualities superficially, taking up her lexicon of virtues but applying their own definitions and prejudices to it. In context, I want to suggest, these qualities take on a special, powerful meaning, quite inverted in value. Moore purposely assumes the traditional "household" virtues and attributes in order to redefine them in the action of her poems. Moore's "feminine" virtues and manners do not glass-in or soften reality, do not trivialize experience or diminish the claims of the self, but on the contrary become in various ways the chief sources of energy in her work. Continually in her poetry and in her prose Moore shows a close relationship between moral and technical virtue. As Geoffrey Hartman has observed in a brief note on the poet, "her style does not embody a morality, it is one."* The

---

*Selections from the notes by Geoffrey Hartman appearing on the jacket of *Marianne Moore Reads from Her Own Works*. Reprinted by permission of Geoffrey Hartman.[11]

central morality of her style (and the chief source of its vitality) is a resistance to the complacencies of thought and language, to a tendency to accept given forms as descriptive of the world as it is. This is not a passive resistance, for it works in alliance with her mental voracity, continually readjusting the line and pushing against the limits of language. Moore's access to this central concern with the limits of language is through a conventional but redefined femininity. Or, conversely, the breaking up of our assumptions about certain types of virtue and manner is a natural instance of a larger concern for resisting complacencies of thought and language.

This is not, for Moore, an explicitly feminist issue. She nowhere indicates that she thinks of her poems or the values they advocate as particularly "feminine." In fact most of the animal figures that demonstrate these qualities are given male pronouns. But it seems only natural that Moore should select the attributes most readily applied to her as the focus of her efforts to rediscover language. Whether these qualities are a natural or inherited part of her femininity, however, one feels in reading her poems that a man could not have seen the potential in such qualities that Moore has seen and exploited.

One of Moore's favorite categories of virtue, observed throughout her poetry and criticism, is humility, with its analogues, restraint, and modesty. What a nineteenth-century reviewer said of the woman poet Felicia Hemans has been said in other ways (in the quotations above) of Moore: "she never forgets what is due feminine reserve."[12] Indeed, Moore learned well the lesson of Bryn Mawr president Carey Thomas which she quotes in her essay on the "impassioned emancipator": she "behaved not with decorum but with marked decorum."[13] This does not mean that Moore practiced humility without sincerity. Rather, she discovers in it a special value: "humility is a kind of armor." Critics usually take this to mean that by playing down the self, by making few overt claims to authority and power, we avoid subjecting ourselves to envy or attack. Moore's descriptiveness, her extensive use of quotation, her choice of peripheral subject matter, her circumlocution, are all pointed to as technical counterparts of her moral predilections. But what Moore, with Carey Thomas, understood is that strength and power are not necessarily stifled or even contained, but are on the contrary nurtured through acts of self-protection. Aggressive, indecorous, intolerant behavior wastes energy and creativity which can be better sustained and wielded with a certain guardedness. She quotes Thomas' remark: "Bryn Mawr must not be less guarded because it is good."[14] Juhasz and others tend to see nothing but the armor, neglecting what is achieved by its use. Moore compromises nothing in her "self-protective" humility; she gains. Though the idea of "feminine reserve" may conventionally imply an attitude appropriate to inferiority, Moore does not even pretend to weakness. She shows humility to be a reserve, in the sense of a reservoir of power. At the end of "In This Age of Hard Trying," for instance, Moore shows how an apparent "inconsequence of manner" is more effective and durable than aggressive certitude.

IN THIS AGE OF HARD TRYING,
NONCHALANCE IS GOOD AND

"really, it is not the
>> business of the gods to bake clay pots." They did not
>>> do it in this instance. A few
>>>> revolved upon the axes of their worth
>> as if excessive popularity might be a pot;

they did not venture the
>> profession of humility. The polished wedge
>>> that might have split the firmament
>>>> was dumb. At last it threw itself away
>> and falling down, conferred on some poor fool, a privilege.

"Taller by the length of
>> a conversation of five hundred years than all
>>> the others," there was one whose tales
>>>> of what could never have been actual—
>> were better than the haggish, uncompanionable drawl

of certitude; his by-
>> play was more terrible in its effectiveness
>>> than the fiercest frontal attack.
>>>> The staff, the bag, the feigned inconsequence
>> of manner, best bespeak that weapon, self-protectiveness.

(CP, 34)*

Humility, a guarded manner, has the advantage of taking the listener offguard. And Moore practices her point in a number of ways here. The prosaic, conversational tone, the long, meandering, run-on lines and shifts of figurative level, give the impression of nonchalance. She is not, she seems to suggest, writing anything so grand as a poem. But the design is present, though unobtrusive, acting on our imaginations almost without alerting us. We hardly notice, though we subliminally hear, the careful rhymes, the subtly extended metaphor, the logic of the tale, so that the final lines have a special bold effect in their paradoxical clarity.

---

*All lines quoted from Marianne Moore's poetry are taken from *The Complete Poems of Marianne Moore* (New York: Viking, 1967). Selections from the following are reprinted with permission of Macmillan Publishing Company, Inc. and by permission of Faber and Faber Ltd. from *The Complete Poems of Marianne Moore*: "In This Age of Hard Trying" (p. 484), "When I Buy Pictures" (pp. 499-500), "An Octopus" (pp. 504-5), "Sea Unicorns and Land Unicorns" (p. 502), "Novices" (p. 497), and "Sojourn in the Whale" (p. 506), copyright © 1935 by Marianne Moore, renewed 1963 by Marianne Moore and T. S. Eliot. "The Paper Nautilus" (p. 494) copyright © 1941 by Marianne Moore, renewed 1969 by Marianne Moore. "His Shield" (p. 486), copyright © 1951 by Marianne Moore, renewed 1979 by Lawrence E. Brinn and Louise Crane.

Moore's feminine humility, then, is designing: she wants to create and sustain an interest which overt self-assertion or pronounced form would snuff out. Moore's humility and restraint are not passive defenses but ways of gathering force, as a bow is pulled back in order to carry the arrow farther when it is finally released. Such motives and strategies are at work in many of her best poems, especially "The Plumet Basilisk," "The Frigate Pelican," "To a Snail,"and "The Pangolin," poems about animals she admires for elusive strengths similar to those she displays in her writing. The end of humility is not self-protection for its own sake so much as "gusto," the spark released in the discovery of and enthusiasm for what is out of our control. In language, "humility is an indispensable teacher, enabling concentration to heighten gusto."* Whereas humility associated with women usually implies something negative, a withdrawal, a deference, Moore shows its positive outcome. She is one woman for whom humility is not an end but a means of inspiration and expression.

Humility is not armor against the aggressions of the world on the self so much as against those of the self on the world, against the "disease, My Self," as she calls it. To impose the self and its accumulated structures on the world is to narrow the world and trap the self, a self-defeating gesture. "In Distrust of Merits" takes this theme up directly, but it is always present obliquely in Moore's verse. For her, humility "keeps the world large," preserves a place for something beyond the self that keeps us from complacency and satiation, consequently keeping us alive.

"His Shield" (CP, 144) is the poem quoted most often in connection with Moore's idea of the armor of humility. She says it directly: "his shield was his humility." The poem warns against "greed and flattery," insisting that "freedom" is "the power of relinquishing what one would keep." Bravado does not please or improve anything, it simply attracts contenders, and wastes energy fighting them off. "Be dull, don't be envied or armed with a measuring rod." Don't attract envy by flaunting your achievement. This is a traditional code of .femininity, but it usually implies that feminine achievement is incommensurate with envy or pride. Let us see how Moore understands her message.

The poem contrasts two kinds of armor, as several critics have pointed out. Moore finds that the spiny covering of the "edgehog miscalled hedgehog with all his edges out . . . won't do." Instead, "I'll wrap myself in salamander skin." The armor of "pig-fur" aggressing on the outside would scare things off. Its force is its inadequacy. But "asbestos" armor endures rather than extinguishes fire. It allows the outside world to enclose without annihilating the subject. Furthermore, it keeps the edges inside, keeps a fire alive internally rather than exhausting it in consuming ego. The ideal is "a lizard in the midst of flames, a firebrand that is life," who is, to use a phrase from Moore's critical essays, "galvanized against inertia." Where possession, and its verbal equivalent,

---

*From *Predilections* by Marianne Moore. © 1955 by Marianne Moore. Reprinted by permission of Viking Penguin, Inc.15

singleminded assertion, imply stasis and complacency, survival and freedom require the constant readjustment of thought. At the level of the sentence, "humility" does not mean that one should be silent, but rather that language should continually be revised in the presence of what it cannot accommodate.

The utopia represented in the poem is an "unconquerable country of unpompous gusto." Power is not compromised, it is simply redistributed. Presbyter John, the hero of the poem, "styled himself but presbyter." Gusto is generated less out of self-aggrandizing conquest or consumption than out of awareness, out of a perpetually perceived difference between himself and the world, and the preservation of that difference and of desire. Resources are never used up in such a country.

Self-denial sounds like an odd basis for utopian experience, however. How can untapped wealth and power be considered as such? Moore manages to develop a sense of wealth without conquest through symbols of the potential effects of power. "Rubies large as tennis/balls conjoined in streams so/that the mountain seemed to bleed." The mountain only *seems* to bleed, but in doing so it marks a potential encounter. Emblematized strength is perpetual, exerted strength expires. Indeed, the emblem of external battle is only realized internally in the struggle for self-possession. The stream of blood, as the internalized warfare of humility, is only the blood stream, the "firebrand that is life."

If we think of the poet as presbyter, the vitality of Moore's lines comes from investing her thought in a presentation of the external world, hence so many poems in a descriptive mode which obliquely suggest a personal attitude. The oddity and apparent awkwardness of her lines comes from that sense of the inadequacy of the "measuring rod" to deal honestly with particulars. In language, "to relinquish what one would keep" is to continually resist available form. One way she does this is by having different forms displace each other to create a variegated surface. Images cut across each other to deny any rigid hierarchy. The "I" of the poem is swallowed up in description. Moral and discursive languages do not preside over the poem, but take their place in a range of languages: commercial, conversational, descriptive, metaphoric. While her lines expand and digress in pursuit of what is always posited as indefinable, they also create images of the self's internal activity, thereby steadying the flux of exploration. Thus, as Geoffrey Hartman has pointed out, "she achieves a dialogue of one, an ironic crossfire of statement that continually denies and reasserts the possibility of a selfless assertion of self . . . the armor she describes is the modesty whereby the self is made strong to resist itself, but also strong to assert its being against voracious dogmatism."[16] The abnegation of self ultimately satisfies the self, for it widens the sphere of response, the self being continually discovered through response to the external world. It declares knowledge a matter of process rather than possession, and it ensures the continuance of that process. The aggressive self is identified in the conquest of one form over another, an impulse to narrow and exclude, which finally entraps the self in the form it has imposed. But the humble self flourishes in the multiplicity of form, identifying with none. It neither narrows its domain nor can be narrowed by the force of others, for it exists in resisting closure. Humility, restraint, paradoxically conduce to freedom.

The armor of humility appears as a recurrent theme and technique in the critical essays as well. "Humility, Concentration and Gusto" opens in the more than metaphorical context of war.

> In times like these we are tempted to disregard anything that has not a direct bearing on freedom; or should I say, an obvious bearing, for what is more persuasive than poetry, though as Robert Frost says, it works obliquely and delicately. Commander King-Hall, in his book *Total Victory*, is really saying that the pen is the sword when he says the object of war is to persuade the enemy to change his mind.[17]

Such talk of persuasion would seem on the side of the porcupine's edgy, aggressive "battle dress." But what is persuasive, it turns out, what has bearing on freedom, is humility.

> We don't want war, but it does conduce to humility, as someone said in the foreward to an exhibition catalogue of his work, "With what shall the artist arm himself save with his humility?". Humility, indeed, is armor, for it realizes that it is impossible to be original in the sense of doing something that has never been thought of before. Originality is in any case a byproduct of sincerity; that is to say, of feeling that is honest and accordingly rejects anything that might cloud the impression, such as unnecessary commas, modifying clauses, or delayed predicates.[18]

One should not speak from ambition, then, but from honest feeling. The work, as one early critic of "female poetry" said, should "come from the heart, to be natural and true."[19] Humility begins in this essay as a principle of simplicity and "quiet objectiveness," the reduction of self-assertion and the elevation of the external "impression." This is what Ransom "admired" in Millay, "a vein of poetry which is spontaneous, straightforward in diction, and excitingly womanlike; a distinguished objective record of a woman's mind."[20] But humility becomes, as the essay goes on, a principle of difficulty standing for "the refusal to be false." When associated with "sincerity," the principle of humility and restraint becomes an agent of "gusto" by continually turning up a difference between the ways things are described and the way things are. "Gusto thrives on freedom," Moore explains, and freedom is preserved by failures of formal closure, by linguistic deviation. Daniel Berkeley Updike, Moore tells us, "has always seemed to me a phenomenon of eloquence because of the quiet objectiveness of his writing."

> And what he says of printing applies equally to poetry. It is true, is it not, that "style does not depend on decoration but on simplicity and proportion"? Nor can we dignify confusion by calling it

> baroque. Here, I may say, I am preaching to myself, since, when I am as complete as I like to be, I seem unable to get an effect plain enough.[21]

But this is sophisticated humility on Moore's part. What is persuasive is her preaching to herself. Certainly we would not expect her to be less complete than she would like to be, so what might seem like ornament or excess in her verse is justified as honesty. Humility, which upholds an ideal of quiet objectiveness, of simplicity and proportion, also upholds sincerity, which will not force a perception into a dishonestly neat structure. What results from this ironic conflict is a lively play of impulses through a highly variegated, rebellious surface. Though she will not make public claims to "originality," her poems are certainly idiosyncratic and individual, and invite the interest of a public into the special world of a private enchantment.

Moore often speaks of her "natural reticence" in explaining the disobliging difficulty of some of her work. Conventionally, natural reticence belongs to woman's lesser capacity for logical assertion. As a supposedly intuitive rather than analytical creature, woman naturally has trouble being articulate: language is a system of codification and dissection. Moore herself says "feeling at its deepest tends to be inarticulate." But in her verse, once natural reticence gives way to speech it paradoxically causes an overflow of words.

The extreme digressiveness of surface in Moore's poetry has perplexed many critics. Juhasz sees it as deliberate evasiveness, her way "of not talking about what she is talking about and talking about what she is not talking about."[22] Roy Harvey Pearce criticizes her "gossipy" quality and her "uncertainty as to direction." Though Pearce doesn't label these qualities "feminine" he implies as much, and Ransom is explicit. Woman's mind "has no direction or modulation except by its natural health."[23] In other words, women live without purpose or focus beyond their immediate daily cares, to which they respond with inarticulate emotions. Their minds cannot sustain a logical argument or coherent structure because they have no powers of memory or projection, because they live in a continuous present.

Moore takes this digressive mode of thought and examines its special advantages. The mind that follows "its natural health" has a capacity for nuance which evades us where there is "too stern an intellectual emphasis." The "steam roller" mind crushes "all the particles down into close conformity." "As for butterflies, I can hardly conceive of one's attending upon you." The "aimless" mind, like "the magic flute" illogically weaves "what logic can't unweave." It is closer to the center of experience, alive to changes of an unconscious voice. It has a greater capacity for discovery, not blinded by its own hypotheses. It is more inclusive; it has more variety. Through her unwieldy, non-hierarchical structures, her elongated, loquacious sentences, Moore achieves a sense of "continuous present," a sense of the poem in process, the mind experiencing and discovering itself. Moore's prosody works to this same end, through inconspicuous syllabic measure, through dispersed rhyme and run-on lines. Ransom thinks women are always weak on form "because they are not strict enough and expert enough to manage forms, in their default of the discipline under which men are trained."[24] Moore's form is indeed not uniform or abstractly applied; it depends upon movement and changes inflection, unleashing new impulses as they are called up.

George Hartman has been unusually sensitive to the force of Moore's "gossipy" meanderings.

> . . . one reads her poems less for their message (always suffused) than for the pleasure of seeing how style may become an act of the living—the infinitely inclusive and discriminating—mind.
>
> This mind, or rather Miss Moore's, is "an enchanting thing;" it takes us by its very irrelevancies. Here too everything is surface; she talks, so to say, from the top of her mind and represents herself as a gossip on the baroque scale. But secretly she is a magician, and distracts on purpose. While her message eludes us through understatement, the poem itself remains teasingly alive through the overstatement of its many tactics, till we accept the conventional rabbit, glorified by prestidigitation. Yet the magic of language becomes intensely moral on further acquaintance and her crazyquilt of thoughts, quotations and sounds resolves into subtler units of meaning and rhythm. The free (but not formless) verse helps break up the automatic emphases of traditional syntax, and respects the more dynamic shifts of the inner, and not merely spoken voice.[25]

Moore's elusive surfaces involve a moral prudence as well as an aesthetic one. She wants to dodge self-consciousness. What male critics have called a certain "fussiness" in Moore, she calls "unconscious fastidiousness" in which she finds "a great amount of poetry." What she seems to describe with the phrase is a kind of impulsive persistence in attempting to manage unmanageable material. Moore sees "unconscious fastidiousness" as an important part of the nurturing process, and imitates tha process in her poems. Maternity is the subject of "The Paper Nautilus," and in comparing it to poetry she alters the conventional view of both. We conventionally think of maternal affection as a soft, graceful attitude, and similarly Moore's poetry has been prized, condescendingly, for its "relaxed ease." But the poem describes the process of nurture as a struggle beneath a surface of gentleness, a highly precarious restraint of power. Here unconscious fastidiousness means a high level of attentiveness without the imposition of rigid design which might impede natural development. The health of the eggs somehow depends upon maximum power and maximum restraint. The juxtaposition of "the ram's-horn cradled freight" and "a devil-fish" and her eggs reinforces this tension. Later we are told of the shell's relative delicacy (like a wasp nest) and of its strength (like Ionic columns and the force of Parthenon sculpture). The tension described in holding back Hercules is clarified through a notion of a "fortress of love" but not relieved. We have metaphors of maximum impulse without the expiration of energy in action. The paper nautilus must "hide" her "freight" but not "crush" it. The same goes for poets. They too are "hindered to succeed."

> For authorities whose hopes
> are shaped by mercenaries?
>   Writers entrapped by
>   teatime fame and by
> commuters' comforts? Not for these
>   the paper nautilus
>   constructs her thin glass shell.

(CP, 121)

The poem starts by distinguishing two kinds of form, one which is complacent and commercial, generated by petty ambition, (and the association of mercenaries and commuters suggests a male domain) and another kind which will not "entrap" the writer or the audience. Appropriately, Moore will not "entrap" herself and her subject by restricting the tenor of this other kind. Rather, after an initial reference to writers, she shifts into a metaphor for metaphor itself: the shell in which our impression of the world can take shape without calcifying. But the shell is importantly the source and product of a maternal affection, a desire to nurture, in order finally to release the growing object. Her shell does not contain the eggs, or in terms of poetry, is not "the thing itself."

The feminine code of sacrifice says one must "relinquish what one would keep," and this is often applied to maternal relationships. But Moore changes this idea, in an artistic context, to a mode of freedom, not just a duty. Thus "the intensively watched egges coming from/ the shell free it when they are freed." And the mother is free from her state of tension. Freedom, that is, requires differentiation.

We are curious when we sense something like ourselves yet different. Moore knows that observation is always in a way self-interested. Indeed, language is fundamentally of the self and not of the other, so self-expression is inevitable. Her mind follows likeness and finds difference, and again likeness, in the form of statements that are qualified, images which clash, rhymes that are interrupted, deviating detail, almost any form of verbal differentiation. In the process she does not accomplish "objectification" (curiosity is not satisfied) but something more interesting: a composition which metes out likeness and difference, visual and aural as well as semantic. The composition has the rhetorical power both to make associations and to suggest its own limits, since these verbal differences are made to seem like the difference between the world and what we say about it. Moore's compositions are trails of associations which conduct the reader to their source. This identification occurs not only as our vicarious experience of her mental flux, but through her final, subtle self-portraiture. Moore begins by presenting an object apparently for its own sake, but in the process of describing it she borrows the object as a figure of her own activity. This self-portraiture is not the point of arrival of the poet's search for unity or for the thing itself, but a kind of parting embrace of words and things, a form of possession or appropriation that leaves the thing untouched while its ghost performs the function of analogy. Moore pursues the contours of objects for what she can discover of herself, but precisely because she learns about herself through observation of the external world, she can never declare her motive or speak of herself directly. "Imaginary possession" allows her to make associations without assumptions. She never gets to the point at which the idea subverts the observation.

The narcissists and sophisticates in the art world are the constant butt of Moore's satire, though they are "deaf to satire." In "Novices," for instance, she criticizes the "supertadpoles of expression" so attentive to their own egos

so that they do not know "whether it is the buyer or the seller
who gives the money"—
an abstruse idea plain to none but the artist,
the only seller who buys and holds on to the money.

* * *

they write the sort of thing that would in their judgment
interest a lady;
curious to know if we do not adore each letter of the alphabet
that goes to make a word of it—

(CP, 60)

These "Will Honeycombs" who "anatomize their work," whose art is highly rational and symmetrical, are "bored by the detailless perspective of the sea," too absorbed in flattering themselves with their intellectual conquests to recognize the irrational power of nature. Moore contrasts their style with "the spontaneous unforced passion of the Hebrew language," which derives its "tempestuous energy" from a complete surrender to the sublimity of nature. In their example Moore shows that the self grows larger by imaginatively embracing something beyond its rational control.

But Moore is not simply advocating unconscious spontaneity or self-annihilation. Moore's is a highly conscious art, its objects derived primarily from books, not wild nature. It is the activity of tracing an "other," of knowing it in relation to oneself, as similar and different, that interests her, and she has called this "imaginary possession." With imaginary possession the mind is free to make associations, but at the same time knows them as such and does not identify them as exclusive truths. The task of "When I Buy Pictures," for instance, is to give both the illusion of a figure in the world who does not affect it, and to make a gesture of possession, to bring what is seen under the control of language.

WHEN I BUY PICTURES

or what is closer to the truth
when I look at that of which I may regard myself as the
imaginary possessor,
I fix upon what would give me pleasure in my average moments:
the satire upon curiosity in which no more is discernible
than the intensity of the mood;
or quite the opposite—the old thing, the medieval decorated hat-box,
in which there are hounds with waists diminishing like the waist
of the hourglass,
and deer and birds and seated people;

(CP, 48)

The game of imaginary possession involves discretion and humility, not prohibition:

Too stern an intellectual emphasis upon this quality or that
detracts from one's enjoyment.
It must not wish to disarm anything; nor may the approved
triumph easily be honored—
that which is great because something else is small.

(CP, 48)

Of course these are not "average moments"; they are moments of luminosity, selected for their suggestiveness. The difference is that between selection which reveals a will and transformation which emblematizes a will. Moore does not simply direct her imagery toward a final or overarching intention. Her mind is attentive to the properties of each object and each word as it occurs. Age suggests images of age: hatboxes which bear images of old-fashioned hounds that are shaped like hourglasses whose waists remind her of time's waste and as these waists diminish the imagery narrows its reference to the matter of fact: deer, birds, and seated people. The coherence of a part takes her to the next, without rejecting the influence of the immediate details. But while avoiding "too stern an intellectual emphasis" a surprisingly complex range of associations, built upon the problems of time, distance and complexity, emerges in the movement from one image to the next, at no cost to the surface randomness of local association:

It may be no more than a square of parquetry; the literal
biography perhaps,
in letters standing well apart upon a parchment-like expanse;
an artichoke in six varieties of blue; the snipe-legged hieroglyphic
in three parts;

the silver fence protecting Adam's grave, or Michael taking
Adam by the wrist.

(CP, 48)

Parquetry, artichoke, biography, hieroglyphic are all patterns of one kind or another. The range is inclusive and humorous. These orders are mocked, but shown to be natural. "Literal biography" is a contradiction reduced to its formal elements, letters standing well apart. We are directed through meaningless "orders" to consider our desire for possession, and the poem moves to emblems of our fall. These unite the previously separate and random problems of time, distance, and complexity raised in the imagery. Poems suppose a hierarchy of elements, but the rhetoric of the list resists our locating ourselves anywhere in particular in the poem. Moore quite consciously tempts our desire for architectonic, mythic structures, our need to privilege the "heroic" moment. She wants these associations while she restrains them from blocking their natural contexts. One does not forfeit the self, then, one does not resign all "views"; one simply explores them discreetly.

Of course the poem itself is a picture for sale. The satire on curiosity is a picture of ourselves since it is, finally, the intensity of the mood which is at issue. Its "opposite," the picture of receding things, draws the curious figure on until it becomes a mirror ("when I look at that of which I may regard myself"). The self does get expressed, through its own enchantment with something else, and this, I think, is what Virginia Woolf means in *A Room of One's Own* when she speaks of a woman's ability to get close to the fountain of creative energy.

While Moore's poetry is in a way "impersonal," in that the self is not the focus or dominant presence, we feel the movement of a distinct personality throughout. Indeed, Moore's very resistance to formal closure becomes for her a means of self-relevation. The "minor defects" of form, as she called unassimilated elements, are marks of style. And it is in style that we know this poet, not in subject or assertion. Though she never advocates "originality," the ambition to supersede the forms others have created, she is a great defender of "idiosyncrasy," an inevitable expression of "honest vision." Idiosyncrasy is connected with sincerity, a kind of non-competitive, oblique presentation of self; it does not require a personal subject or a show of power; it challenges no one.

Emily Watts, in *The Poetry of American Women*, identifies Moore's verse with a tradition of "feminine realism." What she and other critics are pointing to in the use of this term is the combination of "mundane realities," "simple human and natural situations," and "natural sense objects," with ethical generalizations or "household morality." The feminine mind neatly integrates nature and morality. Randall Jarrell, for one, strongly objects to Moore's poetry on the basis of this integration. In clear sexual categories he challenges what he sees as Moore's domestic falsifications, upholding instead the male vision of amoral nature and its corresponding cosmic ambition.

But Moore has transformed the structure of feminine realism (which links observation to ethical generalization) in a number of ways. While she does detail nature, she celebrates her subjects for their recalcitrance. And the morality that accompanies these pictures is one of resisting the mind's impulse to circumscribe experience. In "Sea Unicorns and Land Unicorns," (about the Unicorn Tapestries) Moore points out that the unicorn remains "a puzzle to the hunters." Only the virgin knows him:

> Thus this strange animal with its miraculous elusiveness,
> has come to be unique,
> "impossible to take alive,"
> tamed only by a lady inoffensive like itself—
> as curiously wild and gentle;

> (CP, 78)

All the poems follow a dictum of resistance even while they move through an apparent structure of observation-moral, for they continually propose definitions only to unravel them. "Integration, too tough for infraction," integration of the mind and the external world, of ethos and nature, is the goal of Moore's poetry, not its claim. And it is based on "efforts of affection" and not on aggression. It is achieved through process, through an open-ended dialectic of observing and making observations, in a continuous present.

While Moore follows the tendency in "feminine realism" to keep an eye on the external object, she is distinctly modern in her awareness of the limits of language to present that object. Moore's "descriptions" break up the conventions of composition, not to protect the self but to bring language into a more adequate relationship to experience, to discover a new realism which resists the habits of mind and eye. But what such resistance to referential conventions does, finally, is bring us into a closer awareness of the surface of language. By blocking the easy transfer from word to picture of meaning, by continually shifting the flow of counters and intruding on conventions which we too readily naturalize, Moore reminds us that we are not actually seeing, but only reading. This technique is especially effective in her poem "An Octopus," a long description of a glacier that concludes with a moral of "relentless accuracy." The extreme difficulty of accurately perceiving the object creates a corresponding difficulty in the words. Often the lengthy and cumbersome sentences lose their syntactic hold on us. We forget the subject or antecedent in the tow of subordinate clauses. Colons and semicolons are suspended between groups without an easy sense of their relation. Appositions become subjects with their own appositions in turn. Participial phrases go on for several lines until we cease even to anticipate their subjects. Where conventional "realism" trusts the parts of speech to represent reality, Moore's language continually demonstrates their failure. In its attempt to circumscribe the viscous presence, the language of "An Octopus," for instance, doubles back on itself with lines that refer outwardly to the objective experience, and inwardly to the experience of reading. "Completing the circle, you have been deceived into thinking that you have progressed." "Neatness of finish! Neatness of finish! Relentless accuracy is the nature of this octopus/ with its capacity for fact." Such self-reflective imagery admits that ultimately the "morals" we derive are not natural but represent our efforts to come to terms with nature. In that sense all of Moore's ethical generalizations have to do with her poetic activity.

"Neatness of finish" and "relentless accuracy" sound, in isolation, like mundane lessons. But in the context of this poem they present an enormous challenge to the eye and mind. And Moore proves the point she is making, for instead of rounding off the description with this abstract conclusion, she returns to the particular. She adopts, in the end, a policy of accuracy more relentless than before:

> Is "tree" the word for these things
> "flat on the ground like vines"?
> some "bent in a half circle with branches on one side
> suggesting dust-brushes, not trees;
> some finding strength in union, forming little stunted groves
> their flattened mats of branches shrunk in trying to escape"
> from the hard mountain "planed by ice and polished by the wind"—
> the white volcano with no weather side;
> the lightning flashing at its base,
> rain falling in the valleys, and snow falling on the peak—
> the glassy octopus symmetrically pointed,
> its claw cut by the avalanche
> "with a sound like the crack of a rifle
> in a curtain of powdered snow launched like a waterfall."

(CP, 76)

The breathlessness of the passage pulls us away from the organizing frame of grammar and syntax and hurls us into the midst of detail. Ethical generalization is returned to the level of perception. And yet even in the midst of detail, the mind makes associations. In this case the associations simply remind us of the controlling presence of language. At the end of the mountain is a curtain of snow; at the end of the poem—is a curtain of snow, the page. Her humility denies both the claims of an achieved realist and those of an achieved moralist; but her struggle for integration is vital and rewarding.

Moore transforms and toughens our understanding of familiar virtues when she uses them as stylistic devices. Humility, affection, reserve, are not passive but dynamic and vital modes of response. They do not protect but rather sustain the self in experience. In her redefinition and revaluation of what have been seen as "feminine" modes of identity, Moore displays a larger, encompassing concern to avoid all complacencies of mind. No container will hold her gusto.

You have been compelled by hags to spin
gold thread from straw and have heard men say:
"There is a feminine temperament in direct contrast to ours

which makes her do these things. Circumscribed by a
heritage of blindness and native
incompetence, she will become wise and will be forced to give in.
Compelled by experience, she will turn back;

water seeks its own level":
and you have smiled. "Water in motion is far
from level." You have seen it, when obstacles happen to bar
the path, rise automatically.

(CP, 90)

In describing Ireland, Moore has obliquely celebrated the resilient power of the "feminine temperament." Ireland survives and deepens its identity by a combination of persistence and responsiveness. By rising to meet the shapes experience presents rather than either retreating or imposing artificial forms, Moore sustains a vital, creative contact between her self and her surroundings.

NOTES

1. T. S. Eliot, rev. of *Poems* and *Marriage*, by Marianne Moore, *Dial* LXXV (December 1923) rept. in *Marianne Moore: A Collection of Critical Essays*, ed. Charles Tomlinson (Englewood Cliffs, N.J.: Prentice Hall, 1969), p. 51.

2. Randall Jarrell, "Her Shield," from *Poetry and the Age* by Randall Jarrell (1953) rept. in *Marianne Moore: A Collection of Critical Essays*, p. 114-24.

3. R. P. Blackmur, "The Method of Marianne Moore," from *The Double Agent, Essays in Craft and Elucidation* by R. P. Blackmur (New York: Arrow, 1935) rept. in *Marianne Moore: A Collection of Critical Essays*, p. 86.

4. T. S. Eliot, Preface to *Selected Poems* by Marianne Moore (New York: MacMillan, 1935), rept. in *Marianne Moore: A Collection of Critical Essays*, p. 61.

5. John Crowe Ransom, "Woman as Poet," *The World's Body* (New York: Charles Scribners's Sons, 1938) pp. 77-78.

6. John Crowe Ransom, "On Being Modern With Distinction," *Quarterly Review of Literature*, no. 2 (1948), rept. in *Marianne Moore: A Collection of Critical Essays*, p. 102.

7. Roy Harvey Pearce, *The Continuity of American Poetry* (Princeton: Princeton University Press, 1961), pp. 366-75.

8. Suzanne Juhasz, *Naked and Fiery Forms: Modern American Poetry by Women* (New York: Harper and Row, 1976) pp. 33-56.

9. Marianne Moore, *Dress and Kindred Subjects* (New York: Ibex, 1965).

10. The major archive of Moore documents is in the Rosenbach Museum, Philadelphia; the literary executor is Clive Driver.

11. Geoffrey Hartman, "Notes" for *Marianne Moore Reads From Her Own Works*; Yale Series of Recorded Poets.

12. Quoted in Emily Stipes Watts, *The Poetry of American Women from 1632 to 1945*, (Austin: University of Texas, 1977), p. 69. Watts does not name the reviewer or the source.

13. Marianne Moore, "M. Carey Thomas of Bryn Mawr," in *The Marianne Moore Reader* (New York: Viking, 1961).

14. Ibid.

15. Marianne Moore, "Humility, Concentration and Gusto," from *Predilections* (New York: Viking, 1955), p. 20.

16. Geoffrey Hartman, notes.

17. Moore, "Humility, Concentration and Gusto," p. 82.

18. Ibid., p. 83.

19. Quoted in Watts, *The Poetry of American Women from 1632 to 1945.* p. 69. Watts does not name the source.

20. John Crowe Ransom, "Woman as Poet," p. 104.

21. Marianne Moore, "Feeling and Precision," from *Predilections* (New York: Viking, 1955), p. 7.

22. Juhasz, *Naked and Fiery Forms*, p. 42.

23. Ransom, "Woman as Poet," p. 78.

24. Ibid., p. 103.

25. Geoffrey Hartman, notes to *Marianne Moore Reads from Her Own Works.*

16
THE CONSTRUCTION OF
AMBIGUITY IN *THE AWAKENING*:
A LINGUISTIC ANALYSIS

Paula A. Treichler

The central narrative of Kate Chopin's novel *The Awakening* can be said to concern Edna Pontellier's struggle to define herself as an active subject, and to cease to be merely the passive object of forces beyond her control.[1] But the precise nature of this struggle, as well as its emotional and psychological dimensions, is less easily articulated.* One textual counterpart to this complexity is the ongoing syntactic interplay between active and passive voice which parallels, and not infrequently undermines, the overt narrative. The relationship between formal grammatical patterns and obvious narrative meaning shapes our understanding of Edna's changing consciousness and serves as an index to its vicissitudes. The verb "awaken," from which the novel's title and central metaphor derive, formally complicates in a similar way the active and passive elements of Edna's experience. Both transitive and intransitive, it can take a grammatical object but does not have to: someone can awaken, can be awakened, can awaken someone else. The title of the novel, a noun, is structurally unspecified and can draw on all these possibilities. Similarly, the novel's personal pronouns are revealing: one could argue that *The Awakening* charts Edna Pontellier's growing mastery of the first person singular, and that when this

---

*As Cynthia Griffin Wolff, "Thanatos and Eros," p. 449, writes, most critics see the novel "as growing out of an existential confrontation between the heroine and some external, repressive force"; others see the struggle as largely internal. The forces against which Edna is seen to struggle include familial and social demands, Victorian culture, the constraints of marriage and of a male-dominated society and civilization, Romantic myths and illusions, the restraints of Creole society, interpersonal relationships, her "emotionally improverished childhood" (Sullivan and Smith), maternity, matrimony, her female need for dependency, "her passional nature's drive for fulfillment" (Spangler), eros, death, and sleep.

"I" has been created, the book has successfully completed its mission and comes to an end.

The close analysis of verbal form remains a relatively uncommon approach to fiction in general, and to *The Awakening* in particular. Yet it permits us to study the crucial intersections between form and meaning which presumably are part of any literary experience. Thus we find that the book asserts from the outset the ambiguities of Edna's own role in her awakening and suggests, too, that out attempts as readers to delineate this role precisely may fail: that no unambiguous reading is possible. The form of the language, in other words, insists that the problems of Edna's situation are genuine and cannot be fully resolved; the meaning of the novel exists, in part, in its verbal form.

At the same time as the book progresses, the seemingly artless, even childlike, simplicity of Chopin's style gives way to a rather complicated and intense reading experience. In fact the language offers a verbal resolution to the novel's narrative problems which is nearly perfect, and which, in its craft, transcends the profound contradictions and ambiguities of the story.

I

Edna Pontellier first appears in *The Awakening* when her husband perceives her in the distance as "a white sunshade that was advancing at snail's pace from the beach"; as it moves closer, we learn that "beneath its pink-lined shelter were his wife, Mrs. Pontellier, and young Robert Lebrun."[2] Thus the literal object we are first shown gives way to her official designation as "his wife" and at last to her proper name, at its most formal. (Only later is she regularly called "Edna Pontellier" or "Edna," a naming device that regulates our distance and sympathies.) This view of Edna as an object is made explicit when her husband looks at her "as one looks at a valuable piece of personal property which has suffered some damage"(4). The image is more than an ironic comment on the nature of the Pontelliers' conventional marriage, for Edna is to be an object in a much wider sense.

She is often, for example, a grammatical object. In an early scene she sits outside crying, angry and upset after her husband's complaints and trivial conversation have awakened her out of a sound sleep (the literal awakening here gives psychological plausibility to the metaphor). This passage offers the first overt signal of Edna's discontent—our first entry to her consciousness coincides with the beginnings of her awakening:

> An indescribable oppression, which seemed to generate in some unfamiliar part of her consciousness, filled her whole being with a vague anguish. It was like a shadow, like a mist passing across her soul's summer day. It was strange and unfamiliar; it was a mood.
>
> (14-15)

Though the narrative asserts that Edna is unusually moved, the language disguises her emotional involvement. She does not really participate in the sentence at all: Chopin does not even choose to say that Edna "feels oppressed," but rather presents the experience of oppression as something remote, existing without relationship to her. The syntactic subject of the sentence is "oppression," an abstraction whose concrete reality is further reduced by being "indescribable"; the formal and virtually content-free sequence of syllables offers little genuine information. The oppression has originated somewhere in "her consciousness" yet *she* has not generated it, and now it fills "her whole being with a vague anguish." No real causative agent is identified, though certainly the passage creates a sense of threat and dramatic opposition. Edna is the silent, baffled receptacle for feelings that fill her mindlessly, as though she were a hollow vessel. Both the content and formal elements of the passage sustain this picture. Further, the repeated indefinite pronoun "it" contributes to the sense of vague threat. The whole passage, in fact, is aggressively global and nonspecific, embodying a kind of verbal groping which duplicates Edna's dim, and at this point tentative, perception of the events that are coming to occupy her consciousness. As she tries to clarify her sense of oppression, she moves further from it: "It was like a shadow, like a mist passing across her soul's summer day" (another image of her as an object, a summer landscape that mist and shadows pass across). Though technically concrete, these nouns refer to the most insubstantial and transient of things; Edna, trying hard to view her oppression as temporary, is drawn by their impermanence. The construction "it was" somewhat weakens her attempt by asserting, more or less in the voice of an objective narrator, that the oppression indeed does exist—in contrast, for example, to the more equivocal verb phrase "seemed to generate" in the preceding sentence. Altogether, the words prepare us for the next turn of Edna's consciousness: "It was strange and unfamiliar; it was a mood." The words "strange" and "unfamiliar" commit Edna to the domain of her subjective consciousness where the threat can no longer be externalized. The suddenness with which we come to "it was a mood" suggests how she arrives, in panic, at a rationalization to reduce the threat: a mood is the most comforting and commonplace of all explanations for the inexplicable ways in which people, especially women, feel and behave, and thus serves, for the time being, to reassure her that her feelings are acceptable. Restored to relative normalcy, she becomes suddenly conscious of the mosquites and goes inside to sleep.

This introduction to Edna's consciousness is marked by language drawn from a world of formal abstraction. Its elements recur frequently in the novel—the abstract nouns and adjectives, dense with Latinate prefixes and suffixes, the chain of prepositional phrases, the serviceable "it was" construction. We are given the sense that forces are at work, but they remain disguised, stubbornly unobservable, their point of origin and locus ambiguous and shadowy. Yet these abstract and "unreal" verbal elements acquire in the course of the book a convincing reality of their own. Indeed, they emerge as the dominant and unchanging reality behind the illusory visions that Edna experiences and become, in consequence, virtual protagonists in the novel's verbal drama. In the process we grow used to the language that at first distanced us from Edna's experience, and learn to recognize the grammar and vocabulary, the verbal territory, that mark the progress of her awakening. What appears to begin as needlessly abstract, awkward, and uninviting language comes to signal the complicated struggles of Edna's most essential self.*

Just before the "indescribable oppression" passages I have been discussing, Edna is presented differently:

> The tears came so fast to Mrs. Pontellier's eyes that the damp sleeve of her *peignoir* no longer served to dry them. She was holding the back of her chair with one hand; her loose sleeve had slipped almost to the shoulder of her uplifted arm. Turning, she thrust her face, steaming and wet, into the bend of her arm, and she went on crying there, not caring any longer to dry her face, her eyes, her arms.
>
> (14)

Although this passage occurs in the same narrative context and also portrays Edna overcome by emotion, the mode of presentation establishes for Edna a strong and clear physical presence which in some ways challenges the notion of her passivity and helplessness. The nouns, pronouns, and verbs are concrete and visual, and describe not her "being" nor her "consciousness" but her sleeve, her arm, her face. Though "tear" and "sleeve" are the syntactic subjects in the first sentence, they do not crowd our sense of Edna herself; no more in control of the tears than she is of the oppression, she is nevertheless palpably *there* in the words and images of the narrative description. The passage does little more than catalogue Edna's clothes and the individual parts of her body, and does not particularly invoke the presence of a thinking self; yet the pronoun "she" anchors her physical self to the language (just as the pronoun "it" reinforced the vagueness of her oppression and further abstracted its reality).

Though Edna is behaving "passively," the repeated pronoun "she" and the concrete actions she performs inevitably help to create a portrait of her as forceful and independent, demonstrably capable of action. The passage illustrates another of the book's pervasive sentence structures, in which Edna's name or the pronoun "she" makes up the head noun phrase and serves as syntactic subject—and for the most part semantic subject, that is, performer of action, as well. (Compare the long paragraph that describes Edna's preparations for sleep

---

*Thus the conjunction of abstract noun with abstract adjective recurs at critical points. For example: "contradictory impulses" (33), "shadowy anguish" (33), "abiding truth" (66), "awakened being" (116), "futile expedients" (146), "incomprehensible longing" (139), "appalling and hopeless ennui" (145), "extraneous impression" (145), "despondent frame of mind" (158), "external existence" (219), "radiant peace" (187), "awakening sensuousness" (199), "feverish anxiety" (220), "vague dread" (288), "inward agony" (288), "outspoken revolt" (288).

at Madame Antoine's, p. 93; Edna is the nominal or pronominal subject of seven of the eight sentences in the passage and her name or "she" or "her" occurs 22 times.)

Per Seyersted has proposed that Chopin's ongoing exploration of behavioral alternatives for women led in her writing to "an interplay between her self-assertive and self-forgetting heroines" that amounted to "a running dialogue with herself on woman's lot."* In *The Awakening* these alternatives are explored simultaneously, not simply through the presentation of different kinds of women—Edna, Adele Ratignolle, Mademoiselle Reisz, Madame Lebrun—but through the linguistic presentation of Edna herself. A key example is Edna's childhood memory " 'of a summer day in Kentucky, of a meadow that seemed as big as the ocean to the very little girl walking through the grass' "; sharing this memory with Adele Ratignolle, Edna at first speaks of herself as the little girl, someone else, removed in time and space; only then does she shift to the first person and identify the little girl with herself, at the present time: " 'sometimes I feel this summer as if I were walking through the green meadow again: idly, aimlessly, unthinking and unguided' " (43). This is the emblematic image of Edna's duality: the body moves through the field as though swimming, without clear direction or purpose, without consciousness except, perhaps, as the body's silent witness. The image is striking, as though her body has always lived its life, but apart; now, it is beginning to be invaded with increasing aggression by consciousness, whose enroachment at first takes place in highly noncommittal language (marked, for example, by the repeated negating affixes *-less* and *un-*).

The first part of the book establishes contradictions and dualities, presumably to parallel what the narrative tells us about Edna—the "contradictory subtle play of features" (7), her "dual life" (35). She is continually baffled by her behavior and feelings, and fluctuates between apparent self-knowledge and apparent self-deception. Her perceptions are hedged in modals and conditional structures, negatives, and relative clauses. Any sense of guiding consciousness is undercut by verbal signals of doubt and hesitation. The caged birds that open the novel establish immediately the sense of constrained potential that marks these first chapters. When Edna does experience "a first breath of freedom" (48), it is compared to wine and intoxication, images of deceptive euphoria that suggest only an illusory loss of restraint. The first sentence of Chapter VI, the short chapter that establishes the "voice of the sea" refrain, offers us similar

---

*Per Seyersted, *A Critical Biography*, pp. 111, 113. Other readers have also seen the novel as a contrast between active and passive modes of action. Wheeler writes that Edna awakens to an "awareness of being a 'subject' rather than an 'object' " (123). Mademoiselle Reisz, writes Wolff, is "an active agent who has defined her relationship to the world. Edna, by contrast, is passive" (466). According to Seyersted, she "craves to be an active subject rather than a passive object" (143). Sullivan and Smith argue that the novel's "see-saw narrative stance" presents both a "feminist heroine" and a passively "shallow self-deceiver" (73). Allen suggests that Edna's choice not to be a wife and mother is "positive, active, and courageous," while her conformity to the role would have been "negative, passive, and docile" (227).

complications: "Edna Pontellier could not have told why, wishing to go to the beach with Robert, she should in the first place have declined, and in the second place have followed in obedience to one of the two contradictory impulses which impelled her" (33). Not only are we *told* that Edna's own behavior baffles her, the sentence itself is a wordy puzzle through which we must work our way, in suspense to the heart—"one of the two contradictory impulses." The repeated modals and negatives, the mixture of active and passive voice, the almost clinical vocabulary, discourage Edna's too-close scrutiny of these "impulses"—and discourage us as well. This last point is important. For while the contradictory verbal signals underscore both Edna's own doubts and the contradictions we are told her character includes, they also thwart our own tendencies, as readers, to respond to the narrative from a single perspective.

But the verbal complications I have been describing fall away on the night Edna learns to swim, an event that integrates both modes of syntactic presentation and triumphantly celebrates a unity of emotions and will. The evening begins with the family entertainment at which Mademoiselle Reisz is asked to play the piano. Edna's unexpectedly passionate response to the music transcends the stolid domestic texture of the evening; to her own astonishment, the customary gentle, poetic images are absent, and in their place "the very passions themselves were aroused within her soul, swaying it, lashing it, as the waves daily beat upon her splendid body. She trembled, she was choking, and the tears blinded her" (66). The response is an escalated version of her earlier crying, and again she is described as being at the mercy of forces beyond her control. But not only are these forces more concrete here, the figurative parallel between passions and waves (and soul and body) gives way at once to real waves as the guests walk down to the beach and Edna learns to swim.

She has been trying to learn to swim all summer, but "a certain ungovernable dread hung about her when in the water, unless there was a hand nearby that might reach out and reassure her" (70). Like the earlier oppression that filled her, "ungovernable dread" has "hung about her"—another globally vague picture which admits no guiding consciousness and shows Edna paralyzed and impotent, the passive recipient of instructions from others. Now there is a change:

> But that night she was like the little tottering, stumbling, clutching child, who of a sudden realizes its powers, and walks for the first time alone, boldly and with over-confidence. She could have shouted for joy. She did shout for joy, as with a sweeping stroke or two she lifted her body to the surface of the water. (70)

We find our way through the cluster of adjectives and commas to Edna's triumph: animated and active herself, engaged and roused, she can transform a figure of speech into a real shout of joy. The grammatical shift from "could have" to "did"—like the shift from the little child to Edna herself—signals real changes in her behavior and understanding. Her shout fuses body and consciousness.

Similarly, the passage fuses the contrasting verbal patterns I have described. It begins with "she," but the simile that follows deflects us momentarily from Edna herself with its explicit comparison of her to a child. Both the pronoun "that" and the definite article "the" give the images a still, emblematic quality that characterizes the entire scene. The participles—"stumbling," "tottering," "clutching"—are concrete and visual, and though they suggest faltering and vulnerability, they are intransitive, thus active, not passive. The digression has added suspense: the child "of a sudden realizes its powers" and walks "boldly and with over-confidence"; now Edna's action breaks through the mentalistic language of this symbolic picture, as though the "she" that began the sentence has gathered power that is now released. "She could have shouted for joy. She did shout for joy. . . ." This is one of the most unambivalent expressions of active force in the book: Edna passes from the metaphorical to the actual and offers a verbal model, in miniature, for what the story is about. The passage ends in the wholly immediate and concrete, "as with a sweeping stroke or two she lifted her body to the surface of the water."

Like the scene as a whole, the passage makes clear that swimming has both sensual and spiritual dimensions, and its risks are both sexual and political: "She wanted to swim far out, where no woman had swum before" (70-71). Edna's experience of the water is immediately, passionately sensuous, but its spirtual and political dimensions are continually affirmed: "A feeling of exultation overtook her, as if some power of significant import had been given her to control the working of her body and her soul" (70). We may dwell for a moment on this sentence, which not only relates the swimming experience to both body and soul explicitly but also formally fuses the passive and active elements of Edna's situation. "Exultation," in the first clause, is the familiar abstract noun: as a replacement for "oppression," only the nature of the emotion has changed; formally, Edna remains in the sentence the passive object of abstract forces beyond her control. But then the burden of responsibility shifts when the power is given to her: though still the recipient of this gift, the "her" which is the object of "given" is also the subject of the infinitive "to control." The grammatical simultaneity of "her" as object and subject is equivalent to the fluctuating and sometimes paradoxical images that interlace subject and object, self and other, container and contained, inner and outer. For a moment at least, Chopin creates a perfect verbal merging between the forces that act on Edna from outside her and the imperatives of her own self, between the abstractions of consciousness and the concrete language of her physical world. Nowhere does the narrative voice achieve a fuller sense of integration than in this passage: "She turned her face seaward to gather in an impression of space and solitude, which the vast expanse of water, meeting and melting with the moonlit sky, conveyed to her excited fancy. As she swam she seemed to be reaching out for the unlimited in which to lose herself" (71).

The celebratory language and physical beauty of the scene, however, should not make us forget the threat, signalled first by the description of the little child who walks "with over-confidence" and echoed in words like "reckless," "intoxicated," and "overestimating her strength." Though she may wish "to swim far out," she can in fact only manage a short distance; unaccustomed even to this exertion, she is overcome by exhaustion and a vision of death, and can barely swim back to shore. This experience, together with other features of the scene, deliberately invokes the earlier "voice of the sea" refrain and its sinister promises:

> The voice of the sea is seductive; never ceasing, whispering, clamoring, murmuring, inviting the soul to wander for a spell in abysses of solitude; to lose itself in mazes of inward contemplation.
> The voice of the sea speaks to the soul. The touch of the sea is sensuous, enfolding the body in its soft, close embrace.   (33)

This passage conceals in poetic metaphor the threat which emerges suddenly when Edna, in the swimming scene, experiences both a vision of death and a real danger of drowning. Seduced by the sea's space and solitude, Edna seeks to lose herself in its mazes. The sea may speak to the soul, but its seduction of the body is a more literal and risky enfolding.

The swimming scene gives substance to what has only been metaphorical suggestion; it is the turning point in the novel which offers us, in a rush, a sudden access to Edna's possibilities and an expanded vision of her situation. (We did not know until this scene, for example, that Edna had even been trying to learn to swim.) This conversion of metaphor to experience gives the scene its power. The confusion and hesitance of Edna's earlier behavior fall away as she takes her life, literally, into her own hands. In the scene that follows, speaking to Robert and then to her husband, she uses the first person pronoun with far greater authority than before, describing her feelings and her will. As a reading experience, the swimming scene is a triumph. For Edna, in perfect and dangerous solitude, an "I" has been created.

II

In her childhood Edna crossed "a meadow that seemed as big as the ocean," moving her arms "as if swimming when she walked" (41). The second section of the novel moves from ocean to city, where walking becomes, for Edna, something of an emotional and spiritual equivalent to swimming.

Her walking gives her some degree of physical freedom. " 'I always feel so sorry for women who don't like to walk,' " she says later. " ' They miss so much—so many rare little glimpses of life; and we women learn so little of life on the whole' " (278). But to her husband, this mobility is dangerous. " 'She goes tramping about by herself,' " he tells Dr. Mandelet to indicate the seriousness of her mental condition, " 'moping in street-cars, getting in after dark. I tell you she's peculiar' " (171). Their divergent points of view may remind us that the subtitle of *The Awakening*, originally its title, is "A Solitary Soul." Solitude is a critical theme of the novel, closely related to the existence of the self and its responsibilities.

Edna's physical mobility parallels a tentative kind of self-exploration. When her husband and children leave, and she is alone at last, she experiences "a radiant peace" (187), "A genuine sigh of relief," "a feeling that was unfamiliar but very delicious" (188). "She walked all through the house, from one room to another, as if inspecting it for the first time" (188). The language recalls an earlier scene at Madame Antoine's, when Edna inspected each part of her body, "observing closely, as if it were something she saw for the first time" (93). But Edna comes to realize that she will not find peace in her husband's house. Once she has "resolved never again to belong to another than herself" (208), she must seek a new space, and she makes plans to move into the "pigeon house" around the corner. Edna's freedom to move around—to walk at random, to dine out, to visit the race track—mimics the mobility of the men in the novel, who are always off somewhere—the club, New York, Mexico. Yet it is merely the freedom that Edna wants, not the masculine world it represents—a world which all the male characters, to different degrees, belong to, and which Chopin seems repeatedly to question.*

During Edna's periods of solitude, she achieves some measure of peacefulness and of control over her day-to-day activities. As Margaret Culley points out, Chopin permits us some glimpse of Edna alone by obligingly removing the men in her life from the novel for extended periods of time. Though it is not clearcut, her solitary self-sufficiency does contrast with her dependence on men when they are around. I do not agree with Patricia Meyer Spacks that dependence is the chief issue in the novel, but certainly the masculine presence affects Edna's behavior as well as the language she uses, which is characterized by the familiar abstract nouns, stiff formal phrases, a sense of abstract passivity, and by the distancing "it was/there was" construction. With all her relationships to men unresolved—to Robert, to Arobin, and to her husband—she acknowledges at last

---

*Cigars and newspapers are the props that Chopin sardonically furnishes for the male characters. When the novel opens, Robert is too young, poor, and inexperienced for cigars, and must make do with cigarettes, which he rolls himself. Mr. Pontellier, on the other hand, has earned the right to cigars and to the world of masculine economic and sexual power they stand for. Cigars may seem a rather obvious emblem of this power, but the men in the novel make few appearances without one, and this mildly subversive caricature of male privilege seems clearly intended. On the night Edna learns to swim, she sits outside in the moonlight—first with Robert, who smokes cigarettes, and then alone, in defiance of her husband. He counters her revolutionary mood with a show of power: he drinks wine, puts up his feet, and smokes a cigar while he waits. Finally outlasted, her mood broken, she goes in, pausing to ask him if he's coming. " 'Yes, dear,' " he answers, " 'Just as soon as I have finished my cigar.' " This is communication of a potent form, and when Robert later returns from Mexico, he too shifts to cigars: " 'I suppose I'm getting reckless,' " he tells Edna, " 'I bought a whole box.' " Leaving for Mexico neither Edna's provider nor her lover, he returns aspiring to be both: This almost cartoonlike assertion announces his acquisition of adult male status. Edna's statement that "I am no longer one of Mr. Pontellier's possessions to dispose of or not" violates the rules of this world of established masculine potency and shatters Robert's vision of a dignified transaction between gentlemen. It is to traditional roles and masculine codes, to men and cigars, that Robert's farewell note is loyal.

that "she wanted something to happen—something, anything; she did not know what" (196). This is one of the first concrete admissions of Edna's active involvement, of her actively wanting something. The semantic uncertainty does not lessen the force of the verb. Her awakening consciousness, peaceful only in solitude, plays against her awakening sensuality, which depends for its fulfillment on the masculine world that alienates her.

Much of the narrative tension of the novel, as well as a host of images and metaphors, has seemed to be building toward the moment when Edna will at last commit adultery and experience an explicitly sexual awakening. For Seyersted, the scene in which Edna sleeps with Arobin is the novel's "single, crucial paragraph" where Chopin "explodes the myth of the noble, undivided passion."[3] As we might expect, the passage is powerful:

> Edna cried a little that night after Arobin left her. It was only one phase of the multitudinous emotions which had assailed her. There was with her an overwhelming feeling of irresponsibility. There was the shock of the unexpected and the unaccustomed. There was her husband's reproach, looking at her from the external things around her which he had provided for her external existence. There was Robert's reproach, making itself felt by a quicker, fiercer, more overpowering love which had awakened within her toward him. Above all, there was understanding. She felt as if a mist had been lifted from her eyes, enabling her to look upon and comprehend the significance of life, that monster made up of beauty and brutality. But among the conflicting sensations which assailed her, there was neither shame nor remorse. There was a dull pang of regret because it was not the kiss of love which had inflamed her, because it was not love which had held this cup of life to her lips (219).

This passage asserts that sexual intercourse leaves Edna shocked and overwhelmed, that the "mist had been lifted" to reveal that sexual pleasure can occur without either marriage or love—that it can, indeed, occur with a barely respectable man she does not even especially like. But the language of the passage is curious, and does not quite fulfill our expectations. Though Edna took the initiative in responding to Arobin's kiss ("she clasped his head," 218), and thus implicitly was responsible, she is no longer in active control. Far from reinforcing her emotional commitment to the experience, as the swimming scene so clearly did (as when she achieved the "power . . . to control the working of her body and her soul," 70), this passage displaces her from the action almost entirely. Its syntactic construction is as extreme as any in the book. "There was" or "it was" occurs ten times, repetitively asserting the existence of feelings and responses, but denying Edna any connection to or responsibility for them. In part perhaps, Chopin's wariness led her to report her heroine's responses to sexual gratification without personally committing her to them, but this does not fully account for the stiffness and distance of the passage. At the moment when Edna should be wholly awakened, alive and present, the language removes her. At the moment when her body should be fully engaged, abstractions absorb her experience.

Body is invaded by consciousness; the link cannot be undone. We may have believed that *The Awakening* has been building toward Edna's sexual fulfillment, but we are wrong. It cannot be, this language says; both body and spirit are awakening toward some final end, and this is not it. The book's verbal complications here thwart our temptation to read this passage as a release or a solution. As the pages that follow make clear, Edna's "problem" is never simply one of achieving the freedom to make sexuality possible or to forsake paternalistic conventions; it is rather a question of how one can live in the world with both oneself and others. It is also a question of how a woman who has achieved a self—has become an "I"—can live in the world. The book builds toward a rather brutal exploration of the physiological consequences of women's choices. Here, as elsewhere, we see and hear connections which are not explicit. We carry the language of the novel along with us as we read.

This process is exemplified when Edna, in the midst of her elegant dinner party several nights later, suddenly experiences a total assault by the abstract forces, so familiar to us now, that have threatened her from the beginning:

> But as she sat there amid her guests, she felt the old ennui overtaking her; the hopelessness which so often assailed her, which came upon her like an obsession, like something extraneous, independent of volition. It was something which announced itself; a chill breath that seemed to issue from some vast cavern wherein discords wailed. There came over her the acute longing which always summoned into her spiritual vision the presence of the beloved one, overpowering her at once with a sense of the unattainable. (232)

That this language occurs at this point, when Edna is discovering personal freedom and overt sexuality, is ominous. Our recognition of the lexical and syntactic patterns duplicates, perhaps, Edna's acceptance of this turn of emotional events; the phrase "the old ennui" suggests how commonplace the oppression, once so "strange and unfamiliar" (14), has become. That oppression, introduced long ago, has solidified and thus become more genuinely threatening. It is now poignantly localized: unlike her first experience of oppression, "which seemed to generate in some unfamiliar part of her unconsciousness" (14), it here announces itself as "a chill breath that seemed to issue from some vast cavern wherein discords wailed." Again she is "overtaken," "come upon," "overpowered"—but now the earlier "mist" and "shadows" have given way to the permanence of a "vast cavern" of solid rock. To an extraordinary degree the passage compresses the verbal elements that have troubled Edna: the abstraction, vagueness, passivity that have characterized these moments of awakening consciousness.

Yet why should this language occur here? Why should it here threaten Edna's new life with a foreshadowing of despair and death? Using such language as evidence, Sullivan and Smith argue that Edna in the course of the book experiences "a series of depressions that become suicidal," that the facts of her life "paint a consistent portrait of the kind of woman who might commit suicide because she was denied love by a man important to her."[4] We might then read the dinner party scene as a corruption of the innocence of the family entertainment at Grand Isle: when, for example, Robert's decadent brother Victor hums Robert's song, it is for Edna the transforming vision. Wolff, similarly, describes Edna's "sense of inner emptiness" (for example, the "vast cavern" image), which she attributes to a "schizoid" personality, and an "infantile life-pattern."[5] Allen's analysis of male critics' responses to the novel notes their virtually uniform castigation of Edna for failing in her duties as a wife and mother; yet much of the same irritation and righteous outrage pervades these psychological studies, which seem to view Edna's depression as a result of her individual failures and personal maladjustments. But this analysis fails to account for our experience of the novel as a reading experience; and I would argue that the language, here and elsewhere, continually asserts the existence of an independent, impersonal state of affairs over which Edna has little control. Analysis of the central metaphor will clarify the argument.

III

Chopin achieves her effects by building up, over time, a network of images, words, verbal refrains, and grammatical textures, often through simple and quite artificial repetition, until the language we remember is continually energizing the language on the page. This growing resonance of language and imagery makes complex and sensuous what is essentially straightforward prose. In the closing chapters of *The Awakening*, this cumulative density is apparent, and contributes to the drama and sense of narrative completion that the reading experience creates.

Chopin's central metaphor of waking and sleeping, for example, depends on more than a hundred references to literal and metaphorical awakening, sleeping, and dreaming. At first the words themselves tempt us to make some fairly conventional equations: sleep means blindness, inertia, passivity, death; awakening means energy, activity, vision, life. Nothing in the prose denies us these meanings. But gradually, as they are linked to specific words, images, and narrative developments, the novel's unique associations supplant the personal and literary associations we have brought to it. By the time we reach the final scenes, most of the key words have occurred before and resonate with a verbal history internal to the text. This process of cumulative association—this intricate and increasingly paradoxical interweaving of meanings—radically changes their impact. Whatever we accept as the meaning of the novel must take into account this process of transformation.

The process can be briefly sketched. In an early scene, Edna is literally awakened by her husband. The night she learns to swim, her sleep is "troubled and feverish, disturbed with dreams" that leave fleeting impressions the next day

upon "her half-awakened senses" (82). Her sensuality is later said to be awakened by Arobin (199), while Edna attributes her awakening to Robert (283).
Elsewhere her awakening seems self-generated. The ambiguous structure of the
word "awakening" encompasses these definitions, permitting Edna to be
awakened, to awaken someone else (as she awakens Robert, 83), or simply to
awaken spontaneously (as she does on p. 94). Critics have noted that the act
of awakening (like sleeping) figures both literally and symbolically in the novel
(see Wheeler or Wolff, for example), and most of the key scenes, in fact, play
upon these events. But the density and complexity of verbal reference are
critical. Repeated references make clear Edna's "awakening sensuousness"
(199); yet after Arobin kisses her hand, she feels like a woman who "realizes
the significance of [unfaithfulness] without being wholly awakened from its
glamour" (201-2). She is simultaneously, in other words, awakening *to*
sensuality and awakening *from* it. Because in Chopin, the individual line or
paragraph is inevitably subordinate to the cumulative verbal effect, such
paradoxical usage thwarts any single perspective or definition.

When Edna meets Robert in the garden and returns with him for the final
time to her little house, the imagery of sleeping, awakening and dreaming
intensifies. " 'Robert,' " Edna asks him as he sits in shadow, "as if in a reverie,"
" 'Are you asleep?' " (280). This same question opened the intricate, political
battle of wills between Edna and her husband the night she learned to swim
(78 ff.). Here, it opens an exchange between Edna and Robert which parallels
the earlier scene and clarifies Chopin's position in this novel on relationships
between women and men. When Edna leans down and kisses Robert, she takes
control of her life (as she did with Arobin) and shatters his evasive reticence;
at first it seems that what she earlier characterized as a "delicious, grotesque
impossible dream" (81) is coming true, for Robert confesses his own " 'wild
dream of your some day becoming my wife' " (281). But in shock and surprise
Edna replies " 'Your wife!' " and in this exclamation reveals the vast distance
that separates her earlier consciousness from that which now tells Robert, " 'You
have been a very, very foolish boy, wasting your time dreaming of impossible
things when you speak of Mr. Pontellier setting me free! I am no longer one of
Mr. Pontellier's possessions to dispose of or not. I give myself where I choose' "
(282).

Edna explicitly rejects her role as a possession and an object, and it is
significant that she refers to her husband formally as "Mr. Pontellier"; for it
was as "Mrs. Pontellier" that the novel introduced her and almost at once referred to her as both an object and a possession. Her statement at this point recalls
her inward determination, earlier, "never to belong to another than herself"; but
now she expresses herself aloud, and it is her new language, perhaps, that
frightens Robert as much as what she says. It was in this language that she
confronted him in an earlier scene and demonstrated the same mastery of the
first person singular pronoun: " 'I suppose this is what you would call unwomanly; but I have got into a habit of expressing myself. It doesn't matter to
me, and you may think me unwomanly if you like' " (276-77). In contrast to
this language of the self are numerous references to literal and figurative voices in

the novel (for example, 72, 109, 134, 243) which for Edna become increasingly unimportant as her own language emerges. By the time the doctor offers meaningful conversation—to "talk of things you never have dreamt of talking about before" (293) —it is a language Edna no longer speaks.

Robert turns pale during Edna's assertion of independence, but she does not yet recognize that they are at cross-purposes—that her insistence and initiative have at last shattered his vaguely self-congratulatory indecisiveness and, in fact, terrified him. " 'It was you,' " she goes on, " 'who awoke me last summer out of a life-long, stupid dream' " (293). Robert himself has been treated as a part of this dream until now, and so the sudden description of her whole life as a *stupid* dream (and of Robert's dream as a waste of time) confirms that, for Edna, the meaning of the word "dream" has changed: what was "delicious" fantasy is now rejected as delusion.

Chopin introduced the metaphor of sleeping and awakening by rooting it in reality when Edna was awakened by her husband. Now Edna is called away to be with Adele Ratignolle during childbirth, and as she sits at her bedside, the central metaphor is once more transformed into literal reality:

> Edna began to feel uneasy. She was seized with a vague dread. Her own life experiences seemed far away, unreal, and only half remembered. She recalled faintly an ecstasy of pain, the heavy odor of chloroform, a stupor which deadened sensation, and an awakening to find a little new life to which she had given being, added to the great unnumbered multitude of souls that come and go. (288)

This passage is of critical narrative importance, for together with Edna's response to the birth process itself and her exchange with Doctor Mandelet, it makes clear that for women the birth of children is a central and inescapable issue. It is a philosophical as well as a physiological fact, for Edna having just declared her love for Robert, comprehends with vivid clarity the inescapable link between sexual fulfillment, childbirth, and responsibility for those "little lives." In the passage, multiple verbal connections come together: for example, the phrase "heavy odor of chloroform" binds an earlier fragment "heavy with sleep" to Arobin's "narcotic" presence and to the "heavy odor of jessamine" (231) at Edna's dinner party; earlier, when Arobin and Robert have both left, Edna "stayed alone in a kind of reverie—a sort of stupor" (269); the stupor which deadens sensation recalls the Ratignolles' marriage of "blind contentment" (145). The drugged stupor of childbirth, its deadened sensations, resolves in women's terms the conventional paradox that out of death comes life. But the passage also gives specific reality to the sense of alien forces that has governed Edna's awakening consciousness: her original experience of "indescribable oppression" is in fact clearly described here. The "vague dread" that seizes her recalls her earlier "vague anguish," the "ungovernable dread" she experienced in the water, and the "vague dread" that has filled Adele: in *The Awakening*, the source of this dread, the source of the oppression, lies in the reality of the female body. This reality is the source, in turn, of life's compelling illusions.

Edna's revelation leaves her "stunned and speechless with emotion," for its corollary is that her own sexual awakening is as deluded as her previous life has been; it is merely part of the "stupid life-long dream." Dazed, speaking as much to herself as to Doctor Mandelet, she completes the vision: " 'The years that are gone seem like dreams—if one might go on sleeping and dreaming—but to wake up and find—oh! well! perhaps it is better to wake up after all, even to suffer, rather than to remain a dupe to illusions all one's life' " (292). The deliciousness of the dream is at the root of its deceptive power. The "cup of life" that sexual passion hold's out is nature's narcotic, which both intoxicates and drugs—" 'a decoy,' " as the doctor says, " 'to secure mothers for the race' " (291). Edna accepts responsibility for her vision. " 'One has to think of the children some time or other,' " she says, speaking in the abstract but at once shifting to the first person: " 'I don't want anything but my own way. . . . Still, I shouldn't want to trample upon the little lives' " (292-93). The change of pronoun signals the self's recognition of responsibility, though not necessarily, as most readings have had it, for her own children; she is no more a "mother-woman" than she has ever been. Rather, she sees the inevitability of the connection, and the "unnumbered multitude" of young lives that result from the illusion of sexual fulfillment. These are "the realities" with which Edna has at last come "face to face"; this is the "alien force" that threatens to invade her.

Characteristically, Edna does not accept this vision without a struggle; her consciousness attempts one last evasion by reviving earlier dreams. "Numb with the intoxication of expectancy" (the language continues to link passion with pregnancy and death), she hopes Robert will have fallen asleep so that she can "awaken him with a kiss" and "arouse him with her caresses" (294). "She could picture at that moment no greater bliss on earth than possession of the beloved one" (293). But as the vocabulary itself should tell us, none of this is to be. Instead, we learn how dense the language has become when Edna finds the house empty and reads Robert's farewell note (" 'I love you. Good-by—because I love you' " 294):

> Edna grew faint when she read the words. She went and sat on the sofa. Then she stretched herself out there, never uttering a sound. She did not sleep. She did not go to bed. The lamp sputtered and went out. She was still awake in the morning, when Celestine unlocked the kitchen door and came in to light the fire. (294)

This "awakening," for Edna, is final. Her faintness momentarily invokes her customary tendency to dream and sleep, but not for long. Unlike the first awakening scene, here she does not cry nor succumb at last to sleep. In perfect solitude and silence, her mind is entirely occupied with itself. The threatening external forces have been internalized within her own body: the language of childbirth underlies the "vast cavern wherein discords wailed." Though the passage holds us fast to Edna's literal behavior, it is no longer purely concrete;

its structures are invaded with meaning. In the terms that the book has created, to be alive is to sleep and to dream; out of the deathlike stupor of childbirth comes life, but conversely, to awaken, as Edna has done, is to die. When her consciousness fully awakens, it undoes itself. The passage doubles as a retrospective catalogue of her consciousness and a preparation for the decision she is making.

IV

Edna enters the final chapter through the eyes of Victor and Mariequita; she is again "Mrs. Pontellier," and her docile, conventional interaction with them informs us that the real Edna is elsewhere. Now as she moves "rather mechanically" toward the beach, we reenter her consciousness which we find has absorbed its external environment and is now "not noticing anything special except that the sun was hot." Edna's analysis of her situation is distanced verbally from her current consciousness by the past perfect tense ("she had done all the thinking which was necessary"), and is offered at this point, after the fact, to the reader. In her despondency, she has seen the inevitable connections between responsibility to one's self and to others, especially to one's children— those that already exist and those not yet born. Adele's plea to " 'think of the children' " does not mean to Edna what it means to her. To Edna, the body enters a duplicitous pact with nature to betray the self; the inevitability of this duplicity makes the children seem like alien antagonists who "overcome" and "overpower" her. As her body awakens and consciousness invades it, its fate becomes clear. To live as the creator and nurturer of "new little" lives perverts the self; to live alone and for herself alone, as Mademoiselle Reisz does, is for Edna impossible. The roots of the word "dream" include both "joy" and "deception"; Edna's vision of reality has robbed her of the possibility of either, and she must put aside all the fictions she has been offered. Maternal love, romantic love, sexual passion, economic independence, artistic achievement, physical comfort, civilized elegance: all, for Edna, are intensely duplicitous.

The paradox is this: Mrs. Pontellier has become an "I" and has mastered in her own speech the use of the pronoun. Her movement through space in the novel—swimming, walking—is important because she is the only female character capable of it: capable of change, capable of learning a new language. But at the point of her final movement, she speaks and embodies a language which cannot be spoken. Only in solitude can the true self speak and be heard.

This is what the last chapter is about. It is a stunning culmination of the novel's verbal patterns that gives them their final transformation. It condenses the processes that have been animating the reading experience and carries us along in a swift and yet often unexpected rush of words and images. The novel's metaphors become, in the last scene, its literal reality. Thus throughout the novel Edna has metaphorically removed her clothing: first she loosened "the mantle of reserve" (35); when Robert left for Mexico "her whole existence was dulled, like a faded garment which seems to be no longer worth wearing" (117-18); as she changes, "she was becoming herself and daily casting aside that fictitious self which we assume like a garment with which to appear before the world" (147-48); after the exhaustion of watching Adele give birth, she lets "the tearing emotion" "fall away from her like a somber, uncomfortable garment, which she had but to loosen to be rid of" (293). Now, as she reaches the beach and changes into her bathing suit, she again transforms the metaphorical into the actual, stripping away her fictitious selves: "But when she was there beside the sea, absolutely alone, she cast the unpleasant, pricking garments from her, and for the first time in her life she stood naked in the open air, at the mercy of the sun, the breeze that beat upon her, and the waves that invited her" (301).

It is thus no surprise that Edna walks literally into the sea. Life and death are inextricably linked, as the language has linked sleeping and awakening. "All along the white beach, up and down, there was no living thing in sight," Chopin writes, yet then at once adds to the scene "a bird with a broken wing," "beating the air above, reeling, fluttering, circling down, down to the water" (301-2). The bird's appearance here underscores the verbal processes of this final chapter, for it too has been a dual image throughout the novel; invoking both the "fluttering wings" of the mother-women and the bruised and exhausted artistic weaklings who, in Mademoiselle Reisz' words, come "fluttering back to earth" (217), the image links childbirth with death and confirms the novel's verbal movement. The obviousness, the expectedness of the image makes clear its participation not in a world of real things but in a visionary verbal structure. The language of Edna's experience supports this reading: "How strange and awful it seemed to stand naked under the sky! How delicious! She felt like some new-born creature, opening its eyes in a familiar world that it had never known" (301). This recalls the earlier comment that Edna had learned "to look with her own eyes; to see and to apprehend the deeper undercurrents of life" (245) —which links this clear-sightedness with the sea.

Edna's final movement into the sea makes literal, in the general way I have cited, the sea's metaphorical seductiveness; the link is explicit, because the "voice of the sea" refrain is repeated. But it forms a stricter parallel with the earlier swimming scene, both in its individual images and in its overall sense of personal will and spirit of victory. Learning to swim—awakening—made Edna's death inevitable. Her vision of death that night, of course, foreshadowed her final suicide. But what is more interesting is that the final scene restores to swimming its literal meaning. The earlier scene promised a metaphorical fulfillment; it promised that Edna's triumph was to be the beginning of a new life; it promised an awakening that was both sensual and spiritual. It *was* that, but its symbolic and metaphorical possibilities were always more appealing than any imaginable reality; similarly, no subsequent reality in Edna's experience ever moved her as much as her own power, while in the water, "to control the working of her body and her soul" (70). Thus she does not return to the sea because it is the ideal lover, or the unlimited she has sought, or a transcendent oneness "in which to lose herself." Rather, she chooses the sea for itself. The joy of swimming is not what it promises or stands for; it is the ultimate end. What seemed metaphorical and symbolic is literal.

Similarly, Edna's suicide translates into narrative reality the verbal elements from which the novel has been built. It enacts the moment during the swimming scene when Edna was simultaneously both active subject and passive object. In the last paragraph, we see as well that the novel's language enacts this paradox, offering us a literal reality hallucinated by a consciousness which no longer exists:

> She looked into the distance, and the old terror flamed up for an instant, then sank again. Edna heard her father's voice and her sister Margaret's. She heard the barking of an old dog that was chained to the sycamore tree. The spurs of the cavalry officer clanged as he walked across the porch. There was the hum of bees, and the musky odor of pinks filled the air. (303)

At the beginning of the paragraph, Edna actively looks into the distance; she is the subject of the next two sentences, though now as a passive listener. Then the spurs clang across the porch, and she is no longer in the sentence at all. Sense impressions and memories float in space. The unique and individual consciousness, the "I," has disintegrated; it is the reader, as much as Edna, who retains the meaning of the cavalry officer. "There was the hum of bees, and the musky odor of pinks filled the air." Just as the novel opened with an image of two birds—an apparently literal image almost immediately undermined by the statement that one of them spoke "a language which nobody understood"— so here the apparently humdrum image of bees and pinks is undermined by the fact that they are as much a part of our reality as Edna's.

The self asserts itself and in doing so undoes itself. Suicide is perhaps the most profoundly ambivalent of all human acts, and one which here confirms the unresolvable ambiguities of Edna's own role in the novel. It represents active passivity, a decision no longer to decide. For Edna, this act translates many of the novel's metaphors into reality, and in turn parallels the critical fact about this story: that it is about a woman learning to perceive reality whose "I" supplants the language of illusion. In determining "never to belong to another than herself," and "to give up the unessential," she transcends the mythologies offered to her, and to us, and this is treated as a triumph, not a failure. No matter what specific interpretations one gives the story's ending, its language has been living its own life and preparing us for this resolution. The profoundly active and passive elements that animate the narrative, the struggles of the self to master a language, are given, in Edna's suicide, their perfect human emblem and perfect literal, and literary, resolution.

NOTES

1. See Priscilla Allen, "Old Critics and New: The Treatment of Chopin's *The Awakening*," Arlyn Diamond and Lee R. Edwards, eds., *The Authority of Experience: Essays in Feminist Criticism* (Amherst: University of Massachusetts Press, 1977); Robert Arner, "The Art of Kate Chopin: Apprenticeship and Achievement," *Louisiana Studies* 14 (Spring 1975); Margaret Culley, "Edna Pontellier: 'A Solitary Soul'," in her edition of *The Awakening* (New York: Norton, 1976), pp. 224-8; Josephine Donovan, "Feminist Style Criticism," *Female Studies* 6 2nd Edition (1973); Ellen Moers, *Literary Women* (New York: Doubleday, 1976); Per Seyersted, *Kate Chopin: A Critical Biography* (Baton Rouge: Louisiana State University Press, 1969); Patricia Meyer Spacks, *The Female Imagination* (New York: Knopf, 1972); George M. Spangler, "Kate Chopin's *The Awakening:* A Partial Dissent," *Novel* 3 (Spring 1970):249-55; Ruth Sullivan and Stewart Smith, "Narrative Stance in Kate Chopin's *The Awakening*," *Studies in American Fiction* 1 (Spring 1973):62-75; Emily Toth, "Comment," *Signs* 1 (Summer 1976):1005; Otis B. Wheeler, "The Five Awakenings of Edna Pontellier," *The Southern Review* 11 (Winter 1975):118-28; Cynthia Griffin Wolff, "Thanatos and Eros: Kate Chopin's *The Awakening*," *American Quarterly* 25 (October 1973): 449-71; Susan Wolkenfeld, "Edna's Suicide: The Problem of the One and the Many," in Culley, ed.; Joan Zlotnick, "A Woman's Will: Kate Chopin on Selfhood, Wifehood, and Motherhood," *The Markham Review* (October 1968), unpaginated.

2. Kate Chopin, *The Awakening* (New York: Capricorn Books, 1964), p. 4. All quotations are from this edition and are documented internally by page number.

3. Seyersted, *A Critical Biography*, p. 171.

4. Sullivan and Smith, "Narrative Stance in Kate Chopin's *The Awakening*," p. 69.

5. Wolff, "Thanatos and Eros," pp. 469, 460, 461.

17
WOMEN'S AUTOBIOGRAPHY IN FRANCE: FOR A DIALECTICS OF IDENTIFICATION

Nancy K. Miller

> Is there, for me, no other haven than this
> commonplace room? Must I stay forever
> before this impenetrable mirror where I
> come up against myself, face to face?
> Colette, *The Vagabond*

The oft-cited and apparently transparent epigraph to Colette's *Break of Day*—"Do you imagine in reading my books that I am drawing my portrait? Patience: it's only my model"[1]—challenges the reader's competence in distinguishing life from art, nature from imitation, autobiography from fiction. Although this inaugural gesture, anticipating both our misreading and our improper labeling of the text, will prove to be more than a simple inveighing against the fallacy of reference, let, us, for the moment, proceed as docile and linear readers. The novel opens with a letter, and the author's first words ostensibly authenticate the document: "This note, signed 'Sidonie Colette, nee Landoy,' was written by my mother to one of my husbands, the second. A year later she died at the age of seventy-seven."[2] The invitation thus extended to seal the identity gap between the "I" of narration and Sidonie Gabrielle Colette is reissued in the second chapter. Defending herself against "one of my

A skeletal form of this essay was presented at NEMLA, April 1977. I am grateful to the Council for Research in the Humanities of Columbia University for the award of a summer stipend (1977) which permitted me to pursue my inquiry in this area. I would also like to thank the students in my graduate seminar, "French Women Writers: Toward a Definition of the Feminine Text," Columbia, Fall, 1977 for their moral and intellectual support during the final elaboration of this essay.

husband's" claims that she could write nothing but love stories, the narrator (a novelist) reviews the history of her fictional heroines and the genealogy of her *name*:

> In them I called myself Renée Néré or else, prophetically, I intro-
> duced a Léa. So it came about that both legally and familiarly, as
> well as in my books, I now have only one name, which is my own.
> Did it take only thirty years of my life to reach that point, or rather
> to get back to it? I shall end by thinking that it wasn't too high a
> price to pay.*

Who is speaking? And in whose name? The luminary warning issued at the very threshold of the text operates like a free-floating anxiety, always there to prevent a comfortable foreclosure. The "I" of narration may, like Colette, have "only one name" but her project is no less ambiguous for that onomastic symmetry.† To bypass that ambiguity would be to assume, for example, that the fiction of *Break of Day* is a page from Colette's autobiography, and hence to perform a "masculine" reading:

> Why do men—writers or so-called writers—still show surprise that a
> woman should so easily reveal to the public love-secrets and amorous
> lies and half-truths? *By divulging these, she manages to hide other
> important and obscure secrets which she herself does not understand
> very well. . . .* Man, my friend, you willingly make fun of women's
> writings because they can't help being autobiographical. On whom
> then were you relying to paint women for you. . . ? On yourself?[3]

"Colette" would have her critics not confuse (by sexual "phallacy") "the illuminated zone" of the feminine sector, love's brilliant disasters, with the darker, shadowy text of the female self, "the true intimate life of a woman."[4] But that intimacy, that maskless self, has to do with "*preference*," and here, we are told, she will "keep silent."[5]

Shall we take "Colette" at her word then? Then what we have are deliberate *fictions* of self-representation, "rearranged fragments of . . . emotional life"[6] as she calls them, and not autobiography after all? Philippe Lejeune, whose *L'Autobiographie en France* constitutes the first attempt to

---

*Colette, *Break of Day*, p. 19. Christiane Makward has pointed out the importance of this evolution in her provocative analysis of patronyms and their relationship both to women's writing and the representation of femininity: "not only is the father's name feminized and stripped of its function (to signify descendance) but it takes the place of a first name. 'Colette' is no longer a first name, a patronym or a pseudonym but *the name* that a free woman took 50 years to make for herself," "Le Nom du Père: écritures féminines d'un siècle à l'autre," paper delivered at the Third Annual Colloquim in Nineteenth-century French Studies, October 1977, Columbus, Ohio.

†As Elaine Marks comments, citing the same passage: if the narrator is "no longer wearing an obvious mask . . . she is, however, wearing the mask of 'Colette.'" And this "Colette" only exposes a self protected by inverted commas. *Colette*, pp. 212-13.

define and classify autobiography in the French tradition, would have it so. He excludes Colette from his repertory, citing her own reluctance to talk about herself; but more to the point, the absence of what he poses as a necessary condition of autobiography: the "autobiographical pact."[7] This pact is a declaration of autobiographical intention, an explicit project of sincere truth telling; a promise to the *reader* that the textual and referential "I" are one. For Lejeune, however confessional a text may seem, without that covenant of good faith, we remain in the realm of fiction.

It seems, perhaps, unregenerate bad will that despite the caveat implicit in "Colette's" jibe at the male reader expecting to find autobiography seeping through the pages of women's literature, we so reluctantly accept her exclusion from the French autobiographical canon. This resistance comes not so much from doubts about the legitimacy of Lejeune's criteria (as they do or do not apply to Colette) but from a hesitation about embracing wholeheartedly any theoretical model *indifferent* to a problematics of genre as inflected by gender. With this hesitation in mind, let us consider instances of those female autobiographers included by Lejeune—George Sand, Daniel Stern (Marie d'Agoult), and Simone de Beauvoir. Taking his criteria as a point of departure, and moving dialectically between the polarities of textual production and consumption, of authorship and readership, we will return in closing—with some stops along the way—to Colette. Thus by virtue of her undecidable relation to the androcentric paradigm Colette will serve as the fiction, the pretext really, which allows us to play with the theory.

*   *   *

Lejeune's nutshell definition of autobiography as the "retrospective narrative in prose that someone makes of his own existence, when he places the main emphasis on his individual life, in particular on the history of his personality,"[8] provides a jumping off place for our excursus. One can then ask the obvious question: is there a specificity to a female retrospective, and where will it make itself felt? To the extent that autobiography, as Diane Johnson has put it, "requires some strategy of self-dramatization" and "contains, as in fiction, a crisis and a denouement,"[9] what conventions, we might then ask, govern the production of a female self as *theater*: that which literally is given to be seen? How does a woman writer perform on the stage of her text? What, in a word, is a one-woman show?

Historically, the French autobiographer, male or female, has had to come to terms with the exhibitionist performer that is Jean-Jacques Rousseau.* Both

---

*For Lejeune, French autobiography begins officially with Rousseau; and he dates the genre as beginning around 1760. As for the response to Rousseau, Lejeune writes: "Rousseau is the only one to say aloud what everyone thinks in private. All the autobiographical pacts that follow are written against Rousseau's disastrous frankness." (p. 82.)

George Sand and her contemporary Daniel Stern take a certain distance from *The Confessions* because of the inclusive quality of his rememorations. Sand, for example, asks in her "pact": "Who can forgive him for having confessed Mme de Warens while confessing himself?"* Daniel Stern takes up the same point, rejecting promiscuity, and concluding that for herself: "I felt neither the right nor the desire, in recalling my own memories, to mix in, inappropriately, those of others."[10] And both issue warnings that the reader hoping for scandalous relevations will be disappointed; their truth, if not their memory, will be selective. Now the problem of selectivity is not a problem for women only. Every autobiographer must deal with it. Chateaubriand, for one, writes in the preface to his memoirs that he will "include no name other than his own in everything that concerns his private life."[11] To some extent, then, this reticence to name names is a matter of historical context: the nineteenth-century backlash to the tell-all stance of Rousseau—especially in the area of the sexual connection, the erogenous zones of the self. But not entirely. The decision to go public is particularly charged for the women writer.

In the preface to her second volume of memoirs, Simone de Beauvoir too goes back to Rousseau: "It may be objected that such an inquiry concerns no one but myself. Not so; if any individual—a Pepys or a Rousseau, an exceptional or a run-of-the-mill character—reveals himself honestly, everyone, more or less, becomes involved. It is impossible for him to shed light on his own life without at some point illuminating the lives of others."[12] But then, following this relative indifference to what we might call the spillover principle, a familiar caveat:

> At the same time I must warn [my readers] that I have no intention of telling them everything. I described my childhood and adolescence without any omissions. . . . I cannot treat the years of my maturity in the same detached way—nor do I enjoy a similar freedom when discussing them. I have no intention of filling these pages with spiteful gossip about myself and my friends; I lack the instincts of the scandal monger. There are many things which I firmly intend to leave in obscurity.[13]

And she adds (in the next sentence): "On the other hand, my life has been closely linked with that of Jean-Paul Sartre. As he intends to write his own life story, I shall not attempt to perform the task for him."[14] It is fair, I think, to assume that

---

*George Sand, *Histoire de ma vie*, in *Oeuvres autobiographiques* (Paris: Gallimard, 1970), Vol. I, p. 13. Béatrice Didier, in "Femme/Identité/Ecriture: A propos de *l'Histoire de ma vie* de George Sand," begins her article with an excerpt from Sand's correspondence: "I confess that I am neither humble enough to write confessions like Jean-Jacques nor impertinent enough to praise myself like the literary lights of the century. Furthermore, I don't believe that private life falls within the purview of the critics." I regret that I did not have access to Didier's interesting analysis before the fact. I refer the reader to the special issue of *La Revue des Sciences Humaines: Ecriture, Féminité, Féminisme*, 168 (1977) in which her article appears, pp. 561-76.

while for all autobiographers already figures of public fiction there is a strong sense of responsibility about speaking out, because being known, they expect their words to have an impact within a clearly defined reader's circle, the female autobiographers know that they are being read as *women*. Women, in the case of Sand, Stern, and Beauvoir (and this is no less true for Colette), known for (or even through) their liaisons with famous men. The concern with notoriety, then, functions as an additional grid or constraint placed upon the truth. Rather, upon "the shaping of the past"* as truth.

Daniel Stern articulates with the greatest insistence the role played by the fact of femininity in the autobiographical venture, and the *gender* of sincerity. She asks a friend in 1850, years before actually writing the first volume of her memoirs: "How do you think a work of this sort written by a woman, by a mother, should be composed? . . . I would favor a grave confession, narrow in scope, disengaged from detail, rather moral and intellectual than real. But I am told that that would be without charm."[15] And 13 years later, in a diary entry (but by this time, it would seem, she has already begun writing): "No, my friend, I won't write my *Memoirs*. . . . My instinctive repugnance has conquered . . . I had conceived of a daring book. Feminine confessions as sincere as and consequently more daring (because of public opinion) than those of Jean-Jacques. Once I thought this book was going to come about: *The Story of My Life* was announced. *I* cannot do it."† The book does get written, however, and in the preface to *Mes Souvenirs* Stern traces the logic of her hesitations: "I was a woman, and as such, not bound to a virile sincerity;" but when a woman's life is not governed by "the common rule . . . she becomes responsible, more responsible than a man, in the eyes of all. When this woman, because of some chance or talent, comes out of obscurity, she contracts, instantly, virile duties."[16] Thus, an exceptional woman, by virtue of that exceptionality, becomes subject to a double constraint: masculine responsibilities and feminine sensitivity. For whatever is wrong in the world, Stern contends, "woman has felt it more completely in her whole being;" if a woman is an instrument more sensitive than a man in picking up the "discordances" of society, however, she must nevertheless be more discreet than a man in rendering those vibrations: "My persuasion being . . . that a woman's pen was more constrained than another's by choice within the truth."[17]

Although, as Georges Gusdorf has written in his well-known essay on autobiography, "the man who tells his story . . . is not involved in an objective and disinterested occupation, but in a work of personal justification," and although

---

*The expression, somewhat out of context here, is from Roy Pascal, in *Design and Truth in Autobiography* (Cambridge: Harvard University Press, 1960), p. 5. Didier makes the same point, "Femme/Identité/Ecriture," p. 561.

†Cited by Vier, *La Comtesse d'Agoult*, p. 255. Thus Stern distances herself from Sand's *Histoire de ma Vie* as well as Rousseau's *Confessions*. Stern comments on Sand's work—based on an incomplete reading—in the following manner: "It seems to me that [the work] is too true or not true enough, and that is not how I would conceive of Confessions," in a letter to Hortense Allart, dated 1855, cited by Vier, footnote 727, p. 307.

such self-justification in the eyes of the world may well constitute "the most secret intention"[18] of any autobiographical undertaking, for Stern (as is true in varying degrees of intensity for Sand and Beauvoir) the self being justified is indelibly marked by what Beauvoir calls "féminitude:"[19] a culturally determined status of difference and oppression. Thus Stern would show (and surely this is the not so very hidden agenda for Sand and Beauvoir) that while a woman may fly in the face of tradition, that is, of traditional expectations for women, particularly in regard to the institution of marriage, she is no less a *human being* of merit; that while on the face of it she is an outlaw, the real fault lies with society and its laws. To justify an unorthodox life by writing about it, however, is to *reinscribe* the original violation, to reviolate masculine turf: hence Stern's defensiveness about the range of her pen. The drama of the self (to return to the histrionic metaphor proposed earlier) is staged in a public theater, and it is *thesis* drama. The autobiographies of these women, to invoke another literary genre, are a defense and illustration, at once a treatise on overcoming received notions of femininity, and a poetics calling for another, freer text. These autobiographies, then, belong to that type of women's writing Elaine Showalter describes as "Feminist": "*protest*" against the "standards of art and its views of social roles," and "*advocacy*" of minority rights and values, including a demand for autonomy."[20] The subject of women's autobiography here is a self both scotomized and overexposed by the fact of her femininity as a social reality.

It should come as no surprise that for women determined to go beyond the strictures of convention, conventionally female moments are not assigned priviledged status. One does not find, needless to say, even metaphorical traces of what Hélène Cixous calls for in her "feminine future:" "the gestation drive—just like the desire to write: a desire to live self from within, a desire for the swollen belly, for language, for blood."[21] Autobiology is not the subtext of auto-bio-*graphy*. It is not, however, entirely repressed. George Sand, for example, who gives birth nine months after her marriage, embraces her pregnancy with pleasure and female solidarity: "I spent the winter of 1822-23 at Nohant, rather ill, but absorbed by the feeling of maternal love that was revealing itself to me through the sweetest dreams and the liveliest aspirations. The transformation that comes about at that moment in the life and thoughts of a woman is, in general, complete and sudden. It was so for me as for the great majority."[22] Forced by her doctor to remain in bed and perfectly still for six weeks, Sand comments: "The order . . . was severe, but what wouldn't I have done to maintain the hope of being a mother?"[23] And the account of childbirth itself, if abbreviated and discreet, is no less positive: "My son Maurice came into the world June 30, 1823, without mishap and very hardy. It was the most beautiful moment of my life, that moment when after an hour of deep sleep which followed upon the terrible pains of that paroxysm, I saw, on waking up, that tiny being asleep on my pillow. I had dreamed of him so much ahead of time, and I was so weak, I wasn't sure not to still be dreaming."[24]

Colette, in that slim volume of reminiscences called *The Evening Star* also gives pregnancy a few pages of retrospective attention. Colette, taken by surprise at age 40, is, in the beginning, less sanguine and more anxious than (the younger and at that point in her life more conventional) Sand: "I was simply afraid that at my age I would not know how to give a child the proper love and care, devotion and understanding. Love—so I believed—had already hurt me a great deal by monopolizing me for the past twenty years."* This concern leads to secrecy about her condition, which when finally revealed to a male friend leads him to say: "You're behaving as a man would, you're having a masculine pregnancy!"[25] The "masculine" pregnancy, however, temporarily gives way to a slightly ironized but no less "feminine" text:

> Insidiously, unhurriedly, the beatitude of pregnant females spread through me. I was no longer subject to any discomfort, any unease. This purring contentment, this euphoria—how give a name either scientific or familiar to this state of preservation?—must certainly have penetrated me, since I have not forgotten it and am recalling it now, when life can never again bring me plentitude. . . . One gets tired of keeping to oneself all the unsaid things—in the present case my feeling of pride, of banal magnificence, as I ripened my fruit.[26]

Despite the euphoria, Colette continued to write: "The 'masculine pregnancy' did not lose all its rights; I was working on the last part of *L'Entrave*. The child and the novel were both rushing me, and the *Vie Parisienne*, which was serializing my unfinished novel, was catching up with me. The baby showed signs that it would win the race, and I screwed on the cap of my fountain pen."[27] The account of childbirth itself is characterized less by benign irony and humorous reticence than by a brutal distancing from the female lot: "What followed . . . doesn't matter, and I will give it no place here. What followed was the prolonged scream that issues from all women in childbed. . . . What followed was a restorative sleep and selfish appetite."[28] But the anaphora already perceptible in the passage cited above ("What followed"/"la suite") continues to structure insistently the narrative of this *hapax*, this unique moment in the writer's life, connecting an undifferentiating and hence (for Colette) negative female bond to a singular and bittersweet experience, her post-partum response to her daughter: "But what followed was also, once, an effort to crawl toward me made by my bundled up little larva that had been laid down for a moment on my bed. What animal perfection! The little creature guessed, she sensed the presence of my forbidden milk, and blindly struggled toward that blocked source. Never did I cry more brokenheartedly. Dreadful it is to ask in vain, but small is that hurt when compared with the pain of not giving . . ."[29] Colette accords a few more paragraphs to her passage into

---

*Colette, *The Evening Star (L'Etoile Vesper)* has been translated by David LeVay (Indianapolis, New York: Bobbs-Merrill, 1973). His translation, however, is so unfaithful to Colette in spirit and style that I have chosen instead to use those passages cited from this volume of *Recollections* as anthologized by Robert Phelps in *Earthly Paradise* (New York: Farrar, Straus, Giroux, 1966); his translator, Herma Briffault, does honor to Colette's text. For those who might wish to consult the passages cited in context, I have provided the page references to the complete translation. Above, Phelps, p. 199; LeVay, p. 132.

motherhood, but as she returns quickly to the "competition between the book and the birth," the saving grace—for her writing—of her "jot of virility,"[30] to conclude with speculation about her own mother's probable reaction to this improbable maternity: "When I was a young girl, if I ever happened to occupy myself with some needlework, Sido always shook her soothsayer's head and commented, 'You will never look like anything but a boy who is sewing! She would not have said, 'You will never be anything but a writer who gave birth to a child,' for she would not have failed to see the accidental character of my maternity."[31]

A writer who gave birth to a child, this *hierarchization* of roles has everything to do with the shape of the autobiographies under consideration here: mothers by accident of nature, writers by design. While marriage (and for Beauvoir the decision—in France, a singularly modern one—not to marry), and childbearing (and again for Beauvoir the decision not to bear children) indeed punctuate the female retrospective, they are not *signifying* moments. They are of course significant; and they are facts of life. But they shape lives rather in counterpoint to the meaningful trajectory: The transcendence of the feminine condition through writing. If there is crisis and drama and denouement, to return to Johnson's lexicon, it revolves around the act of writing. Although Beauvoir is the only autobiographer of this group to oppose in mutually exclusive categories writing and maternity, her assumption of writing as a vocation and as locus of identity is paradigmatic: "I knew that in order to become a writer I needed a great measure of time and freedom. I had no rooted objection to playing at long odds, but this was not a game: the whole value and direction of my life lay at stake. The risk of compromising it could only have been justified had I regarded a child as no less vital a creative task than a work of art, which I did not."[32] Mothers or not, maternal or not,* destiny is not tributary of anatomy in these texts; the important trajectory is intellectual.† The life of the mind, however, is not coldly cerebral but impassioned. Thus Stern describes

---

*The contrast between Sand and Stern is interesting to note. Sand writes, for example, about maternal feelings: "I wasn't deluded by passion. I had for the artist [Chopin] a kind of very intense, very true maternal adoration, but which could not for an instant compete with maternal love ("l'amour des entrailles"), the only chaste feeling that can be passionate." George Sand, *Histoire de ma vie*, Vol. II, p. 433. Stern, for her part, reverses the hierarchy: "Let [women] say and repeat that maternal love surpasses all other forms of love, while they cling to it as a last resort("un pis-aller"), and because they have been too cowardly, too vain, too demanding, to experience love and to understand friendship, those two exceptional feelings which can only germinate in strong souls." Daniel Stern, *Mémoires*, p. 82.

†This valorization of intellectual pursuits is not restricted, it would seem, to women writers in France. In the chapter she calls "Female Identities," Patricia Spacks comments on the autobiographical works of four eighteenth-century English writers, Mrs. Thrale, Mrs. Pilkington, Mrs. Clarke, and Lady Mary Wortley Montagu: "With an almost mythic insistence all four of these women reiterate a theme common in the century's fiction: the female apology, heavily tinged with resentment, for the life of the mind. Men think, therefore exist; women, who—men believed—hardly think at all, have therefore perhaps a questionable hold on their own existences." Patricia Meyer Spacks, *Imagining a Self* (Cambridge: Harvard University Press; 1976), pp. 78-79.

her motivation in becoming a writer: "I needed to get outside of myself, to put into my life a new interest, which was not love for a man, but an intellectual relationship with those who felt, thought and suffered as I did. I published therefore . . ."[33] The cogito for Sand, Stern, and Beauvoir thus would seem to be: I write, therefore I am. Writing—for publication—represents entrance into the world of others, and by means of that passage a rebirth: access to the status of autonomous subject.* The textualization of a female "I" means escape from the sphere inhabited by those "relative beings" (as Beauvoir has characterized women) who experience the world only through the mediation of men. To write is to come out of the wings, and to appear, however briefly, center stage.

Thus, Beauvoir describes the publication of her first novel: "So through the medium of my book I aroused curiosity, irritation, even sympathy: there were people who actually liked it. Now at last I was fulfilling the promises I had made myself when I was fifteen. . . . For a moment it was sufficient that I had crossed the threshold: *She came to stay* existed for other people, and I had entered public life."[34] One arrives then at this curious but perhaps not very surprising paradox: These autobiographies are the stories of women who succeeded in becoming more than *just women*, and by their own negative definition of that condition. Sand, for example, reflecting on Montaigne's exclusion of women from the chapter on friendship by virtue of their inferior moral nature, protests and would exempt herself—at least partially—from that category by virtue of her education:

> I could see that an education rendered somewhat different from that of other women by fortuitous circumstances had modified my being . . . . I was not, therefore, entirely a woman like those whom the moralists censure and mock; in my soul I had enthusiasm for the beautiful, thirst for the true, and yet I was indeed a woman like all the others, sickly, highly strung, dominated by my imagination, childishly vulnerable to the tender emotions and anxieties of maternity.[35]

While Sand in this reflection concludes that "the heart and the mind have a sex," and that "a woman will always be more of an artist and a poet in her life, a man always more in his work" (but objects to an interpretation of that difference as a definition of "moral inferiority"), she no less aspires to transcendence, dreaming of those "male virtues to which women can raise themselves."[36] The question one must now ask is whether the story of a woman who sees conventional female self-definition as a text to be rewritten, who refuses the inscription of her body as the ultimate truth of her self, to become, if not a man, an exceptional woman (hence like a man), is a story significantly different from that of a man who

---

* *"The Story of My Life* is especially and in the end the story of a birth to writing— birth deferred, sometimes occulted, difficult, of which the narrative traverses the entire text . . . this birth becomes . . . the very object of the book." Didier, pp. 567-68.

becomes an exceptional man? (Particularly in this instance of figures who became exceptional by virtue of their writing.)

I see only one way to answer this question: difference is there to be read only if one is determined to decipher what women have said (or, more important, left unsaid) about the pattern of their lives, over and above what any person might say about his. I say "his" deliberately. Not because men in fact lead genderless lives, but because the fact of their gender is given and received literarily as a mere *donneé* of personhood; because the canon of the autobiographical text, like the literary canon in general does not interrogate gender as a meaningful category of reference or of interpretation. This is not to say, however, that the male autobiographer does not inscribe his *sexuality*. And Rousseau is hardly silent on the matter. But when Rousseau, for example, writes at the beginning of the *Confessions*: "I want to show my fellow men ("mes semblables") a man in all nature's truth,"[37] he conflates in perfect conformity with the linguistic economy of the West maleness and humanity, as do most of the critic-consumers of autobiography cited in these pages. To speak of difference, therefore, is to perform a diacritical gesture, to refuse the politics of denegation and concomitantly a neutral (neuter) economy of both textual production and consumption.* The difference of which I speak is located in the "I" of the beholder, in the *reader's* perception and identity. I would propose, then, as a first working hypothesis, the notion of gender-bound reading: a practice of the text that would recognize the status of the reader as differentiated subject, a reading subject named by gender and committed in a dialectics of identification to deciphering the inscription of a female subject. Let us consider briefly now a less docile reading of our autobiographers, and of Colette.

Toward the end of *The Evening Star*, Colette imagines a publisher asking her: " 'When will you make up your mind to give us your memoirs?' " And has herself answer: "Dear publisher, I will write them neither more, nor better nor less than today."[38] She thus rejects the specifically autobiographical project as repetition. And suddenly wonders about an earlier female writer and autobiographer:

How the devil did George Sand manage? Robust laborer of letters that she was, she was able to finish off one novel and begin another within the hour. She never lost either a lover or a puff of her hookah by it, produced a twenty volume *Histoire de ma vie* into the bargain, and I am completely staggered when I think of it. Pell-mell, and with ferocious energy she piled up her work, her passing griefs, her

---

*If there is, as Cixous maintains, a "*marked*," that is, masculine writing (Hélène Cixous, "The Laugh of the Medusa," p. 379.), there is no less a "marked" reading: a masculine mode of reception. Unless we are willing to abandon the literature of the past, the literature by women I mean, waiting to find the inscription of femininity at some future time, we must find another way to read; failing that we will indeed come up dry.

limited felicities. I could never have done so much, and at the moment when she was thinking forward to her full barns I was still lingering to gaze at the green, flowering wheat.[39]

Colette, reading Sand, wonders about that life: the weave of writing, love, happiness, unhappiness. And makes the comparison to her own: she/I. If, as Gusdorf suggests, the "essence of autobiography" is its "anthropological significance,"[40] Colette is a good *reader* of autobiography because the text of another's life sends her back to her own (which has been the challenge of autobiography since Augustine). Why Sand, and how does Colette think back to Sand? Having introduced, as we saw earlier, the question of memoirs, and having rejected the undertaking, Colette then imagines her image in a publisher's eyes: "God forgive me! They must expect a kind of 'Secret Journal' in the style of the Goncourt brothers?"[41] By ellipsis Colette rejects this negative and implicitly masculine, dirty secrets model. Instead, thinking about how much time and what sacrifices were involved in the elaboration of her own life's work—"It has taken me a great deal of time to scratch out forty or so books. So many hours that could have been used for travel, for idle strolls, for reading, even for indulging a feminine and healthy coquetry"[42]—Colette makes a feminine connection: how did Sand manage?

This structure of kinship through which readers as women perceive bonds relating them to writers as women would seem to be a "natural" feature of the autobiographical text. But is it? Are these autobiographies the place par excellence in which the self inscribed and the self deciphering perform the ultimate face to face? I don't think so. Despite the identity between the "I" of authorship and the "I" of narration, and the pacts of sincerity, reading these lives is rather like shaking hands with one's gloves on; and white gloves at that. What is one to make of such *decorous* communication? To the extent that autobiography, like any narrative, requires a shaping of the past, a making *sense* of a life, it tends to cast out the parts that don't add up, or what we might think of as the flipside of the official *reconstructed* personality. Still, autobiography can incorporate what Roy Pascal has called the "cone of darkness at the centre;" indeed, as he comments, "it seems to be required of the autobiographer that he should recognize that there is something unknowable in him."[43] One has the impression reading Stern,* Sand, and Beauvoir that the determination to

---

*I must here, somewhat belatedly, distinguish between Stern's *Mes souvenirs* (1806-1833) and her *Mémoires* (1833-1854). Both were published posthumously, in 1880 and 1927, respectively. The later text, which is an account of her love affair with Liszt, is extraordinarily "personal" and moving. However, the volume itself is a construction, a compilation made by the editor, Daniel Ollivier. It includes journal entries (hers and Liszt's), notes, and fragmentary chapters of the *unfinished Mémoires*. (As one might imagine, the journal is the more passionate, disturbed and disturbing document.) Stern herself seems to have favored this installment of her life's story. In a letter dated 1867, cited by Vier (*LaComtesse*, p. 262), Marie d'Agoult writes: "I am just finishing the second volume of the *Mémoires*: the story of passion that will not be a masterpiece, but *my*

have their lives make sense and thus be susceptible to *universal* reception blinds them, as it were, to their own darkness; the "*submerged* core," "the sexual mystery that would make a drama."*

But should we give up so easily? We are given in the autobiographies clues telling us where to look, or not to look, for what Colette calls the "unsaid things." When Beauvoir, for example, describes the stakes of her *fiction* writing, how she wanted to be read, she tells us something important about her *other* self:

> I passionately wanted the public to like my work; therefore like George Eliot, who had become identified in my mind with Maggie Tulliver, I would myself become an imaginary character, endowed with beauty, desirability, and a sort of shimmering transparent loveliness. It was this metamorphosis that my ambition sought . . . I dreamed of splitting into two selves, and of having a shadowy alter ego that would pierce and haunt people's hearts. It would have been no good if this phantom had had overt connections with a person of flesh and blood; anonymity would have suited me perfectly.[44]

Sand points us in the same direction, by denegation:

> It was inevitably said that *Indiana* was my person and my story. It is nothing of the sort. I have presented many types of women, and I think that after reading this account of the impressions and reflections of my life, it will be clear that I have never portrayed myself ["mise en scène"] as a woman ["sous des traits féminins"]. I am too much of a romantic ["trop romanesque"] to have seen the heroine of a novel in my mirror. . . . Even if I had tried to make myself beautiful and dramatize my life, I would never have succeeded. My *self*, confronting me face to face would always have been a chilly reminder ["refroidie"].[45]

---

masterpiece;" italicized in the text. As I will argue, if one is reading to discover, uncover, a female self, the corpus must be expanded by breaking down the barriers of genre; rather, the hierarchies of the canon: Fiction, autobiography, correspondence, diaries, and so on. Here, Vier's remarks on reading the *Mémoires* with the correspondence are very much to the point: "It is Marie whom the *Mémoires* portray; the letters give us glimpses of the Countess d'Agoult; the former is fragile and passive, the latter chatelaine and suzeraine; the former belongs completely to the man she loves and admires, the latter knows herself to be an original mind and senses in herself a literary vocation." Vol. I, p. 175.

*Pauline Kael, reviewing Lillian Hellman's *Julia* with *Pentimento*, the filmic fiction with the autobiography, *The New Yorker*, October 10, 1977, p. 100-01. Not surprisingly, Hellman's conclusion to the volume of her memoirs called *An Unfinished Woman* (New York: Bantam, 1974), points to the dangers lurking in the passion for a coherent self: "I do regret that I have spent too much of my life trying to find what I called 'truth,' trying to find what I called 'sense'. I never knew what I meant by truth, never made the sense I hoped for. All I mean is that I left too much of me unfinished because I wasted too much time. However." p. 244.

By suggesting, as I am, that a *double* reading—of the autobiography with the fiction—would provide a more sensitive apparatus for deciphering a female self, I am not proposing a giant step backwards in the history of criticism, a return to the kind of biographical "hermeneutics" that characterizes a Larnac (in his *Histoire de la littérature féminine*). Larnac, like Colette's hypostasized male reader in *Break of Day*, reads all women's fiction as autobiography: "In the center of every feminine novel, one discovers the author. . . . Incapable of abstracting a fragment of themselves to constitute a whole, they have to put all of themselves into their work."[46] It is not, of course, a question of saying, as Larnac does, Indiana is George Sand (in female drag).

Rather, I am proposing a dialectical practice of reading which would privilege *neither* the autobiography *nor* the fiction, but take the two writings together in their status as text. Such a reading has recently been undertaken, modestly and brilliantly, by Germaine Brée in an essay on George Sand entitled "The Fictions of Autobiography." Brée isolates what she calls the "matrix of fabulation"* and analyzes its function in both the autobiography and the fiction. The matrix is that structure through which Sand deals with the problem of origins and identity. Brée decodes the Sandian inscription of the self, allowing the " 'fictional fiction' " and the "fictions of autobiography"[47] to illuminate each other. Because of the historical protocol and mythical taboos that have governed women's writing until very recently, and beyond that their very notion of a self, not to perform an expanded reading, not, in this instance, to read the fiction *with* the autobiography is to remain prisoner of a canon that bars women from their own texts.

And Colette?

Let us return briefly to the epigraph from *Break of Day*. Early in the novel, the narrator gives us a portrait of her mother taking stock at the end of her life. The metaphor used for this putting into perspective of the past is that of a painter before a canvas: "She stands back, and returns, and stands back again, pushing some scandalous detail into place, bringing into the light of day a memory drowned in shadow. By some unhoped-for art she becomes—equitable. Is anyone imagining as he reads me, that I'm portraying myself? *Have patience: this is merely my model.*"[48] In context, then, the epigraph seems to narrow its focus. Indeed, it has been taken to mean that the model in question is "the model of the mother," and that this "affiliation, recognized and reclaimed"[49] constitutes the deep structure of the novel; painter of her mother, and through her mother, herself. This is no less, however, the portrait of the writer as crypto-autobiographer as that actively is described in this same novel: "No

---

*Germaine Bree, "The Fictions of Autobiography," *Nineteenth-Century French Studies* 4, (Summer) 1976, p. 446. Gusdorf himself seems to make a case for a double reading when he remarks: "There would therefore be two versions, or two instances, of autobiography: on the one hand, the confession strictly speaking, on the other, the entire work of the artist which takes up the same subject matter in complete freedom and with the protection of incognito." p. 121.

other fear, not even that of ridicule, prevents me from writing these lines which I am willing to risk will be published. Why should I stop my hand from gliding over this paper to which for so many years I've confided what I know about myself, what I've tried to hide, what I've invented and what I've guessed?[50] Every inscription of the self is an approximation and a projection; a matter of details, shadows, adjustment, and proportion—an arrangement of truths. Still, does the collection of self-portraits make an autobiography? Robert Phelps tried to construct one in a volume called *Earthly Paradise: An Autobiography*[51] in which he strings together moments, passages, from Colette's works in a thematic and roughly chronological continuum. Lejeune, properly, rejects Phelps's construction as just that: one does not ghostwrite an autobiography; the "pact" cannot be concluded by a third party.

How then to conclude?

At the end of an article published two years after *L'Autobiographie en France*,[52] Lejeune renounces his previous attempts to find a definition of autobiography that would be coherent and exhaustive. He looks instead to a history (as yet to be written) of autobiography that would be the history of the way in which autobiography is read—this, having decided that autobiography is as much a *mode of reading*, as a mode of writing. Lejeune, to be sure, is not concerned with female autobiography. But his notion of a contractual genre dependent upon codes of transmission and reception is an important one for our purposes, because it places the problematics of autobiography in reader response.

And Colette?

To read Colette is not, in the final analysis (*pace* Lejeune), to read a woman's *autobiography*. It is, however, to read the inscription of a *female* self:* a cultural fabrication that names itself as such, and that we can identify through the patient negotiation we ourselves make with the neither/nor of "memoirs mixed with fiction, fictions compounded of fact."[53] Colette's textual "I" is not bound by *genre*. For the "real" autobiographers—Sand, Stern and Beauvoir—despite their pact, the locus of identification, I would suggest, is no different. The historical truth of a woman writer's life lies in the reader's grasp of her intratext: the body of her writing and not the writing of her body.

NOTES

1. Cited, for example, and discussed, by Elaine Marks in her excellent study *Colette* (New Brunswick: Rutgers University Press, 1960), p. 213; translation is hers. All future references to *Break of Day*, however, will be drawn from the Enid McLeod translation (New York: Farrar, Straus and Cudahy, 1961). All translations from the French here will be mine unless otherwise indicated.

---

*Female, both as gender, and specifically, as Showalter uses the term in *A Literature of Their Own:* "a turning inward freed from some of the dependency of opposition, a search for identity," p. 13.

2. Colette, *Break of Day*, p. 5.

3. Colette, *Break of Day*, p. 62; italics mine. On the status of the fragmentary love story ostensibly structuring the novel, see Marks, pp. 213-14.

4. Ibid., pp. 62-63.

5. Ibid., p. 45.

6. Ibid., p. 45.

7. Philippe Lejeune, *L'Autobiographie en France*, (Paris: Armand Colin, 1971); pp. 72-73.

8. Ibid., p. 14.

9. Diane Johnson, "Ghosts," *The New York Review of Books* 24 (3 February, 1977) :19; in Lejeune's terms, autobiographical writing itself is an act of "staging": "l'écriture y est mise en scène." *L'Autobiographie*, p. 73.

10. Daniel Stern, *Avant-Propos* to *Mémoires* [1833-1854], (Paris: Calmann-Lévy, 1927), p. 11.

11. Rene'de Chateaubriand, *Mémoires d'Outre-Tombe* (Paris: Flammarion, 1948), Vol. I, p. 547.

12. Simone de Beauvoir, *The Prime of Life* (New York: Harper, 1976), p. 10; translator, Peter Green.

13. Ibid., lost in translation is the italicization of "everything," "*tout*."

14. Ibid.

15. Letter to Hortense Allard, cited by Jacques Vier in *La Comtesse d'Agoult et son temps* (Paris: Armand Colin, 1961), Vol. IV, p. 250.

16. Daniel Stern, *Préface* to *Mes Souvenirs* (Paris: Calmann-Lévy, 1880), pp. viii-ix.

17. Stern, *Mémoires*, p. 11.

18. Georges Gusdorf, "Conditions et limites de l'autobiographie," in *Formen der Sebstdarstellung* (Berlin: Duncker and Humblot, 1956), p. 115.

19. Simone de Beauvoir, "interroge Jean-Paul Sartre," *L'Arc*, (1975):12.

20. Elaine Showalter, *A Literature of Their Own* (Princeton: Princeton University Press, 1977), p. 13.

21. Hélène Cixous, "The Laugh of the Medusa," translated by Keith Cohen and Paula Cohen in *Signs: Journal of Women in Culture and Society* 1, no. 4 (Summer 1976):891.

22. George Sand, *Histoire de ma vie*, Vol. II, p. 32.

23. Ibid., Vol. II, p. 35.

24. Ibid., Vol. II, p. 37.

25. Robert Phelps, *Earthly Paradise* (New York: Farrar, Strauss, Giroux, 1966), p. 169; David LeVay, *The Evening Star* [*L'Etoile Vesper*] (Indianapolis, New York: Bobbs-Merrill, 1973), p. 132.

26. Phelps, *Earthly Paradise*, p. 200; Le Vay, *Evening Star*, pp. 132-33.

27. Phelps, *Earthly Paradise*, p. 203; Le Vay, *Evening Star*, p. 135.

28. Phelps, *Earthly Paradise*, p. 203; Le Vay, *Evening Star*, p. 136.

29. Phelps, *Earthly Paradise*, pp. 203-04; Le Vay, *Evening Star*, p. 136.

30. Phelps, *Earthly Paradise*, pp. 205-6; Le Vay, *Evening Star*, p. 137.

31. Phelps, *Earthly Paradise*, pp. 205-6; Le Vay, *Evening Star*, p. 137.

32. de Beauvoir, *The Prime of Life*, p. 67.

33. Stern, *Mémoires*, p. 215.

34. de Beauvoir, *The Prime of Life*, p. 441.

35. Sand, *Histoire de ma vie*, Vol. II, pp. 126-27.

36. Ibid., Vol. II, p. 127.

37. Jean-Jacques Rousseau, *Les Confessions* (Paris: Garnier-Flammarion, 1968), Vol. I, p. 43.

38. Colette, *The Evening Star*, translation mine; Le Vay, p. 141.

39. Phelps, *Earthly Paradise*, p. 502; Le Vay, *Evening Star*, p. 141. Also cited by Ellen Moers, a propos of Sand's importance in the female literary tradition, *Literary Women* (New York: Doubleday, 1976), p. 11.

40. Gusdorf, "Conditions et limites de l'autobiographie," p. 119.

41. Colette, *The Evening Star*, translation mine; Le Vay, *Evening Star*, p. 141.

42. Phelps, *Earthly Paradise*, p. 502; Le Vay, *Evening Star*, p. 141.

43. Roy Pascal, *Design and Truth in Autobiography*, (Cambridge: Harvard University Press, 1960), pp. 184-85.

44. de Beauvoir, *The Prime of Life*, p. 291.

45. Sand, *Histoire de ma vie*, Vol. II, p. 160.

46. Jean Larnac, *Histoire de la littérature féminine* (Paris: Kra, 1929), pp. 253-54.

47. Germaine Brée, "The Fictions of Autobiography," p. 446.

48. Colette, *Break of Day*, pp. 34-35; italics mine.

49. Michel Mercier, *Le Roman féminin* (Paris: P.U.F., 1976), p. 46.

50. Colette, *Break of Day,* p. 62.

51. cf. footnote 37 supra.

52. Philippe Lejeune, "Le pacte autobiographique," *Poétique* 14 (1973):137-62; cf. especially, 160-62.

53. William Gass, "Three Photos of Colette," *The New York Review of Books* 24 (14 April 1977):12.

18

SNATCHES OF CONVERSATION

Jane Gallop

There is a myth in our culture that women were (in some indefinite past) the silent sex. In this myth (which we might also call a male fantasy construction), women are objects described, not speaking subjects. Female muses might inspire literature, and ladies might be wooed by playful style, but women (as women, as incarnations of the myth of Woman) did not produce culture. However our culture also has another myth about woman's relation to language—the myth of Woman as essentially a liar. According to this tradition, Woman spoke, neither to enlighten with philosophy or science, nor to give her word as the guarantee for some joint enterprise; she spoke to deceive.

"The silent sex" was never considered to be actually non-speaking. Talking constantly, women emitted chatter, gossip, and foolishness. Gushing forth torrents of empty words, babbling contradictorily, all sense canceled out, leaving merely white noise, so much less significant than absolute, "eloquent silence."

Naive men were ensnared by the siren's song, because they took the woman at her word, taking that word out of the context of its unending protean flow. So women were called liars, and their speech, not conforming to solid male rules of logic, clarity, consistency, deemed nonsense.

Smart men knew better. They paid women no mind. So women became the silent sex, by dint of not being heard.

Thus the dealings of men-as-men with women-as-women (which are, after all, sexual relations) had to be predicated upon the body of knowledge compiled by men (the compilers of knowledge, speakers of sense) about Woman. Although this lore was inadequate and often in disagreement with women's utterances about themselves, there was nothing to be done. Women could not be trusted to tell the truth about themselves. Women's statements about their sexuality were notoriously subject to the distortions of flirtatious modesty and manipulative docility. Knowledge, to be useful, must transcend the intersubject dynamics in those actions. It was impractical to listen to women's chatter, for it offered no information that could be processed and reliably applied in some quest for greater power.

So theories of woman's sexuality remained inadequate. Feminism, recognizing the mechanism by which women's talk was dismissed as idle chatter, demanded that women be heard. And so women came to speak their sexuality, not in the old private way: highly-charged exchanges between confidantes or conversations between lovers. Out of feminism arose public female discourse on women's sexuality.

The most serious and sophisticated product of this speaking out is *The Hite Report*, whose very title declares the scientific credentials of the work. To prove that women are capable of theorizing (being logical, consistent, disinterested) about their sexuality, Shere Hite gives her book all the trappings of science (long methodological introduction, voluminous appended charts full of numbers). Hite places herself in the tradition of male sexologists (*The Kinsey Report*, the fictional *Chapman Report*), yet would keep her special status as a woman. The contradiction inherent in this position is important and vexatious: it is the problem of "public female discourse": how to gain the logic and authority of science without losing the authenticity of confession.

In an attempt to analyze this contradiction, we will look at a less illustrious example of women making their sexuality public—Nancy Friday's *My Secret Garden*. The title here is sexy (vaginal even), rather than drily scientific. The book sells through the titillation of confession; nonetheless, the author's explicit intention, borne out by the format, is to break women's silence and aid in their liberation.

Our two representatives of public female discourse focus, as one might expect from the divergent tones of their titles, upon different aspects of female sexuality. Hite prefers the sheer mechanics of sex, thus reporting a level-headed female sexuality, one of control and scientifically predictable results. *My Secret Garden* presents the fantasies which supplement mechanics, inviting us into the lush, irrational world of passion. Yet both books share the conviction that sense can be made from woman's eroticism, that light and order (male logic, discursive seriousness) can be brought to the murky tangles of the female genitalia/mind.

Their common fantasy is no bold new dream, no virginal daughter of Modern Feminism or the Sexual Revolution. This fantasy has long been part of Western (male) culture: the dream of imposing order upon mute, dark confusion, of channeling female gush into logical categories, of bringing woman's hidden powers into the open where they might be harnessed.

Perhaps the most graphic example of this traditional fantasy is Denis Diderot's *Les Bijoux Indiscrets* (The Indiscreet Jewels). The hero of that novel, the monarch Mangogul, asks a genie for the power to learn the truth about women's sexual adventures. He wants this power because one cannot trust what women say, because women dissimulate in their conventional pretense of chastity. The genie gives him a ring which when directed towards a woman causes her to speak clearly and distinctly, not from her mouth, but from her "jewel," her nether parts. These "snatches of conversation" seem to fulfill the desire for the unmediated word of the thing itself. The nether parts no longer are a dark mystery, but speak frankly and articulately. The novel presents a mixture of the jewels' confessions and reactions to and theorizing about this "chatterbox" phenomenon.

Just as a dream within a dream is often closer to "reality"; so in this fantasy world the insatiably curious monarch has a dream which might be said to lay bare the philosophical underpinnings of the tale. In this chapter, pointedly titled "Chapter XXXII, Perhaps the best and least read of this story," Mangogul dreams he is walking about in a highly unstable building full of undernourished cripples in rags. Despite the obvious lacks in both building and men, he is forced to acknowledge they have a certain beauty. The dreamer learns that he is in the "region of hypotheses" and that these people are *systématiques* (which is to say, they arrange diversity into systematic worlds by means of hypotheses). Then Mangogul sees a child approach who grows with each step until it reaches colossal proportions. This child, he is told, is Experience, whose arrival causes the edifice of hypotheses to shake and crumble. Informed by Plato (the healthiest of the *systématiques*) that "this edifice has but a moment left,"[1] Mangogul flees. The child arrives; the building falls; and Mangogul wakes up.

Mangogul dreams of the triumph of empiricism over a priori hypothesis, and his sexual investigations can be seen as a rejection of all the lovely, faulty hypotheses about women and as an empiricist's effort to learn the facts, to gather unprejudiced data. This is precisely the philosophy behind *The Hite Report*: "what should be done is to look at what women are actually experiencing, what they enjoy, and when they orgasm—and then draw conclusions. In other words, researchers must stop telling women what they *should* feel sexually, and start asking them what they *do* feel sexually."[2] Hite would first gather the data, and only then create, a posteriori, a "new theory of female sexuality" (p. 11).

This new theory advocates that women take control of their own stimulation, have power over their own bodies. In the place of reproductive coitus as the basic sexual paradigm, Hite posits masturbation. The truth of woman's sexuality can be found in what the woman does when she is alone, when, unswayed by interpersonal dynamics and cultural pressures, woman can follow her "natural instincts" (v. p. 59 and 243). Dropping the impartial mask of the researcher, Hite becomes an applied sexologist, as she counsels: "don't wait for the Right Man to be dependent on [in finding fulfilling sex], but create your own good situation— which can include yourself as being the Princess Charming" (p. 255).

The liberated woman, heroine of this new theory of female sexuality, would be in frank and lucid communication with her genitalia. Her hidden parts would speak sensibly to her, and she would know their secrets, so that she (that is, her rational self) might control them and her destiny, rather than being overpowered by a passionate loss of self. As Peggy Kamuf commented, "Woman masturbating is to her own sexuality (in control of it, mastering it—master-bating) what the Sultan is to female sexuality."

Mangogul's mistress Mirzoza feared the cruel potential of his magic ring. "She knew the sultan's curiosity, and she hadn't sufficient confidence in the promises of a man who was less in love than he was tyrannical to be free from worry" (Ch. VI, p. 15). The curious imperialist, with his ravenous will to power through knowledge, would use his charm over women, not to love them or give them (or even himself) pleasure, but to strip them of their powers (dissimula-tion, coquetry, baffling inconsistency).

We are distinguishing here between two different sorts of "power(s)." Mangogul possesses a certain worldly power (command, control) which he can expand through knowledge (reason, logic). This is in contrast to Mirzoza's "powers." The first, expressed in the singular, is a monolithic authority which would subjugate everything to its unified rule. The second, expressed in the plural, consists of various abilities and charms that can be used strategically to influence other people's actions. Drawing upon the traditional mythology, we characterize consolidated/consolidating power as male, and plural, tactical powers as female, although we are fully cognizant of the fact that both real men and real women desire, strive for, and attain (to a certain extent) "power" and both men and women turn their persuasive "powers" (charms) to the manipulation of others. The central difference is that power (which is always a dream of power, a fantasy never quite achieved) would be an absolute attribute of a monadic self, not contingent upon situation; whereas (feminine, strategic) powers are always powers over others, dependent upon a given intersubjective dynamic.

Hite, like Mangogul, would banish all mystery which stands in the way of self-determination and control (monadic power). Masturbation is chosen as the primary model of female sexuality, because it is the most efficient method of attaining orgasm: "There is no great mystery about why a woman has an orgasm. It happens with the right stimulation, quickly, pleasurably, and reliably" (p. 270). In this scientific, non-mystic, non-ecstatic, sexuality, pleasure is allowed, but there is a premium on efficiency and predictable causality.

Although from time to time *The Report* concedes that orgasm might be overemphasized at the expense of emotion and interpersonal relations, the privileged position of orgasm in unavoidable, given the empiricist dream behind the new theory. This dream sexology would gather its data without having to deal with the psyche and its irritating (female) tendency to cloud facts with opinions, desires, and fantasies. In an extreme moment, the book betrays this white-coat fantasy when in defense of masturbation as the paradigm of female sexuality, it gratuitously mentions that "As a matter of fact, the highest cardiac rates of all the orgasms . . . studied occurred during female masturbation" (p. 192).

Taken out of context, it seems absurd that the goal of sexual activity should be the sheer height of cardiac rate. Yet within the dream of a logical eroticism, an eroticism of control and power, striving in the spirit of Scientific Progress and the Technological Revolution toward the bigger and the better, there is nothing more desirable than that which can be measured by instruments, rather than judged by a subject.

Predictably, a mathematical fantasy also makes an appearance in *Les Bijoux Indiscrets* (Ch. XVII), in the account of a journey to an uncharted isle. In this fantasy-within-a-fantasy, people have genitals of various geometric shapes. Before two people can marry they are examined to ensure that they possess interlocking parts. Besides the morphological criterion, sexual temperature must match. Special thermometers measure "tempérament" (that lovely eighteenth-century word for passion which etymologically suggests measurable heat). Yet we are told in the novel that even these extreme "measures" are not sufficient to squelch infidelity, which is rampant on this island.

Although we turned to *Les Bijoux Indiscrets* in an attempt to delineate the empiricist fantasy that structures recent attempts to make women speak their sexuality, the novel is much more than such a univocal reading would make it. It includes not just that dream, but a criticism of it. Such is the effect of a mathematical allusion in the very title of the novel. "Discret" in French means not only "discreet," but also "discrete"—that is, separable into parts, countable. If the jewels are "indiscrete" they are not countable, and are the derision of the mathematical fantasy. When the sultan reads the report of mathematically arranged unions in the uncharted isle, Mirzoza leaves the room offended. In a sense our criticism of Hite's white-coat fantasy puts us in the position of Mirzoza and her opposition to Mangogul's imperialism. In a way the present text is a restaging of Diderot's novel.

More than a collection of forced confessions "direct from the source" (so to speak), more even than a philosophical allegory, *Les Bijoux Indiscrets* is the history of a love affair, of the power struggle between two lovers, which is actually each one's fight not to be totally overwhelmed by the other. Mangogul might strike out alone with his ring to wrest sexual secrets from the women of his kingdom, but it is always in order to bring back a report to Mirzoza, to score a victory in their private and well-matched battle of the sexes.

Mirzoza is an exceptionally accomplished storyteller, a Scheherazade who regaled her royal lover with the sexual adventures of the town until one day she ran dry. We are told in one breath (Ch. III, p. 6) both that she ran out of stories and that she had "peu de tempérament." Mangogul and Mirzoza have reached an impasse: she is no longer putting out either verbal or vaginal enchantments. She suggests (testing his love) he look elsewhere in the court for entertainment. He gallantly counters that no one tells stories as well as she. But she replies (not won over from her suspicions and fears so easily) that, regardless, he'll "more than make up in content what he may lose in form" (that is, he might prefer her, but all the variety will certainly make up for the inadequacy of any particular woman/storyteller). She may be testing him out of jealous fear, but in his own insecurity he reads this as her indifference. So he goes to a genie to enlist aid in gaining access to (the truth about) all the women in his kingdom.

The explicit plot has Mangogul merely in search of tales of the ladies' romantic dalliances, but he asks for access to the truth about these women in the most equivocal terms: saying he would like to "procure some pleasures at the expense of the women of my court." The genie thinks Mangogul wants to have sexual commerce with all these women, but Mangogul assures him that he only wishes to know their adventures, "that's all." So he is given the ring.

Immediately upon possession of this new power, the sultan goes to try it on his mistress. Yet as he is about to attain full possession of his love's secret interiority (and discover why she no longer "puts out"), he becomes frightened of what he might learn and in his agitation awakens her so that she forbids him (under penalty of loss of her love) to use it on her. Afraid to find out that she is not faithful, Mangogul has caused his first attempt to founder. With all his power the Man is powerless before someone whose love he wants.

At the close of the novel Mangogul finally does make Mirzoza's "jewel" speak. He takes advantage of her when she is in a swoon. The story has a happy ending: her vagina tells her love for him, so he has no more use for the ring and returns it to the genie. The entire baroque path of the novel is but a deferral of this confrontation. The fantasy of sexual expertise (domination of alterity by a monadic power) is belied by the intricacies of desire which include a need to hear the voice of the loved one's desire.

Of course Diderot's book is a novel, so it is no wonder that sexual research is given emotional motivation. Yet we find that Nancy Friday offers us a similar pretext for her non-fiction study of women's fantasies. Apparently discourse about sexuality tends to be not very far removed from its context. Like sexuality, it is always wound up with emotional situations, intersubjectivity. It is only the white-coat fantasy that allows us to imagine that either sexual activity or discourse about sexuality could ever be purified of subjective content. It is the same white-coat fantasy that subtends the belief that there can be a discourse about sexuality that is not sexual talk, a scientific discourse that is not vulgar, but clean and sterile. (Mangogul pointed his ring at women's vaginas from a distance, he did not have to get his hands dirty.)

My Secret Garden opens with a long, explicit, unprefaced sexual fantasy which the reader supposes to be an example of the subject matter collected by Friday. The fantasy reaches its climax, and the reader is shocked, in the afterglow of this very sexy scenario, to read the following " 'Tell me what you are thinking about,' the man I was actually [in bed with] said, his words as charged as the action in my mind. As I'd never stopped to think before doing anything to him in bed, I didn't stop to edit my thoughts. I told him what I'd been thinking. He got out of bed, put on his pants and went home."[3]

Nancy Friday begins her book with this account of its origin. That sexual encounter, which made her feel ashamed, unloved, and unnatural for having sexual fantasies, planted the seed for *My Secret Garden*. That intimate pretext repeats itself in a more professional discourse. Some years later, happily married to a man who encourages her sexual fantasizing, Friday wrote a novel that included a chapter which was a narration of a sexual fantasy of the heroine.

"[Friday's] editor, a man, was put off. Her fantasies made the heroine sound like some kind of sexual freak, he said" (p. 4). If the sexual encounter of the first pages was the moment of conception for *My Secret Garden*, it was in this confrontation with her editor that the fantasy collection was born. The first incident created a need to speak her psychic sexuality privately, but the second impelled her to bring it out into the world.

My Sexual Garden is her retort to those two men, who would prefer her silence because her speech threatens them. She was vulnerable to their rejection, because, as she says, they "hit [her] in that area where women, knowing least about each other's true sexual selves, are most vulnerable" (p. 5). So Friday sets out to learn the truth about women in order to arm herself for the battle of the sexes.

Mangogul brought back his revelations of female truth to Mirzoza as a tactic to arouse her desire. He reports back all the women's lack of constancy. Although Mirzoza persists in her claim that, despite all the damning evidence, women can love faithfully, she refuses to allow him to turn his ring on her, thus refusing to allow her "jewel" to prove her claim for women's virtue *and* speak her faithful love. Thus each report to Mirzoza of an application of the ring is another goad to get her to prove her love by allowing him to make her "jewel" speak that love (allowing him to arouse her desire). Likewise Friday recounts all these women's secret thoughts so that men will consider her a normal, natural women (so they will desire her). Although this book brings women together as confidantes and sisters, that sorority's function is to enhance their charm for men. Women are to gain liberation and power so as to increase their powers over men. Like Mangogul, as we have read him, Friday's ideal heroine would search not for some uncompromising, non-contingent strength, but for strategic powers over the opposite sex.

Unlike Hite—who glorifies masturbation as the solitary uncompromised jubilation of the autonomous ego wherein woman can be strong, free, and exercise a practical, controlled sexuality—Friday advocates an autoerotic schema that is vulnerably intersubjective, rather than the closed godlike circle of individual fulfilling herself.

Nancy Friday might well ask Shere Hite point blank, "If sex is reduced to a test of power, what woman wants to be left all alone, all powerful, playing with herself?" (p. 7). Actually, this rhetorical question appears in the context of Friday's criticism of Women's Liberation—a sympathetic criticism which embraces feminism's goals but regrets the strident tones of its demands for power. *The Hite Report* privileges efficient, reliable sexual stimulation. Yet if sex were fun, would we want to get it over with as quickly as possible? If it were a game, would we want to be certain of the outcome?

Our reading tries to draw attention to what is at once the major fault and the greatest contribution of *The Hite Report*. Hite really has broken women's silence and brought their "underground" sexuality out into the open. In the pages of her book, women's voices can be heard in all their rich diversity. But inasmuch as Hite's science fantasy compels her to organize those voices into a "new theory," which is to say, inasmuch as she wishes to overthrow the old theories and usurp the place of the male sexologist, she necessarily comes to occupy that male place.

The "new theory" sounds astonishingly like the old: is the mere fact of theorizing a sufficiently powerful common denominator to attenuate the effect of any divergent content? All theories of sexuality have failed. Is any possible theory doomed to inadequacy because desire must exceed and frustrate logical consistency?

Optimistic about the possibilities for a fresh start, *The Hite Report* begins with a rejection of past contributions in the field: "Researchers, looking for statistical 'norms,' have . . . all too often wound up *telling* women how they should feel rather than asking them how they do feel" (p. 11). [Male] researchers have thrust language upon passive women, whereas Hite's questioning would attentively stimulate women to respond. The model for good sexual research is structurally analogous to the pattern for good sex. Hite asks; women respond. But then Hite tells them what their responses mean.

Although Hite would like to speak from an impartial position, high above any unscientific influences, she cannot. The fantasies which energize her for the tremendous task of "a nationwide study of female sexuality" prejudice her in favor of certain findings. She wants to ground her theory in Experience, but the only way to gain access to, interpret, and communicate women's experience is through language. Once dealing with and in language, it is no longer simply a question of gathering scientific data. The researcher, rather than immune in some metalinguistic ether, is embroiled in the middle of an intersubjective situation, where what is said always has in view a desired response from the interlocutor. The speaker does not merely convey information; she wants to please, irritate, arouse, or deceive the listener.

Hite is sorely tempted to have recourse to a natural female sexuality ("masturbation provides a source of almost pure biological feedback—it is one of the few forms of instinctive behavior to which we have access" [p. 59]) which has been deformed by an artificial, overlaid culture whose main agent is language. But she is dissuaded from the biological model because that is precisely the tactic of the old (repressive, male) theory of female sexuality, which posits a natural, reproductive feminity that has fallen into dysfunction through the decadence and neurosis of modern culture. Eschewing the naturalistic paradigm (in spite of her white-coat fantasy), she arrives at a philosophy of free will: "Sex and all physical relations are something *we* create: they are cultural forms, not biological forms" (p. 432).

Do *we* create cultural forms? Clearly we have not in the past—woman's sexuality has been patterned by already existing forms. One might argue that men created those self-serving patterns, and now it is time for women to do likewise. However, autonomous, solitary individuals (male or female) cannot create cultural forms ex nihilo according to whim, any more than one can communicate by making up words. Sexuality, like language, is inescapably intersubjective. If one monadic psyche wanted to structure a sexual exchange according to her caprice, she would need an already understandable means of communicating the new form. The attempt to pattern sexual intercourse after masturbation runs up against the same barrier as the effort to express one's own peculiarity in language.

Fortunately, people do not formulate propositions (sexual or otherwise) merely from the wish to impose their autonomous will upon the passivity of others. Inasmuch as sexuality and language always include a need to elicit a response from an other, they can only be adequately understood in relation to that response. To try to isolate the truth of desire by reducing it to the well-defined, straightforward sterility of masturbation produces an image as deceptive as words in a dictionary—devoid of irony, rhetoric, and flirtatious word play. Of course meaning ascertained outside of context is clearer, crisper, and more easily manipulated; but it is naively innocent of the game theory which determines all worldly intercourse.

The major discrepancy between Hite and her subjects is that she, in search of scientific data, favors strong, clear, calculable responses whereas they, in quest of love and happiness, even power, are interested in diverse, less clearly measurable factors. This distinction determines a dynamic tension played out in *The Report* between the Woman whose voice Hite longs to hear and the women who actually speak. She succeeds in getting women to testify because of her evident desire for their testimony. Women gave more than the questionnaires asked for; and that more was a sexual response (rather than a response *about* their sexuality). They reacted as is customary when urged to talk about sex; they got aroused ("I liked the questionnaire. I've been doing it at work for the past week and have hurried home at five o'clock every day horny horny horny" [p. 50]). They felt desired and returned that desire.

It is Hite's evident desire for all these women to give signs of their desire, to speak their desire, that makes her questionnaire and her book so seductive. Having exposed her desires to the powerful sexual expert, a woman craves some proof of the researcher's love, some response beyond impassive science. One woman, getting personal if not explicitly sexual, wrote "I like these questions very much. Filling them out I got the desire to know you in person, and continue our questions and answers" (Hite, p. 524). Continued in person these questions and answers would be more embarrassing, and all the more exciting. As another woman put it, "I haven't had sex with another woman, except verbally—I think women often make love by talking a certain way, at least I do" (Hite, p. 399).

I *do not want to reduce* a scientific study, and its very real contribution to knowledge about women's sexuality, *to a mere sublimation.* But no sexology can be above the sexual register, or else it would lose its validity as a contact with the truth of sex. There is no sexual metalanguage (hence the impossibility of a successfully impartial sexual theory). Seduction is often carried on by means of erotic talk; talk about sex (as disinterested as it might pretend to be) is sexy.

NOTES

1. Denis Diderot, *Oeuvres romanesques* (Paris: Garnier, 1962), p. 117.
2. Shere Hite, *The Hite Report* (New York: Dell, 1976), p. 60.
3. Nancy Friday, *My Secret Garden* (New York: Pocket Books, 1974), p. 2.

19
WRITING LIKE A WOMAN

Peggy Kamuf

In what has become the handbook of archetypal criticism, Northrop Frye's *Anatomy of Criticism*, the critic contrasts two types of poets in this fashion: "The poet who writes creatively rather than deliberately is not the father of his poem. He is at best a midwife, or more accurately still, the womb of Mother Nature herself. Her privates he, so to speak."[1] Implicit, of course, in Frye's analogy is the hierarchical distinction of high poetry from baser productions. The vehicle for this distinction is the difference between fathers and mothers which, in a tautological fashion, is understood as the difference between noble, disciplined creation and the unmentionable processes of procreation. To be the father of a poem is to stand at a certain remove and to present the child to the world from a dignified posture. To be the mother, one must lie supine, spread-legged, exposing the ignoble locus of the child's generation—the womb, so to speak. With that last little phrase, Frye reminds us that, of course, he is using a figure of speech. No poet is literally a mother of poems. We can only use such a description by way of analogy, which is to say already at a certain remove. In Frye's analogy, the "creative" poet is *like* a mother which is, after all, not the same thing as being a mother in a literal sense. Like the "deliberate" poet, the "creative" poet is seen to be finally a father as well, but one who has stooped to imitate a mother's posture— "so to speak."

A feminist critic, reacting to the same passage from Frye that we have just quoted, writes: "Do I, then, as a woman poet write from the phallus of Father Nature, his privates I 'so to speak'?"[2] If by the father's phallus one means the metaphoric sign of the signifying process itself, then, well, yes. Using language—whether as poet or critic—we are all, more or less, in the position of a father, the parent of mediation.

Now, what I have just written would seem to be wholly out of place in a book on women and language. To concede at the outset that it is the father

284

who speaks and says "I" is to close the debate even before it is opened. Nevertheless, this is where we must begin to talk about women and language, women in language, if we are to end up at any distance from where we started. The opposite strategy, which from the outset assumes a clear distinction between masculine and feminine discourse, runs the risk of merely corroborating the father's position in the end. How this works can best be seen by considering an example from recent feminist literary criticism.

The opening chapter of Patricia Meyer Spack's *The Female Imagination* is on theorists (Simone de Beauvoir, Mary Ellman, and Kate Millett), and it concludes in this fashion: "So what is a woman to do, setting out to write about women? She can imitate men in her writing, or strive for an impersonality beyond sex, but finally she must write as a woman: what other way is there?"[3] Spack's study puts together readings of a list of literary works by women in order to determine how, in her phrase, one "writes as a woman." However, by limiting the field to works whose authors are women, the critic finally gets caught in the kind of biological determinism, which, in other contexts, is recognized as a primary instance of antifeminist sexism. Consider, for example, this passage from the prologue:

> Surely the mind has a sex, minds *learn* their sex—and it is no derogation of the female variety to say so. At any rate, for readily discernible historical reasons women have characteristically concerned themselves with matters more or less peripheral to male concerns, or at least slightly skewed from them. The differences between traditional female preoccupations and roles and male ones make a difference in female writing. Even if a woman wishes to demonstrate her essential identity with male interests and ideas, the necessity of making the demonstration, contradicting the stereotype, allies her initially with her sisters. And the complex nature of the sisterhood emerges in the books it has produced.[4]

Spack's concept of female writing is one which must expand to include the works of a woman (de Beauvoir is her primary example) "who wishes to demonstrate her essential identity with male interests and ideas." Although the author sets out with a statement of faith in a psychological or cultural differentiation which can be characterized sexually ("Surely the mind has a sex . . ."), she abandons this intuition without a second thought when she must account for a woman who, by her own reckoning, has a "male" mind. By adopting the biological distinction of male/female to define a cultural phenomenon, the critic demonstrates the impossibility of limiting that definition to what it "is" for, as it turns out, it "is" also what it "is not." By "female writing," we discover, Spacks quite banally understands works signed by biologically determined females of the species.

If the inaugural gesture of this feminist criticism is the reduction of the literary work to its signature and to the tautological assumption that a feminine "identity" is one which signs itself with a feminine name, then it will be able to produce only tautological statements of dubious value: women's writing is writing signed by women. Western culture has, of course, traditionally reserved a separate category for the intellectual or cultural productions of women, intimating their special status as exceptions within those realms where to "think male thoughts" is not to be distinguished from thinking in universals. Coming out of that tradition, we are also formed in the cult of the individual and the temptation which results to explain to ourselves artistic and intellectual productions as expressions, simple and direct, of individual experience. However, if these are principles establishing the grounds of a practice of feminist criticism, then that practice must be prepared to ally itself with the fundamental assumptions of patriarchy which relies on the same principles.

If, on the other hand, by "feminist" one understands a way of reading texts that points to the masks of truth with which phallocentrism hides its fictions, then one place to begin such a reading is by looking behind the mask of the proper name, the sign that secures our patriarchal heritage: the father's name and the index of sexual identity.

To ignore the signature which attributes a literary work to its author is to attempt to discard the involuntary reflexes of a modern reader schooled in the categories of basic literary history. One cannot easily contrive to be blind to that which one has been taught to see with such directed focus. But what if one were to take an anonymous work, that is, work which, in the absence of a signature, must be read blind, as if no known subject had written it? Perhaps, only perhaps, thus blinded, one has a chance to see what has become a blind spot in our enlightened culture.

*   *   *

The text known as *The Portuguese Letters* was first published in Paris in 1669. It consists of five letters, in French, undated and unsigned, apparently written by a woman in a Portuguese convent to an unnamed French officer who, after conducting a brief and passionate love affair in Portugal with the author of the letters, has returned to France. Briefly summarized, the letters chronicle the gradual realization on the part of their author that the French officer had probably never seriously envisioned remaining in Portugal or taking Mariana (the name the author gives herself) back to France with him. Mariana finds herself in the humiliating position of having been an easy mark, because of her nun's naiveté, for the seductive maneuvers of the duplicitous French gentleman. Abandoned, she must struggle with her desire, which, although robbed of its object by the separation and by the discovery of the lover's unworthiness, grows to be all the more virulent and disruptive. By the fourth letter in the series, however, Mariana has shifted to a predominantly accusatory tone in an effort to overcome what she terms her feminine weakness which keeps her prey to the deceptive charms of her lost lover and tempts her to adopt a self-deceptive interpretation of her situation. In the fifth letter, she announces her decision to break off the correspondence with the Frenchman and describes, in relatively dispassionate language, the self-inflicted violence which has separated her less from her lover than from her own passion.

The title page of the first edition of this work states that it is a translation but identifies neither the author nor the translator. In a preface, the editor disclaims that he can provide such information: "I have managed, after much care and trouble, to obtain a correct copy of the translation of five Portuguese letters written to a noble gentleman who served in Portugal. . . . I know neither the name of him to whom they were addressed nor the name of the translator, but it seemed to me that I would be doing them no disservice by making the letters public."[5] Quite soon after they appeared and attained a quick popularity in the Parisian literary salons, the debate began as to their authenticity since many readers apparently chose to understand the editor's preface in terms of the literary convention of "found letters." In the three centuries since, literary historians and critics still have not managed to resolve the question of attribution beyond a reasonable doubt, although relatively few readers have doubted the letters' value as a classical masterpiece of extraordinary intensity and composition. The partisans of their authenticity attribute this achievement to the spontaneous genius of a forgotten nun in the grip of a formidable passion for a faithless lover; the partisans of the literary convention argue that only a tighly controlled and deliberately executed art could have produced such a brilliantly expressive work, and that therefore the author must have been a member of the Parisian literary elite. As it happens, this debate has generated a corollary argument: the first, that the author of the original letters was a woman; the second, that their author (not translator) was a man.

During most of the nineteenth century, the authenticity position held sway. This was so, in part, because in 1810 a literary researcher named Boissonade believed he had found the key to the identities of both the nun and her French lover in a marginal note inserted in his copy of the 1669 edition. He confidently informed the literary public that the nun's name was Mariana Alcaforada and that, while she was a nun at Beja in Portugal, she wrote the letters to the comte de Chamilly, also called the comte de Saint-Léger. There followed upon Boissonade's discovery a long period of research in Beja which painstakingly unearthed from oblivion the past of Sister Mariana da Costa Alcoforado who had taken vows at the convent of Our Lady of the Conception convent in 1663 and had died there in 1723, dates which lent an historic plausibility to the letters. By 1890 both French and Portuguese scholars had agreed that the question of attribution of the text was settled and that they had identified the real Portuguese nun. Accordingly, the work was henceforward to be listed as belonging to the Portuguese national literature, and the French version catalogued as an anonymous translation from the original.

Not everyone, however, was satisfied with this conclusion, most particularly an English researcher named F. C. Green who published an article in 1926 contesting the authenticity theory. His research in both Paris and Beja turned up inconsistencies between the biography of Mariana, as far as it could be recovered, and certain chronological and geographical references in the letters. Moreover, he discovered in the Bibliothèque Nationale in Paris a copy of the original publisher's permit from 1669 for the text of the letters. The permit was issued to the name of Guilleragues for several works to be published together, one of which was simply referred to as "Portuguese letters." It began to appear to Green, and subsequently to others, that Guilleragues, a minor poet and lettrist from the salon of Mme de Sablé and a correspondent of Racine's, had been responsible not only for the publication of the letters but for their entire composition.

Few scholars followed up on the suggestions of Green's research until, in 1954, Leo Spitzer published a stylistic analysis of the text which purported to prove once and for all the conventional, literary origin of the letters and to disallow finally the argument of their spontaneity or authenticity. As a result of these two important pieces of research, the editors at Garnier undertook to issue a new edition of the text which would assemble all the documents from the history of the debate over its origin and make a definitive declaration of attribution. The task was given to F. Deloffre and J. Rougeot who, in 1962, published the first edition of the *Portuguese Letters* which designated an author on the title page: Guilleragues. The edition was generally greeted with appreciation by other scholars and the question of attribution finally laid to rest.

This abbreviated history of the controversy over the *Portuguese Letters* gives some notion of the issues in the two camps. In the pages that follow, I would like to analyze some of the significant moments in the last chapters of the controversy so as to highlight, insofar as possible, the critical choices and presuppositions which have underwritten the various interpretations of the text's genesis and consequently its significance. The point of this exercise is to clear the way for a blind reading of a text written, perhaps, in a woman's hand.

*   *   *

In their introduction to the definitive edition already mentioned, Deloffre and Rougeot choose the analogy of the paternity suit to characterize the judgment of attribution of the text.[6] As Northrop Frye does in the passage cited above, this analogy invites us to consider the author as the parent of the text, more exactly as the father of the text. Once again in this instance, the parental metaphor implies fatherhood exclusively even when, as is the case here, one of the contenders for the title of "parent" might be more aptly called the "mother" of the text. At closer look, moreover, one finds that the issue of paternity versus maternity is very nearly reproduced in the principal argument over a spontaneous versus a literary, conventional composition of the letters. In other terms, either the text is what it appears to be on the simplest level of comprehension or it is a contrived appearance and thereby other than what a "naive" reading might lead one to judge. This characterization, which differentiates between simple appearance and more complex reality, echoes, of course, the Platonic distinction of perceptible from ideal forms and, more specifically, the differential values which our culture assigns to maternity and paternity. Consider, for example, this observation from Freud's discussion of the patriarchal function in *Moses and Monotheism:*

> This turning from the mother to the father [the triumph of patriarchy over matriarchy] points . . . to a victory of intellectuality over sensuality—that is, an advance in civilization, since maternity is proved by the evidence of the senses while paternity is an hypothesis, based on an inference and a promise. Taking sides in this way with a thought-process in preference to a sense perception has proved to be a momentous step.[7]

Freud is here simply re-stating a fundamental assumption of what we know as culture: that the movement away from the unmediated maternal bond toward the mediated (or hypothetical) paternal bond is the motor of cultural advance. On the level of the individual, this advance proceeds from the moment of the physical separation from the mother's womb to the psychological separation through the various stages of Oedipal conflict and resolution. On the collective level, the movement is away from the recognition of the matriarchal alignment toward the valorization of the paternal origin and patriarchal authority.

Freud, however, is led to ask the one question which this neat description of psycho-cultural history cannot answer: the question of the authority which, at the origin, authorizes the father's authority: ". . . in the case of some advances in intellectuality—for instance, in the case of the victory of patriarchy— we cannot point to the authority which lays down the standard which is to be regarded as higher. It cannot in this case be the father, since he is only elevated into being an authority by the advance itself."[8] The origin of the father as origin is lost in an aporia. The authority of patriarchy relies on our failing to ask the question which Freud implicitly poses, on our refusing to think the absence, at the origin, of an origin.*

In the situation of the literary text we are considering, the authorial first cause is similarly not in evidence. Just as masking the aporia at the origin of patriarchal authority has been the chief occupation of western metaphysics since Plato, so too literary hermeneutics has found itself principally concerned— and not only in the instance we are considering—with grounding any system of interpretation in the presence of an author at the conception of the work. Thus, for example, the question for Deloffre and Rougeot is simply who the father/author was and not whether this text, or any text, can claim such a legitimate and traceable ancestry.

Deloffre and Rougeot document at length the history of the search for

---

*I am indebted to Jane Gallop for bringing these passages from Freud to my attention and for working out with me their implications for the rest of my analysis.

the father of the *Portuguese Letters.* One witness they bring forward is Jean-Jacques Rousseau, who was among the earliest readers to suggest that things were not as they appeared:

> Women, in general, show neither appreciation nor proficiency nor genius in any part. They can succeed in certain short works which demand only lightness, taste, grace, sometimes even philosophy and reasoning. They can acquire scientific knowledge, erudition, talents and anything which can be acquired through hard work. But the celestial fire which heats and engulfs the soul, the genius which consumes and devours, that burning eloquence, those sublime raptures which transmit delight to the very foundation of the soul will always be lacking from women's writings. They are all cold and pretty like their authors. They may show great wit but never any soul. They are a hundred times more reasonable than they are passionate. Women know neither how to describe nor experience love itself. Only Sappho and one other deserve to be counted as exceptions. I would bet everything I have that the *Portuguese Letters* were written by a man.[9]

Deloffre and Rougeot quote this passage in extenso, as reproduced here, although ostensibly it is only the last sentence which interests them. Manifestly, they would like to disassociate themselves from Rousseau's syllogistic reasoning and rescue the conclusions of his argument from the principles which produce them. "Without getting involved in this discussion of principle, let us look at the facts, and, since we are asked to judge a paternity suit, let us hear from the partisans of both theses."[10] A set of "facts" they find particularly persuasive are those uncovered in Leo Spitzer's important study on the *Portuguese Letters.* One could hardly have wished for a more authoritative word on the subject. Let us therefore briefly examine how the father of modern stylistics confers legitimacy on this bastard text.

Spitzer enters into the dispute with this admonishment of all the researchers who have preceded him:

> One would think that just plain good sense would have led literary historians not to attack the problem of the attribution of a text without first having elucidated its exact meaning. It is only once this meaning is well established that we will be able to retrace the causal forces which presided at the elaboration of a work, while, if the work itself remains poorly defined, the causal force (the personality of the author) will remain necessarily obscure. . . . I maintain in effect that if the critics had recognized from the outset the *artistic* value of this collection of letters, they would not have hesitated to deny the other alternative, that of "authentic" letters, written in Portuguese by some nun exhumed from the archives of "history." If we can prove the unity of artistic conception and

> execution of the five French letters then any "naturalist" theory or "evolutionary" descendance from the Portuguese original is excluded.[11]

The note of ridicule suggested by the proliferation of inverted commas at the end of this passage is but a first sign of Spitzer's disdain for any and all naive readers of the letters, in particular for the critics who have gone before and who should have known better.

As he makes clear in this opening statement, Spitzer intends to prove that the artistic conception and execution of the work is manifest on every level. It is incumbent upon every scholar who recognizes this artistic value to deny the alternative of a non-literary conception and execution, to deny, in other words, that "some nun exhumed from the archives of 'history' " had anything to do with the text as we read it. Already here, however, even before Spitzer begins his detailed and most often brilliant analysis of the five letters, one realizes that, in the end, we will not be handed definitive proof, but only a *probable* explanation. That is, it will be demonstrated that it is highly unlikely that anyone unfamiliar with and unpracticed in the refined classical discourse on passion which was common in seventeenth-century Parisian salons could have reproduced an exemplary model of that discourse. Improbable, but of course not impossible. The judgment which Spitzer makes rests upon our common acceptance of the model of probability. This model, from the mathematical operations of statistics, has another, not dissimilar use in the special context to which Spitzer makes frequent reference: the set of literary conventions compiled by the code of *vraisemblance* or verisimilitude, and even more specifically, the classical content of that code. With this is mind, we understand Spitzer to be arguing as follows: while it is not impossible that someone named Mariana Alcoforado wrote these five letters, it is highly *invraisemblable*.*

Before we consider the specific use Spitzer makes of the concept, let us review the general description of *vraisemblance* as it is understood by contemporary literary history. Our guide in this will be Gérard Genette's own review of this classical code in his article "Vraisemblance et motivation."[12]

The *vraisemblance* of a classical play or prose narration is seen as determined by two factors which, because they mutually reinforce and imply each other, are frequently collapsed into a single concept. First, one can distinguish the notion of likelihood or probability that derives from the opposition of the general to the singular, the essential to the accidental. "Truth only produces things as they are while *vraisemblance* produces them as they must be. Truth is

---

*I have decided not to translate this term and its derivatives 1) in order not to have to deal with their ungainly English equivalent "verisimilitudinous" and "univerisimilitudinous", and 2) because these translations are not only cumbersome but inexact since *vraisemblance* implies both likelihood and "real-seeming" according to literary conventions.

almost always defective by the intermingling of the singular conditions which compose it. Nothing is born into the world which does not move away from the perfection of its idea at birth. One must look for origins and models in *vraisemblance* and in the universal principles of things where they are protected from the corruption of the material and the singular."[13] The birth image at the center of this passage signals already the implication of patriarchal ideology in this concept of probable essences and leads us to the other level at which *vraisemblance* functions: respect for a socio-political norm. Genette writes that "*vraisemblance* and the code of social propriety (*bienséance*) are joined by the same criterion which is 'all that conforms to public opinion'. This 'opinion', real or supposed, is almost precisely that which today we would call an ideology, that is, a corpus of maxims and prejudices which constitutes at the same time a vision of the world and a system of values."[14] As a "vision of the world" *vraisemblance* provides a standard for logical judgments—probability. As a "system of values" *vraisemblance* catalogues a social group's ethical judgments, its ideology. But as the two can never be rigorously divorced from each other, it follows that what a particular society judges to be logical or probable is always bound up with a prior determination of what is deemed proper.

The frequently cited example of the controversy provoked by Corneille's *Le Cid* illustrates this double determination of *vraisemblance*. The play's critics protested the representation of Chimène as a woman who marries her father's murderer. This representation was condemned widely as either immoral or improbable, but both reproaches were joined in faulting the play's *vraisemblance*. It is impossible, thus, to separate that which shocks the public's moral sensibility (Chimène's *improper* act—an honorable woman *should not* marry her father's murderer) from that which clashes with their sense of logical probability (Chimène's *unlikely* act—an honorable woman *would not* marry her father's murderer). That the protests, however, clearly separated historical or singular reality fom general or essential truth (*vraisemblance*) is made evident by the fact that one of the play's most outspoken detractors, Mlle. de Scudéry, could write: "It is true that Chimène married the Cid, but it is not *vraisemblable* that a woman of honor marries her father's murderer."[15] Historical reality is not the model for vraisemblance. On the contrary, vraisemblance is that code according to which a society imposes an ideological order on historical, material reality—on all that which is "born into this world."

Returning now to Spitzer's essay, we can perhaps determine how the manipulation of the criterion of vraisemblance affects the central question of the text's genesis. It should be repeated that Spitzer's analysis of the letters does not proceed on the assumption that it can determine the sex of the author on the basis of stylistic or formal aspects of the work but only that such an analysis can decide the question of literary or non-literary conception. The first problematic lies presumably outside the jurisdiction of stylistics. In effect, it would defeat the principal understanding of this procedure which sets out to find an "artistic" rather than a "naturalistic" (Spitzer's terms) impulse behind the letters if one would then propose to support that demonstration with a stylistic profile of the author's sex identity, thereby sending the argument back into the camp of the "naturalists." Spitzer, we must believe, is far more objective than, for example, Rousseau, for he eschews any confidence in sexual stereotypes when the question is one of literary style. However, such stereotypes are not so easily dispatched.

One senses, for instance, that part of Spitzer's conviction derives from what would be shocking about this text if one knew it to be "authentic." His distaste for this alternative focuses on the central situation of a woman who transgresses not only the fundamental interdictions for her sex but also the devotional vows of a Christian religious order. At moments, one almost expects his analysis to veer off into the sort of revulsion with which another reader of the letters, Barbey d'Aurevilly, rejected the notion of their authenticity. Deloffre and Rougeot characterize Barbey's reaction as one of "horror at the idea that a nun, the spouse of Jesus Christ, could have written such impieties."[16] Spitzer, with considerably more restraint, simply denies the probability of Mariana's blasphemous behavior: "The fact that one finds no trace in our letters of a grave conflict between religion and love . . . could indicate to what extent love's monomania has replaced any religious life in Mariana–but *one would expect* on the part of a real nun at least passing allusion to prayer, to the sacrament and to ritual. [The] ascendancy of sentimentality in her expression *would better suit* a literary character from high drama than a humble sister" (my italics).[17] The added italics are meant to emphasize the two points of juncture between this moment in Spitzer's analysis and the double determination of *vraisemblance*: probability, or the essential as opposed to the singular ("one would expect . . .") and propriety ("her expression would better suit . . ."). The only context in which Spitzer can explain (and excuse) Mariana's improbable and unsuitable lack of guilt and torment, self-loathing even, is that of seventeenth-century literary convention: "Is it not an accepted principle of the seventeenth century to proscribe any representation of Christian sacrament from the secular theater, a principle which has also influenced this 'epistolary drama'?" In other words, that a real nun might forsake all allusion to her religious training and give herself over completely to the secular language of passion goes against normal expectation and shocks one's sense of propriety, whereas a literary conventional nun is fully expected to do so. It is *invraisemblable* that one would find no trace of religious devotion in a "real" nun's correspondence, but in a literary context this improbability becomes, on the contrary, the mark of *vraisemblance* or what the literary audience has come to expect by virtue of convention. Thus, on the specific point Spitzer is here discussing, there is assumed to be a fundamental contrast between an authentic portrayal and a *vraisemblable* portrayal because of the classical prohibition of direct religious representation. Notice, however, that this assumption is itself grounded in the system which it invokes as a standard of measure since it supposes that in the absence of such an artificial prohibition a nun in Mariana's situation would show signs of a "grave conflict between religion and love." Spitzer thereby has recourse to the literary criterion of *vraisemblance* in order to determine the non-literary status of a phenomenon. In effect, Spitzer must argue both that the text conforms to the rules of *vraisemblance* and is therefore a conventional work *and* that it contradicts these rules, thereby demonstrating its inauthenticity.

Anyone familiar with the rest of Spitzer's critical work knows that he is thoroughly versed in the seventeenth-century code of *vraisemblance* and realizes better than most the implications of Boileau's famous reminder to would-be poets: "The true may sometimes not be *vraisemblable*;" or of Montaigne's more intolerant observation: "It is foolish presumption to go about disdaining and condemning as false that which does not seem *vraisemblable.*" Nevertheless, as we have seen, Spitzer subtly invokes both ideological propriety and its neutral mask, probability, in order to disdain and condemn as false the text's (possible) authenticity. The subtlety of that analysis can be appreciated when it is placed beside the sort of clumsy psychological determinism one finds in another proponent of the theory of the literariness of the *Letters*, Wolfgang Leiner, who routinely interchanges terms like "true," "authentic," and *"vraisemblable."* In a move similar to Spitzer's, Leiner takes the inconsistencies to be proof of the letters' *vraisemblance* and ultimately what he calls their "psychological authenticity:" ". . . it seems to me that it is precisely the inherent contradictions in the text, contradictions which deprive the work of any 'historical credence', which contribute to its achieving a psychological authenticity . . . . [Guillragues] directed all his attention to the study of feminine psychology. And it is there that he has succeeded in giving a *vraisemblable* and authentic portrait."[18]

Is it going too far to suggest that these two critics so prefer the idea that Mariana is, to quote Leiner, the "original creation of a French author of the classical period" that they are willing to overlook the logical distortions in their argument? That the contrary hypothesis of "authentic" letters offends not their sense of logic but their sense of propriety? By cementing in place the vision of the letters as a literary production, their interpretations operate as a kind of shield between them and whatever is shocking or scandalous in this text written (possibly) in a woman's hand. It is as if by placing a mediator— Guilleragues—between themselves and the Mariana of the letters they can confine or defuse whatever elements remain too unmediated. Their experience as critics (that is, as someone who reads literature at a distance mediated by the knowledge of tradition and who has learned to overcome the "naive" desire to suspend disbelief) is perhaps put in question by a work which may have more than the conventional claims to authenticity, for example, as "found letters." Confused reasoning helps maintain that critical stance.

Of course, we have focused thus far on only one moment in Spitzer's analysis, a moment when the argument appears to stumble into the ideological circularity of *vraisemblance*. There are, to be sure, many other lines of reasoning which the critic mobilizes to support his central argument. However, at the risk of being impertinent (beside the point, but also "insolent or saucy in speech or manners," according to the *Oxford English Dictionary*; impertinence, thus, like *invraisemblance*, conflates the concepts of the inessential and the socially improper), let us shift our focus from the apparent center of the essay—the stylistic analysis of the *Portuguese Letters*—to its marginal regions, the notes at the bottom of the page. This is the region proper (so to speak) to the impertinent argument, the space reserved for inessential discourse. What we find there is not only Spitzer meddling in an issue which is beside the point of his article but the evocation of another instance of the impertinent woman—Heloise.

Spitzer takes up the issue of the resemblances between Heloise's correspondence with Abelard and the anonymous seventeenth-century letters in an exceedingly long note which pursues a double argument, both the subjects of controversy among other literary historians:[19] 1) that this correspondence, re-published in an early seventeenth-century edition of Abelard's complete works, served as a model for the *Portuguese Letters*; and 2) that the letters from Heloise to Abelard were probably largely re-written (perhaps even entirely invented) by the latter when he was composing his autobiographical memoir, *Historia calamitatum*.

The note is structured by three moments: first, Spitzer points to the medieval correspondence as a model for the classical one, thereby placing the *Portuguese Letters* in the line of a tradition, specifically that of an imagined or unsolicited correspondence; second, this initial comparison must be justified by a discussion of the controversy over the authorship or authenticity of the Heloise correspondence, which Spitzer decides, peremptorily, in favor of Abelard's partial or complete re-editing; third, Spitzer returns to the question of imitation or influence and finds several more instances when the author of the *Letters* was probably drawing upon the invention of the author of Heloise's letters to Abelard. One instance he cites is particularly charged. Spitzer writes:

> the idea of the amorous couple violating the respect of the convent at Beja by their amatory relations would seem to come from the episode recounted by Abelard in the fifth letter on his visit to the convent of the nuns at Argenteuil and the scene of "libertinage" which took place in the refectory. One could explain by this literary origin a motif whose *invraisemblance* has shocked critics of the *Portuguese Letters*. [20]

By first setting up the Heloise/Abelard correspondance as an "origin" of Mariana's letters, and then arguing for the "literary" status of this origin, Spitzer submits the shocking *invraisemblance* of the transgressive motif to a double mediation. The text is thus given a father—Abelard—and is re-inserted in the chain of mediating explanations. As Mariana and Heloise became merely fictional interlocutors, the texts in which they figure lose their shock value. The ideological order of paternity is once again ratified and the works return to the code of *vraisemblance*. However, Spitzer's displacement of first Mariana and then Heloise in view of this re-assertion of a mediating authority leaves us to consider the implications of the *original* paternity of Abelard.

The fact that, although castrated, Abelard is the father to whom these bastard texts must finally return only serves to underline that by paternity one understands first of all a relation to mediation.* By this logic, it is precisely because Abelard is the castrated "spiritual" father (and not in spite of it) that he is in the best position to fulfill the role as origin of the process of generation. By affixing the mark of Abelard to these letters, Spitzer assures the protective presence of a mediator, a father, who receives the child/text at the moment of birth and wraps it in the conventions of culture.

The process of restoration of the father's name does not end with Abelard or even Guilleragues. There is still another father-figure to whom a debt is owing, still another mediator who serves to explain and contain the Mariana of the *Portuguese Letters*. He is the absent lover to whom the letters are addressed; but in order to reach him, Spitzer must abandon his critical principle of explicating the work only in terms of its own internal structure. Here, instead, near the end of his essay, Spitzer directs our attention to the probable *reality* of Mariana's French officer, his *nature*, his *objective* image.

> We never know where we are with regards to what the beloved officer *really* was, in and of himself. One even wonders if certain of Mariana's phillipics . . . are not meant to give us a glimpse, in a very feeble and passing light, of the *objective* image of a brilliant French officer. . . . Are not even his polite and harmless responses to her reproaches, which cause the rupture, an indication of the temperament of a well-balanced nobleman who cannot be impolite to a woman? He's a ladies' man . . . But what of it? Isn't it *natural* for a young and ebullient officer of aristocratic birth, "likeable," unmarried . . . ? It is also quite characteristic that Mariana never tells us the name of her lover, she who does identify her own role in the drama under the name of Mariana. She never thinks of putting him before her and giving him a *reality* outside of herself. We are in the presence of a "narcissistic" love . . . . It is not the infrequent and cold responses of the lover but the narrowness of her image of him that killed Mariana's passion.[21]

Mariana stands accused of upstaging her lover, of usurping his place at the center of the event. The critic judges her passion to be pathologically "narcissistic" and takes as a foremost sign of this distortion the failure of the text of that passion to record the lover's name. It remains resolutely a bastard text which will not acknowledge the "natural" order of a noble society and thereby give the ladies' man his due.

One can only speculate why Spitzer interpolates this justification of the French officer. The reference to an extra-fictional reality represents, as I have

---

*In general, "castration" is the term which in psychoanalysis describes the stage of psychic development that follows upon the resolution of the Oedipal conflict, that is, the child's acceptance of the father's mediation and renunciation of the phallic immediacy of the mother.

already noted, a departure from the basic procedure of the rest of the study. Why does Spitzer choose finally to understand the whole work in terms of Mariana's narrow image of her lover—that "brilliant," "polite," "well-balanced," "likeable," "young and ebullient officer of aristocratic birth"? What prompts him to suggest that one can read these epithets hidden behind Mariana's more unflattering language? Since his leading argument has been an attack on the blindness of other critics who were too ready to believe in Mariana's "reality," this passage could be read as a final parry intended to clarify once and for all the opposition illusion/reality, blindness/insight. In this final and definitive version, it is Mariana who is blind to the reality of her lover, and her blindness has in turn obfuscated the issue of the text's "original" generation for more than three centuries of literary history. Mariana's passion is, in this version, an illusion, a fiction behind which stands the only reality: a man's quite natural philanderings.

*   *   *

Spitzer, as I think I have shown, wants to give this text a father, some "deliberate" poet (to use Frye's phrase again) who can confer with his name and his art a legitimacy on these unsigned letters. What that father represents is a clear intentionality, realized or given expression in the written work and recovered through the work of interpretation. Moreover, the same would apply if one were to argue, against Spitzer, that the letters are "authentic" rather than "literary." This interpretation understands merely a different intentionality and therefore a different realization, but it functions equally to ratify the position which belongs to the father. To affix a signature—a determinate intentionality—to a text, whether as we read or as we write, is to attempt what Spitzer tries to do with this essay: contain an unlimited textual system, install a measure of protection between this boundlessness and one's own power to know, to be this power and to know that one is this power.

To whom or to what do we attribute a text like the *Portuguese Letters* if it is not to some finite intentionality which must differ according to whether the work is, finally, fiction or autobiography, a man's imagined scene or a woman's lived experience? How can one read a work in the absence of the concept of an author and hence authorial intention? This question is essentially the same as the question of origin which we earlier saw Freud trip over in his apology of patriarchy: it supposes that a system of differential values (for example, culture or language) was set in operation by a non-differentiated term, that is, an origin uncontaminated by the differential structure it inaugurates. Likewise the author's intentionality would have to lie somewhere outside—behind, beneath, before—the text which it informs and grounds. In order, however, to effect a workable critique of the first notion—which gives transcendental authority to patriarchal values—one must re-appraise the second as well by reading the author's "intention" (and indeed by reading the "author") as itself already marked within the chain of differences which it can neither originate nor control.

The *Portuguese Letters*, then: written by a "man," by a "woman," as "fiction," as "authentic letters"? We may of course still want to provide some answers to these questions, but such empiricism cannot be counted on to lead us outside the circle of its own pre-ordained tautologies of what is woman's writing, man's writing, fictional, or authentic. If, on the other hand, the theory and practice of writing *as* a woman—to recall the phrase encountered earlier—are to be in any measure critical levers with which to displace the imponderable weight of patriarchy, then it is only to the extent that we bear down at the most vulnerable point, that interval where essence risks seeping out into pretense. For "as a woman" is also a simile, a comparison which associates two terms through resemblance and which can diminish but never abolish their difference. Only with this simile the effect is the contrary: "a woman writing as a woman"—the repetition of the "identical" term splits that identity, making room for a slight shift, spacing out the differential meaning which has always been at work in the single term. And the repetition has no reason to stop there, no finite number of times it can be repeated until it closes itself off logically, with the original identity recuperated in a final term. Likewise, one can find only arbitrary beginnings for the series, and no term which is not already a repetition: " . . . a woman writing as a woman writing as a . . ."

So where can this lead us or leave us? Writing as a woman . . . no place, but neither is it a perfect tautological circle. Rather, it leads through whatever it has meant, will mean, and can mean (as well as all it has *not* meant, will *not* mean, and can *not* mean) to be "as and like" a woman, as if a woman were something one is—or is not—purely and simply. Reading a text as written by a woman will be reading it *as if* it had no (determined) father, *as if*, in other words, it were illegitimate, recognized by its mother who can only give it a borrowed name.

In all likelihood, someone named Guilleragues wrote the work we know as the *Portuguese Letters* but suppressed that fact on the title page, leaving a blank where one normally looks to find an author's name. If filling in that blank with a proper name has been the work of more than three hundred years, it nevertheless leaves us with the task of reading that text as if it had never known its father.

NOTES

1. Northrop Frye, *Anatomy of Criticism* (Princeton: Princeton University Press, 1957), p. 98.
2. Annis V. Pratt, "The New Feminist Criticisms: Exploring the History of the New Space," in *Beyond Intellectual Sexism: A New Woman, A New Reality*, ed. Joan I. Roberts (New York: McKay, 1976), p. 179.
3. Patricia Meyer Spacks, *The Female Imagination* (New York: Knopf, 1975), p.35.
4. Ibid., p. 7.

5. *Lettres portugaises, Valentins et autres oeuvres de Guilleragues*, eds. F. Deloffre et J. Rougeot (Paris: Garnier, 1962), p. vii; my translation.

6. ". . . let us look at the facts, and, since we are asked to judge a paternity suit, let us hear from the partisans of both theses." Ibid.

7. *The Standard Edition of the Complete Works of Sigmund Freud*, (London: Hogarth Press, 1949), p. 23; p. 114.

8. Ibid., p. 118.

9. Jean-Jacques Rousseau, *La Lettre à d'Alembert sur les spectacles* (Paris: Garnier-Flammarion, 1967), pp. 199-200; my translation.

10. *Lettres portuguises*, eds. Deloffre, Rougeot, p. vii.

11. Leo Spitzer, "Les *Lettres portugaises*," *Romanische Forschungen* 65 (1953):95; my translation.

12. Gérard Genette, "Vraisemblance et motivation," in *Figures II* (Paris: Seuil, 1969), pp. 71-77

13. Ibid., p. 73; my translation.

14. Ibid.

15. Ibid., p. 71.

16. *Lettres portugaises*, eds. Deloffre, Rougeot, p. vi.

17. Spitzer, "Les *Lettres portugaises*," pp. 117-18.

18. Wolfgang Leiner, "De Nouvelles considerations sur l'apostrophe initiale des *Lettres portugaises*," *Romanische Forschungen* 78 (1965):562; my translation.

19. For a detailed refutation of Spitzer's argument about the Abelard correspondence, cf. E.P.M. Dronke, "Heloise and Marianne," *Romanische Forschungen* 72 (1960): 224ff.

20. Spitzer, "Les *Lettres portugaises*," pp. 111-12.

21. Spitzer, "Les *Lettres portugaises*," pp. 121-22; all but the first italics are mine.

20
READING READING:
ECHO'S ABDUCTION OF LANGUAGE

Caren Greenberg

Myth has been widely used as a critical tool, yet a precise definition of what constitutes myth and its function in criticism remains problematic. Thematic critics refer to texts containing explicit references to various Greek or Roman myths; historical critics trace the use made of those myths over certain time periods. Feminist critics, along with some psychoanalytic critics, often depart radically from the first two by dealing mostly with problems of archetypes not generally derived from the Greco-Roman tradition. For the remaining psychoanalytic critics, those influenced by Freud and Lacan, the use of myth is both more psycho-sexually oriented and more structural. Uniting all these concerns, the structural notion of myth, that is, the concept of myths as stories whose purpose is to specify and to explain otherwise unexplained relationships among people or phenomena, allows for the inclusion of all these critical approaches. The application of myth to criticism is, and should remain, varied, but one particular relationship has barely been examined through the organizing grid of myths: the relationship between the reader and the text.

In a largely non-literary context, Freud proposed an interpretation of the Oedipus myth which, through the delineation of the Oedipal triangle (father-mother-son), purported to explain the development of male sexuality in the individual. Further, in *Totem and Taboo*, Freud maintained (be it through structural analogy, blind androcentrism, or an accurate perception of the patriarchy), "that the beginnings of religion, ethics, society, and art meet in the Oedipus complex."[1]

Literary critics have certainly not gone out of their way to question that all-encompassing contention. In Louis Fraiberg's *Psychoanalysis and American Literary Criticism*,[2] Freud's analysis of the Oedipus legend is treated at great length, its universal nature goes virtually unquestioned, and it suffers no competition from alternate Freudian myths: narcissism, for example, is never mentioned. *The Practice of Psychoanalytic Criticism*[3] contains articles which use the Oedipus complex or Oedipal anxiety to explain such authors as More, Dickens, Kafka, Yeats, and Shakespeare, along with many of their works. Even outside of the overtly psychoanalytic context, the Oedipus myth reappears with inordinate frequency. One peculiar aspect of this is its insistent recurrence as object of analysis. The most noteworthy example is Claude Lévi-Strauss' early analysis of the Oedipus myth in *L'Anthropologie structurale*—despite his own assertion that the Oedipus myth "lends itself poorly to a demonstration" of his method.*

These are only a few of the overwhelming number of possible examples of the critical obsession with the Oedipus myth. We cannot help but notice, along with René Girard, "the permanence, many thousands of years old, of the Oedipal myth, the irrevocable nature of its themes, the quasi-religious respect with which modern culture continues to surround it."[4] The Oedipus myth is as old as the patriarchy, and it survives in modern criticism in a way that no other myth (not even Orpheus, not even Pygmalion) survives. As we have already seen, myth is usually a socially useful story, one which serves to explain some phenomenon which is not otherwise accounted for. It thus serves to overcome uncertainty or to explain away violence. Whatever the Oedipus myth was once meant to elucidate, Freud's use of the myth to characterize the development of male sexuality has established its usefulness and thus its continued status as myth in our own patriarchal society.

Returning to the subject of criticism, we can hypothesize that the interest

---

*Claude Lévi-Strauss, *L'Anthropologie structurale* (Paris: Plon, 1958), p. 235. Because the English translation by Claire Jacobson and Brooke Grundfest Schoepf [*Structural Anthropology* (New York: Basic Books, 1963), p. 213] downplays these disclaimers, I have provided my own translation of Lévi-Strauss' statement on the question of the unsuitability of the Oedipus myth: "Let us take as an example the Oedipus myth, which offers the advantage of being known by everyone, so that we can dispense with telling the story. No doubt this example lends itself poorly to a demonstration. The Oedipus myth has come to us in fragmentary and late versions which are all literary transpositions, inspired more by moral or esthetic concerns than by religious tradition or ritualistic usage, assuming that such concerns ever were present in relation to it. But [. . . .] we simply want to illustrate—without drawing any conclusions about the myth itself—a certain technique, the use of which is probably not legitimate in this particular case, because of the uncertainties just mentioned." The reason everyone knows the Oedipus myth is that Freud discussed it in the context of the Oedipus complex. Despite Lévi-Strauss' excuses, the fact remains that the myth is, on the contrary, very useful to his purpose, for it allows a discussion of a myth of male sexuality without the acknowledgment that that is the topic of the discussion. Consequently, it is not too surprising that where his analysis of the Oedipus myth was long considered a revolutionary model for literary criticism, his more recent works on different cultural myths, though widely read and considered by many specialists to be technically better, have had no comparable impact. Without question, the methods developed by Lévi-Strauss are outstanding, but one cannot help but wonder if their impact would have been as widely appreciated if he had chosen another myth.

afforded the Oedipus myth by many critics springs from a narcissistic desire on the part of the critic to examine *his* own sexual development. This brand of critic and criticism is a logical outgrowth of the academic patriarchy (or filiarchy), and it is with no biological connotation, though with a very definite psycho-sexual one, that I will refer to Oedipal (or male) criticism and the Oedipal (or male) critic, and that I will correspondingly use the masculine pronoun in italics to designate psychosexual rather than biological masculinity.

Those critical texts which use the Oedipus myth as their model or structure are suggesting that the myth is a kind of reading. A major benefit of seeing the myth as a description of a reading is that the myth becomes a new text—one about reading, a particular relationship with language—which can in turn be read. It is therefore possible to analyze the critic's relationship to the text by analyzing the myth according to which the reading is structured.

When it is used to explain male sexuality, the Oedipus myth is interpreted as the drama of the son attempting to move into the role of the father through the appropriation of his power and his pleasure in the form of the wife/mother. According to René Girard: "[Oedipal] identification is a desire *to be*, which one seeks, naturally, to fulfill by *having*, that is, by the appropriation of the father's objects. The son, Freud writes, seeks to replace the father in all regards; thus, he seeks to replace him in his desires, to desire that which he desires."[5] The mother, as the object of desire, is the point of intersection between father and son; and since she is the key to the son's identification with the father, she is also the point of intersection between masculine power and pleasure.

The mother's body, as a point of intersection and contention becomes symbolic: a sexual battleground important not because of her own intrinsic power, but rather as a mark of the father's power. In this sense, the wife/ mother's body fulfills the first requirement of a language system: it marks something other than itself.

If she is to play the role of the text, the mother must also be legible, that is, the symbolism of her body must be decipherable. This requirement corresponds to the unconscious nature of the Oedipal conflict which can be brought to light by the analyst. Legibility is represented in the Oedipus myth by Oedipus' ignorance of his own crimes and his subsequent recognition of them. For the mark of Oedipus' crimes is Jocasta: she carries the royal power once belonging to Laius and confers it upon Oedipus, along with Laius' sexual pleasures. As point of intersection between father and son, she is also the mark of Oedipus' crimes: the herdsman recognizes her as the woman who had given him the baby Oedipus.

When Oedipus thus learns of his patricide and incest, his first reaction is to go after Jocasta with a sword, to eliminate the mark of his crimes. But Oedipus is too late; Jocasta has already hung herself. Once Jocasta's dual sexual role as mother and wife is recognized, her body hangs dead, a mark of incest and patricide, of sexuality and of death. The text, Jocasta's body, is a residue of Oedipus' successful reading.

An Oedipal form of reading suggests specific relationships among reader, text, and author. The myth implies that the roles at both ends of the creative process are essentially male and that the mediating text is female—and dead.* Laius, as king and father to Oedipus, first gave meaning to Jocasta as "she whom one must marry in order to become king" and "she who could render Oedipus' lovemaking incestuous." In this way, Laius is author of the text Jocasta: he renders her meaningful. Oedipus is forced into the role of the reader, decoding the message of pleasure and power which Jocasta's body at first hid and later revealed. An Oedipal reading is one which involves a struggle for power and pleasure; the relationship between the author and critic is a political and sexual power-play for the possession and the pleasure of the text.

Oedipal reading suffers from many limitations. The very elements which make the Oedipus myth so useful in the discussion of male sexuality tend to deny the importance of the woman, since she acquires meaning only as the symbol of the father's power. Woman is the text in the Oedipus myth, and if we pursue the analogy, the fate of the text (and therefore of language) in the Oedipal reading process parallels the fate of women in the patriarchy: both are without intrinsic value and gain importance only to the extent that they signify something other than themselves.†

Since the major blind spot in Oedipal reading is its insensitivity to the text, the most apparent loss is attention to the stuff of the text, language. In

---

*Hélène Cixous has made this comment about the male view of the relationship between women and death: "They say that there are two things which cannot be represented: death and female genitals. Because they need femininity to be associated with death; they're erect from fear! for themselves! They *need* to be afraid of us." *La Jeune née* (Paris: 10/18, 1975), p. 126. My translation.

Further, on the question of the disappearance of the woman, Cixous writes, "Either woman is passive or she does not exist. What is left of her is unthinkable or unthought. Which is to say that she is not thought about, that she isn't included in the binary oppositions, she does not form a couple with the father (who does form a couple with the son)." Cixous, p. 118. My translation.

†The overriding importance of reference to the nonlinguistic world suggests that Oedipal critics are primarily concerned with the discovery of empirical reality or a statement of "truth." It is therefore possible to include among the Oedipal critics those literary historians and psychoanalytic critics who seek historical and biographical information in literary texts. Yet, some more recent critics are not exempt from the search for truth. Levi-Strauss claims, for example, that myths manifest themselves through many different versions and that it is possible to relate them in a grid which reveals what he calls the "mythic structure." He does so as an anthropologist, seeking information about a culture through the dissection and redistribution of texts. [See Lévi-Strauss, *L'Anthropologie*, especially pages 240-41.] It would be tempting to hypothesize about the Oedipal nature of much early structural criticism inspired by the social sciences. In fact, the essential difference between early structuralism and contemporary semiotics may very well be the shift in concern from external reference (which ultimately subjugated the text to "reality") to internal reflexivity. This shift is apparent in the work of Roland Barthes. In 1968 Barthes wrote, "In the multiplicity of writing, everything is to be *disentangled*, nothing *deciphered*;

orderto correct this lack, an alternate, perhaps adjunct, myth should prove useful. Rather than abandoning female textuality to the simple status of corpse, as is the case of Jocasta, the Echo myth, wherein the female body exists in relation to language, provides an alternative to Oedipal reading. In two versions of the Echo myth the relationship between the female body and language allows us to reconstruct—or to construct—a myth about the nature of female textuality. By female textuality, I mean a non-Oedipal relationship to the text: one in which the relationship of the reader to language is recognized as essential, where the reader perceives the stuff of the text as intrinsically important.*

The Echo and Narcissus version of the myth appears in Ovid's *Metamorphoses.*[6] Echo sees Narcissus while he is hunting and falls in love with him. From the outset Echo is described as still having a body and as being afflicted with her peculiar speech. There is a digression which explains the origin of her problem: Echo had been punished by Juno because by entertaining her with chatter, Echo had kept the goddess from discovering Jove's sexual infidelity. Since it was linguistic prowess that had allowed Echo to trick Juno, the goddess took her revenge on Echo's verbal talents. After this brief history, the Echo and Narcissus narrative is resumed. Burning with love, Echo is nonetheless incapable of initiating conversation with Narcissus. All she can do is repeat the last part of Narcissus' utterances in order to offer herself to him. When Narcissus is lost he calls out to his friends—cries which Echo tailors to her own needs in order to designate a meeting place. The one initiative she can take is physical: Echo tries to throw her arms around Narcissus. He pulls away, saying that he would rather die than give her power over him, and Echo responds by saying that she gives him power over her. Her physical advances rejected, Echo runs off and pines away for Narcissus' love. First, her body shrivels up, leaving only her bones and voice. The bones then harden into stone and only the voice remains to repeat Narcissus' dying words and sounds.

---

the structure can be followed, 'run' (like the thread of a stocking) at every point and at every level, but there is nothing beneath: the space of writing is to be ranged over, not pierced; writing ceaselessly posits meaning ceaselessly to evaporate it, carrying out a systematic exemption of meaning. In precisely this way literature (it would be better from now on to say *writing*), by refusing to assign a 'secret', an ultimate meaning, to the text (and to the world as text), liberates what may be called an anti-theological activity, an activity that is truly revolutionary since to refuse to fix meaning is, in the end, to refuse God and his hypostases—reason, science, law." [Roland Barthes,"The Death of the Author," in *Image-Music-Text*, trans. Stephen Heath (New York: Hill and Wang, 1977), p. 147.] In our terms, this amounts to total advocacy of non-Oedipal criticism. Yet, the article ends with a statement which recreates the critical Oedipal crisis: "The birth of the reader must be at the cost of the death of the Author." [Barthes, p. 148.] By 1973 Barthes totally shifted his critical emphasis to "the pleasure of the text," and gave his total attention to the stuff of the text and its relationship to the reader, rather than to its referential capacities. [See Roland Barthes, *Le Plaisir du texte* (Paris: Seuil, 1973).]

*The Echo myth is not put forth here as a more real or true critical relationship to the text, rather it is proposed as one example, amidst myriad possibilities, of a feminist form of reading.

The origin of Echo's problem shows her being punished for having veiled male sexuality from a woman. The chatter that Echo puts forth, a fictional text, diverts Juno from knowledge rather than informing her. The truth is there to be learned, but a female text substitutes itself for that truth in much the same way that Jocasta kept Oedipus from knowledge, despite her potential legibility. When Juno takes her revenge, she does so exclusively on the linguistic function: Echo's body remains intact. Echo still exists as an individual, language still emanates from her, but it is in the form of repetition. Echo still performs linguistically; she is able to choose how much of the end of an utterance she wants to repeat. She remains a speaker because she can produce language which is in relation to her desires.

Narcissus' problem is that he is lost, out of place. His cries are as lost as his body, and they go out to an unknown receiver in an unknown location. When Echo first returns Narcissus' words, before he has seen her, he remains confused. Once she presents herself to him, arms outstretched, Narcissus' words are localized, not in their original topos, but in a new one. Like a printed text, Echo's body provides a new location for his words, and Echo's voice provides a new reading of his text. At this point, Echo's body stands instead of Narcissus' body as a point of origin for his speech, but her body is at the same time a locus of her own sexual desire. She is different from Narcissus to the extent that her desires are different. (Once Narcissus falls in love with his own image, his desires are identical to Echo's—he loves Narcissus—and the fate of his body is similar as well.)

When Echo's bodily condensation begins and the soft tissues dry and shrivel, the erotic nature of her body disappears. As her individual erotic physical characteristics disappear, she is reduced to a locus of the function of repetition. When at last the bones petrify, even the *trace* of the function disappears: it is marked only by its occurrence and by its passive instrument, the rocks. No longer an agent of repetition, Echo is the repetition. In fact, no longer Echo, she becomes an echo or echoing.

The Echo and Pan version of the myth is recounted in Longus' *Daphnis and Chloe*[7] In this version, Echo is intact physically and linguistically at the start. Raised by the nymphs and muses, she is an expert musician as well as a virgin who shuns the company of males. Pan is incensed by her for two reasons: her musical competence puts her into competition with him, and her devotion to maidenhood causes her to reject his advances. Pan takes his revenge by sending the shepherds and goatherds to rip Echo's body apart and to scatter the pieces which are still singing. The pieces of her body are hidden away by the Earth, but the music and Echo's voice continue to imitate all sounds—including Pan's pipes. When Pan hears his music repeated, he pursues the sound. No longer in search of sexual satisfaction, he is searching for what he believes to be his own student.

While the Echo of this version does repeat language as well as music, the emphasis is on music. Music is structured sound; in relation to language, it is form without content. Similarly, Echo's body is form without emotional content, beauty without sexual desire. The parallel between the music and Echo's body seems justified given the interdependence between bodily disintegration and the loss of creativity in this version. Unlike the Echo who loves Narcissus, this Echo apparently suffers no peculiarity of speech until her body is destroyed. During her lifetime, she maintains her original body structure and can produce musical harmony. When Pan seeks vengeance, he seeks vengeance on unity: the structural integrity of the speaker is diffused, as Echo's body is undone by Pan's violence. The imitation or echoing which results is the one element of language which is not disorganized by this dissemination: the repetition function. Repetition survives diffusion because, as language re-pre-senting itself, it requires no agent, it needs no place of origin.

In the Narcissus version, Echo's body came to conform to her linguistic ability—or inability. For Pan's Echo, on the contrary, the dispersion of body parts atomized the speaker's control over language. Thus, this loss of control over language carries with it the loss of personal location, a loss of body, but the two versions of the myth depict this change in very different ways. Still, there are two ways in which the versions can be related to one another.

First, working on the assumption that a reading comprising the two should reduce them to their points of similarity, we find that only three intersecting elements survive the comparison: the name Echo, her fading body, and the repetition function. The name Echo and her body both indicate the female repeater, so that we are left, if we wither the versions further, if we reduce their differences from one another to a bare minimum (or skeleton), with the repeater and the repetition function. Both versions effect the transformation of the locus or agent of repetition into the function of repetition. Reduced to this minimum, the myth can be interpreted as an example of the relationship between the textual *corpus* and the reading function. As the pages turn, as Echo's body disappears, as the text-object loses its importance and the reading function gains priority, the reading replaces the text.

My examination of this hypothetical reading gives this result because my essential premise was that readings could be discussed rather than texts. My criticism reenforces my own notion: I have narcissistically used the text Echo in order to speak my own theory. I seem to end up repeating myself. It is the same tautological form of demonstration which pervades the notion of myth or of structure in literary criticism: in short, it is the same prejudice about the text's submission to criticism that has given the Oedipal critic such power to exert *his* sexuality through the Oedipus myth. The difficulty seems to grow out of a kind of narcissistic reductionism: the critic reduces the text to a repetition of *himself*.

A second way to deal with the Ovid and Longus versions is to put them into a complementary relationship to one another rather than into a reductive one. The two versions can be fused to offer further information about one another. By reading a composite of two versions, by somehow allowing Echo to talk to herself, we may begin to learn something about the nature of her textual-ity. A reading based on complementarity results in a circular pattern of strict structuring and the explosion of structures. Thus, the Echo which Pan despises carries the mythic, skeletal structure to which her love for Narcissus has reduced her: virginal and perfect. But Echo's mythic body *dismembered* is the myth disseminated and become versions, the Word disseminated and become words, the end of Echo as an active agent of language and the beginning of her subjection to her function. Within every torn piece of her textual body remains the one feature which recalls the original myth, repetition. Already repeating and non-virginal, Narcissus' Echo can be seen as one of the pieces of Pan's Echo.

This construct allows for many tempting interpretations. The alternation between structuring and dissemination bears a rather strong resemblance to erection and dissemination. This clue should not be ignored, for, since both versions are about Echo, the variables come from the two male figures, Narcissus and Pan. Thus, when we relate the two versions, what we have done in fact is relate the two males: Narcissus' desire for self-containment with Pan's desire for the Other (or others). That the myth should allow a reading of a male sexual experience is hardly odd.

At this point, we can begin to formulate some hypotheses concerning the place of the female text within this male-dominated situation. Why must the text be eliminated? Why must Echo be picked to shreds or ignored? The underlying threat posed by the text and exposed in this reading is that without textual violation, the mark or body which remains may be a locus from which language may seen to emanate; the text may seen to be a speaker, and, further, a speaker which speaks about itself, expresses its own desires. The danger of Echo's bodily integrity, the threat of Echo's ability to originate speech or music, is the implicit threat to Narcissus' narcissism—the threat that the locus of repetition might have its own, different body, that the repetition might be distorted, the text not be transparent: in short, that he might *not* be in love with himself.

All of this can be read from/into the versions of the Echo myth, but an examination of what Echo *can* do with language, an examination of the ramifications of linguistic repetition by a sexual other, should help explain why the text needs killing within the context of Oedipal criticism.

In the Narcissus version, it is possible to see Narcissus as an author in that he originates the words which Echo will repeat. However, if we continue to see Echo as the text, the notion that Narcissus adequately fills the role of reader seems unfounded. Narcissus seeks no truth, and he unravels no mysteries as Oedipus did. He only wants to find his friends. Instead, he finds his own reflection, a text which he recognizes neither as a reflection nor as a representation of himself. If Narcissus is a reader, he is a bad one, because he is unaware of the text *qua* text. To whom, then, is the reading function relegated in this version? When Narcissus rejects Echo's love, she repeats his words in such a way as to express her own love for him. Echo's repetition is, therefore, a reading. Echo has abducted the first person pronoun, and the negation of passion simultaneously becomes expression of passion.

In short, repetition by a different-sex speaker is a creative act of reading involving a new locus of desire and a non-Oedipal act of identification. Identification in this case does not render the identifier identical to the text, in the way that Oedipal identification makes the son's desires conform to those of the father; instead, it changes the meaning of the text, it changes the desires. Earlier, we quoted René Girard as saying that Oedipal identification "is a desire *to be*, which one seeks, naturally to fulfill by *having*." Echo's abduction of language reverses the process of conformity, the "desire *to be*," required by Oedipal identification. When the object of desire is language, when the object of desire is the first person pronoun, identification, even repetition, is something else: it is the transformation of the meaning of language. The necessary ambiguity of language makes repetition an act of radical change: where once there was no desire, the words come to express desire. Where once the first person subject was male, it is now female. Language is not simply transvestite here, it is transsexual. That is, it conveys both male and female sexual desires and not merely male and female roles.

The Pan version presents a different problem. While Pan does produce music and words, they do not take on a body—a textual body—during Echo's lifetime. Echo is actually a musical competitor. The only way in which she is a text is from Pan's perspective as a body worth violating, as a locus of pleasure. Echo is an author (an inspirer of passion, as well as a musician), and her music and passion are consonant with her body. Pan, the avid reader, can decipher her only by dissecting her. In the Pan version of the myth Echo is not so much a text as an author.

These two readings of the versions lead to a joint reading which may provide two very different myths about the notion of reading. On the one hand (the male hand), if we follow the notion of sexual desire, Pan, the reader, is chasing Echo, the text, who in turn is chasing Narcissus, the author. No wonder the text must disappear; how else would the critic ever understand the author? We come back to the Oedipal notion that the text must be transparent.

On the other hand (the female hand this time), the two versions may be linked not by a chain of desire, but by textual functioning. By this I mean that the notions of some *real* author and some *particular* reader and some corpse or *book* are given over to something else: the text as a locus of processes. For, if Echo is in one version an author and in another version a reader and in both versions a text, then relating these two versions is relating these functions. The acceptance of the critical act as creative rather than destructive and the creative act as something of a reading (of self, of other texts, of the reader, for example) permits Echo to read Echo and Echo to write Echo. The text in this case is no longer some female cadaver, rather it is, if not a speaker, at least a teller about itself and its associated processes. The text is creating itself and the reading process continues the text's participation in the creative process. If the text can come to be seen as a locus of processes, as speaking itself, then it can cease being represented by and occupying the political position of dead women. It will no longer be open to critical or creative dominance. In order to effect this change, it is not so much that roles need to be reversed; that is, for example, it is not particularly necessary that the text suddenly become seen as a male entity dominated by female critics. Instead, domination or mastery of the text must disappear as a political necessity of criticism.

Since a text is obviously not intrinsically male or female, the only value there can be in assigning it a gender derives from the critic's concern with power or pleasure. If the text is a set of processes—one of which is a transsexual one, as we suggested in the case of Echo's repetition—the use of gender as a way of further conceptualizing the text becomes fruitless. This is not to say that the text has nothing to do with pleasure or power, perhaps even sexual pleasure and power, but that this sexuality may not be gender-related.

The possibility that the text contains transsexual processes brings us back to Oedipus, who, although he kills a man (his father) is left with a female corpse which marks not only his crime of patricide but also that of incest. This transsexual marker for transgressions of power and pleasure should already have led us to suspect that the text must be sexually ambivalent, but, because the vehicle of that ambiguity, language, is nowhere put into question, the textual process is overshadowed by the facts that Oedipus has learned. The Echo myth proposes an essential relationship between the text's reworking of language and Echo's abduction of language as a vehicle of her own desire.

NOTES

1. Sigmund Freud, *Totem and Taboo*, trans. A. A. Brill (New York: Vintage Books, 1946), p. 202.
2. Louis Fraiberg, *Psychoanalysis and American Literary Criticism* (Detroit: Wayne State University Press, 1960).
3. Leonard Tennenhouse, ed., *The Practice of Psychoanalytic Criticism* (Detroit: Wayne State University Press, 1976).
4. My translation. The original French reads: "La permanence plusieurs fois millénaire du mythe oedipien, le caractère imprescriptible de ses thèmes, le respect quasi religieux dont la culture moderne continue à l'entourer [. . . .]" René Girard, *La Violence et le sacré* (Paris: Bernard Grasset, 1972), p. 120. Patrick Gregory's translation, *Violence and the Sacred* (Baltimore: The Johns Hopkins University Press, 1977), reduces Girard's forceful description of the power of the Oedipus myth to the statement "that modern culture continues to hold it dear," (P. 81) a rather peculiar understatement.
5. Girard, *La Violence*, p. 237. My translation. Gregory's translation reads, "The identification is a desire *to be* the model that seeks fulfillment, naturally enough, by means of appropriation; that is, by taking over the things that belong to his father. As Freud says, the son seeks to take the father's place everywhere; he thus seeks to assume his desires, to desire what the father desires" (p. 170).
6. Ovid, *The Metamorphoses*, trans. Horace Gregory (New York: The Viking Press, 1958); and, trans. Rolfe Humphries (Bloomington: Indiana University Press, 1955). Glimpses of the development of the Echo myth in our culture can be found in Louise Vinge, *The Narcissus Theme in Western European Literature Up to the Early 19th Century*, trans. Robert Dewsnap, Nigel Reeves, et al. (Lund: Gleerups, 1967).
7. Longus, *Daphnis and Chloe* in *Three Greek Romances*, trans. Moses Hadas (New York: Bobbs-Merrill, 1953), pp. 45-46.

21
UNMAKING AND MAKING IN
TO THE LIGHTHOUSE

Gayatri C. Spivak

This essay is not necessarily an attempt to illuminate *To the Lighthouse* and lead us to a correct reading. It is rather an attempt to use the book by the deliberate superimposition of two allegories—grammatical and sexual—and by reading it, at moments, as autobiography. This modest attempt at understanding criticism not merely as a theoretical approach to the "truth" of a text, but at the same time as a practical enterprise that produces a reading as part of a much larger polemic.* I introduce *To the Lighthouse* into this polemic by reading it as the story of Mr. Ramsay (philosopher-theorist) and Lily (artist-practitioner) around Mrs. Ramsay (text).

*　　*　　*

Virginia Woolf's *To the Lighthouse* can be read as a project to catch the essence of Mrs. Ramsay. A certain reading of the book would show how the project is undermined; another, how it is articulated. I will suggest that the undermining, although more philosophically adventurous, is set aside by Woolf's book; that the articulation is found to be a more absorbing pursuit.

On a certain level of generality the project to catch the essence of Mrs. Ramsay is articulated in terms of finding an adequate language. The first part

---

*The simplest articulation of the polemic, which "starts" with Martin Heidegger's approach to the tradition of philosophy, is still Jacques Derrida's *Of Grammatology* (Baltimore: Johns Hopkins University Press, 1976), pp. 157-64. I have tried to follow Derrida's suggestion regarding productive or "forced" readings in my piece (in preparation) "Marx after Derrida."

of the book ("The Window") looks at the language of marriage: is Mrs. Ramsay's "reality" to be found there? The third part of the book ("The Lighthouse") uncovers the language of art: Lily catches Mrs. Ramsay in her painting. Or at least, a gesture on the canvas is implicitly given as a representation of a possible vision (implicitly of Mrs. Ramsay or the picture itself):

> With a sudden intensity, as if she saw it clear for a second, she drew a line there, in the centre. It was done; it was finished. Yes, she thought, laying down her brush in extreme fatigue, I have had my vision.[1]

The second part of the book couples or hinges I and III. In Part I, Mrs. Ramsay is, in the grammatical sense, the subject. In Part III, the painting predicates her.* I could make a grammatical allegory of the structure of the book: Subject (Mrs. Ramsay)–copula–Predicate (painting). That would be the structure of the proposition, the irreducible form of the logic of non-contradiction, the simplest and most powerful sentence. Within this allegory, the second part of the book is the place of the copula. That too yields a suggestive metaphor. For the copula is not only the pivot of grammar and logic, the axle of ideal language, the third person singular indicative of "to be"; it also carries a sexual charge. "Copulation" happens not only in language and logic, but also between persons. The metaphor of the copula embraces Mr. Ramsay both ways. As the custodian of the logical proposition ("If Q is Q, then R . . ."), he traffics in the copula; and, as father and husband, he is the custodian of copulation. Lily seeks to catch Mrs. Ramsay with a different kind of copula, a different bridge to predication, a different language of "Being," the language not of philosophy, but of art. Mr. Ramsay has seemingly caught her in the copula of marriage.

A certain rivalry and partnership develop between Lily and Mr. Ramsay in Part III. But this rivalry and partnership do not account for Part II, where the search for a language seems strangely unattached to a character or characters. One is tempted to say, this is the novel's voice, or, here is Woolf. I will suggest that, in this strange section, the customary division between work and life is itself vague, that the language sought here is the language of madness.

Within the grammatical allegory of the structure of the book, it would run thus: the strongest bond, the copula in the proposition, the bastion of language, the place of the "is," is almost uncoupled in the coupling part of *To the Lighthouse*. How does that disarticulation and undermining take its place within the articulation of the project to catch the essence of Mrs. Ramsay in an adequate language?

---

*This sort of allegorical fancy should of course not be confused with the "narrative typology" outlined in Tzvetan Todorov, "Narrative Transformations," *The Poetics of Prose*, trans. Richard Howard (Ithaca: Cornell University Press, 1977), pp. 218-33. Todorov indicates in that essay the precursors of his own approach.

I. THE WINDOW

The language of marriage seems a refusal of "good" language, if a good language is that which brings about communication. When she speaks, Mrs. Ramsay speaks the "fallen" language of a civility that covers over the harshness of interpersonal relations. (The most successful—silent—communication between herself and her husband is to deflect his fury at Mr. Carmichael's request for a second helping of soup!) When she and Mr. Ramsay speak to each other or read together, their paths do not cross. She knows marriage brings trouble, yet, when she speaks of marriage, it is with complete and prophetic optimism. Her own privileged moments are when words break down, when silence encroaches, or when the inanimate world reflects her. In the end she turns her refusal of discourse into an exclamation of triumph, the epitome, in this book of a successful con-jugal (copulative) relationship.

All of section twelve presents conjugal non-communication with a light touch. I quote two moments: "All this phrase-making was a game, she thought, for if she had said half what he said, she would have blown her brains out by now" (106). "And,"

> looking up, she saw above the thin trees the first pulse of the full-throbbing star, and wanted to make her husband look at it; for the sight gave her such keen pleasure. But she stopped herself. He never looked at things. If he did, all he would say would be, Poor little world, with one of his sighs. At that moment, he said, "Very fine," to please her, and pretended to admire the flowers. But she knew quite well that he did not admire them, or even realize that they were there (108).

If I were reading the relationship between her knowledge and her power, I would remark here on her matchmaking, or her manipulation of men through deliberate self-suppression. But I am interested only in establishing that she relies little on language, especially language in marriage. Her privileged moments (a privilege that is often nothing but terror), are when words disappear, or when the inanimate world reflects her. One such terrifying moment of privilege is when the men cease talking and the sea's soothing song stops:

> The gruff murmur, . . . which had kept on assuring her, though she could not hear what was said . . . that the men were happily talking; this sound, which had . . . taken its place soothingly in the scale of sounds pressing on top of her . . . had ceased; so that the monotonous fall of the waves on the beach, which for the most part . . . seemed consolingly to repeat over and over again as she sat with the children the words of some old cradle song . . . but at other times . . . had no such kindly meaning, but like a ghostly roll of drums remorselessly beat the measure of life. . . . —this

sound which had been obscured and concealed under the other sounds suddenly thundered hollow in her ears and made her look up with an impulse of terror.
They had ceased to talk: that was the explanation (27-28).

Why should language be an ally for her, or promise any adequation to her selfhood? Her discourse with "life," her "old antagonist"–her "parleying" (92)–though not shared with anyone, is "for the most part" a bitterly hostile exchange. Her sexuality the stage for action between son and husband, does not allow her more than the most marginal instrument and energy of self-signification: "There was scarcely a shell of herself left for her to know herself by; all was so lavished and spent; and James, as he stood stiff between her knees, felt her rise in a rosy-flowered fruit tree laid with leaves and dancing boughs into which the beak of brass, the arid scimitar of his father, the egotistical man, plunged and smote, demanding sympathy" (60). It is not surprising that, when she feels free (both to "go" and "rest"), "life sank down for a moment," and not only language, but personality and selfhood were lost: "This core of darkness could go any-where. . . . Not as oneself did one find rest ever . . . but as a wedge of darkness losing personality . . ."(96).

Any dream-dictionary would tell us that knitting stands for masturbation. A text-dictionary would alert us that one knits a *web*, which is a text. Woolf uses the image of Mrs. Ramsay's knitting (an auto-erotic textuality) strategically. It may represent a reflexive act, a discursivity. It emphasizes the second kind of privileged moment that is Mrs. Ramsay's secret: when she leans toward inani-mate things, which reflect her. The structure of that reflection is indeed that of sexual intercourse (copulation) and of self-mirroring in the other. Within that structure, however, she is, in this last move, the object not the subject, the other not the self. The moment of self-privilege is now its own preservative yielding to the world of things.

Imagining herself as a wedge of darkness, she "looked out to meet that stroke of the Lighthouse, the long steady stroke, the last of the three, which was her stroke" (96). I must think of "stroke" as the predicate, the last stroke in the three-stroke sentence (S is P) of the house of light, which, as any dictionary of symbols will tell us, is the house of knowledge or philosophy. If Mrs. Ramsay recognizes her own mark in being predicated rather than in subjectivity, she is still caught within copulation. As Woolf knits into her text the image of a suspended knitting she moves us, through the near-identification ("like," "in a sense") of mirroring, to deliver a satisfying image of the threshold of copulation ("a bride to meet her lover"):

> She looked up over her knitting and met the third stroke and it seemed to her like her own eyes meeting her own eyes. . . . It was odd, she thought, how if one was alone, one leant to inanimate things; trees, streams, flowers; felt they expressed one; felt they became one; felt they knew one, in a sense were one. . . . There

rose, and she looked and looked with her needles suspended, there curled up off the floor of the mind, rose from the lake of one's being, a mist, a bride to meet her lover (97-98).

"One" can be both "identity" (the word for the unit), and "difference" (an impersonal agent, not she herself); "in a sense" might be understood both "idiomatically" and "literally" (meaning "within a meaning").

But these are not the last words on Mrs. Ramsay in "The Window." Mostly she remains the protector (13), the manager (14), the imperialist governor of men's sterility (126). At the end of her section she mingles charmingly, as women will, the notions of love, beauty in the eye of the male beholder, and power. By refusing to *say* "I love you," she has taken away his power to deny it; by saying "you were right," she has triumphed:

> She never could say what she felt. . . . He was watching her. She knew what he was thinking. You are more beautiful than ever. And she felt herself very beautiful. . . . She began to smile, for though she had not said a word, he knew, of course he knew, that she loved him. . . .
> "Yes, you were right." . . . And she looked at him smiling. For she had triumphed again. She had not said it: Yet he knew (186).

And what of the language of academic philosophy, Mr. Ramsay's tool for making a connection between subject and predicate? Words come easily to him. Woolf shows him to us as he plans a lecture (67). He assimilates the leaves of the trees into leaves of paper: "Seeing again the . . . geraniums which had so often decorated processes of thought, and bore, written up among their leaves, as if they were scraps of paper on which one scribbles notes in the rush of reading . . ." (66). And he finds them dispensable: "He picked a leaf sharply. . . . He threw away the leaf" (67).

The most celebrated formulation of Mr. Ramsay is through the image of the keyboard-alphabet. Here is the traditional copular proposition in the service of the logic of identity and geometrical proof: If Q is Q, then R is. . . .*

"For if thought is like the keyboard of a piano, "—is it? never mind, this is the exclusivist move, taking for granted a prior proposition, that lets the copula play—"divided into so many notes, or like the alphabet is ranged in twenty-six letters all in order, then his splendid mind had no sort of difficulty in running over those letters one by one . . . until it had reached, say, the letter A." Q is an interesting letter, starting "questions," "quid," "quod," "quantity,"

---

*It is not insignificant that he draws strength for his splendid burst of thinking from a glance at that safe symbol, *his* wife-and-child as a functioning unit: "Without his distinguishing either his son or his wife, the sight of them fortified him and satisfied him and consecrated his effort to arrive at a perfectly clear understanding of the problem which now engaged the energies of his splendid mind" (53).

"quality," and of course, "q.e.d." "Q he could demonstrate. If Q then is Q–R– . . . 'Then R . . .' " (54).

"But after Q? What comes next?" After the discourse of demonstration, the language of "q," comes the discourse of desire. If only he could reach R! Could identify the place in thought with the initial letter of his own name, his father's name, and his son's! If Mrs. Ramsay repeatedly endorses the copulation of marriage—as in the case of the Rayleys—for the sake of a maternalist genealogy, Mr. Ramsay would exploit the copulation of philosophy for the sake of paternalistic appropriation.* But the Rayleys' marriage comes to nothing, and Mr. Ramsay is convinced "he would never reach R" (55).

II. TIME PASSES

I do not know how to read a roman à clef, especially an autobiographical one. I do not know how to insert Woolf's life into the text of her book. Yet there is a case to be made here. I will present the material of a possible biographical speculation, adumbrate a relationship between life and book that I cannot theoretically present, consider the case made, and give a certain reading.

Since the printing date inside the cover of *To the Lighthouse* is 1927, it seems clear that the war in "Time Passes" is the Great War of 1914-1918. The somewhat enigmatic sentence that begins its last section is, "then indeed peace had come" (213). Lily, the time-keeper of the book, tells us that the events of "The Window" were "ten years ago [in 1908]." Shortly thereafter, Mrs. Ramsay "died rather suddenly" (194).

The Stephen family (the "real" Ramsays) had visited Talland House in St. Ives (the "real" location of *To the Lighthouse*) for the last time in 1894. Julia Stephen (the "real" Mrs. Ramsay, Virginia Woolf's mother) died in 1895. In a certain sense, "Time Passes" compresses 1894-1918—from Mrs. Stephen's death to the end of the war.

For Woolf those years were marked by madness. She broke down after her mother's death in 1895, after her father's death in 1904, once again in 1910, briefly in 1912, lingeringly in 1913, most violently in 1915 (as "Time Passes" ostensibly begins). From 1917 on, there was a period of continued lucidity. In 1919 (as "Time Passes" ostensibly ends) *Night and Day* was published. In the next section, I will argue that it is significant that *Night and Day* is "about" her painter-sister Vanessa Bell.

---

*Here are bits of Mrs. Ramsay's maternalistic endorsement of marriage. "Divining, through her own past, some deep, some buried, some quite speechless feeling that one had for one's mother at Rose's age" (123). "All this would be revived again in the lives of Paul and Minta; 'the Rayleys'—she tried the new name over. . . . It was all one stream. . . . Paul and Minta would carry it on when she was dead" (170-71). As for Mr. Ramsay's enterprise, the irony is sharpened if we remind ourselves that Virginia Stephen's father was engaged in compiling *The Dictionary of National Biographie*.

I should like to propose that, whatever her writing intent, "Time Passes" narrates the production of a discourse of madness within this autobiographical roman a' clef. In the place of the copula or the hinge in the book a story of unhinging is told.

Perhaps this unhinging or "desecrating" was not unsuspected by Woolf herself. One is invited to interpret the curious surface of writing of Virginia Stephen's 1899 diary as a desecration of the right use of reason. It was written in "a minute, spidery, often virtually illegible hand, which she made more difficult to read by gluing her pages on to or between Dr. Isaac Watt's *Logick/ or/ the right use of Reason/ with a variety of rules to guard against error in the affairs of religion and human life as well as in the sciences.* . . . Virginia bought this in St. Ives for its binding and its format: " ' Any other book, almost, would have been too sacred to undergo the descration that I planned.' "[2]

At the beginning of "Time Passes," the sense of a house as the dwelling-place of reason and of light as the sign of reason are firmly implied. It is within this framework that "certain airs" and an "immense darkness" begin to descend (189, 190). Human agency is attenuated as the house is denuded of human occupancy. "There was scarcely anything left of body or mind by which one could say, 'This is he' or 'This is she.' Sometimes a hand was raised as if to clutch something or ward off something, or somebody laughed aloud as if sharing a joke with nothingness. . . . Almost one might imagine them" (190). The soothing power of Mrs. Ramsay's civilized language is wearing away into indifference. The disintegration of the house is given through the loosening of the shawl she had wrapped around the death's head: "With a roar, with a rupture, as after centuries of quiescence, a rock rends itself from the mountain and hurtles crashing into the valley, one fold of the shawl loosened and swung to and fro" (195- 96).

(The covering of the death's head by the shawl in "The Window" is a marvelous deceptive deployment of undecidability. Cam, the girl-child, must be reminded of the animal skull; James, the male child, not; Mrs. Ramsay covers it, draws Cam's attention to what is under, and Jame's to what is over, and puts them to sleep by weaving a fabulous tale.)

There are glimpses of the possibility of an accession to truth in this curiously dismembered scene; but at the same time, a *personal* access is denied:

> It seemed now as if, touched by human penitence and all its toil, divine goodness had parted the curtain and displayed behind it, single, distinct, the hare erect; the wave falling; the boat rocking, which, did we deserve them, should be ours always. But alas, divine goodness twitching the cord, draws the curtain; it does not please him; he covers his treasures in a drench of hail, and so breaks them, so confuses them that it seems impossible that their calm should ever return, or that we should ever compose from their fragments a perfect whole or read in the littered pieces the clear words of truth (192-93).

I cannot account for, but merely record that strange twinge of guilt: "it does not please him." The guardian of the truth behind the veil is no longer the beautiful but lying mother; it is rather the good God-father, for "divine goodness" is a "he" and he "covers his treasures," hides his genitals, in what would customarily be a "feminine" gesture. This sexual shift—for the author of *To the Lighthouse* is a woman—also indicates a denial of access. The next bit of writing about a vision of truth is given as "imaginations of the strangest kind—of flesh turned to atoms." Man and woman are rendered to "gull, flower, tree, . . . and the white earth itself" (199). "Cliff, sea, cloud, and sky" must "assemble outwardly the scattered parts of the vision within" (198). Human agency is now dispensable. And access to truth is still denied. For "if questioned," the universe seemed "at once to withdraw."

In another move within the same paragraph, "the absolute good" is seen as "something alien to the processes of domestic life," processes that would, in the manner of Mrs. Ramsay, keep the house of reason in order. Through a silent gap between two sentences, Woolf brings us back to those domestic processes, as if to ward off the menace of madness at any price. By way of a logically unacceptable "moreover," "the spring," one of the agents in the outer world, constitutes a domestic and feminine image recalling not only Mrs. Ramsay but pointing genealogically, in the next sentence, to her daughter Prue. Yet here too, only the dark side of domesticity may be seen: "Prue died that summer in some illness connected with childbirth" (199).

Earlier in that paragraph "the minds of men" are called "those mirrors . . . those pools of uneasy water." And indeed, as human agency is turned down, light begins a narcissistic troping that produces an extra-human text: "Now, day after day, light turned, like a flower reflected in water, its sharp image on the wall opposite" (194). Mrs. Ramsay's shawl is changed into a silent writing that envelops sound: "The swaying mantle of silence which, week after week in the empty room, wove into the falling cries of birds, ships hooting, the drone and hum of the fields, a dog's bark, a man's shout, and folded them round the house in silence" (195). "The empty rooms seemed to murmur with the echoes of the fields and the hum of the flies . . . the sun so striped and barred the rooms" (200).

The last image brings us back to the vague imagery of guilt and torture, a humanity-excluding tone that is also heard when the narcissism of light and nature turns to masturbation: "The nights now are full of wind and destruction. . . . Also the sea tosses itself ['tossing off' is English slang for masturbation], and should any sleeper fancying that he might find on the beach an answer to his doubts, a sharer of his solitude, throw off his bed-clothes and go down by himself to walk on the sand, no image with semblance of serving and divine promptitude comes readily to hand bringing the night to order and making the world reflect the compass of his soul" (193). Nature is occupied with itself and cannot provide a mirror or a companion for the human seeker of the copula, the word that binds.

It is the War that brings this narrative of estrangement to its full destructive potential: "Did Nature supplement what man advanced? . . . With equal complacence she saw his misery, his meanness, and his torture. That dream, of sharing, completing, of finding in solitude on the beach an answer, was then but a reflection in a mirror, and the mirror itself was but the surface glassiness which forms in quiescence when the nobler powers sleep beneath? . . . to pace the beach was impossible; contemplation was unendurable" (201-2).

Before this large-scale estrangement, there was some possibility of truth in the never-fulfilled always troping and uncoupling narcissism of the light, and in the bodiless hand clasp of loveliness and stillness with their "scarcely disturbed . . . indifference" and their "*air* of pure integrity" (195). There was comfort in the vouchsafing of an answer (however witless) to the questions of subject and object: "The mystic, the visionary, walking the beach on a fine night . . . asking themselves 'What am I,' 'What is this?' had suddenly an answer vouchsafed them, (*they could not say what it was*) so that they were warm in the frost and had comfort in the desert" (197-98; italics are mine).

Indeed, "Time Passes" as a whole does not narrate a full encroachment of the discourse of madness. Even in the passage that describes what I call a large-scale estrangement, there is a minute trace of comfort, hardly endorsed by the author. It is perhaps marked in the double-edged fact that in this woman's book, complacent and uncooperating nature is feminine, and she shares with the human mind the image of the mirroring surface. In the following passage, however, the absence of a copula between "nature" and "mind," leading to a lustful wantonness of blind copulation cum auto-eroticism, seems the very picture of madness rampant:

> Listening (had there been any one to listen) from the upper rooms of the empty house only gigantic chaos streaked with lightning could have been heard tumbling and tossing, as the winds and waves disported themselves like amorphous bulks of leviathans whose brows are pierced by no light of reason, and mounted one on top of another, and lunged and plunged in the darkness of daylight (for night and day, month and year ran shapelessly together) in idiot games, until it seemed as if the universe were battling and tumbling, in brute confusion and wanton lust aimlessly by itself. . . . The stillness and the brightness of the day were as strange as the chaos and the tumult of night, with the trees standing there, looking up, yet beholding nothing. The mirror was broken (202-3).

The disappearance of reason and the confusion of sexuality are consistently linked: "Let the poppy seed itself and the carnation mate with the cabbage" (208). Now all seems lost. "For now had come that moment, that hesitation when the dawn trembles and night passes, when if a feather alight in the scale it will be weighed down . . . the whole house . . . to the depths to lie upon the sands of oblivion" (208-9).

But the feather does not fall. For in the long "wanton lust" passage it is a coupling that only *seems* onanistic. The differentiation of night and day, if almost obliterated (itself a possible copulation—night is day is night is day), is restored in the last image of the eyeless trees. Further, the *possibility* of a perspective from "the *upper rooms* of the empty house" of reason is broached. And Mrs. McNab the charwoman is allowed the hint of a power to recuperate the mirror. She stands in front of the looking glass, but we are not sure she contemplates her image. The copula is uncertain. Does she say "I *am* I [my image]," as Narcissus said *iste ego sum*? All we have is a parenthesis: "(she stood arms akimbo in front of the looking glass)" [203].

Thus Mrs. McNab halts disaster in the allegory of a reason menaced by madness, an ontology on the brink of disaster by the near-uncoupling of the copula. She is related to "a force working; something not highly conscious" (209). Once again, the copula between her and this description is not given. They simply inhabit contiguous sentences.

The house is rehabilitated and peace comes as "Time Passes" comes to an end. But the coupling between "Window" and "Lighthouse" (or the predication of Mrs. Ramsay's "is-ness") remains open to doubt. When "the voice of the beauty of the world" now entreats the sleepers to come down to the beach, we know that there are times of violence when a sleeper may entreat and be brutally refused. And indeed the voice murmurs "too softly to hear what it said—but what mattered if the meaning were plain?" (213). Is it? Woolf does not make clear what the "this" is in that further entreaty the voice "might resume": "why not accept this, be content with this, acquiesce and resign?" (214). We are free to say that "this" is the limits of language.

III. THE LIGHTHOUSE

In the third section Woolf presents the elaborate story of the acquisition of a vision of art. We must compare this to the affectionately contemptuous and brief description of Mr. Ramsay preparing his lecture. Lily would create the copula through art, predicate Mrs. Ramsay in a painting rather than a sentence. Before reading that story, I must once again present certain halting conclusions that would link life and book.

It seems clear to every reader that "Virginia Woolf" is both Cam and Lily Briscoe. In Cam at seven, as in "The Window," she might see, very loosely speaking, a kind of pre-Oedipal girlhood: "I think a good deal about . . . how I was a nice little girl here [at St. Ives]. . . . Do you like yourself as a child? I like myself, before the age of 10, that is—before consciousness sets in."[3] Cam is tied up with James (as Shakespeare with Shakespeare's sister in *A Room of One's Own*), a shadow-portrait of Virginia's brothers Thoby and Adrian. *Together* Cam-James go through an Oedipal scene that involves both father *and* mother as givers of law and language, and thus they allow Virginia Woolf to question the orthodox masculinist psychoanalytic position.* But that is not my subject here. I must fix my glance on Lily.

Lily is the same age (43) as Woolf when she began *To the Lighthouse*. Lily has just gone through the gestatory ten years taken over by "Time Passes," and Woolf has a special feeling for decades:

> Every 10 years, at 20, again at 30, such agony of different sorts possessed me that not content with rambling and reading I did most emphatically attempt to end it all. . . . Every ten years brings, I suppose, one of those private orientations which match the vast one which is, to my mind, general now in the race. I mean life has to be faced: to be rejected; then accepted on new terms with rapture. And so on, and so on; till you are 40, when the only problem is to grasp it tighter and tighter to you, so quick it seems to slip, and so infinitely desirable is it. (L II. 598-99)

But Lily is a painter. She "is" also Virginia's artist-sister Vanessa Bell. There is that curious incident between Lily and Mr. Ramsay, where, "in complete silence she stood there, grasping her paintbrush" (228). It is a situation often repeated between Vanessa and Leslie Stephen.[4] There is also the fact that this book is the laying of a mother's ghost, and it is to Vanessa that Virginia directs the question: "Why did you bring me into the world to go through these ordeals?" (L II. 458).

Lily begins or finishes her painting just after "peace had come." At the "actual" time of the Armistice, Virginia was finishing a book about Vanessa: "The guns have been going off for half an hour, and the sirens whistling; so I suppose we are at peace. . . . How am I to write my last chapter in all this shindy? . . . I don't suppose I've ever enjoyed any writing so much as I did the last half of *Night and Day*. . . Try thinking of Katharine [the heroine] as Vanessa, not me" (L II. 290, 295, 400). Lily, as she is conceived, could thus be both artist (Virginia) and material (Vanessa), an attempted copula ("the artist *is* her work") that must forever be broken in order that the artist survive.

If I knew how to manipulate erotic textuality, I should read the incredible charge of passion in the long letters to Vanessa, addressed to "Dearest," "Beloved," "Dolphin." Is it too crude to say that the sane, many-lovered, fecund Vanessa was a kind of ideal other for Virginia? She wrote that she wanted to confuse the maternity of Vanessa's daughter. And there are innumerable letters where she asks Vanessa's husband, Clive Bell, or her lover Duncan Grant, to caress the beloved vicariously for her. I quote one of those many entreaties: "Kiss her, most passionately, in all my private places—neck—, and arm, and eyeball, and tell her—what new thing is there to tell her? How fond I am of her husband?" (L I. 325). If indeed Lily, Mr. Ramsay's contender and Mrs.

---

*The references to Freud are elaborated in my discussion of Luce Irigaray's reading of Freud's "Femininity" later in this essay.

Ramsay's scribe, is the name of Vanessa-Virginia, only the simplest genitalist view of sexuality would call her conception androgynous. But, as I must continue to repeat, I cannot develop that argument.

Let us talk instead of Lily's medium: it is writing and painting. Always with reference to Vanessa, Virginia wonders at the relationship between the two: "How strange it is to be a painter! They scarcely think; feelings come only every other minute. But then they are profound and inexpressible, tell Nessa" (L II. 541). And in the book: "If only she could . . . write them out in some sentence, then she would have got at the truth of things. . . . She had never finished that picture. She would finish that picture now" (219-20). "Her mind kept throwing up from its depths, scenes, and names, and sayings . . . over that glaring, hideously difficult white space, while she modelled it with greens and blues" (238). "How could one express in words these emotions of the body? . . . Suddenly, . . . the white wave and whisper of the garden become like curves and arabesques flourishing round a centre of complete emptiness" (266). A script, half design, half word, combining words and picturing, getting at the truth of things, expressing the body's feelings, this is Lily's desired "discourse." "But what she wished to get hold of was that very jar on the nerves, the thing itself before it had been made anything" (287). Woolf's language, or Lily's, like all language, cannot keep these goals seamless and unified. It is the truth *of* things, the feelings *of* the body, and, as we can easily say since Derrida, "any" is always already inscribed in "the thing" for it to be open to being "made anything."* So she too, like the philosopher, must search for a copula, for her goal, however conceived, also splits into two. In a most enigmatic wish, perhaps she wishes beauty to be self-identical, as Q *is* Q: "Beauty would *roll itself up*; the space would fill" (268; italics are mine). She wants to bridge a gap and make a sphere, not merely by a love of learning (philosophy) but a love of play, or a play of love: "There might be lovers whose gift it was to choose out the elements of things and place them together and so, giving them a wholeness not theirs in life, make of some scene, or meeting of people (all now gone and separate), one of those globed compacted things over which thought lingers, and love plays" (286). Perhaps she wants to erase "perhaps" and make first and last coincide: "Everything this morning was happening for the first time, perhaps for the last time" (288).

She grasps at two "visions" that ostensibly provide a copula, a bridge between and beyond things. The first: "One glided, one shook one's sails (there was a good deal of movement in the bay, boats were starting off) between things, beyond things. Empty it was not, but full to the brim. She seemed to be standing up to the lips in some substance, to move and float and sink in it, yes,

---

*I am referring to the idea of supplementarity. Derrida has suggested that, if a hierarchical opposition is set up between two concepts, the less favored or logically posterior concept can be shown to be implicit in the other, supply a lack in the other that was always already there. See "The Supplement of the Copula," Tr. James Creech and Josué Harari, *Georgia Review* 30 (Fall 1976):527-64.

for these waters were unfathomably deep" (285-86). Alas, since this is language, one can of course find traces of division here if one looks, if one wants to find them. But even beyond that, this sense of plenitude is betrayed by a broad stroke, the incursion of "temporality," and the rhetoric of measure, of the "almost." For "it was *some such* feeling of completeness *perhaps* which, *ten years ago*, standing *almost* where she stood now, had made her say that she must be in love with the place" (286; italics are mine).

The other vision is of Mrs. Ramsay. It is introduced gently, parenthetically, on page 290. "A noise drew her attention to the drawing-room window—the squeak of a hinge. The light breeze [we are reminded of the empty house of 'Time Passes'] was toying with the window . . . (Yes; she realized that the drawing-room step was empty, but it had no effect on her whatever. She did not want Mrs. Ramsay now.)" By means of a delicate workwomanlike indirection, Lily makes the vision mature through eight-and-a-half pages. She is then rewarded:

> Suddenly the window at which she was looking was whitened by some light stuff behind it. At last then somebody had come into the drawing-room; somebody was sitting in the chair. For Heaven's sake, she prayed, let them sit still there and not come floundering out to talk to her. Mercifully, whoever it was stayed still inside; had settled by some stroke of luck so as to throw an odd-shaped triangular shadow over the step. It altered the composition of the picture a little. (299)

How is this indefiniteness ("somebody," "whoever," "by a stroke of luck") transformed into the certitude and properness of a vision? Through *declaring* this indefiniteness (a kind of absence) as a definiteness (a kind of presence), not through the fullness of presence itself. It is, in other words, turned into a *sign* of presence. The "origin of the shadow" remains "inside the room." It is only the shadow that is on the steps. Lily *declares* that the origin of the shadow is not "somebody" but Mrs. Ramsay. And, paradoxically, having forced the issue, she "wants" *Mr.* Ramsay, now, for he too reaches R only through a sign or symbol. He gets to the Lighthouse, although he "would never reach R." The "metaphorical" language of art falls as short of the "true" copula as the "propositional" language of philosophy. As Woolf writes, "One wanted" the present tense of "that's a chair, that's a table, and yet at the same time, It's a miracle, it's an ecstasy." But all one got was the past tense of "there she sat," the insubstantiated present perfect of "I have had my vision," the negative subjunctive of "he would never reach R," the adverbial similetic clauses of "as if he were saying 'there is no God,' . . . as if he were leaping into space" (308). The provisional copula, always a linear enterprise, a risky bridge, can only be broached by deleting or denying the vacillation of "Time Passes," by drawing a line through the central section of *To the Lighthouse*. "With a sudden intensity, as if she saw it clear for a second, she drew a line there, in the centre" (310).

It would be satisfying to be able to end here. But in order to add a postscript to this allegorical reading of *To the Lighthouse*, I must dwell a moment on Lily's sexuality. Is she in fact androgynous, self-sufficient?

I would like to remind everyone who cites *A Room of One's Own* that "one must be woman-manly or man-womanly" is said there in the voice of Mary Beton, a persona.[5] Woolf must break her off in mid-chapter and resume in her authorial voice. Who can disclaim that there is in her a longing for androgyny, that artificially fulfilled copula? But to reduce her great texts to *successful* articulations of that copula is, I believe, to make a mistake in reading.

In an uncharacteristically lurid and unprepared for passage Lily holds the fear of sex at bay:

> Suddenly . . . a reddish light seemed to burn in her mind, covering Paul Rayley, issuing from him. . . . She heard the roar and the crackle. The whole sea for miles round ran red and gold. Some winey smell mixed with it and intoxicated her. . . . And the roar and the crackle repelled her with fear and disgust, as if while she saw its splendour and power she saw too how it fed on the treasure of the house, greedily, disgustingly, and she loathed it. But for a sight, for a glory it surpassed everything in her experience, and burnt year after year like a signal fire on a desert island at the edge of the sea, and one had only to say "in love" and instantly, as happened now, up rose Paul's fire again (261).

The erotic charge that I would like to see between Virginia and Lily-Vanessa does not preclude the fact that Woolf makes Lily Briscoe repress, exclude, rather than accommodate or transcend, this vision of Rayley as phallus in order to get on with her painting. And the relationship she chooses—as Mr. Ramsay chooses to say "If Q is Q . . .,"—is gently derided for its prim sensitive exclusivism: "She loved William Bankes. They went to Hampton Court and he always left her, like the perfect gentleman he was, plenty of time to wash her hands" (263).

Has she no use for men then? My point is precisely that she makes use of them. They are her instruments. She uses Tansley's goad—"They can't write, they can't paint"—to keep herself going. And she uses Mrs. Ramsay's imagining of Charles Tansley to change her own. "If she wanted to be serious about him she had to help herself to Mrs. Ramsay's sayings, to look at him through her eyes" (293). "Through William's eyes" (264) she gets Mrs. Ramsay in grey. But her most indispensable instrument is Mr. Ramsay.

(Leslie Stephen died nine years after his wife, without ever returning to St. Ives. One could almost say that he is brought back to life in *To the Lighthouse* so that the unfinished business of life can be settled, so that he can deliver Vanessa-Virginia's vision.)

I am thinking, of course, of the double structuring of the end of the book. As Lily paints on the shore, Mr. Ramsay must sail to the lighthouse. "She felt curiously divided, as if one part of her were drawn out there— . . . the lighthouse looked this morning at an immense distance; the other had fixed itself doggedly, solidly, here on the lawn" (233-34). Mr. Ramsay on his boat is the tool for the actualization of her self-separation: a sort of shuttling instrumental copula. It is always a preserved division, never an androgynous synthesis. "So much depends, Lily thought, upon distance" (284). With the same sort of modal uneasiness as in "I have had my vision," she can only say "he must have reached it" (308) rather than "he has," when Mr. Ramsay springs upon the rock.

Let me say at once that I must read the alternating rhythm of Lighthouse-canvas in the last part of the book as a copulation. To sleep with father in order to make a baby (a painting, a book) is supposed to be woman's fondest wish. But, here as well, Woolf gives that brutal verdict a twist. For the baby *is* mother—it is a sublimated version of Mrs. Ramsay that Lily would produce— whereas Freud's point is that the emergence of this wish is to learn to hate the mother. Woolf's emphasis falls not on the phallus that reappears every other section, but on the workshop of the womb that delivers the work. In fact, in terms of the text, Mr. Ramsay's trip can begin because Lily "decides" it must. "She decided that there in that very distant and entirely silent little boat Mr. Ramsay was sitting with Cam and James. Now they had got the sail up; now after a little flagging and hesitation the sails filled and, shrouded in profound silence, she watched the boat take its way with deliberation past the other boats out to sea" (242).

IV. POSTSCRIPT

Knowledge as noncontradiction (identity) is put into question in "The Window"; it is shown to be based on nothing more immutable than "*if* Q is then Q," and Mr. Ramsay's "Character" is shown to be weak and petulant. Marriage as copulation is also devalorized in "The Window"; it is shown to be a debilitating and self-deceived combat, and Mrs. Ramsay's "character" is shown to be at once manipulative and deceitful, and untrusting of language. "Time Passes" allegorically narrates the terror of a (non-human or natural) operation without a copula. "The Lighthouse" puts into question the possibility of knowledge (of Mrs. Ramsay) as trope; for a metaphor of art is also a copula (the copula is, after all, a metaphor) that joins two things.

Lily does not question this impasse, she merely fights it. She makes a copula by drawing a line in the center, which can be both an invitation to fill in a blank or a deliberate erasure. If the latter, then she erases (while keeping legible) that very part of the book that most energetically desires to recuperate the impasse, to achieve the undecidable, to write the narrative of madness, —"Time Passes'—for that section is "in the centre."

But Lily's "line in the centre" is also part of a picture, the picture is part of a book, there is a product of some kind in the story as well as in our hands. I can read this more fully as an allegory of sexual rather than grammatical production: it is not only that Lily decides to copulate, she also shows us her womb-ing. A great deal of the most adventurous criticism in philosophy and literature for the last 15 years has been involved with putting the authority of the proposition (and, therefore, of the copula) into question.* This questioning has been often misunderstood as an invitation to play with the copula. I reserve the occasion for arguing that this "new criticism" in fact asks for what might be called the "feminine mode of critical production."† Here I am reading *To the Lighthouse* as if it corrects that possible misunderstanding. As if it suggests that, for anyone (and the generic human exemplar is a woman) to play with the copula is to go toward the grim narrative of the discourse of madness and war. One must use the copula as a necessarily limited instrument and create as best one can.

(This is not as far-fetched as it might sound. In a recent essay in *Screen*, Stephen Heath collects once again the evidence to show how close the questioning of the copula comes to the psychoanalytic description of hysteria, "the female ailment," where the patient is not sure if she has or has not a penis.[6] And Derrida, trying to catch Jean Genet's mother Mme. Genet in his book *Glas*, as Lily tries to "catch" Mrs. Ramsay, stops at the fetish, of which no one may be sure if it signifies the possession or lack of a penis.[7] In this part of my essay I am suggesting that *To the Lighthouse*, in its emphasis not merely on copulation but on gestation, rewrites the argument from hysteria or fetishism.)

In her reading of Freud's late essay "Femininity" the French feminist Luce Irigaray suggests that Freud gives the girl-child a growth (warped) by penis-envy (pre-Oedipally she is a boy!) because the Father (a certain Freud) needs to seduce through pronouncing the Law (42, 44), because once "grown," she must console and hide man's anguish at the possibility of castration (6, 74) and because she is made to pay the price for keeping the Oedipus complex going (98). And then Irigaray asks, why did Freud not articulate vulvar, vaginal, uterine stages (29, 59), why did he ignore the work of the production of the child in the womb? (89).[8]

---

*Once again I am thinking of the deconstructive criticism of Jacques Derrida. The proposition is dismantled most clearly in *Speech and Phenomena and Other Essays on Husserl's Theory of Signs*, trans. David Allison (Evanston: Northwestern University Press, 1973). Among other texts in the field are Jacques Lacan, "La Science et la vérité," *Ecrits* (Paris: Seuil, 1966), pp. 855-77 and Gilles Deleuze, *Logique du sens* (Paris: Minuit, 1969).

†It is from this point of view that the many helpful readers' reports on this study troubled me as well. They reflected the desire for theoretical and propositional explicitness that, via Woolf and the "new criticism," I am combating here: "There is something coy about this paper and all its 'copulas,' but at the same time, the reading of Wolf [sic] is genuinely suggestive and I found myself ever convinced by the power of what seemed a pun [it is in response to this that I wrote my first paragraph]. It is difficult to understand just what the author's interest in language (as a formal system, with copulae, etc.) is concerned with, where it comes from and why she thinks it should lead to the sorts of insights she discovers. Some sort of theoretical explicitness would help here!"

I know, of course, that the text of Freud has to be banalized in order to be presented as a sexist text. I know also that, in that very text that Irigaray reads, Freud hints at his own fallibility in a sentence that is no mere rhetorical gesture: "If you reject this idea as fantastic and regard my belief in the influence of lack of penis on the configuration of femininity as an *idée fixe*, I am of course defenceless."[9] But I do not write to dispraise Freud, simply to take a hint from Irigaray's reading of Freud.

I am proposing, then, that it is possible to think that texts such as Woolf's can allow us to develop a thematics of womb-envy. I hasten to add that I do not advance womb-envy as a "new" or "original" idea. From Socrates through Nietzsche, philosophers have often wished to be midwives or mothers. I am only placing it beside the definition of the physical womb as a lack. I speculate that the womb has always been defined as a lack *by* man in order to cover over a lack *in* man, the lack, precisely, of a tangible place of production. Why does man say he "gives" a child to a woman? Since we are in the realm of fanciful sex-vocabularies, it is not absurd to suggest that the question of "giving" might be re-formulated if one thought of the large ovum "selecting" among millions of microscopic spermatozoa, dependent for effectiveness upon the physiological cycles of the woman. Freud finds the ovum "passive."[10] It is just as appropriate to point out that, if one must allegorize, one must notice that the uterus "releases," "activates" the ovum. It is simply that the grave periodic rhythm of the womb is not the same as the ad hoc frenzy of the adjudicating phallus. And so forth. I hope the allegoric parallels with *To the Lighthouse* are clear. I am of course not discounting penis-envy, but simply matching it with a possible envy of the womb. As Michel Foucault has written, "it's not a question of emancipating truth from every system of power . . . but of detaching the power of truth from the forms of hegemony (social, economic, and cultural) within which it operates at the present time."[11] This might be the secret of "the rivalry and partnership" between Lily Briscoe and Mr. Ramsay that I mention on the opening page of the essay.

To conclude, then, *To the Lighthouse* reminds me that the womb is not an emptiness or a mystery, it is a place of production. What the hysteron produces is not simply the contemptible text of hysteria, an experimental madness that deconstructs the copula. As a tangible place of production, it can try to construct the copula, however precarious, of art. I am not sure if this ennobling of art as an alternative is a view of things I can fully accept. I can at least honor it as an attempt to articulate, by using a man as an instrument, a woman's vision of a woman;* rather than to disarticulate because no human hand can catch a vision, because, perhaps, no vision obtains.

---

*This aspect of the book allows me to justify our use of theories generated, surely in part by historical accident, by men.

NOTES

1. Virginia Woolf, *To the Lighthouse* (New York: Harcourt, Brace & Company, 1927), p. 310. Subsequent page references are included in my text.

2. Quentin Bell, *Virginia Woolf: A Biography* (New York: Harcourt Brace Jovanovich, 1972), p. 65.

3. Virginia Woolf, *The Letters of Virginia Woolf*, ed. Nigel Nicholson, Vol. II: 1912-1922 (New York: Harcourt Brace Jovanovich, 1976), p. 462. Subsequent references to the *Letters* are given in the text. Volumes I and II are indicated as L I and L II respectively.

4. Virginia Woolf, *Moments of Being*: unpublished autobiographical writings, ed. Jeanne Schulkind (Sussex: Sussex University Press, 1976), p. 124.

5. Virginia Woolf, *A Room of One's Own*, Harbinger Books edition (New York: Harcourt, Brace and World, 1929), p. 108.

6. Stephen Heath, "Difference," *Screen* 19.3. (Autumn 1978):56-57.

7. Jacques Derrida, *Glas* (Paris: Galilée, 1974), p. 290b.

8. Luce Irigaray, "La tache aveugle d'un vieux reve de symétrie," *Speculum: de l'autre femme* (Seuil, Paris, 1974). Subsequent references to this essay are included in my text. For a critique of Irigaray's position, read Monique Plaza, " 'Phallomorphic Power' and the Psychology of 'Woman': a Patriarchal Chain," *Ideology and Consciousness* 4 (1978):5-36.

9. Sigmund Freud, "Femininity," *The Complete Psychological Works of Sigmund Freud*, ed. James Strachey (London: The Hogarth Press, 1961), XXII, 132.

10. Ibid., p. 114.

11. Interview with Michel Foucault, *Politique-Hébdo*, no. 247 (Nov. 29-Dec. 6, 1976), p. 33. Trans. by Colin Gordon, "The Political Function of the Intellectual," *Radical Philosophy*, no. 17 (Summer 1977).

NAME AND TITLE INDEX

Pamela, 210
Pan, 305-06, 307, 308
"Pangolin, The," 226
"Paper Nautilus, The," 231
Pascal, Roy, 262, 268
Pearce, Roy Harvey, 223, 229
Pentimento, 269
Pepys, Samuel, 261
Petrarch, 207
Phelps, Robert, 264, 271
Philips, Katherine Fowler, 211
Philipsen, Gerry, 38-39
Pilkington, Mrs., 265
Pinckney, Eliza Lucas, see Lucas, Eliza
Pisan, Christine de, 206
Plaisir du texte, Le, 303-04
Plato, 289
"Plumet Basilisk, The," 226
"Poet as Woman, The," 222
Poetics of Prose, The, 311
Poetry of American Women, The, 234
Political Leadership Among Swat Pathans, 172
Portuguese Letters, The, 286, 288, 290, 294, 295-96, 297-98, see also *Lettres Portugaises*
Power, Eileen, 206
"Power in Speech: A Review of Women's and Men's Speech," 26
Practice of Psychoanalytic Criticism, The, 301
Price, Vincent, 175
Psalms, 191
Psychoanalysis and American Literary Criticism, 300
Pygmalion, 301

Questions and Politeness: Strategies in Social Interaction, 131
Quintilian, 206

Racine, 288
Ransom, John Crowe, 222, 228, 229
Rapp, Rayna [formerly Reiter], 37
Recollections, 264
Regeneration Through Violence, 198
Reiter, Rayna (Rapp), 32, 35
"Requests and Responses in Children's

Speech," 160
Revue des Sciences Humaines: Eriture, Féminite', Féminisme, 261
Reynolds, Myra, 207
Rich, Adrienne, ix, 49, 63
Richardson, Samuel, 210, 214
Riegelhaupt, Joyce F., 35
Rights of Man, 69
Rights of Woman, 69
Ritchie, Marguerite, 75
"Roman, est-il chose femelle? Le," 208
Room of One's Own, A, 50-51, 205, 234, 319, 323
Rossetti, Christina, 222
Rougeot, J., 288, 290, 293
Rousseau, Jean-Jacques, 260, 261, 262, 267, 290, 293
Rowson, Susanna, 201

Sablé, Mme. de, 288
Sacks, Harvey, 157
Sand, George, 260, 261, 262, 263-64, 265-66, 267-69, 270, 271
Sapir, Edward, 14-15, 17
Sappho, 290
Saraga, Esther, 65
Sartre, Jean-Paul, 261
Saussure, Ferdinand de, 47
Schegloff, Emanuel, 157
Schoepf, Brooke Grundfest, 301
"Science et la vérité, La," 325
Screen, 694
Scudéry, Mile. de, 215, 292
"Sea Unicorns and Land Unicorns," 235
Second Sex, The, 48
Seitel, Peter, 40
Seneca, 205, 212
Sense and Sensibility, 210
Sentences in Dialog, 157
Seyersted, Per, 243, 248
Shakespeare, 11, 205-06, 301, 319
She Came to Stay, 266
Showalter, Elaine, 207, 263, 271
Shuy, Roger, 131
Sidney, Sir Philip, 212
Sido, 265

SUBJECT INDEX

accent: regional, 13, 150, 151; standard 151, 153, 154 (*see also* dialect)

address, 9, 79-91 passim, 117, 118; Black-White differences in, 82, 84

address form: endearment, 79-91 passim, 116; in-group, 115, 128; regional differences in, 82, 83, 84, 85; respect, 79-91 passim, 102, 103; studies, 18; zero, 79, 80, 83, 86, 87, 88, 90, 91

Africa (*see* Madagascar, Senegal, Tanzania)

age: as social variable, 9, 18, 19-20, 71, 82, 83, 84, 86, 89, 90, 103, 104, 118, 119, 144, 145, 146, 147, 148

aggravation, 159 (*see also* directive)

allegory, 278, 310, 311, 312, 319, 324-25

ambiguity, 21, 40, 41, 70, 73, 74, 75, 76, 77, 86, 90, 201, 239-56 passim, 259, 308, 309

America (*see* Latin America, United States)

Amerindian (*see* Mayan, Yana)

analogy, 232, 284, 288

androcentrism, 7, 260, 325 (*see also* generic masculine)

androgyny, 151, 155, 320, 323, 324

anger, 39, 66, 85, 91, 117, 127, 143, 174-185 passim

apology, 114, 115, 116

art, language of, 310, 311, 322

Asia (*see* Atjehnese, India, Indonesian, Japanese)

assertion: logical 229; negative, 30, 124

assertive speech, 28, 37, 98, 119 (*see also* strategy)

association, process of, 232, 233, 234, 236, 250

assumptions, 3, 6, 8, 9, 10, 20, 21, 37, 38, 41, 60, 125, 222, 223 (*see also* expectations)

Atjehnese, 41

attitudes in speech community, 4; effect on style, 120, 125, 126-27, 129, 142-43, 150, 151, 153, 154; toward women, 5, 6-7, 8, 77, 152

Austria, 29, 143, 148

author, 49, 51, 53, 260, 286, 287, 288, 289-90, 292, 297, 298, 302, 303, 303-04, 307-08; probability model of, 293

authority (*see* power)

autobiography, 211, 212, 258-271 passim, 295, 297, 310; French tradition of, 260; as mode of reading, 271 (*see also* fiction, novel)

auto-eroticism (*see* masturbation)

behavior, 8, 20, 77, 150, 183; aggressive, 224; blasphemous, 293; condescending, 90; constraints on, 133; control over, 38; deferential, 118; feeling and, 174, 175, 179, 181, 183, 184, 185; instinctive, 281; intentional, 182; linguistic, 19, 26, 27, 32, 89, 104, 141, 148, 149; male/

167, 224, 242, 245, 254; first person, 50, 239, 246, 252, 254; indefinite, 241, 242; second person, 15; third person, 242, 243 (*see also* generic masculine, "I")
pronoun-envy, 65, 70
prosodic patterns, 16, 58, 65, 84, 96, 97, 102, 108, 111, 118, 120, 128
proverbs, 40-41
psychoanalysis, 176, 180, 181, 182, 183, 250, 289, 296, 300, 301-02, 319, 324, 325, 326 (*see also* identification, Oedipus complex)
public (*see* domestic/public, speech: public, publishing)
publishing, 63, 211, 212, 215, 266, 267, 286, 288

question, 19, 20, 32, 89, 160; direct, 85; negative, 128; rhetorical, 30, 124, 125, 128, 280; tag, 17, 18, 19, 96,

reader, 11, 21, 49 51, 52, 244, 258, 260, 267, 268, 271, 300, 302, 303, 304, 307, 308
reading, 49, 52, 239, 248, 254, 298, 306-08; allegorical, 322; ambiguity of, 240; blind, 288; creativity of, 49; double, 270, 288, 315; feminist, 51, 286, 304; forced, 310; of Freud, 325-26; function, 306; gender-bound, 259, 267, 270; (inter) subjectivity of, 49, 51, 52, 280, 306, 315; Oedipal, 302, 303, 304, 306; plurality of, 52, 240, 250, 278, 288, 302; process, 49, 50; self-, 175; skills, 148
reference, 47, 48, 51, 64, 69, 70, 73, 75, 250, 251, 258, 267
register (*see* slang style)
repertoire (*see* linguistic resources)
repetition, 20, 128, 250, 298, 304-08, 309
request, 85, 87, 114, 124, 126, 128, 161, 162, 163, 166, 168, 169

(*see also* directive)
respect, 39, 91, 117, 118
respectability, 37, 38
rhetoric, 47, 65, 119, 124, 125, 128, 207, 212, 213, 214, 216, 231, 234, 282, 321, 326; classical, 205, 209; Latin, 205, 206, 207, 216
ritual, 14, 41-42, 118, 119, 128, 132, 145, 293
rule, 3, 4, 14-15, 31, 32, 40, 73, 89, 140

schismogenesis, 131
self, 38, 222, 223, 225, 226, 228, 231, 232, 234, 237, 242, 243-44, 245, 247, 249, 253, 254, 256, 313 (*see also* difference, "I," "other")
semantics, 120, 124, 132 (*see also* meaning)
semiotics, 47, 303-04; sign, 46, 47, 322, 323; signified, 47, 48; signifier, 47, 48, 49, 50; signifying process, 50, 285, 303
Senegal: Wolof, 39
separation of spheres: female/male, 31, 32, 33, 35, 118, 134, 201, 202, 209 (*see also* domestic/ public, sex role)
service encounter, address in, 79-91 passim; defined, 80
sex differences: in language use, 3, 13-21 passim, 26-37 passim, 39, 40, 41, 71, 72, 74, 83, 93, 96, 103-04, 106, 140-49 passim, 157-69 passim, 172-73 passim, 191, 285 (*see also* speech: men's, speech: women's); in linguistic innovation, 59, 60, 148; in linguistic socialization, 48, 58 (*see also* norms: different); in literary education, 205-08 passim; in service personnel's address toward, 90-91; in social organization, 165, 169, 172-73 passim; in speech evaluation of others, 151 (*see also* sex role)

speech community, 14-15, 17, 67, 113; defined, 140

speech evaluation, 41, 42, 65, 69-77 passim, 106-110, 151, 152, 153, 155

standard, 47, 64, 75; address, 87, 88, 89, 90; form, 111-12, 131, (*see also* dialect, norms)

statistical analysis, 107, 150, 152, 154

status (*see* social status)

stereotypes, 7, 9, 10, 16, 17-18, 38, 58, 59, 60, 65, 71, 95, 117, 140, 150, 151, 154, 208, 293

story-telling, 14-15, 32, 145, 148, 162, 163, 164, 278

strategy, 11, 17, 20, 21, 27, 29, 38, 62, 65, 77, 95, 113-134 passim, 157-73 passim, 226, 280, 281, 285; accomodation, assimilative, 154; active restraint, "humility," 222-37 passim; collaborative, 19, 32, 64, 165-69 passim; communicative, 30; competitive, 19, 64, 157-64 passim, 169-70 passim; deliberate ambiguity, 239-56 passim; elaboration, 32, 87, 121, 163; and "feminine" style, 113; finesse, 31; flattery, 62; (in)direct, 14, 30, 39, 40, 112, 128, 172; laughter, 163; non-confrontative, 39; politeness, 31, 113, 114, 121, 124, 125, 128, 129, 131; plural 276, 277; 280; presentational, 37; ridicule, 64, 65, 290; and "speaker's-eye view," 133; subterfuge, 31 (*see also* speech act, style)

structuralism, 300, 301, 303-04, 306 (*see also* criticism)

style: Ciceronian, 212, 216; epistolary, 213, 215; feminine, 20, 94, 97, 98, 99, 102, 103, 104, 105, 106, 107, 111, 113, 128, 223, 225, 226, 230, 232, 234, 237 (*see also* writing: "like a woman"); "gossipy," 223, 229, 230; literary, 47, 53; models for, 208; plain, 209, 213, 215, 216;

preaching/declaiming, 128; separation of, 209; sexual register, 282; verbal, 17, 19, 32, 33, 38, 39, 40, 89, 111, 113, 117, 129, 160, 239; (*see also* form, slang, strategy)

stylistics, 21, 47, 290, 293

subject, 48, 50, 51, 53, 226, 231, 234, 313, 318; autonomous, 266; female, 267; gender-marked, 51; reader as, 267; speaking, 274; syntactic, 242, 245, 311, 314

subjectivity, 49, 52, 279, 313 (*see also* reading)

supplementarity, 321

syntax, 58, 111-12, 165, 166, 167, 169, 170, 236, 239-56 passim (*see also* form, grammar)

taboo, 14, 63, 270

Tanzania, 40 (*see also* Buhaya)

Tenejapa, 30, 114, 117-33 passim

text, 21, 48, 49, 51, 52, 53, 258, 259, 260, 264, 270, 278, 286, 287, 288, 289, 291, 294, 295, 300, 302-05, 306, 308-09; authenticity of, 287, 294; female, 303, 304, 305, 306-08, 310

textual analysis, 239-56 passim, 310-26 passim

textuality, 304, 307, 308; auto-erotic, 313; erotic, 320

transformation: metaphorical projection as 200; of nature, 189, 196; process of, 42, 250, 254

trope, 317, 318, 324 (*see also* metaphor)

truth(s): aesthetic, 208; access to, 278, 316, 317; arrangement of 271; desire, 282; exclusive, 232; guardian of, 317; historical, 271; masks of, 286; Oedipal criticism and, 303-04; possibility of, 318; power of, 326; pursuit of, 208, 269, 280, 307; of sexuality, 276-77; shaping of past as, 261; sources of, 213; of text, 310; of things, 321; universal, 52; and *vraisemblance*, 291, 292

ABOUT THE EDITORS AND CONTRIBUTORS

SALLY McCONNELL-GINET teaches linguistics at Cornell, where she earlier held visiting appointments in philosophy and Women's Studies. Her principal research interests in linguistics have been in the areas of English syntax/semantics and sociolinguistics. She has published and spoken on the topic of language and the sexes and has drawn on her several years of experience with a linguistics/ Women's Studies course in helping to edit this volume.

RUTH A. BORKER received her Ph.D. from the University of California, Berkeley in 1974. She has taught and published in the areas of anthropology of women, ethnography of communication, and symbolic anthropology, and her editorial work on this book was begun while she was Assistant Professor of Anthropology and Women's Studies at Cornell. She now has a research affiliation with the Language Behavior Laboratory in Berkeley and has recently undertaken a study with Daniel Maltz of the development of sex-specific models of communication.

NELLY FURMAN is Associate Professor in the Department of Romance Studies at Cornell University, where she teaches nineteenth-century French literature. She has been actively involved in the development of the Cornell Women's Studies Program and has taught and published on feminist topics. She collected and edited the literary materials for this book.

BOWMAN K. ATKINS, formerly research assistant on the Duke Law and Language Project, also worked on the Duke Language in Advertising Project. A graduate student in anthropology at Cornell University, he is currently studying language attitudes in Thailand.

PENELOPE BROWN, who received the Ph.D. in Anthropology from the University of California, Berkeley in 1979, is currently living in Cambridge, England where she is working on the analysis of natural conversations in Tzeltal and in English. She is a member of the collective which teaches a course on Women in Society at the University of Cambridge and is active in local feminist campaigns.

BONNIE COSTELLO has written articles on several women poets and has just completed a book-length manuscript on the work of Marianne Moore. She held a Mellon Faculty Fellowship at Harvard University during 1979-80 and is an Assistant Professor of English at Boston University.

JOSEPHINE DONOVAN edited *Feminist Literary Criticisms, Explorations in Theory* (University of Kentucky, 1975) and is the author of *Sarah Orne Jewett* (Unger, 1980) as well as numerous articles on women's literature and feminist literary criticism. Her current research is on the women writers of the New England "local color" school. She resides in Portsmouth, New Hampshire.

JANE GALLOP teaches French at Miami University in Ohio. She wrote a dissertation entitled "Intersexions: A Reading of Sade with Bataille, Blanchot and Klossowski," and her forthcoming book, *Psychoanalysis and Feminism in France*, is being published by Macmillan.

HOWARD GILES, Reader in Social Psychology at the University of Bristol in England, has authored and edited numerous publications, among them nine books that are concerned with developing a social psychology of language that emphasizes intergroup communication. His coauthors in this volume, PHILIP SMITH, CAROLINE BROWNE, SARAH WHITEMAN, and JENNIFER WILLIAMS, have also been part of the social psychology research group at Bristol.

MARJORIE HARNESS GOODWIN is an Assistant Professor in Anthropology at the University of South Carolina. Her Ph.D. research at the University of Pennsylvania focused on how children at play organize such everyday conversational activities as gossip, arguing, greeting, leave-taking, and story-telling. She has published articles drawing on these materials in *American Ethnologist* and *Sociological Inquiry*; her ongoing research continues this interest in analysis of naturally occurring conversations.

CAREN GREENBERG is an Assistant Professor of French at the University of Rochester. She has published and spoken on the relationship between feminism and contemporary French criticism. A specialist in the seventeenth century, she is currently working on a book about the structural relationship between baroque and libertine French literature.

PEGGY KAMUF is Associate Professor of French at Miami University. Her work on seventeenth- and eighteenth-century texts, as well as psychoanalysis and feminist topics, has appeared in *Diacritics* and *Romantic Review*. She is currently preparing a study of some early fictions of woman's desire.

ANNETTE KOLODNY, whose Ph.D. is in English and American Literature, has taught at Yale, British Columbia, and New Hampshire. She has published actively in early and contemporary American literature and cultures, women's studies, and feminist literary criticism. *The Lay of the Land* (University of North Carolina, 1975), combined these interests by presenting a feminist analysis of American pastoral writing; her follow-up study of women's writing about the American frontiers is being prepared with support from the Rockefeller and Guggenheim Foundations.

CHERIS KRAMARAE [formerly Kramer] teaches courses on language and gender and on the ethnography of speaking at the University of Illinois, where she is Associate Professor of Speech Communication. She has published many articles on women and language, and her book, *Women and Men Speaking: Frameworks for Analysis*, is forthcoming from Newbury House, which will also publish *Language and Sex II*, which she is coediting with Nancy Henley and Barrie Thorne. She is U.S. editor of *Women's Studies International Quarterly* and edited the June 1980 issue devoted to gender and language.

JOAN MANES received her Ph.D. in linguistics from the University of Pennsylvania in 1976 and has been Assistant Professor of Anthropology at the University of Virginia since 1974. She combines an interest in semantics with a concern for the ethnography of speaking and, in general, for a sociolinguistic approach to the study of language.

WENDY MARTYNA, Assistant Professor of Psychology at University of California, Santa Cruz, is co-editor of *Women and Men: Changing Roles, Relationships, and Perceptions*. She received her Ph.D. from Stanford and has published a number of articles on language and the sexes as well as on other topics in the social psychology of the sexes and on death and dying.

NANCY K. MILLER was a Mellon Fellow in the Humanities at Columbia University, 1976-78, and is now Assistant Professor of French at Columbia. Her book, *The Heroine's Text: Readings in the French and English Novel, 1722-1782*, is being published by Columbia University Press, and her articles have appeared in *Diacritics, Signs, Eighteenth-Century Studies, Women and Literature, and L'Esprit Créateur*.

PATRICIA C. NICHOLS received her Ph.D. in linguistics from Stanford University, where she was one of the founders of the international newsletter, *Women and Language News*. Her dissertation dealt with Gullah, a Creole spoken in coastal South Carolina and Georgia by descendents of West African slaves, and she is now doing a comparative study of white rural speech in the same area.

She has published several articles on her sociolinguistic research and has lectured in English, linguistics, and education at San José State University since 1976.

WILLIAM M. O'BARR conducted field research among the Pare in Tanzania in 1967-68 and again in 1972. He directed the Law and Language Project at Duke University from 1974-77 and in 1977 expanded his research to include advertising language. In addition to the several papers he has written, he is a co-author of *Tradition and Identity in Changing Africa* and a co-editor of *Language and Politics* and *Survey Research in Africa*. He is Professor of Anthropology at Duke University.

NAOMI SCHEMAN is Assistant Professor of Philosophy at the University of Minnesota, where she also teaches in the Women's Studies Program. A graduate of Barnard College and Harvard University, she formerly taught at the University of Ottawa. Her interests include feminist theory and philosophy of mind, and is working on a critique of individualist theories of the emotions.

GAYATRI CHAKRAVORTY SPIVAK is Professor of English at the University of Texas. Her books are *Myself Must I Remake: The Life and Poetry of W. B. Yeats* (1974) and a translation of Jacques Derrida's *Of Grammatology* (1976). In preparation is a book-length study of Deconstruction, Feminism, and Marxism, and she has published numerous articles on poetry, literary and critical theory, and feminism.

PAULA A. TREICHLER studied philosophy at Antioch College and received her Ph.D. in psycholinguistics from the University of Rochester. Since 1972, she has been an administrator at the University of Illinois and is presently Assistant Dean for Student Affairs at the Schools of Basic Medical Sciences and Clinical Medicine at Urbana-Champaign. Her research has focused on communicative behavior, language, and feminist literary criticism, and she has taught several Women's Studies courses at the University of Illinois.

NESSA WOLFSON received her Ph.D. from the Department of Linguistics at the University of Pennsylvania. Since 1976, she has been Director of the Program in Educational Linguistics at the Graduate School of Education of the University of Pennsylvania. Her research interests include sociolinguistics, discourse analysis, and the teaching of English as a second language.